The Southern Marches of Imperial Ethiopia

EASTERN AFRICAN STUDIES

Revealing Prophets
Edited by David M. Anderson & Douglas H. Johnson

East African Expressions of Christianity
Edited by Thomas Spear & Isaria N. Kimambo

The Poor Are Not Us
Edited by David M. Anderson & Vigdis Broch-Due

*Potent Brews**
Justin Willis

Swahili Origins
James de Vere Allen

Being Maasai
Edited by Thomas Spear & Richard Waller

Jua Kali Kenya
Kenneth King

Control & Crisis in Colonial Kenya
Bruce Berman

Unhappy Valley
Book One: State & Class
Book Two: Violence & Ethnicity
Bruce Berman & John Lonsdale

Mau Mau from Below
Greet Kershaw

The Mau Mau War in Perspective
Frank Furedi

Squatters & the Roots of Mau Mau 1905–63
Tabitha Kanogo

Economic & Social Origins of Mau Mau 1945–53
David W. Throup

Multi-Party Politics in Kenya
David W. Throup & Charles Hornsby

Empire State-Building
Joanna Lewis

Decolonization & Independence in Kenya 1940–93
Edited by B.A. Ogot & William R. Ochieng'

Eroding the Commons
David Anderson

Penetration & Protest in Tanzania
Isaria N. Kimambo

Custodians of the Land
Edited by Gregory Maddox, James L. Giblin & Isaria N. Kimambo

Education in the Development of Tanzania 1919–1990
Lene Buchert

The Second Economy in Tanzania
T.L. Maliyamkono & M.S.D. Bagachwa

Ecology Control & Economic Development in East African History
Helge Kjekshus

Siaya
David William Cohen & E.S. Atieno Odhiambo

Uganda Now
Changing Uganda
Developing Uganda
From Chaos to Order
Religion & Politics in East Africa
Edited by Holger Bernt Hansen & Michael Twaddle

Kakungulu & the Creation of Uganda 1868–1928
Michael Twaddle

Controlling Anger
Suzette Heald

Kampala Women Getting By
Sandra Wallman

*Political Power in Pre-Colonial Buganda**
Richard Reid

Alice Lakwena & the Holy Spirits
Heike Behrend

Slaves, Spices & Ivory in Zanzibar
Abdul Sheriff

Zanzibar Under Colonial Rule
Edited by Abdul Sheriff & Ed Ferguson

The History & Conservation of Zanzibar Stone Town
Edited by Abdul Sheriff

Pastimes & Politics
Laura Fair

Ethnicity & Conflict in the Horn of Africa
Edited by Katsuyoshi Fukui & John Markakis

Conflict, Age & Power in North East Africa
Edited by Eisei Kurimoto & Simon Simonse

Property Rights & Political Development in Ethiopia & Eritrea
Sandra Fullerton Joireman

Revolution & Religion in Ethiopia
Øyvind M. Eide

Brothers at War
Tekeste Negash & Kjetil Tronvoll

From Guerrillas to Government
David Pool

A History of Modern Ethiopia 1855–1991
Second edition
Bahru Zewde

Pioneers of Change in Ethiopia
Bahru Zewde

Remapping Ethiopia
Edited by W. James, D. Donham, E. Kurimoto & A. Triulzi

Southern Marches of Imperial Ethiopia
Edited by Donald L. Donham & Wendy James

*A Modern History of the Somali**
Fourth edition
I.M. Lewis

* forthcoming

The Southern Marches of Imperial Ethiopia

Essays in History & Social Anthropology

Edited by

DONALD DONHAM
Department of Anthropology
Emory University

&

WENDY JAMES
Institute of Social Anthropology
University of Oxford

James Currey
OXFORD

Ohio University Press
ATHENS

Addis Ababa University Press
ADDIS ABABA

James Currey Ltd
73 Botley Road
Oxford
OX2 0BS

Ohio University Press
Scott Quadrangle
Athens, Ohio 45701, USA

Addis Ababa University Press
Addis Ababa University
PO Box 1176
Addis Ababa, Ethiopia

First published by Cambridge University Press 1986

Second impression 2002

2 3 4 5 06 05 04 03 02

British Library Cataloguing in Publication Data
The southern marches of imperial Ethiopia : essays in
history and social anthropology. - (Eastern African studies)
1. Ethiopia - History - 1889-1974
I. Donham, Donald L. (Donald Lewis) II. James, Wendy, 1940–
963'.06

ISBN 0-85255-794-9 (James Currey paper)

Library of Congress Cataloguing in Publication Data
is available on request

ISBN 0-8214-1449-6 (Ohio University Press paper)

Printed and bound in Britain
by Woolnough, Irthlingborough

No sooner has the peasant unloaded the tribute due to the lord than the latter 'congratulates' the peasant for having come just at the right time to be sent to the lord's measured lands somewhere beyond the Awash, from which the peasant is supposed to bring a load of *ṭef*. The toil-worn peasant supplicates, pleads and laments:

'Oh, Sire, it is harvest time in our area and if I do not harvest now, before the approaching rains, Sire, I will be finished, evicted, uprooted. Oh, Sire!'

No heed to his pleadings and lamentations. He must go to the measured estate and collect the load of *ṭef* as the lord ordered. The peasant has no choice and he submits. Cursing the day he was born, like the Biblical Job, he takes to his heels in the direction of the Awash. At the estate, the inevitable happens. The lord's representative engages the peasant in the renovation of the lord's house there. That takes a whole week's work. Only then does the peasant reach Addis Abeba with the load of *ṭef*. At Addis another task, another order! Endless! The peasant now collects the whole lot of grain – that from the Awash estate which he would have to have ground into flour and that he himself had brought earlier – and stores them properly.

While he does this, he runs out of his own provisions and in the hope of keeping his belly full hangs about feast places – and comes back exhausted, sick, and diseased. Like a sick old dog with his head resting on a heap of animal dung, the peasant passes his last torturous and agonizing days below the fence of the lord's compound. When at last he dies, the lord's household servants carry out the body on a stick and after a few scratchy digs, they 'bury' him in a ditch.

Oh, the peasant's donkey! No problem, somebody has helped himself to it as the peasant lay dying below the fence.

A lady living nearby asks a lady of the lord's household: 'Sister, I saw a dead body leaving your household for burial today. Who could he possibly be?'

'Don't mind him, sister,' retorts the lady from the lord's household, 'he was not human born; he was only a *gebbar*.'

Asbe Hailu, *Birhanina Selam*, 1927

Contents

List of illustrations — *Page* ix
The contributors — xi
Preface — xiii

I The making of an imperial state

1 Old Abyssinia and the new Ethiopian empire: themes in social history — 3
DONALD DONHAM

II Renegotiating power and authority

2 Neḳemte and Addis Abeba: dilemmas of provincial rule — 51
ALESSANDRO TRIULZI

3 From ritual kings to Ethiopian landlords in Maale — 69
DONALD DONHAM

4 Institutionalizing a fringe periphery: Dassanetch–Amhara relations — 96
URI ALMAGOR

III Reorienting kinship and identity

5 Lifelines: exchange marriage among the Gumuz — 119
WENDY JAMES

6 A problem of domination at the periphery: the Kwegu and the Mursi — 148
DAVID TURTON

IV Expanding tribute and trade

7 Coffee in centre–periphery relations: Gedeo in the early twentieth century — 175
CHARLES W. MCCLELLAN

8 Vicious cycles: ivory, slaves, and arms on the new Maji frontier 196
PETER P. GARRETSON

9 On the Nilotic frontier: imperial Ethiopia in the southern Sudan, 1898–1936 219
DOUGLAS H. JOHNSON

Epilogue 246
WENDY JAMES

Notes 250
Select bibliography 294
Index 299

Illustrations

PLATES

1 The Emperor Menilek and Empress Ṭaytu. From the 'Mission Ozil' album of 1908, in the Institute of Ethiopian Studies, Addis Abeba. Photographed by Donald Donham *page* 25

2 Women grinding flour at the residence of a *ras*. From the 'Mission Ozil' album of 1908, in the Institute of Ethiopian Studies, Addis Abeba. Photographed by Donald Donham 54

3 *Dejazmach* Gebre Igzīabihēr. Photograph made available to A. Triulzi by courtesy of the family 57

4 *Grazmach* Hilla in 1951 (from A. E. Jensen, editor, *Altvölker Süd-Äthiopens*) 90

5 Emperor Haile Selassie visits the Dassanetch. The Governor of Gamo-Gofa presents a girl with candy, while the Emperor looks on. Photographed by Uri Almagor, December 1968 111

6 This picture, from an album in the Institute of Ethiopian Studies, Addis Abeba, entitled 'Mission Addis Ababa-Roseires 1919–20', is almost certainly of Shaykh Hamdan Abu Shok of Gubba, from the survey expedition of G. W. Grabham and R. P. Black. Photographed by Donald Donham 128

7 Gumuz women and children. Photographed by Wendy James, August 1975 131

8 A newly married wife of an exchange marriage, still in seclusion and heavily veiled, is led from her hut by a girl of her husband's village. Photographed by Wendy James, August 1975 132

9 Weighing of ivory, probably for taxation purposes, at a customs gate outside Addis Abeba. From the 'Mission Ozil' album of 1908, in the Institute of Ethiopian Studies, Addis Abeba. Photographed by Donald Donham 208

10 A minor chief of the south-west, out hunting. From the 'Mission Ozil' album of 1908, in the Institute of Ethiopian Studies, Addis Abeba. Photographed by Donald Donham 209

11 Anuak chief of Gambela, photographed by the Bonchamps Mission, 1897–8; from an album in the Institute of Ethiopian Studies, Addis Abeba. Photographed by Donald Donham 212

MAPS

1 Modern Ethiopia and its lowland surroundings 18
2 Major languages in modern Ethiopia 19
3 Macro-regions in Ethiopia 22
4 Ethiopian provincial boundaries, 1935 29
5 Ethiopian provincial boundaries, 1970 30
6 Towns in Ethiopia, *c.* 1935 31
7 Towns in Ethiopia, *c.* 1973 32
8 Location map for case studies. Numbers correspond to chapters 36
9 The Blue Nile Basin: to illustrate Chapters 2 and 5 53
10 Maale and its surroundings 79
11 The Omo Basin: to illustrate Chapters 3, 4, 6 and 7 86
12 The Upper Nile Basin: to illustrate Chapters 8 and 9 198

FIGURES

1 The royal compound of Maale 73
2 A Mursi–Kwegu settlement 152
3 Ethiopian ivory exports 211

TABLES

1 The changing balance of power over Maale in the twentieth century 77
2 Succession to the kingship in Maale 82
3 Primary products used to pay patrons in Gedeo 181
4 Gedeo extended-family size correlated with *gibir* payments 183
5 Arms, ivory and cattle rates of exchange, 1901–35 234

The contributors

Note: For details of published books mentioned here see select bibliography

URI ALMAGOR is Senior Lecturer in the Department of Sociology and Social Anthropology, Hebrew University of Jerusalem. His doctorate was from Manchester University, where he has been Simon Research Fellow, and he has recently been a Visiting Professor at Harvard University (1984–5). He carried out field work among the Dassanetch from 1968 to 1970 and has since done field work among the Herero of Botswana (1975–9, intermittently). His publications include a monograph on the Dassanetch, *Pastoral Partners*.

DONALD DONHAM is Assistant Professor of Anthropology at Stanford University, California, where he previously gained his Ph.D. He was a Research Associate of the African Studies Centre in Cambridge during 1978–9, and has carried out field research in Maale, Ethiopia, in various periods during 1974–5 and 1982–4. His monograph *Work and Power in Maale, Ethiopia* has recently appeared.

PETER P. GARRETSON is Assistant Professor of History at Florida State University. He has previously taught in the University of Khartoum and obtained his Ph.D. from the School of Oriental and African Studies, University of London, in 1974, for a study of the history of Addis Abeba. Having grown up in Ethiopia, he has spent many years there doing research. He has published several articles on Ethiopian history and is preparing a book.

DOUGLAS H. JOHNSON was Assistant Director for Archives, Juba, the Sudan, 1980–3. In 1982 he also held a Fulbright-Hayes Senior Research Grant. He carried out field work among the Nuer of the Sudan in 1974–6 for his Ph.D. at UCLA. He is preparing a book on the history of Nuer prophets, a collection of documents on Nuer history, and has published a number of articles on aspects of Sudanese history.

WENDY JAMES is Lecturer at the Institute of Social Anthropology, University of Oxford, and a Fellow of St Cross College. Among previous appointments she has taught in the University of Khartoum. She gained her D.Phil. from Oxford for research among the Uduk and neighbouring peoples of the Sudan in periods between 1966 and 1969, and has since undertaken field research among various groups in western Ethiopia (1974–5), and in the town of Juba, the Sudan (1982–3). Her publications include a monograph, *'Kwanim Pa: The Making of the Uduk People*, to which she is preparing a sequel on religion and morality.

DAVID TURTON is Senior Lecturer in Social Anthropology in the University of Manchester, having previously gained his Ph.D. from the London School of Economics and Political Science. He has carried out field research among the Mursi of Ethiopia (1968–70, 1973–4 and 1982–3). He has published several articles on the Mursi and has collaborated with Granada TV in making anthropological films (*The Mursi*, 1974; and *The Kwegu*, 1982).

CHARLES MCCLELLAN is Assistant Professor of History, Radford University, Virginia. He worked with the Peace Corps in Debre Marcos, Ethiopia, from 1967–70, and carried out field research in Sidamo from 1974–5, gaining his Ph.D. from Michigan State University. In addition to published articles, he has a forthcoming monograph on Gedeo.

ALESSANDRO TRIULZI is Associate Professor of Subsaharan African History at the Istituto Universitario Orientale of Naples, Italy. He conducted research in Ethiopia from 1971–3, particularly among the Bertha and Oromo of western Wellegga. He obtained his Ph.D. from Northwestern University. He has published numerous articles on western Ethiopia, co-edited historical work and written a monograph on the history of Bela Shangul, *Salt, Gold and Legitimacy: the History of a No-Man's Land.*

Preface
to first impression

By 1974, the year in which Ethiopia saw Emperor Haile Selassie I deposed and a new revolutionary government installed, a younger generation of scholars had become engaged in the study of the peoples and history of the country. It was already a thoroughly 'post-colonial' period in the development of African history and social anthropology, although recent advances in these subjects had not yet been brought fully into the world of 'Ethiopianist' scholarship. The anticipation of social reform and political change so widespread in Ethiopia in the early 1970s invited, then, a rethinking of older approaches. A new awareness of the part that humbler peoples could play in history began to shape the work of both Ethiopian and foreign researchers. Historians were asking questions which took them from the royal chronicles and capitals which had been the *locus* of their predecessors' enquiry into the exploration of local sources and even face-to-face enquiries in 'the field'. Anthropologists were, at the same time, sensing a need to extend the context of their understanding of remote 'tribal' peoples, and finding this more appropriately in the recent development of the imperial Ethiopian state than in the aeons of speculative 'culture history'.

Against this background, the present book took shape. Donald Donham first planned an informal workshop for a number of those who had recently carried out field research in Ethiopia, and this was held under the auspices of the Cambridge African Studies Centre in July 1979, at Clare Hall. He then organized a follow-up conference at Monterey, California, in March 1982, entitled 'Society and History of Imperial Ethiopia: The South, c. 1880–1974'. Substantial funding was provided by the National Endowment for the Humanities (U.S.A.), supplemented by the Hewlett Fund at the Center for International Studies and by the African Studies Center, both of Stanford University. An editorial committee of Donald Donham, Wendy James and Peter Garretson drew up guidelines for revision of the papers in order that a number could be composed into an integrated book. It was intended that this book should open up a fresh perspective on Ethiopian society, by drawing upon the lives, memories and opinions of those lesser-known people of the southern provinces who had most recently 'become Ethiopians'.

The present volume is the outcome of our efforts, and we offer it as a new view, a picture of 'another Ethiopia' which may be unfamiliar to many readers. It corresponds neither to the well-known image of the grand old kingdom of the Lion of Judah, nor to that of its remoter regions as a separate kaleidoscope of 'tribes'; nor does it assume an easy process of the mutual blending of cultures. We bring into focus for the first time the story of the *political interaction* between the expanding imperial state on the one hand, and the peoples of its new southern frontiers on the other. The events of this story have shaped the present-day society of places and peoples throughout the regions south of the old Abyssinian kingdom, and indeed far beyond the borders of the modern state.

The first chapter sets the scene with an overview of the social dynamics of the highland polity, and its transformation into a modern empire. Succeeding chapters offer a series of original case studies, each locally placed within the southern peripheral regions, and each analysing an aspect of that locality in the light of its relationship with the imperial centre over time. In the order in which we present them, the chapters introduce and develop a number of common themes: in particular, transformations in patterns of leadership and authority; changes in the fabric of ethnic and personal identity along with the re-working of kinship and marriage ties; and the all-pervasive consequences of the extension of economic demand through tribute and trade, which in the Ethiopian case led, rather than followed, the expansion of imperial rule. The cases have been deliberately selected as a geographical series, from the inner periphery of the highlands west of Addis Abeba through the southwest to the remote southern boundaries of the modern state and beyond, into the Sudan.

By concentrating on a part of the empire, we do not wish to preach academic or political balkanization. On the contrary, we hope to have demonstrated something of the general nature of interconnections between the Ethiopian centre and the various parts which make up the whole. From a grassroots perspective, these have often been exploitative; but to reveal the interconnections at least reminds us of the rôle of the provinces and frontier regions in the making of a remarkable nation. Without the contributions of Ethiopia's southern peoples, whose sweat and blood go unrecorded in 'Ethiopianist' annals, the Battle of Adwa in 1896 might not have been won and Menilek II might not have gone on to build his empire. Ethiopia might never have played the part it did in the modern political arena, nor might it have become, as it did, an international symbol of African statehood and civilization. If this is an ambiguous legacy (as in much historical 'progress'), then at least the following papers accept the ambiguity and attempt to avoid political simplifications.

Peter Garretson's historical vision played an important part in the formulation of this book, and as he was unable to continue his part in the editorial work because of ill health, we are glad to acknowledge his contribution here. We also wish to express our debt to all those who participated in the project by preparing papers, contributing to discussion at our meetings, writing to us, helping to revise and edit drafts, and of course typing, retyping and word-processing. We are indebted to the care and skill of Stella Seddon for the preparation of the Index. Friends and family have given freely of their time in providing help throughout, and here we would like to give special thanks to Nancy Donham.

We have leaned quite heavily on the facilities of both the Department of Anthropology at Stanford and the Institute of Social Anthropology at Oxford. Sandy Robertson in Cambridge has kept an avuncular eye on the project from the start and we are grateful for his help and encouragement.

Also, we wish to acknowledge our obligation to colleagues and friends in Ethiopia, for their support in various ways over the years, support without which little of this work could have been done. We have benefited also from their advice and criticism. Almost all of the contributors to this book have enjoyed association with Addis Abeba University and with the fine research tradition of the Institute of Ethiopian Studies and the Department of History in particular. We offer this book in the spirit of the same research tradition.

Finally, we are glad to announce that a number of further papers from our project are to appear in the *Journal of Northeast African Studies*, published by the African Studies Center at Michigan State University.

May 1985 W. J.

Preface
to first paperback impression

The present volume of essays by anthropologists and historians traces the story of the intimate connection between the Ethiopian political centre and its outlying provinces and border regions over the period of approximately a century, from the 1880s up to 1974. During that period, the Ethiopian 'centre' consisted of a newly consolidated monarchy, which in the context of European imperial claims to large swathes of territory in North East Africa, extended its own geographical reach and a kind of imperial control over the peoples of its southern and western hinterlands. This spatial extension, together with a growing need for military defence of the new Ethiopia in the face of European expansionism, led to heavy impositions by the imperial state upon local economies and communities across the country.

In 1974, the last emperor, Haile Selassie I, was overthrown and replaced, not by democracy, but by an increasingly authoritarian form of state socialism. The country was eventually led by Haile Mariam Mengistu, generally seen as a brutal dictator, whose regime itself was replaced in 1991 after a period of resistance by several armed regional movements. Shortly after this, as the outcome of a long-running and deeply founded regional struggle, Eritrea achieved independent statehood. The new Ethiopian government, with strong Western backing, has pursued a policy of the devolution of powers to all its constituent regions, conceptualized and redefined spatially as a series of local nationalities or ethnic groups. Over the decades of struggle and civil war in the country since the end of the imperial era, many Ethiopians have left their country and formed new communities in the diaspora, these often supporting material improvements in their particular home areas along with a rising pride in local culture and heritage.

Relationships between the Ethiopian centre and its peripheries have thus changed more than once in substance, and in spatial format, since 1974. The present volume, although first published in 1986, is therefore a matter of past history in many ways as it does not take the story beyond 1974. However, the essays here were completed at a time when it was already clear that the geo-political space of Ethiopia was changing for good, under the projects of state socialism. An element of hindsight at that time gave a sharper edge to our analysis of the conditions under which local peoples lived during the former imperial rule, and in a way *The Southern Marches of Imperial Ethiopia* already called out for a sequel when it first appeared. Its methods and approach were also seen to mark a number of innovative departures, and these invited further working out in the new conditions. To anthropologists, *Southern Marches* demonstrated a range of ways in which the interpretation of local case materials must proceed in relation to an understanding of wider historical contexts. For Ethiopia – unlike most of the rest of Africa – that context was provided by the re-consolidation and expansion of an indigenous empire, associated with a cultural core – Orthodox Christian, and Amharic- or Tigrinya-speaking. From the turn of the twentieth century onward, power was exerted from a hierarchy of administrative centres dominated by the newly established city of Addis Ababa. Analysed against this background, the social and cultural patterns of particular Ethiopian peoples can be seen, in many ways, as responses to or engagements with this wider arena.

To historians of Ethiopia, on the other hand, *Southern Marches* marked other turns. Ethiopian history, like a good deal of historical writing, had been focused on metanarratives of the nation – in the case of Ethiopia, the preservation of its independence against all colonial odds. Emperors' lives, their battles and foreign intrigues, from Tewodros to Yohannes to Menilek to Haile Selassie, furnished a seemingly natural way to shape stories and to distinguish periods. *Southern Marches*, in contrast, looked at the project of state-making from the point of view of the southern peripheries. There, the darker side of history came into focus – the assertion of cultural superiority by the Orthodox Christian core, the serfdom and slavery, and the extraction of resources in demand by the world market. Like much other work at the time, *Southern Marches* demonstrated the value of a history 'from below' expanded by new sources such as local memory, oral history, and the indirect evidence contained in sedimented custom.

The socialist regime of Mengistu planned, and implemented, dramatic projects of land reform, agricultural development through planned settlements, and political modernization across the county. The government of that time mobilized record numbers of people for military purposes, and responded to periods of famine and insecurity by the mass transportation of people from one place to another. The human geography of the country was overhauled further as the effects of civil war, and involvement in the struggles of neighbouring countries, spread over the land. The overthrow of Mengistu's regime in 1991 was followed by the new government's policy of transforming the standing of peripheral regions and peoples within the state. This has led to a round of fresh enquiries about the nature of the new regions, and the welfare of their peoples. The methods of locating anthropological analysis in widening spatial frameworks, and approaching history from the grassroots up, have been widely accepted as appropriate to these topics. As editors of the present volume, we were finally encouraged to put together a new set of studies, some by contributors represented here who had managed to follow through what had been the fate and experience of regions they already knew, and others by younger scholars from a range of countries (including Ethiopia) who had embarked on research either during the socialist period, or after it, during the new government headed by Meles Zenawi from 1991. The result is now published as *Remapping Ethiopia: Socialism and After* (edited by Wendy James, Donald L. Donham, Eisei Kurimoto and Alessandro Triulzi, Oxford/Athens OH/Addis Ababa, James Currey Publishers/ Ohio University Press/Addis Ababa University Press, 2002). We are glad to announce this new publication as the long-anticipated sequel to the present volume. *Southern Marches* was very well received, but the original hardback edition has now been out of print for many years. As it provides such a clear starting point for the changes which have taken place in the post-imperial era, to which *Remapping Ethiopia* is devoted, we are pleased that James Currey, Ohio, and Addis Ababa University Press have undertaken to issue the present paperback edition as a companion. We would like to thank all three sets of publishers, along with our original publishers at Cambridge University Press, who have made it possible for readers to have easy access to both volumes and thus to be able to trace continuities and transformations of regional experience from the old Ethiopia to the new.

Assistance with publication costs was given by Emory University, Atlanta, and by the Istituto Universitario Orientale of Naples. We would like to express our gratitude for this help, which has been applied to the production costs of the paperback impression and in support of the locally-available edition being brought out by Addis Ababa University Press.

DLD, WJ

Note on transcription

In transcribing Amharic terms the following simplified system has been adopted, except for a few proper names where usage is well established. The seven vowel orders are represented as e, u, ī, a, ē, i, o. Distinctive consonants include ch, j, sh, zh, and ny. Glottalized explosives are indicated by a dot under the letter. Plural noun forms are avoided, number being indicated by context alone. Diacritical marks and symbols for languages other than Amharic have been kept to an absolute minimum.

I The Making of an Imperial State

1

Old Abyssinia and the new Ethiopian empire: themes in social history

DONALD DONHAM

During the scramble for Africa by European powers, Ethiopia – alone in Africa – remained free.[1] After an earlier period of disunity in the old Abyssinian empire, the nineteenth century saw the rise of new centralizing monarchs with Tēwodros II (1855–68) and Yohannis IV (1871–89).[2] By the end of the nineteenth century, a third emperor, Menilek II, had managed to bring all of the Abyssinian north under his control (1889), to defeat Italy's attempt at colonization (1896), and to conquer peoples of the southern marches (a process more or less complete by 1900). That history, the story of the making of imperial Ethiopia, is now relatively well-told, at least in outline.[3] Ethiopian chronicles, diplomatic correspondence, treaties, and European government archives have all been used to describe the great men (less often the great women), their knowing political moves and skilful diplomatic designs.

But another story remains untold, for there were many 'others' who helped make twentieth-century Ethiopia. These other Ethiopians lived their lives mostly in the periphery rather than at the political centre; they were local governors sent from Addis Abeba, northern settlers out to seek their fortunes at the frontiers and, most of all, they were the common peasants, tenants, and slaves created in the wake of Menilek's expansion into the south. It is these other Ethiopians and the history which they made that are the subject of the essays that follow.

Of course, there were also common folk in the north, the heartland of Abyssinian empires. Indeed, one of the themes of this introductory chapter is the relationship between traditional forms of social inequality in the north and those created on the southern frontier in the twentieth century. And there was an ancient northern periphery, the *dar ager*, particularly lowland areas to the west, that seems to have provided a model, at least in part, for the one created in the south.[4] But given the paucity of recent field research in the far north of Ethiopia and given the more immediate experience of a whole zone of southern peoples in being incorporated into the empire, we have chosen to focus the present collection of essays on the southern marchlands – roughly from the Abbay (Blue Nile) counterclockwise to the Awash River.

In general, it might be argued that such frontiers – with their clash of powers and of cultural assumptions – render patterns of all societies especially sharply. They provide a perspective not afforded by other vantage points. Such appears to be the case for Ethiopia at least, for the view from the marchlands that the following chapters develop places the analysis of both the traditional Abyssinian north and the newly-incorporated south in a somewhat different light from hitherto. Until recently, northern society has been analysed, mostly by historians, in terms of the structure of its imperial centre, while southern societies have been studied, mostly by anthropologists, as if they had few links with that centre.[5] The notion of frontier, in contrast, connects centre to periphery, and so provides a way of linking the history and social anthropology of Ethiopia. The result here is not one grand, integrated 'historical anthropology'. The reader, no doubt, will be able quickly to separate the anthropologists from the historians, if only because of the latter's particular addiction to the footnote. Still, a genuine exchange of information and techniques has taken place, an exchange in which each side has used the other to extend its own disciplinary horizons.

THE NATURE OF CENTRAL IMPERIAL INSTITUTIONS: CULTURAL THEMES

If the following essays treat particular sections of the southern periphery, this first chapter must consider the centre, for it is impossible to understand the periphery without some appreciation of the type of centre that dominated it. Abyssinian institutions from the pre-nineteenth-century period provided the basis for the new Ethiopian state.[6] What was the nature of those institutions? This question is perhaps best approached by way of recent discussions (in history) of the concept of feudalism and (in social anthropology) of the work of Jack Goody. Let me begin with the latter.

In a number of publications spanning the last two decades, Goody has built up a contrastive model of the political economies of traditional Eurasian versus African social systems.[7] Briefly, the starting point of Goody's argument is technology, and the crucial consideration is whether or not the plough is present. In Eurasian social systems that depend upon plough cultivation, land becomes a scarce factor of production. Accordingly, social stratification is based upon land ownership, both sons and daughters inherit property so that women tend to marry only within their own class, and there are marked differences between élite and commoner cultures. Without the plough, all of this is reversed in Africa: stratification systems are not based upon control over land, women do not inherit significant property and so they marry across social strata, and there are few differences in élite versus commoner culture. Traditional Abyssinia is a critical case to examine against this background. For Abyssinia was geographically African, but it was the single exception in sub-Saharan Africa in having intensive plough cultivation. Does Abyssinia fit the 'Eurasian' model that Goody has constructed?[8]

As Goody's model would predict, there was a class system based upon differential rights with respect to land in Abyssinia. (Below I shall have occasion to question, however, just what those rights meant and how closely they approximated to European ones.) Low-caste artisans, with whom Abyssinians neither ate nor intermarried, were prohibited from owning land at all. Neither did slaves own land, but over a number of generations they were often able to integrate themselves into the common peasantry. The peasantry included both 'tenants' and landowners. 'Tenant' households, *chisennya* (the name comes from the word for smoke *tīs*, the idea being, according to one Ethiopian authority, that 'tenants' could be removed from their fields as easily as smoke) consisted of persons who cultivated the *rist* lands of others.[9] *Rist* or *ristī* (Amharic and Tigrinnya respectively), were rights of production held by ordinary peasants and passed on to their children through both fathers and mothers. 'Tenants' and *rist*-holders do not appear to have been differentiated classes, at least in areas on which we have information; rather, 'tenancy' was one way that access to land was matched to the labour supplies of households as they changed over the developmental cycle.[10] Finally, in contrast to 'tenants' and landholding peasants, an élite held rights with respect to land both in terms of production, *rist*, and in terms of claims on tributes from *rist*-holders. The latter kind of right, *gult* or *gultī*, involved a grant from the imperial centre and theoretically was not hereditary. When it did pass from one generation to the next, a *gult* grant was inherited by only one child, sibling, or more distant relative, usually male.

While this system of differentiated rights with respect to land did tend to produce marriages within the same stratum of Abyssinian society, a sharp differentiation of élite versus commoner cultures did *not* develop, according to Allan Hoben and Merid Wolde Aregay.[11] There were differences of course: 'Large houses perched on hills, crowds of servants and retainers, conspicuous consumption of food and drink, and fine clothing are the symbols of *mekwannint* [noble] status. The noble also cultivates dignified manners which contrast with the roughness of the peasant. Soft, measured speech eschewing any sign of excitement is the hallmark of the *mekwannint* mien.'[12] But these marks of status were not such that an ordinary person, given the required resources, could not cultivate them. The extent of actual status mobility is difficult to estimate. Occasionally, commoners did rise and pass on advantages to their children, even if the higher and entrenched stratum of the élite refused initially to intermarry with such new arrivals.[13]

It is not simply that contrasts in status culture were few in Abyssinia – the image of society itself was different from that of traditional Europe. According to Hoben, the European idea of society as composed of functionally interdependent layers of fundamentally different kinds of persons – those who prayed, those who fought, those who worked – was absent from Abyssinia.[14] Rather, all men were thought to be basically the same, even if chance and personal destiny had rendered them temporarily unequal. Connections between the élite and the peasantry were emphasized by the descent system. Since descent was reckoned bilaterally through both parents, almost any commoner could trace a relationship to local nobles. The resulting ideology of kinship between classes made the Abyssinian concept of society quite different from the European:

> In the northern Ethiopian model all men are ultimately seen as pursuing the same goals in a rather Hobbesian manner, and social integration and order depend on men's being firmly controlled through a pyramidal network of personal dyadic ties of subordination and superordination. These differing conceptions of social order [Ethiopian versus European] are expressed metaphorically in statements about the relationship between the segments of society. In the European metaphor the parts of the body politic are linked to the parts of the body; in the Ethiopian metaphor the relationship of the élite to the peasantry is one of horseman and horse.[15]

It seems that domination, one might almost say exploitation, was much less mystified in Abyssinian than in European discourse. No biological metaphor 'naturalized' inequalities. The very word in Amharic for nobility, *mekwannint*, derives indirectly from the verb *konene* which means to discipline, to constrain, to inflict pain.[16] The word for lord, *melkenya*, derives indirectly from the verb *meleke* meaning variously to vanquish, to govern, to expropriate.[17] The notion of extraction in particular was evident in the phrase commonly used to describe the appointment of lords to fiefs: they were sent 'to eat' their respective countries.[18]

This unadorned system of force and extraction – the horseman riding the horse – was thought to be necessary to maintain a hierarchy among otherwise similar human beings. Disorder arose when underlings were not constrained and disciplined – metaphorically, when they were permitted to eat to their 'satisfaction'. 'A person . . . [freed from dependency relationships] is considered "satisfied" because he needs no one and therefore there is no one to control his behavior by means of the threat of withholding goods and services necessary for his survival. A commonly known proverb expressed this: *ṭigab taamach ya*[*sa*]*diral*. "Too much satisfaction will tempt you to sleep with your wife's relatives." If one becomes too "satisfied", he will take more than he has a right to.'[19]

The notion of constraint and extraction to prevent 'satisfaction' seems to have pervaded the major inequalities in Abyssinian society: the relation between God and his Orthodox Christian believers, that between lords and their followers, and finally that between husband–fathers and their wives and children. With regard to the first, fasting was and is *the* symbol of adherence to Ethiopian Orthodox faith. Its centrality can be appreciated when fasting is seen as God's extraction designed to constrain sinful human nature, to keep believers in line, and to prevent the 'satisfaction' that encourages people to take more than they have a right to. The relationship between lords and their following was seen in much the same light; in fact, the word for the lord's demesne, the field worked by the corvée labour of his peasants, was *hudad*, the same word for the difficult and long Lenten fast.[20] Finally, husband–fathers played the same role of disciplining their wives and children. According to a common saying: *sẽtinna ahiya yale dula aykenam* ('A woman and a donkey can't be kept straight without the stick').[21]

The danger of 'satisfaction' was no doubt a theme emphasized in élite ideology. Existing in tension and contradiction with it was the perhaps stronger notion of the ever-present possibility of taking more than the élite considered to be one's right, the idea that with a little luck anyone could rise in society.[22] In the words of the nineteenth-century traveller Plowden, 'Each man considers himself as born to great destinies, and the smallest spark sets fire to this ambition . . .'[23] Again, the workings of the bilateral system of descent encouraged this, for almost everyone saw himself or herself as descended from local notables. 'The myth of common descent with the nobility . . . told every farmer that he, too, had right and noble ancestors but a few generations back, and that he, too, or perhaps his seed, could once again rise to office through military service and claim a share of his rightful hereditary estate and seigniories.'[24]

Much of social life was devoted, in fact, to realizing strategies of upward mobility, and this underlay the strong sense of individualism in Abyssinian culture that Donald Levine has emphasized: the lack of significant ties of solidarity that would unite households horizontally, the consequent dominance of vertical ties of patron–client relationships, and the constant attempt of persons to rise in this system by manipulating ties to superiors.[25] Given the commitment to the possibility of upward mobility, superiors were not looked upon so much as legitimate holders of power but as useful for protecting and bettering one's own position. According to one saying, 'The wise man bows low to the great lord and silently farts.'[26]

If domination itself was relatively unconcealed, there is good reason to think that commitment to social mobility was the central myth of Abyssinian society.[27] Observer after observer has commented on the military ethos of Abyssinian society, the pervasive ideal of military glory, the hope of every individual (except those in the priesthood) to rise into the nobility through feats of great bravery in war: 'It is, indeed, impossible to sum up in terms that are too strong the attraction of the military life for the Ethiopians . . . The humblest villager once he was armed and mounted on his sorry nag, with even one ragged squire trotting at his side, had become a real man on the road to fortune and adventure.'[28]

Upward mobility, often through military exploits, did perhaps take place, enough to give the ideology some confirmation in actual experience. But the principal direction of change in most periods was surely downward.[29] Given the probable greater reproductive rate of noble households, and given the appreciable, if small, rate of upward mobility, there were never enough fiefs to go around. Consequently, a fraction of those on top were continually pushed downward. And as part of the élite was pushed downward into the peasant sector, peasants themselves faced the ever-present danger of losing land and of falling below the minimum amount required to subsist. This aspect of experience must have conditioned the cultural patterns that Donald Levine has described:

> To know the Amhara peasant at all closely is to appreciate how cautious he is about the intentions of others. He does not assume that he can count on others, though they may make promises. Before engaging in any secular transaction, such as lending money to a neighbor, entering into litigation, or taking on a servant, he insists on securing a guarantor (*wass*) who agrees to make good for damages caused by the man he is backing.[30]

Ironically, downward mobility may have further strengthened the illusion of kinship between classes.[31] In any case, class consciousness among those at the bottom of the system was not developed. According to Donald Crummey, 'Class conflict there undoubtedly was, but . . . [from the seventeenth to the early twentieth centuries] it rarely expressed itself openly; and certainly never in spectacular uprisings. Abyssinian social history is markedly less turbulent and markedly more stable than that of medieval Europe.'[32]

In sum, it is true that Abyssinia, with plough cultivation, had a class system based upon different kinds of rights with respect to land. But the second step in Goody's argument appears not to hold: namely, that Abyssinian society, unlike Eurasian examples, had little differentiation between élite and commoner cultures. Elite styles, of course, differed from peasant ones in so far as the control of economic resources was involved, but full-blown status cultures seem not to have developed.[33] Instead, élites and peasants were united by a system of bilateral descent and by cultural values that portrayed all men as basically equal. What accounts for this 'peculiarity'? The answer, or at least part of the answer, can be introduced by proceeding from cultural patterns to political organization, and by considering the second area of discussion – whether Abyssinian society can be analysed as 'feudal'.

THE POLITICAL AND ETHNIC DYNAMIC OF ABYSSINIAN SOCIETY

At the outset, one must note the remarkable pervasiveness of feudal imagery and concepts used by Western and later by Ethiopian analysts of Abyssinia. Writers as different, one would have thought, as American liberals, Soviet Marxists, and Ethiopian nationalists have converged in seeing Abyssinian society as 'feudal'. If feudalism has served more as an evocative image than as a defined social type, how are we to evolve a concept more suitable for comparative analysis? For clarity, I have chosen to focus the present discussion in relation to the work of two comparative historians, Marc Bloch and Perry Anderson, who have attempted to develop a restrictive definition of feudalism.

> A subject peasantry; widespread use of the service tenement (i.e. the fief) instead of salary, which was out of the question; the supremacy of a class of specialized warriors; ties of obedience and protection which bind man to man and, within the warrior class, assume the distinctive form called vassalage; fragmentation of authority – leading inevitably to disorder; and, in the midst of all this, the survival of other forms of association, family and State . . .[34]

Thus goes Bloch's famous definition in *Feudal Society*. Donald Crummey has comprehensively reviewed each part of this definition and the extent to which Abyssinia fits or departs from it.[35] Here, I would like to concentrate on the one portion of the definition – the presence of fiefs and the fragmentation of authority – that characterizes Abyssinian society most closely. What I hope to show, however, is that the political dynamic of enfiefment – its developmental tendency over time and its consequences for ethnic identity – is markedly different from that of medieval Europe or Japan. This pattern is crucial for understanding twentieth-century history on the Ethiopian frontiers, for it underlay all centre–periphery interactions.

Fiefs there undoubtedly were in Abyssinia. The word for fief, *gult*, indicated a granting away of 'sovereignty'.[36] A *gult* was a grant of power to dominate. A lord granted a fief had the right to collect tribute, both in kind and in corvée labour from peasants who lived on the land. And he enjoyed juridical rights over his subjects, the right to settle all disputes, subject only to appeal to the crown. In return for these, the lord was expected to maintain a personal army and to provide military support for the centre whenever he was called upon.[37] As Taddesse Tamrat has observed, the owner of a *gult* '. . . was basically different from a landlord in that he had originally no right on the land itself, but only on the peasants living and working on it. The ownership of the land remained in the hands of the local people, who passed it on to their descendants according to their own customary laws.'[38]

The granting of fiefs certainly fragmented authority. Once the emperor had appointed a lord to a provincial *gult*, the lord had complete power to appoint all the functionaries under him. He could, for example, confer military titles (which marked off the élite) up to the rank below his own, his own title having been conferred by the emperor. As Enrico Cerulli, who observed the system in the 1930s, emphasized, the only way that the emperor could influence the appointment of his followers' followers was to revoke the appointment of his follower.[39] Each link in the hierarchy was a personal one, and each person was bound only to those immediately above and below. As more than one European traveller found to his rue, local officials could ignore a letter from the emperor permitting travel, unless it was endorsed by their own immediate superior. A number of common sayings capture the fragmentation of authority; perhaps the most direct is, 'A dog knows his master but not his master's master.'[40]

Max Weber called attention to the structural difference between polities in which an emperor manages to support his followers out of imperial revenues and those in which followers are supported by fiefs.[41] In the first case, an emperor retains power of appointment and reappointment, while in the second, a hereditary stratum of lords tends to develop, thus weakening the power of central authority. In Europe and Japan, fiefs became hereditary, and it was out of the relative stability provided by hereditary fiefs that the notion of orders as legally defined strata with their own cultures developed. Abyssinian society, though it depended upon fiefs, never reached the end point in Weber's continuum. It seems that neither the emperor nor regional chiefs decisively won the struggle to control fiefs. The powers of each waxed and waned in different periods, local governors always being reshuffled to some extent during times of strong imperial control. As a consequence, a society-wide élite stratum with its own high culture never crystallized. In its stead a core–periphery structure developed in which fiefs in core areas tended to become more or less hereditary while those in peripheries were more firmly controlled by emperors. Emperors' strength, it will be quickly seen, rested in large part on their success in extending peripheries.

Hereditary fiefs in core areas were conditioned by the particular workings of the Abyssinian class system. Peasants in core Abyssinian areas often voiced their support for the appointment of governors hereditary to their own areas.[42] This was not the result simply of primordial attachments to regional identities, though these tended to develop to some degree over time, but was the outcome of a peculiar coincidence of peasants' class interests with those of local élites. Governors, because of the judicial power which they exercised over their provinces, inevitably had the opportunity – legitimate and illegitimate – to gain control of land in hereditary *rist* tenure.[43] Rights to *gult* gave them power over the people on the land, but newly-acquired *rist* rights afforded actual productive control over the land. A new governor, one from outside the hereditary line of past governors (who had already accumulated their *rist* lands), meant therefore that the area controlled by local peasants was automatically decreased. As the new governor and his entourage acquired *rist* rights, some peasants were obliged either to accept the status of tenants, to clear new lands (usually in short supply), or to emigrate.

As peasant demands to be ruled by their own noble houses suggest, core areas had a number of traditional ways of resisting imperial control. In fact, the whole notion of *rist* lands as sacred hereditary property, and peasants' willingness to litigate over them literally for decades, must have developed out of centuries of resistance to exploitation. *Rist beshī ametu lebalebētu* ('*Rist* after a thousand years still belongs to the owner'), according to a common proverb. Such forms of resistance in core areas pushed the more extreme forms of domination to the periphery, and this process was continually re-enacted as peripheries – at least those in the highlands to the south suitable for plough cultivation – were transformed into core areas as local peoples took on Abyssinian identity. This process of Abyssinianization, uneven and by no means complete, was neither an easy nor an automatic process. It was force that ultimately changed the local cultural equation. This emerges clearly in Taddesse Tamrat's study of the fourteenth and fifteenth centuries:

> All the Christian provinces in the north were originally acquired by wars of conquest . . . He [the king] appropriated all the people and their land, and reserved every right to dispose of them according to his wishes. He executed all resistance fighters who fell into his hands, and reduced to slavery other captives of war . . . These acts of cruel repression were deliberately committed . . . to force the people to surrender and to give them a terrible example of the destructive force of the Christian army in case of further revolts.[44]

Abyssinianization involved three principal components: the spread of the *rist* system of land tenure, the adoption of Amharic, and the expansion of the Orthodox church. The spread of the *rist* system is not yet well understood, but historians from Conti Rossini to Taddesse Tamrat have suggested, on the basis of the information that does exist, that *rist* regularly evolved out of *gult* grants made in peripheral areas.[45] This could have taken place in a number of different ways, but basically the process seems to have involved the settlement of a number of Abyssinian men, usually soldiers, on *gult* grants in the periphery, their intermarriage with local women, and, over time, the establishment of a local élite of mixed parentage. When this local élite was pushed downward in society, as the emperor transferred the *gult* grant to new settlers or as wars overturned local conditions, its remnants often apparently claimed *rist* rights. This claim would have been logical in view of maternal descent ties, for it was their mothers' people who had traditional rights to live on the land. Later *rist* holders saw themselves as descendants of the first colonists – colonization, *akinyinet*, always being surrounded by an aura of creativity, discovery, and Christian merit.[46] A variety of local tenure systems were, then, transformed into *rist*, bilateral descent constructs being crucial in the process of amalgamation.

The spread of Amharic, *lisane nigus* ('the king's language'), was an integral part of this process of cultural transformation. For peoples in peripheral regions, the political motivations for learning Amharic were great, for they could not claim rights that peasants traditionally enjoyed in core areas without speaking the language of those who sought to take those rights away. As with bilateral descent, the very structure of Amharic appears to retain vestiges of its rôle in colonization. M. Lionel Bender, following earlier scholars, has recently called attention to Amharic's peculiar combination of an undeniably Semitic vocabulary with a very un-Semitic syntax – a syntax closer to the languages of peoples continually absorbed by the Abyssinians.[47] This combination is characteristic of languages that develop from pidgins, those simplified means of communication that sometimes develop between two social groups, one hierarchically superimposed upon the other. As Bender emphasizes, this theory of the origin of Amharic is still speculative, but there is no doubt that the language continually spread, finally transforming the linguistic map of southern Abyssinia.

The expansion of Orthodox Christianity was the last aspect of the tripartite process of Abyssinianization and, like the ability to speak Amharic, it was contradictory in class character: that is, it at once legitimated Abyssinian society and its traditional inequalities and undermined the superexploitation that took place in the peripheries.[48] This last point can be seen in the church's condemnation of the enslavement of Christians. For those on the frontiers, then, Christian identity promised an escape from the worst aspects of Abyssinian domination, and at times peoples on the southern periphery begged northern emperors to make them Christian.[49] Except for the fourteenth and fifteenth centuries, however, the impulse toward evangelization of the marchlands was weak in Abyssinian history.[50] In the core, church and state were intimately intertwined, and emperors regularly gave *gult* grants known as *semon* to churches and monasteries just as they did to nobles, these ecclesiastical bodies being supported by tributes from peasants just as were local governors.

It was out of this core–periphery structure and the uneven, gradual conversion of parts of the periphery into core areas that Abyssinian ethnic categories developed and took on their salience. A full analysis of this complex phenomenon is beyond my competence, but I want briefly to comment on three categories that assumed overall importance in Abyssinian discourse: Amhara, Shanḳilla, and Galla. Because it was mainly Amharic-speaking peoples that directed and accomplished Abyssinian expansion from the thirteenth century, the category of Amhara naturally took on high prestige: *Amara yazzal injī aytazzezim* ('The Amhara is to rule, not to be ruled').[51] As many Ethiopians have pointed out, however, 'Amhara' is *not* a traditional tribal identity that depends primarily upon descent. As we have just seen, peoples on the periphery, or at least some of them, could 'become' Amhara over the generations. The category 'Amhara' denoted rather a particular position at the centre of the core–periphery structure which I have described. Amhara were, first of all, Orthodox Christians. Second, they spoke Amharic. And, an aspect that I have not mentioned so far, they were not markedly negroid in racial features.

The label Shanḳilla had a more pointed reference to race: Shanḳilla were, simply, blacks. Both Guidi and Baeteman, for example, translate Shanḳilla as negro.[52] Shanḳilla were blacks who lived in the lowland wildernesses (*bereha*) unsuitable for plough cultivation. They constituted, as it were, a permanent periphery that was never incorporated into the Abyssinian core. During the two millennia that Semitic-speaking peoples expanded from far northern Ethiopia southward, the line between Abyssinia proper and the Nilo-Saharan speaking peoples in the lowlands to the west was an exceptionally stable boundary. Abyssinians crossed it primarily for continuous slave raids, and slavery provides the strong secondary meaning of Shanḳilla. Peoples designated by the term were, essentially, reservoir populations of potential slaves, seen almost as part of the natural environment of the Abyssinian state.[53]

Although they were incorporated in great numbers, Shankilla were not thought to be proper marriage partners for Abyssinians, and the descendants of informal Abyssinian–Shanḳilla sexual unions (which were quite common) were stigmatized by a set of terms that could discriminate between degrees of admixture going back seven generations: *willaj*, *finnaj*, *ḳinnaj*, *aselleṭ*, *amelleṭ*, *manbētē*, and *dereba bētē*.[54] The last was a person of one hundred and twenty-eighth part slave descent. These terms may represent more an attempt at priestly rationalization than the actual practice of Abyssinians; descendants of slaves probably integrated themselves into the Amhara peasantry in most areas before seven generations. Still, the process was a long one, interrupted by the retention of local memories.

If the category Amhara was intimately connected with the centre and Shanḳilla with the periphery permanently beyond the pale (as well as with slaves brought into the core), the notion of Galla in Abyssinian discourse was different.[55] (The category Agaw in the fourteenth and fifteenth centuries may have resembled what I am about to describe for Galla in the better-documented nineteenth century.) Although 'Galla' carried overtones of race and slavery – perhaps particularly to Abyssinians in the far north – its primary meaning seems to have been focused on religion and culture, not on race.[56] Galla were pagans. They were uncivilized. *Ye-Galla çhewa ye-gomen çhoma yelem* ('It's as impossible to find a Galla gentleman as it is to find fat in greens').[57] Or again: *Galla-na shinfilla bīyaṭbutim ayṭera* ('Even if you wash them, stomach lining and a Galla will never come clean').[58] But in fact, some Galla (and a considerable number of Agaw) were finally 'civilized'; over time, they became Amhara. Intermarriage with Christian Galla, while not completely free, was nevertheless extensive. In other words, the category Galla seems to find its semantic centre of gravity in the middle of the opposition between Amhara and Shanḳilla, most distinctively in those parts of the semi-periphery in the process of becoming parts of the core. One well-known myth states that the Galla descended, in fact, from a high-born Amhara lady and a slave.[59] The Galla were, according to this story, descendants of an irregular mixture between peoples in the core and the periphery.

The inter-relationship between ethnic categories in Abyssinia was conditioned by the struggle between emperors and regional nobility to control fiefs. Had the nobility decisively won the battle, had fiefs become strictly hereditary as in Europe, there would have been much less of an expansionary tendency in Abyssinian political economy and, therefore, a different ethnic dynamic. With regard to Europe, Perry Anderson notes that the feudal mode of production was markedly less expansionist than other modes and that 'no medieval state was founded on nationality'.[60] Whatever else can be said about Abyssinian society, it was founded upon a nationality, and it did show a persistent tendency to enlarge itself and to incorporate other nationalities.

Given the nobility's greater power in core areas, it was always in emperors' interests to expand the frontier. And, in turn, it finally behoved peoples in frontier areas to become Amhara, so that the cycle eventually had to be begun anew. Why were the nobility not able to capture full control over fiefs? No causal explanation can be given, but an examination of economic organization in Abyssinia will complement and complete the discussion of themes above.

THE ECONOMIC UNDERPINNINGS OF ABYSSINIAN SOCIETY

Feudal relations of production in Europe, according to Perry Anderson, were characterized by a particular amalgamation of economic exploitation with political authority. In Europe, 'the peasants who occupied and tilled the land were not its owners'.[61] In other words, what Anderson emphasizes is that

European feudal lords tended to have direct productive control over the land they owned as fiefs (even if the exact nature of the control varied from region to region and from period to period). Because lords' power extended into the production process itself, they had clear economic interests in improving techniques. It was not unusual, for example, for lords to introduce new technology – such as watermills, which required a certain threshold population of users to be profitable – and to force all of their dependent peasants to use it in return for fees. Peasants, too, had interests in better technology, for the relatively stabilized system of extractions defined by the 'custom of the manor' gave them everything above the lord's portion.

The rôle of towns and cities was also important in defining the feudal mode of production in Europe, according to Anderson. Urban populations based in trade and manufacture provided the principal demand for the food stuffs that lords and peasants produced with increasing efficiency. This demand was able to express itself relatively freely given the way that urban centres were politically organized. Feudal lords did not control towns; instead, urban centres grew up as self-governing communes. The pattern of economic interaction between town and countryside that resulted gave rise to sustained growth.

All of this was different in Abyssinia. Most importantly, Abyssinian fiefs were not bound up with power over the process of production.[62] Instead, lords floated on the top of the economy, so to speak. They sent their agents out at harvest time to collect tributes, often as much as they could, but they played almost no rôle in organizing or directing production. Peasants themselves retained ownership of the land in *rist* tenure. In theory, they could not be displaced by a lord (though in practice, displacement occurred to some extent, particularly on the periphery, as we have seen).

Abyssinian lords' lack of control over the production process was related, in turn, to the insecurity of *gult* tenures. Even in the core, where *gult* tended to stay within the same family, emperors could transfer the office among different members of a family. Without secure prospects of being able to reap the benefits of investment, lords found that the most reasonable strategy was simply a predatory one: to skim off as much surplus as possible from whatever the peasants themselves happened to produce, in whatever way they happened to produce it.

Abyssinian lords had little direct interest, therefore, in technological progress in the basic sectors of the economy (military technology was perhaps a slightly different matter). Merid Wolde Aregay cites the report of a sixteenth-century Portuguese visitor, João de Barros:

> . . . an Armenian who was in those parts happened to make a watermill for the king for grinding wheat and other kinds of grains, which they ground and reground by hand only with great effort. After the king saw how the mill worked, he had it dismantled immediately, for he said that the thing was of no use in his country because he was always moving about his kingdom in encampments and he could not carry machines about that had to be fixed in one place. As if the

device could serve only wherever he himself happened to be and not the people of his entire kingdom![63]

Peasants also had limited interest in technological development, since set levels of extraction defined by the 'custom of the manor' never fully developed. (Indeed, manors as productive organizations were absent.) Levels of tribute gained a certain constancy, but as Richard Caulk showed, peasants were always liable to other exactions, most particularly the support of troops passing through or stationed in their areas.[64] Emperors themselves moved from one province to another, after exhausting the supplies of the first. If peasants produced more, they were often liable only to increased exploitation. This theme was reported by European visitors from Alvarez in the sixteenth century to Grühl in the early twentieth.[65] The result of these factors, and others, was that there was little or no improvement in the basic technology of agricultural production from the twelfth to the nineteenth centuries.[66]

In combination with the more piratical productive relationship that existed between lords and peasants, Abyssinian towns also functioned differently from those in Europe. First of all, the degree of urban development was markedly less, so much so that some observers have assumed that it was non-existent.[67] As Donald Crummey has shown, however, small towns did develop, and by the eighteenth and nineteenth centuries they comprised populations of perhaps 10,000. But these urban settlements provided only a modest demand for grain, and they were not politically independent of local lords. On the contrary, they were often the residential seats of local nobles, and a fair number of townspeople – tax collectors, judges, police – seem to have lived on lords' surpluses.[68] Therefore, no two-way dynamic ensued that promoted the growth of both countryside and town; instead, there was a predominantly one-way extraction of goods by townsmen.

Abyssinian political economy contained, then, little internal impetus to economic expansion. If anything, there was some tendency toward decline and dissolution; as more and more was extracted from peasants, as they were pushed farther and farther, ecological degradation increasingly resulted. Counteracting this tendency was a very active trend toward political expansionism. As core areas economically declined and as peasants there became increasingly adept at resisting imperial exploitation, emperors – if they were to maintain or increase their powers – had to enlarge the empire.

In sum, the nature of *gult* lordship indicates that Abyssinia was neither feudal nor, in Goody's terms, 'Eurasian'.[69] Rather, Abyssinian society appears to sit squarely within the 'African' type of political economy that Goody, and before him, scholars like Max Gluckman have constructed. It is beyond my purposes here to compare Abyssinia with other highly developed African empires in detail (though I believe that such a project will be the next step in placing Abyssinia in proper perspective). What I can do is to put Abyssinian society alongside the generalized model of African political economy that has become widely accepted of late. According to Goody, for example, '. . . African chiefs were sustained by temporary political domination rather than by persisting economic power'.[70] This description exactly characterizes Abyssinian lords – even though the economy over which they presided depended upon plough cultivation. Lords were not landlords.[71] They sat above the production process, using political power to skim off a surplus produced – fairly independently – by those below them.

This aspect of African forms of land tenure was elaborated by Max Gluckman. According to him, African land tenure 'arises from, and is maintained by, fulfillment of obligations to other persons *and not from title to the land itself*' (my emphasis).[72] These obligations grow out of a hierarchy defined first by political status and second by kinship – what Gluckman called 'estates of administration' and 'estates of production'. In the Abyssinian case, these aspects of African land tenure systems correspond precisely to *gult* and *rist*.

That *rist*, as well as *gult*, was a relationship to other persons rather than to the land itself emerges clearly in Allan Hoben's study of Gojjam:

> Most of the distinctive characteristics of *rist* are related to the fact that a field held by *rist* right is not thought of as an enduring unit with fixed boundaries and a permanent location. It is not an object, like a cow or a gun, which a person can dispose of as he pleases. Instead, it represents a share of a much larger tract of land held corporately by the descendents [sic], *through any combination of male and female ancestors*, of a legendary figure who is believed to have first held the tract of land as his *rist* [author's emphasis].[73]

The fields that a person farmed at any one moment represented, therefore, only a fraction of those that he could theoretically claim. Each land tract was subject to overlapping and contradictory rights, and successful men were often able to increase their 'hereditary' *rist* lands through a variety of political stratagems.

The effects of this system of land rights were quite different from the one typical of Western Europe. Most important, the Abyssinian system did not generate a category of landless people who had then to work for others as servants or wage labourers. If a man happened to have many children, his sons and daughters could obtain access to land through strategic marriages and by activating descent ties other than those through their father. Most people managed, one way or another, to obtain substantial amounts of their land rent-free.[74] This meant that land was generally redistributed in relation to demographic and political processes rather than, as in Europe, the reverse. In the so-called European marriage pattern, a household's right to land influenced the most intimate decisions regarding reproduction; high rates of celibacy, late age at marriage, and generally low rates of fertility resulted.[75] None of these were produced by the *rist* system in which title to land itself, in Gluckman's formulation, was subordinated to social relationships involving cognatic descent groups.[76]

The conclusion that Abyssinia was more 'African' than 'Eurasian' has consequences beyond simply placing it in what is arguably the correct pigeonhole. A recognition of African affinity clarifies interconnections within

Abyssinian society that otherwise appear paradoxical. This is the case in particular with emperors' ability to retain some control over *gult* grants – to prevent the nobility from fixing their position in society to the degree that European lords did. Because *gult* grants did not convey power over the production process, they could always be taken away and given to another lord without causing much local economic disruption. It was easier therefore for Abyssinian emperors to keep some measure of central control.

Setting Abyssinia within the range of African societies also highlights the social dynamic that led to the creation of the new southern frontier in the first place. African polities have been called 'absorptive' states, ones in which frontier ethnic groups are regularly incorporated into the dominant ethnic identity, typically through intermarriage. Goody has discussed these processes for the Gonja and Gluckman for the Lozi.[77] In the Abyssinian case, processes of incorporation faced certain barriers; however, in the end even Shanḳilla in core areas became Amhara.

Because Abyssinia was the only major polity in Africa to avoid European colonization for the most part, there has been a tendency, it seems, to assume that it was organized differently from the rest of Africa. This tendency is reinforced by the presence of other traits not found in traditional Africa such as the church, the use of the plough and of writing.[78] But religious beliefs and level of technological development do not mechanically determine the social organization of the economy nor of the polity. That Abyssinian society appears fundamentally 'African' in structure makes the entire historical question of how it survived independently into the twentieth century all the more interesting.[79] In the confrontation of 1896, between one of the strongest African states and one of the weaker European nations, Abyssinia retained its political independence to found the new Ethiopia.

THE RELATIVITY OF CENTRES AND PERIPHERIES IN ABYSSINIA

The discussion above has constructed a model, an outline of Abyssinian society. It remains to set that outline within actual geographical space and real historical time. With regard to space, the effects of geography on Abyssinian society have struck observer after observer. With the exception of the detailed and local work by Volker Stitz, however, analysis has not proceeded much beyond suggestions that technological stagnation may have resulted partly from isolation from world historical forces or that political disunity may have been conditioned by the difficulty of communication across mountainous terrain.[80] Here, I would like to propose a larger-scale, and as yet tentative, analysis by focusing, first, on the escarpment lines that so sharply divide highlands from lowlands in many places and, secondly, on the pattern of rivers and watersheds.

As Map 1 illustrates, the territory finally enclosed within the boundaries of modern Ethiopia was not, as we have come to think of African states, a haphazard collection of ecological zones created only by the fiat of colonial

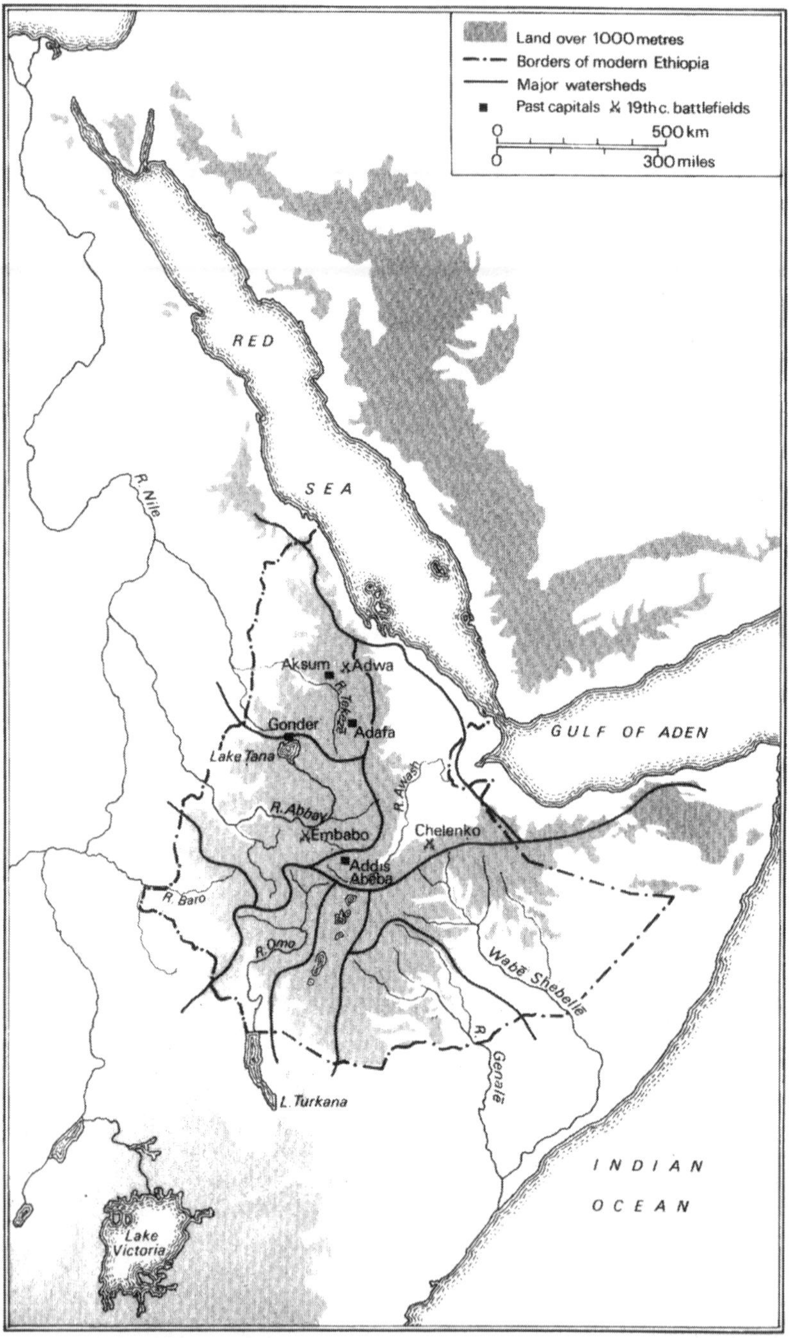

Map 1 Modern Ethiopia and its lowland surroundings

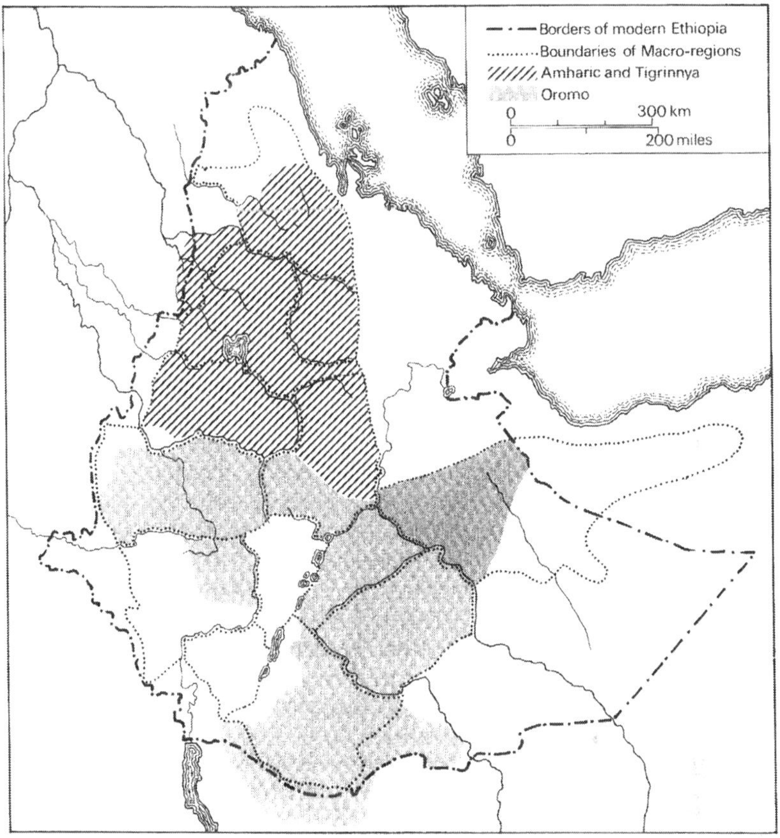

Map 2 Major languages in modern Ethiopia

powers. With the exception of the far north-east and, most importantly, the far south-east, the boundaries of Ethiopia followed the limits of the high plateau. Cool and relatively better watered, the Ethiopian highlands – drained in all directions by the great river systems of the Tekezē, Abbay, Baro, Omo, Genalē, Wabē Shebellē, and Awash – stand in contrast to the lowlands on all sides.

Escarpments, then, were the first feature that tended to define the boundaries of human interaction systems in Abyssinia. This can be seen above in Map 2 which shows the extent of Abyssinia proper, that is, of the Amharic- and Tigrinnya-speaking peoples, by the twentieth century. Abyssinian culture generally did not extend beyond the highlands. Down the escarpment to the west were Nilo-Saharan speaking 'Shankilla' and to the east were the Muslim

Afar. On both sides, the line between highlands and lowlands tended to define the boundary between cultures.

This boundary was, of course, relative to the density of social interaction that took place in the highlands, and certain types of connections across the frontier had a long history. According to Abyssinian ideology, the lowlands were to be avoided – they were wild and dangerous, infested with disease, and inhabited by savages who did not acknowledge God. Despite ideology, lowland wildernesses provided not only reservoir populations for Abyssinian slave-taking but also an escape for nobles who had momentarily lost out in political struggles at the centre. More than once, Abyssinian bandits from élite backgrounds used resources built up in the lowland peripheries through hunting, slaving, and robbery finally to capture legitimate power in the highlands.[81] From the other direction, lowland pastoralists, particularly those on the east, occasionally pushed on to the highlands, often eventually turning themselves into Abyssinians.

The high plateau defined by escarpments did not form a single, homogeneous interaction system. Instead, the pattern of rivers and watersheds exerted a continuous influence on the spatial patterning of connections among peoples. In contrast to most parts of the Eurasian world, rivers did not furnish the grand avenues of communication and trade.[82] Often impossible to cross during the rainy season and un-navigable for any distance, rivers formed instead a second type of barrier to social intercourse. Commenting on the contrast between Abyssinia and Europe, the writer of a British Foreign Office handbook noted:

> In Switzerland, the heights are barren peaks, the valleys are fairly broad and fertile. In Abyssinia, all this is reversed. The heights are mostly open plateaux, the valleys jungle-choked gorges or canyons of great depth. The population lives on the plateaux, and the lines of communication follow the high ground, the valleys being formidable obstacles to traffic.[83]

The lines of high ground – watersheds – appear to have influenced the placement of regional centres. Strikingly, no Abyssinian town in the highlands was located on a river, in contrast to European or Chinese urban centres. Instead, they were inevitably located on high ground, often near a watershed. Many factors went into urban development (defence and the availability of water were only two), but the general influence of geography can be seen in Map 1 which shows the southward shift of political centres over the centuries: Aksum, capital of the Aksumite empire during the first half of the first millennium, near the watershed of the Mereb and the Tekezē; Adafa, capital of the Zagwē dynasty during the twelfth and thirteenth centuries, near the watershed of the two branches of the Tekezē; Gonder, capital of seventeenth- and eighteenth-century Abyssinia, situated in the triangle between Lake Ṭana, the headwaters of the Angereb, and a tributary of the Tekezē; and finally Addis Abeba, capital of modern Ethiopia, located between tributaries of the Abbay and the Awash.

The lines of highest ground also tended to define major trade routes. There were of course exceptions, especially when a major river could be crossed in the dry season in order to save many days of journey; still the effect of the pattern of watersheds on the configuration of trade routes during the fourteenth to the sixteenth century is evident.[84] There were two major routes that can be described in relation to the watersheds shown in Map 1. One went north–south from the Dahlak Islands near the divide between the Tekezē and the Abbay on the one hand and the Awash on the other; the other route travelled east–west from Indian Ocean ports near the divide between the Awash and the Wabē Shebellē. Later centuries saw a branching out from this pattern, but the overall dominance of the two routes appears to have held through the nineteenth century.

More than arteries of trade, these two routes were grand avenues for cultural expansion. Toward the beginning of the second millennium A. D., Muslim religion and power began expanding from the Red Sea coast along the east–west axis, until by the fourteenth century there existed a string of Muslim sultanates from Adal on the coast to Dewaro, Feṭegar, Balē, and finally Hadiya whose territory reached the Rift Valley Lakes.[85] In competition with this development and ultimately destined to overcome it was a similar expansion of Christian power southward along the north–south axis. It was along this route in particular that a string of monasteries was established that would Christianize the highlands to the west.

> . . . during the last quarter of the thirteenth century, the Christians south of Lasta had only occupied a long and very narrow crescent running from the southeastern corner of Begēmdir to the upper waters of the Muger, along the high ridge forming the watershed of the Nile and Awash basins.[86]

Together, the pattern of rivers, escarpments, and watersheds appears to have influenced the definition of what might be called macro-regions in Abyssinia: the largest local units in which people tended to interact – economically, politically, religiously, and linguistically. The effect of regional boundaries was not, of course, narrowly deterministic; particular connections did not always fit within them. Yet, the macro-regions shown in Map 3 do provide a framework in which much of Abyssinian history can be seen as a part of a very broad, if imperfect pattern. Macro-regions appear to be, in Fernand Braudel's famous phrase, a structure of the *longue durée.*

I can illustrate briefly the effects of regional systems on Abyssinian history in four areas: linguistic distributions by the early twentieth century; the definition of provincial political units within Abyssinia; the fragmentation of Abyssinian identity into regional sub-identities; and finally the process by which Shewa became the hegemonic centre of modern Ethiopia. As already mentioned, Abyssinian culture did not extend much beyond the escarpments. Map 2 shows, in addition, that macro-regions tended to act as spatial 'containers' for Abyssinian languages. By the twentieth century, macro-region 1 was inhabited mostly by Tigrinnya speakers, while 2, 3, 4, and the northern part of 5 were dominated by Amharic.[87] In contrast, the Oromo language (which had undergone its own expansion from the south into the

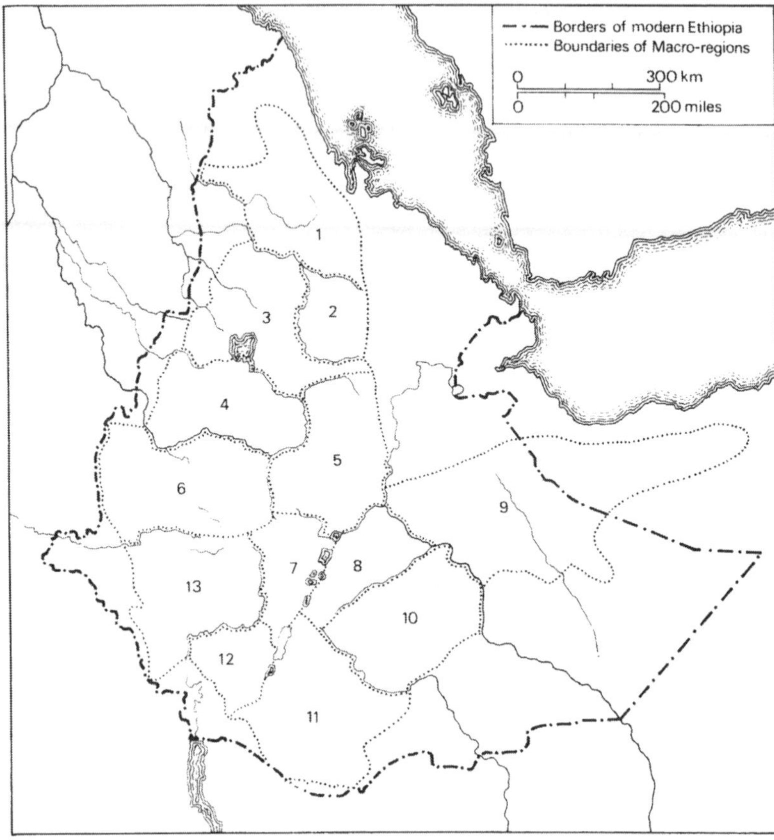

Map 3 Macro-regions in Ethiopia

north beginning in the sixteenth century) was mainly contained by the southern portion of region 5, all of 6, 8, 9, 10, 11, and the northern part of 13.

In regard to the definition of political units, strong Abyssinian emperors managed to consolidate macro-regions into a single weakly integrated polity, but the borders of administrative units one step beneath the emperor – provinces – were always strongly conditioned by macro-regions. Given the available technology of communications and political administration, macro-regions constituted, it seems, the maximum size for provinces. (This effect continued into the present century, as we shall see.) And more often than not, macro-regions were carved up into several provinces, along the lines of minor river systems.

It was in this same context that Abyssinian identity (which until now I have discussed only in regard to the Amhara) was fragmented into a series of regional identities often associated with more or less stable local élites: Tigrai, Begemdir, Lasta, Wag, Gojjam, and Shewa were some of these. In their day-to-day lives, most people probably identified themselves primarily in terms of these regional categories; that is, Gojjamē Amhara tended to see themselves as Gojjamē, Lasta Amhara as Lasta, and so forth. It was only in relation to the permanent periphery of Shankilla slaves and Muslim Afar that Abyssinians saw themselves as members of a more inclusive category: Habesha (both Tigrinnya- and Amharic-speaking peoples).

Each of these ways in which regional systems affected Abyssinian society has been stated in terms of static distributions. Let me comment briefly on the rôle of macro-regions in a historical process – the rise of Shewa and the creation of modern Ethiopia. Shewa was, first of all, strategically placed to capture imperial power; it was located near the heart of the Ethiopian high plateau, the convergence point for trade routes and lines of communication. And, second, it bordered a highland region to the south suitable for colonization. It shared this advantage only with Gojjam, region 4.

Shewan expansion began well before Menilek. From mountain strongholds in the middle of region 5, Shewan rulers began expanding southward against the Oromo in the early part of the nineteenth century.[88] With Menilek's incorporation of Wello to the north in the late 1870s, Shewan rulers had consolidated all of macro-region 5. Thereafter, three battles were crucial in establishing Shewan hegemony over the Abyssinian north and in conquering the south: the battle of Embabo fought near the Abbay–Gibē watershed to the southwest, the battle of Chelenko on the route eastward to the sea, the Awash–Wabē Shebellē divide, and the battle of Adwa fought near the old north–south Christian highway, the Tekezē–Awash divide (for the location of each of these see Map 1).

The first two battles took place while Menilek was still under the nominal authority of king of kings Yohannis. In the 1860s and 1870s Gojjamēs from region 4 had begun expanding across the Abbay into Oromo lands in region 6 – the area to become Wellegga. This region, rich in civet, ivory, coffee, and gold, was the source of many of the goods exported from Abyssinia. To stop Gojjamē expansion and to reserve the south-west for Shewan domination, Menilek sent an army against Gojjam and in June 1882 defeated them at Embabo in the Oromo lands of region 6. In the settlement that ensued, king of kings Yohannis punished both the rulers of Shewa and Gojjam for going to battle (taking away parts of the macro-regions of each) but recognized Menilek's right to the south-west.

Having secured the watershed to the south-west, Menilek's attention turned to the south-east, the old Muslim trade route that gave access to the sea and to international commerce. In this direction, the walled city of Harer, located in the highlands of region 9, was a strategic regional sub-centre. Egyptian forces had occupied Harer in 1875 as a part of a wider and eventually unsuccessful attempt to annex Abyssinia; after their plans for empire failed, Egyptian forces withdrew in 1885, and the way was paved for Menilek to secure the east–west route to the sea (and to make himself independent of the north–south road to the Dahlak Islands). He defeated Harerī forces at Chelenḳo in January 1887. Two years later, Yohannis died fighting the Mahdists, and Menilek became king of kings. It was Menilek's turn then to resist aggressors from the north, and he saved the empire from Western colonialism when he defeated the Italians at the Battle of Adwa in March 1896. As Addis Hiwet has argued, Adwa was momentous in a number of respects.[89] It not only preserved Ethiopian independence, it created Eritrea as an Italian colony; macro-region 1 was split along the Mereb River, the north remaining in Italian hands, the south under Menilek's control.

One consequence of analysing Abyssinian history regionally is that it emphasizes the fact that there was never a single homogeneous periphery. What was 'peripheral' was always relative to a particular level of the hierarchy of centres. In the twentieth century, it might be said that region 5 – Shewa – defined, at the highest hierarchical level, the political centre, while all other areas were peripheral to it. But, one step lower in the hierarchy, Shewa had a centre–periphery structure of its own. The relativity of centre and periphery should be kept in mind in reading the chapters that follow; when authors refer simply to centre and periphery, they always have one level of the hierarchy in mind, not the entire structure.

THE ORGANIZATION OF IMPERIAL ETHIOPIA: CENTRAL INSTITUTIONS

It was, then, as a leader of Abyssinian society – with its particular structure and dynamic, its peculiar spatial organization – that Menilek was able to defeat Italian colonialism and carry out his own imperial expansion into the south. The incorporation of the eight macro-regions of the southern highlands created unprecedented resources at the centre. 'The enlargement of the state multiplied the opportunities for appointment, greatly increased the size of the *mekwannınt* class, and vastly expanded its landed possessions.'[90] Before, in the mid-nineteenth century, Tēwodros' state had rested upon tributes from core Abyssinian regions.[91] By the early twentieth century, these same areas contributed very little to Addis Abeba, with the bulk of state revenues coming from the south.[92] In other words, it seems that exactions from northern peasants lightened, just as those from southern peoples were made more heavy. This subsidy of the core by the periphery, a part of an ancient expansionary pattern, is perhaps *the* secret of modern Ethiopian history. It has often been mentioned that the poorest peasant from the north considered himself superior to any southerner. This cultural expression was not just the result of primordial sentiments; it was underpinned by material inequalities created in the new Ethiopia.

The structural changes that central institutions underwent from 1896 to 1974 are not yet well researched. As Bahru Zewde has observed, all too often analysts, mesmerized by the person of Haile Selassie, have either fallen into a

1 The Emperor Menilek and Empress Ṭaytu. From the 'Mission Ozil' album of 1908, in the Institute of Ethiopian Studies, Addis Abeba.

'great-man' approach to history, or have focused on a vaguely-defined concept of 'modernization'.[93] Here, I would like to consider briefly two developments that dominated the first three-quarters of this century: the creation of a stronger and more centralized bureaucratic state and the increasing commercialization of the economy that led finally to the beginnings of state-directed capitalist enterprises.

These two processes, it seems, did not give rise to a new class that captured state power – that is, to an entirely new kind of society.[94] Rather, they reinforced, at least in the short term, the old Abyssinian class system. This was done by using seemingly modern elements like a standing army, ministerial bureaucracies, national taxation, and codified law to protect the old landed élite. This paradoxical combination of relatively advanced political forms with a backward economy and an ancient class system has led Bahru Zewde to compare early twentieth-century Ethiopia to the absolutist states of Europe during the transition from feudalism to capitalism.[95] As Bahru shows, Ethiopia fits neither the western nor the eastern European sequences. Nevertheless, these patterns of political development in relation to an international system of states, each competing for power, provide a useful backdrop against which to analyse Ethiopia: it was the only traditional African state that survived long enough in the twentieth century to respond internally to challenges posed by the modern world system.

Centralization of power did not proceed evenly during the twentieth century. After 1906, when Menilek was increasingly incapacitated by a series of strokes, there ensued a long struggle for succession that was not finally decided until 1930 when Teferi Mekonnen became king of kings, taking the throne name of Haile Selassie. More than a succession struggle, this contest involved the question of whether Shewan hegemony would survive, and, if so, on what terms. The first challenge came from Ṭaytu, Menilek's wife and the central figure of a northern faction. While Menilek was still alive, Ṭaytu began to mobilize opposition to his chosen heir, a daughter's son, Iyasu, and to encourage support for another of Menilek's daughters, Zewditu (whose marriage to a Begemdir lord she herself had arranged). In 1910 Ṭaytu's attempts were defeated, and she was banished from court politics by a coalition of Shewan lords (many with rich governorships in the south) and *ras* Mīkaēl of Wello, Iyasu's father.[96]

When Menilek died in 1913, he was therefore succeeded by Iyasu. Iyasu, something of a historical enigma, ruled only until 1916. If Ṭaytu's was a northern attempt to subvert Shewan hegemony, it seems that Iyasu's reign was a combined southern-Wello strategy to accomplish the same goal. (It must be remembered that much of Wello was Oromo and that Iyasu's father was from a Muslim Oromo background.) Iyasu established marriage alliances with several important indigenous rulers of the south, most of whom were Muslim, and he appears to have attempted to rally support from southern commoners by de-emphasizing Amhara ethnic identity and Orthodox religion. This threat to core Abyssinian values, plus Iyasu's generally erratic behaviour, quickly alienated the Shewan nobility, and they deposed him in 1916, citing his reported conversion to Islam.

Shewan control of the empire was reasserted in 1916 when Zewditu, Menilek's daughter, was made queen, and Teferi Mekonnen, a son of Menilek's cousin, regent. By a variety of stratagems, Teferi gradually gathered power into his own hands. With Shewan hegemony more or less assured, the over-riding political issue became one of how to respond to the international political economy. Zewditu (by then separated from her Begemdir husband) became the symbolic head of a traditionalist faction whose vision harked back to the nineteenth century when Abyssinia was relatively isolated from the world economy. Teferi, on the other hand, became the leader of the 'progressive' group – the left wing of which Addis Hiwet has called Ethiopia's 'Japanizers'.[97] Aware of their country's economic and political weaknesses *vis-à-vis* Europe, these men sought to use links to the outside to rebuild, to strengthen, and to 'modernize' Ethiopian society (hence the importance of Japan as a symbol of their aspirations).

The 'progressives' finally came to dominate early twentieth-century Ethiopian history. The economy was increasingly commercialized, and the state centralized. These two processes, so intimately intertwined, can be analysed with respect to two major periods separated by Mussolini's occupation of Ethiopia: the first lasted from about 1896 to 1935 and involved gradual changes contained within the confines of the old social system; the second began with fundamental reforms in 1941 and continued at a quickened pace until the revolution of 1974. The pre-occupation period was one in which the overall organization of the state remained more or less Abyssinian – that is, provincial governors still commanded their own armies and were supported by *gult* grants, rather than by salaries. By the end of the period in the early 1930s, Haile Selassie had managed to gain some control over the weakly articulated system; he had created new bureaucratic institutions like the imperial bodyguard and had begun to centralize the collection of customs, but the basic structure of the state remained more or less the same.[98]

Political organization was dramatically reshaped after the emperor was returned to power in 1941 by a British invasionary force and Ethiopian guerrilla fighters. Under the new system, provincial governors no longer controlled their own armies. Nor did they receive *gult* grants that allowed them to take tributes from local peasants. Instead, a national army was created, with a unified hierarchy of command, and a central system of public finance and accounting from which all government officials were supported by salaries in money. Of course, the practice of the new government sometimes departed from its stated ideals, particularly in the early years of the post-Italian period. Still, the organization of the state had been revolutionized, and the degree to which the emperor at the centre could exercise power was very much expanded. By the 1960s, Haile Selassie was personally involved in appointing and reappointing governors down to the level of *awraja* sub-provinces, of which there were approximately one hundred. Given the emperor's base within the Shewan establishment, it is not surprising that Shewans predominated in these and other appointments. In the years from 1941 to 1966, for example, the portion of Shewans appointed to the rank of vice-minister or above was a remarkable 62 per cent.[99]

The political reforms of the early 1940s were directly dependent upon the commercialization of the Ethiopian economy that had begun during the preceding period. In 1904, before the money economy had made much headway, only about one-third of Ethiopian state revenues were in cash.[100] Had the degree of monetization of the economy remained the same, the administrative reforms of 1941 would have been impossible. As Charles McClellan has argued, the type of commodities that entered trade also had to change.[101] In the nineteenth century the most valuable exports had been slaves, ivory, and gold – all easily transportable in relation to their value. Slaves and ivory were not 'produced' at all but were the booty products of Abyssinian predation. By the early decades of the twentieth century, elephant herds were being wiped out, and slaving was becoming increasingly difficult. In this context, the new commodity that did most to transform economic relations was coffee. The construction of the railway from Jibuti to Addis Abeba, completed in 1917, made the export of bulkier products profitable and, in the period from 1920 to 1935, the export of rail-borne coffee – almost all of it produced in the new south – increased fivefold.[102]

The pace of economic change accelerated in the post-Italian period, and Ethiopia began to see the beginnings of capitalist development. The number of industrial enterprises was modest compared to the more developed countries of Africa of the time: 'In 1958 there were only ten small industries in Ethiopia of which one, the Wonji Sugar Mill, was major; the others were flour, soap, cotton, tobacco, brewing and soft drinks, meat and shoes.'[103] By the late 1960s there was a fairly dramatic expansion in industrial production, but even by 1974 the working class – those in paid employment – was minuscule compared to the population still involved in peasant agriculture.[104] The few firms established were mostly joint ventures between the new centralized state and foreign capital – licensed privileges that provided investments for the Ethiopian élite.

All of these changes were integrally tied to aspects of the international political economy. In this respect, modern Ethiopia's relative 'independence' can be misleading. Bahru Zewde has argued, for example, that the beginnings of the development of a more centralized state were partly responsible for the fact that the Ethiopian ruling classes were less united in 1935 than in 1896.[105] In 1935, local nobles who had lost out as the centre began to control peripheral regions more firmly were prime candidates for collaboration with Mussolini's invaders. The occupation itself, from 1936 to 1941, was absolutely critical for later developments. Italian colonialism weakened further the power of local nobles; many either died in the fighting or were disgraced by collaboration. And, economically, not the least of the transformations that Italy left behind was a remarkable system of roads that welded together the macro-regions of Ethiopia in an unprecedented way. Finally, when Haile Selassie returned to Ethiopia in 1941, he was able to reorganize the state partly because of direct British military and civilian aid. The British army policed Ethiopia until 1944 and was used, for example, to put down a revolt against Haile Selassie in Tigrai in 1943 with bombers flown in from Aden.[106] By the early 1950s, the United States took over the rôle of Ethiopia's principal Western backer, and by the late 1960s, Ethiopia received more aid from the United States than all the rest of sub-Saharan Africa put together.[107]

These transformations also affected Ethiopia's internal spatial organization. This can be appreciated by comparing various aspects of the pre- and post-occupation periods. Consider the rationalization that took place in political administration. Before the occupation, provincial administration was based upon a jumble of units, the borders of which were sometimes poorly defined and the sizes and populations of which varied widely. In some cases, two or more provinces, each with its own governor, were combined under a new man's power, while in others, relatively large units were broken down into smaller dominions. In addition, governors of certain provinces were given responsibility (*ḳuraçhinnet*) for others, even though they were not contiguous. As a result, most macro-regions were not unified under one provincial administration, as Map 4 shows.[108] After the Italian occupation, provincial administration was regularized into a system of twelve provinces that followed rather closely the natural boundaries of macro-regions. Map 5 shows

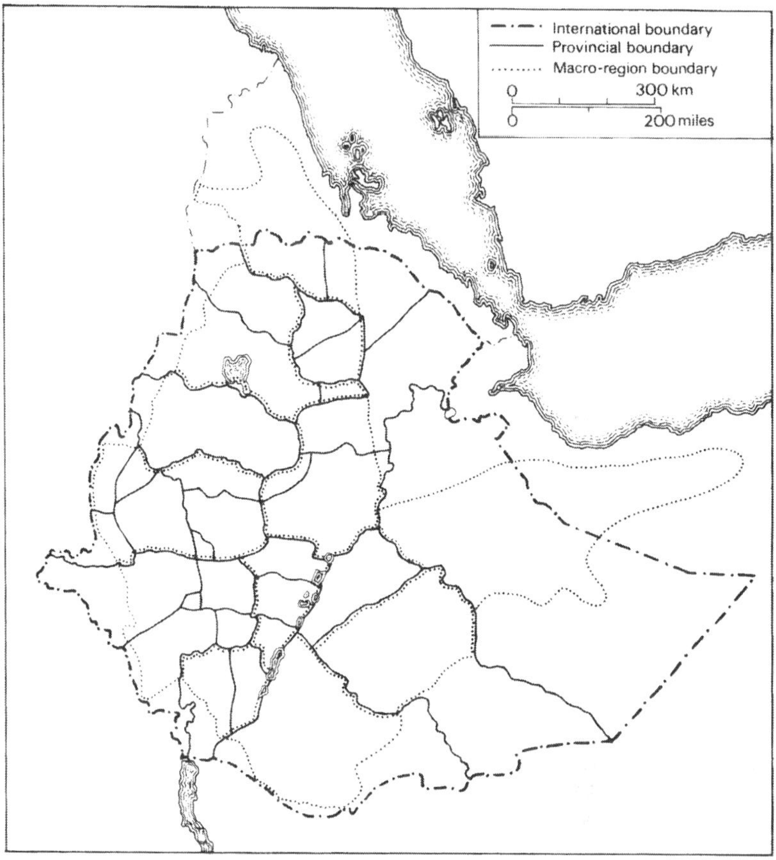

Map 4 Ethiopian provincial boundaries, 1935

that macro-regions 1, 3, 4, 6, 9, 10, 11, and 12 corresponded exactly to provinces.

While the organization of the state was being rationalized throughout the empire, the economic expansion that occurred after 1900 showed a definite southern bias. This can be seen in the spatial patterning of three of the most important innovations in the pre-occupation period: the establishment of banks, the completion of the railway, and the commencement of steamer traffic between Gambela in the south-west and Khartoum in the Sudan. In 1905 Menilek granted a concession to the National Bank of Egypt to set up a bank in Ethiopia. Only one of the branch banks during the pre-Italian period, that of Desē, was located north of Addis Abeba in traditional Abyssinian territory.[109] The railway, as I have said, was another important innovation; in

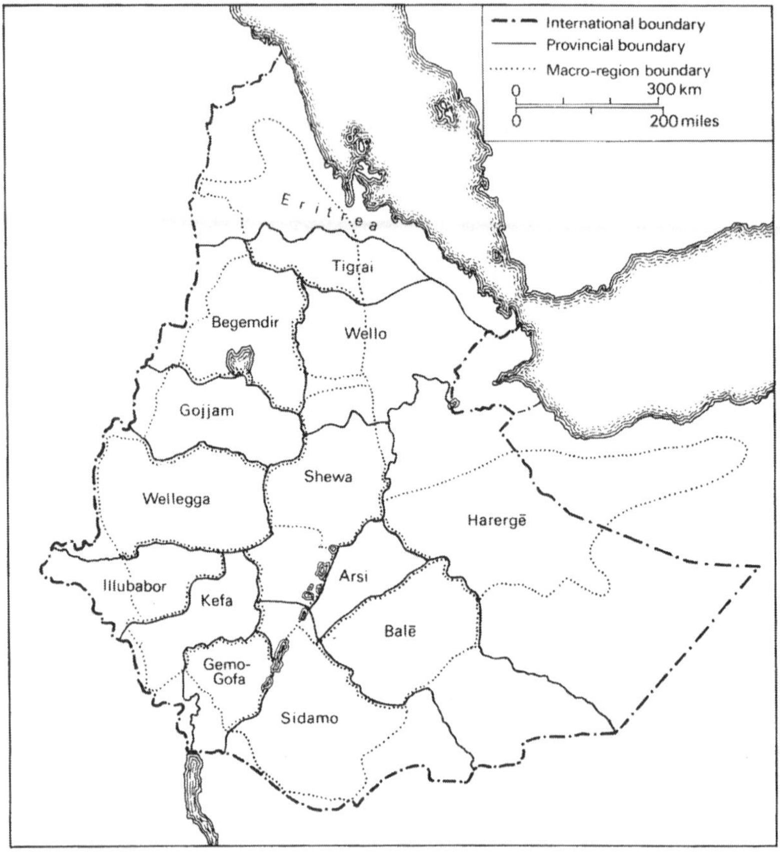

Map 5 Ethiopian provincial boundaries, 1970

many ways it was a modernization of the old Muslim trade route near the Awash–Wabē Shebellē divide. Laid primarily in the lowlands, the rail line was begun in 1897. Dire Dawa was reached in late 1902 and Addis Abeba in 1917.

The last innovation that promoted commercialization was the establishment of a British trading post at Gambela on the Baro River and its linkage by steamboat to Khartoum during the rainy season. After 1904, Gambela became the major point at which Ethiopian and Sudanese trade articulated, but it never effectively competed, as the British hoped it would, with the railway which ended in French-held Jibuti. (This was partly because it was the policy of Ethiopian rulers to channel trade through Addis Abeba and thus through their taxation procedures.) Jibuti cornered 70 to 80 per cent of Ethiopia's total trade before the occupation, while Gambela enjoyed less than 20 per cent.[110] None the less, Gambela's effect in quickening the tempo of

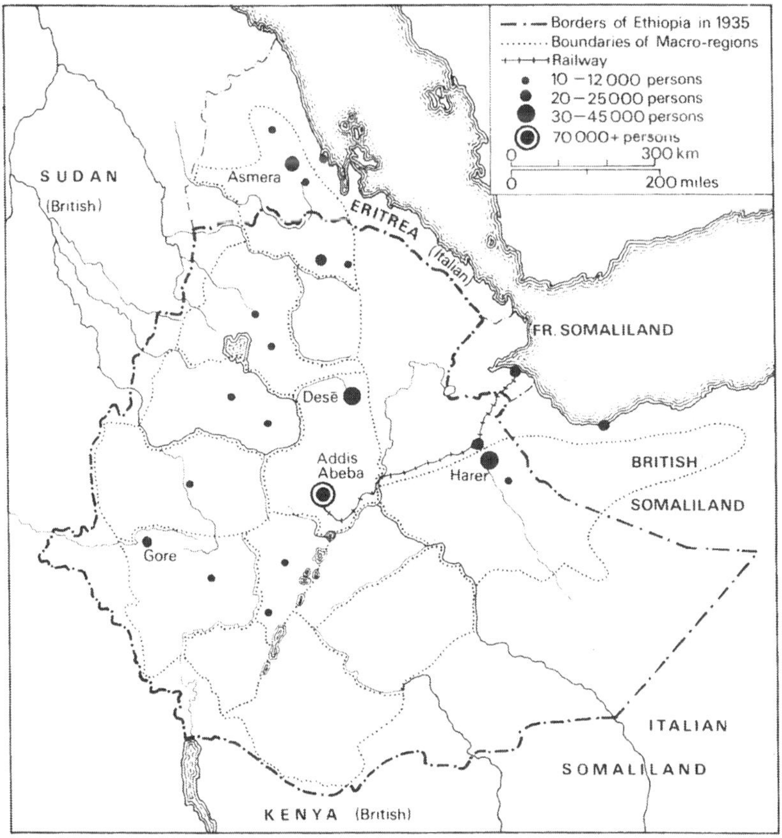

Map 6 Towns in Ethiopia, *c.* 1935

commercialization in the south-west was significant. In 1932, over three thousand tons of coffee, by far the major export, left the post.[111]

The spatial organization of commerce that these innovations helped to create is indicated by the presence and size of towns. As Map 6 shows, the cash economy did not spread evenly across the landscape.[112] Leaving aside Eritrea, already under Italian colonial rule for three decades, Ethiopian territory in the pre-occupation period was dominated by an east–west band of towns at the western end of which was Gore (near the Gambela link to Anglo-Egyptian Khartoum) and at the eastern end of which was Harer (near the railway that led to French held Jibuti). These two towns were the points at which Ethiopia was linked with the world economy. Addis Abeba, at the strategic centre of this band of towns, presided over its workings.[113]

After 1941 the money economy expanded at a faster rate, and towns and

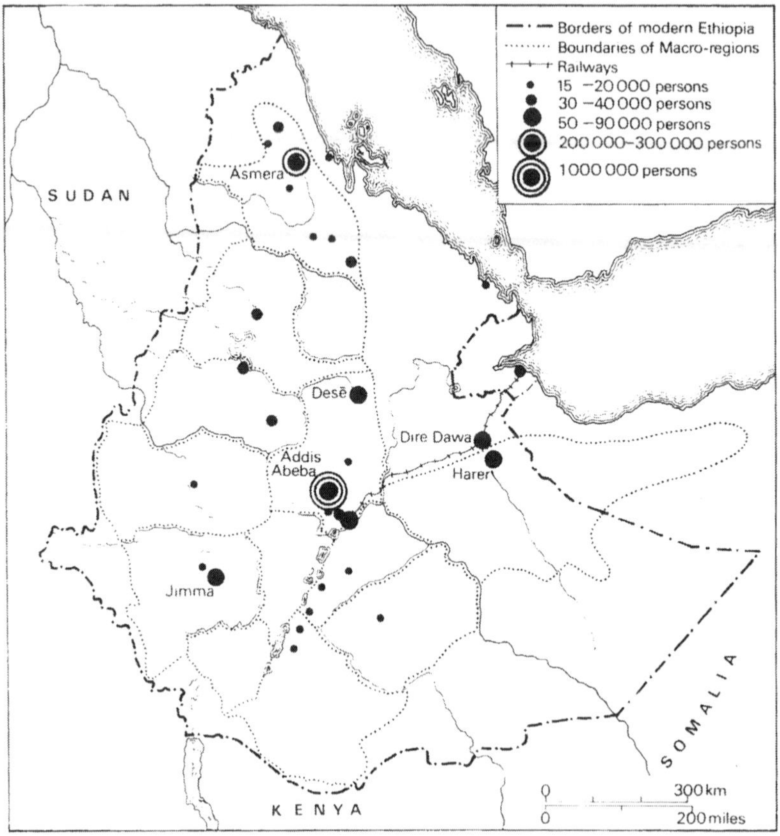

Map 7 Towns in Ethiopia, *c.* 1973

cities grew. As Map 7 shows, the spatial structure of cities still showed a southern centre of gravity.[114] A string of towns grew up in the Rift Valley south of Addis Abeba as mechanized farming began there. And – perhaps most importantly – Addis Abeba and its vicinity grew far faster than other cities. Whereas the urban system of the previous period had been relatively balanced (Addis Abeba was only about twice as large as the next ranking city, Harer, and Harer was less than twice as large as the next town, Desē), that of the post-Italian period was noticeably more top-heavy (by 1975 Addis Abeba was four times as large as the next ranking city, Asmera, and Asmera was about four times larger than Dire Dawa). Toward the end of the period, Addis Abeba had become qualitatively different from the economic and political order that surrounded it. This enclave development, in a way a product of Shewan political hegemony, was encouraged by the concentration of industrial firms in Addis Abeba and its environs. By 1969, about half of all industrial establishments in Ethiopia were located in Shewa, most of them in the vicinity of Addis Abeba.[115]

I have argued that centralization of the state and commercialization of the economy tended to reinforce the old Abyssinian class system, at least in the short term. Over time, labour dues were merely commuted into money. Property rights were reinforced and legally defined, confiscation for political reasons being outlawed.[116] And the power of the landlord class was reinforced to the degree that it was able to keep the rate of taxation on land extremely low. The portion of state revenues drawn from land taxes declined steadily after 1941 until it constituted only about 1 per cent in 1972.[117] (This was in an economy in which approximately 90 per cent of the population was involved in agriculture.) The argument that economic and political changes reinforced the old social structure would be misleading, however, if the long-term tensions and contradictions that these processes created were not also taken into account. At least three of these should be mentioned: the contradiction between bureaucratic and patron–client relationships, the tension between commercial pursuits and the old Abyssinian ideal of lordly redistribution, and the clash between new forms of ethnic consciousness and old definitions of 'Abyssinian'.

At no point did the centralized administration, set up after 1941, approach Max Weber's ideal type of bureaucracy. Abyssinian notions of personal retainership, in particular, precluded much delegation of authority from above. Moreover, salaries were never seen as the sole economic support for bureaucratic offices; like Abyssinian fiefs, offices were more or less licences to extract as much as would appear seemly from those under one's jurisdiction.

> First and foremost, the bond of patrimonial dependence must not be, or seem to be, weakened. No matter how important the position a man occupies, he must not appear to be acting on his own or simply on the authority of his office. Every significant action must appear to have its origin in the person of the emperor . . . Excessive caution – verging on inability to decide any, save the most trivial matters – has been the characteristic trait of successful officials.[118]

This was 'centralization' of a very peculiar type, and the whole administrative system operated only as long as a strong man occupied the centre. In the absence of a rationalized, impersonal bureaucracy, the workings of government depended on paternal guidance from the emperor at the top. This structural 'requirement' appears to have created Haile Selassie as a person as much as he, as a personality, moulded arrangements to his own purposes.

Commercialization of the economy also met barriers. In Abyssinian political economy, wealth had been used primarily to collect followers. Followers increased a leader's military power, which, in turn, gave him (sometimes her) more control over wealth. Tied into this interactive cycle were a set of beliefs and practices which tended to commit peasants and others to a system of social inequality that otherwise might have seemed unjust. The most salient of these was the notion that leaders were military men who led their followers to victory and success – land on the periphery, booty, slaves – and who redistributed their wealth to followers in great feasts. Banquets or *gibir*, ubiquitous in Abyssinian political society, were the stage upon which these values were most dramatically enacted and celebrated.

By the mid-twentieth century, this complex of beliefs and practices no longer made much sense. In particular, local power was no longer *the* avenue to wealth. Increasingly government at the centre took control of local resources such as customs gates and various kinds of taxes that had previously supported the wealth of lords. By the 1950s the principal ways to gain wealth, 'to make money', had changed as commercial enterprises came to dominate the economy. In this new setting, most of the élite lived in Addis Abeba rather than in the countryside, and followers were not needed as before. Lords did not have armies of their own. Indeed, clients had become only a drain on monies that could be more productively invested elsewhere.

The problem that arose was that no new cultural complex developed to legitimate the accumulation of new wealth (as Protestantism had perhaps done in Europe).[119] Instead, there existed much in Abyssinian culture that called it morally into question. If there was any symbolic antithesis in traditional thought to the good lord who distributed wealth to his followers, it was the low-status and niggardly merchant. The very word for merchant, *negadē*, was synonymous with Islam – that which was outside, in opposition to, Abyssinian society. These cultural commitments were by no means dead in 1974. As Asmarom Legesse has observed, it was just the image of the merchant that was used to undermine the legitimacy of Haile Selassie during the revolution. 'The most powerful argument employed by the military to bring down Haile Selassie's government was to list the investments of its members . . . During the week before the abdication, the Dergue gave a detailed, compelling, and totally devastating portrait of the Emperor as a merchant.'[120]

The last and in some ways the most intractable source of conflict created in Haile Selassie's Ethiopia was the developing tension between the definitions of national and ethnic identities. With the multiplication of secessionist movements since 1974, there has been a tendency to read forms of current ethnic consciousness into previous periods. In general, this is a misinterpretation. Reactive and strongly politicized forms of ethnicity occurred late in Ethiopia – developing fully only after the revolution. Just one social identity, that of 'Habesha' or more narrowly 'Amhara', has enjoyed a long and politicized existence in the highlands. Among the groups against which the Amhara expanded, forms of ethnic consciousness seem to have been only weakly developed, at least until the late post-occupation period. Examples include the Agaw, most highland Oromo groups, and the Gurage. These peoples no doubt retained a belief in the worth of their own cultures, but there seems to have been little development of a political critique of the inferior position they occupied *vis-à-vis* the Amhara. The lack of such a reaction must have been related to the processes of incorporation themselves – the fact that women of these groups often married Amhara and that men, particularly high status men with land, often became Amhara. At the far peripheries, among lowland pastoral 'Shankilla' who were not typically incorporated into Abyssinian society, ethnic consciousness seems to have been more developed.[121]

At least two aspects of twentieth-century economic and political change began to transform these patterns of ethnic identification: increasing urbanization and the expansion of education. Because Abyssinian culture equated crafts with outcasts and manual labour done for others with low status, most of the working class of the growing towns in twentieth-century Ethiopia were non-Amhara from the south. The consequence, as William Shack has explained, was an overlay of ethnic identities on the new occupational hierarchies of towns.[122] By the early twentieth century, for example, the word 'coolie' was synonymous with 'Gurage'. As southerners grew successful in new town occupations, they found it difficult (unlike those in the rural economy who accumulated land) to become Amhara, for northern culture continued to regard their occupations as beyond the cultural pale. This turned enterprising men and women back to their own societies. Shack has described the elaboration of Gurage culture that occurred in this context and the intricate set of ties that developed between Gurage in towns and the country.

While the development of towns began to act as a brake on processes of Amharization, the extension of education that occurred in the post-Italian period offered a social context in which ethnicity began to be politicized. Previously, persons who suffered cultural discrimination in Abyssinian society (servants in northern households and to a lesser extent *gebbar* in the south) tended to be placed in contexts in which they did not interact very intensively with others in the same position. Rather, vertical relationships predominated, and it was the very expression of cultural superiority from those in power that led finally to assimilation. Schools were different. As students from non-Amhara backgrounds were drawn into the educational system, they interacted at least as much among themselves as with their teachers. And the 'superior' culture that schools attempted to impart was at least partially contradictory. On the one hand, the stated ideal was one of achievement without regard to cultural background; on the other hand, schools were intimately involved in creating a national identity – one that in many ways simply continued and extended existing categories of 'Habesha' and 'Amhara'.

The strains that these developments entailed began to show only in the 1960s. The organization of the Mecha-Tulema Self-Help Association in 1963 was perhaps one of the first signs.[123] This association of Oromo – which quickly gained members in urban areas, particularly among younger, educated men – raised money for development projects in its homelands. When the association attracted several prominent military men as members and when one of them began, reputedly, to make speeches linking the poverty of Oromo with the northern conquest, the group was outlawed and its leaders jailed. As Christopher Clapham has emphasized, the nature of the Ethiopian

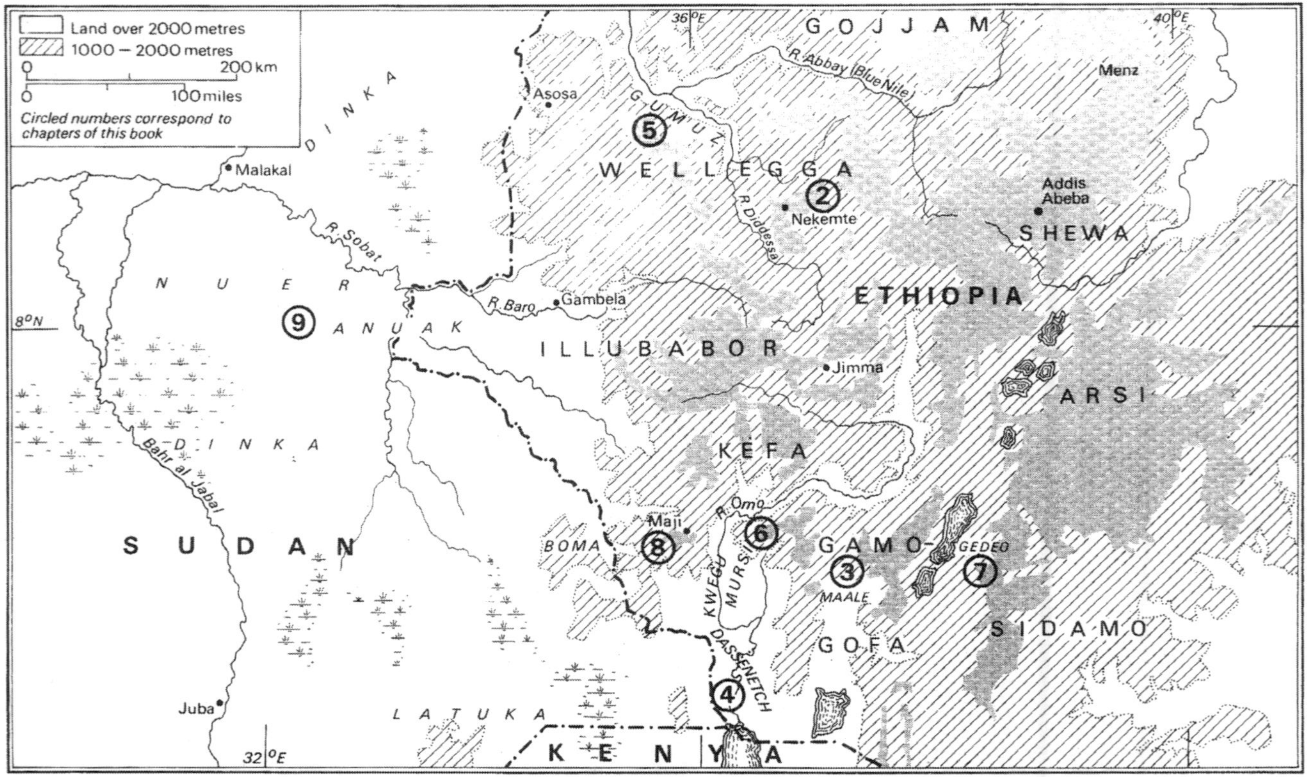

Map 8 Location map for case studies; numbers correspond to chapters

state provided almost no means for demands at the periphery to be translated into action at the centre. Instead, the centre relied principally upon force, and peoples in the periphery faced a limited set of options – 'quietism, partial assimilation through the few inadequate available channels, or revolt'.[124] In the short term, repression worked, but ethnic contradictions lay just beneath the surface of political life, and when the state apparatus began to falter during the early years of the revolutionary process, ethnic movements suddenly appeared in many areas of the empire.

TWENTIETH-CENTURY HISTORY OF THE SOUTHERN MARCHLANDS

At this point in the development of research, it would be impossible for one scholar to analyse the different ways that southern peoples have responded to the pattern of central power just described. Too little research has been done on localities that are differentiated by too many languages and local traditions. The following chapters begin the task with a series of case studies (see Map 8 for their location). Here, finally, I want briefly to outline the general context of Ethiopian rule in the south, introduce the following studies, and then comment on some of the gaps in coverage of this volume.

Twentieth-century political economy in the south has been nothing if not various. It is therefore useful to begin with a typology of how peripheral areas have been linked to the centre. As Alessandro Triulzi argues in his chapter below, this typology must not be understood ahistorically. Regions could change from one type to another, and large regions often exhibited several types of linkage.[125] With these qualifications in mind, it is useful to organize types of centre–periphery linkages into three kinds: (1) those areas, previously independent kingdoms, that were made directly tributary to the crown, (2) those areas where the so-called *gebbar* system was established, where northern governors were appointed and local peoples made into near-serfs, and finally (3) those areas in the far peripheries, lowlands inhabited by hunters, shifting cultivators, and pastoralists. Triulzi's analysis of Neḳemte is an example of the first; Garretson's of Maji, Donham's of Maale, and McClellan's of Gedeo are examples of the second; while James on the Gumuz, Johnson on the Nuer and Anuak, Garretson on various groups in the Maji periphery, Almagor on the Dassanetch, and Turton on the Mursi and the Kwegu fit into the third type.

1 Semi-independent enclaves

The first type of centre–periphery linkage has sometimes been described as one in which local rulers were maintained in their independence and only made tributary to the imperial centre. As Triulzi demonstrates, this characterization can be misleading. While local rulers in Neḳemte, Sayo, Bela Shangul, Ausa, Jimma, and Gubba (the number of these cases was strictly limited) did retain significantly more power than their counterparts in *gebbar* areas described below, they were not independent.[126] A variety of imperial agents were appointed to their provinces to act more or less as spies; in addition, semi-independent rulers were recognized only in areas that were fairly commercialized, and large tributes were the price of their special and precarious status. All were located in the east–west band of territory centred on Addis Abeba that was the most highly commercialized in the empire, and five out of the six were located in the west near the gold-bearing tributaries of the Abbay.

The imposition of demands for tribute on semi-independent rulers affected not only their own territories but also neighbouring peoples, some quite far-flung. Local rulers naturally tried to shift the burden from their own people, where the legitimacy of their rule was based, to surrounding groups – their own peripheries. This can be seen in a number of the following analyses. Sometimes, local rulers slave-raided, as did the rulers of Gubba described by Wendy James. Other times, they attempted to enlarge the territory under their power, as did *dejazmach* Gebre Igzīabihēr of Neḳemte described by Triulzi. Finally, some of the western rulers, as Douglas Johnson shows, set up trade contacts deep into Sudanese territory in order to obtain ivory. All of these expansionary tendencies were related to tribute demands from Addis Abeba, and all affected peoples outside the borders of semi-independent rulers' territories. Centre–periphery relations, therefore, never consisted only of the linkage between particular territories and the centre; an area's fate was also related to the way its neighbours were linked to Addis Abeba.

Over time, the special position of semi-independent rulers was eroded, and their territories reverted to the second mode of domination to be described below. This process began early in the twentieth century and by the time of the Italian occupation, only the rulers of Neḳemte, Bela Shangul, and Ausa remained in their original relationship to the centre.[127] After the occupation, the reforms of 1941 regularized territorial administration. There were no longer pockets of slightly different political structure, though some of the ruling families retained their influence by becoming *awraja* governors under the new arrangements.

2 Gebbar areas

While the economic link drawing tribute from the periphery to the centre in cases like Neḳemte was a direct one, indeed a personal one, that in the second type of area in the south was considerably more indirect. Instead of tribute being funnelled directly to the centre, the greater part was consumed by northern governors and soldiers in the area. This old Abyssinian pattern was intensified after the Great Famine of 1888–92, as Triulzi notes below. It involved *gult* grants to northern governors and soldiers (many of whom were from Shewa), and to local indigenous leaders who became *balabbat*, intermediaries for the administration. *Gult* grants meant that local populations, some of whom had previously lived in relatively unstratified societies, became tribute-paying peasants or *gebbar*.

Let me comment on these two terms, *balabbat* and *gebbar*, both of which have a long history in Abyssinian political economy. The first, *balabbat*, means essentially big man, literally 'one who has a father', that is, a local notable from a family with significant rights over land.[128] It was on this kind of figure that Abyssinian rule had relied in the north; *balabbat* were informal leaders through whom local governors had to work since the Abyssinian state never really penetrated to the level of local communities. This conception of how smaller-scale communities articulated with the state was naturally the one that northerners brought to the south. They made local leaders *balabbat* and attempted to co-opt them into working for the administration by granting them *gult* rights to collect tribute from their erstwhile kinsmen and followers.

Besides *balabbat*, the second key term is *gebbar*. In Abyssinian terms, *gebbar* meant peasant, literally 'tribute-giver'.[129] *Gebbar* were peasants who owned *rist* lands but who were obliged to give tributes to their *gult* lords. These tributes involved part of their crops, corvée labour, and presents to their lords on holidays. This was the system transferred to the south in most of the highlands suitable for northern colonization, with the exception of those few semi-autonomous kingdoms noted above, and those 'unsettled' areas claimed directly by the state, in which evolved a new form of tenancy described below.

As might be expected, the massive reorientation of economic and political relations effected by *gult* grants was introduced and maintained only by force. Garrisons of troops were established in fortified towns (*ketema*) typically strung out near the lines of watersheds on the most commanding mountain-tops. As the name of these soldier-settlers in the south, *neftennya*, 'riflemen', reminds us, northerners by this time were armed with relatively modern weapons. Southerners had almost none, at least in the very early twentieth century. As long as territories were reasonably garrisoned, local peoples had to submit. But as soon as governors removed their armies to fight battles over succession at the centre, as they did after Menilek's illness and death, local peoples often revolted.[130]

Ideally, one-third or one-quarter of settled lands in the south were given as hereditary *gult* to local *balabbat* (in fact the fraction could be much smaller, as in Maale). The rest fell to the government to distribute as *gult* to local governors (who held their rights only as long as they were in office) and to corps of troops (who could pass on their rights to a son if the latter entered the service of the corps). It must be emphasized that these grants did not in theory alienate southerners' lands; the occupants of the land, *gebbar*, were assumed still to own their land, just as in the north.[131] What was granted was the right to take tributes from persons who resided on the land. Governors and soldiers thus became linked with a varying number of southern families who provided them with food through tributes, worked in their houses as personal servants, ground flour, carried water, built houses, fed mules, and generally did anything else that they could be cajoled or forced into doing.

No more forceful account of the situation of *gebbar* exists than that of Asbe Hailu, published in Amharic in 1927 and quoted at the beginning of this book.[132] While clearly polemical, Asbe none the less appears to capture the human dimensions of what it meant to be a *gebbar*. Analytically, how is the position of *gebbar* to be understood? At times in the following essays, we have equated southern *gebbar* with serfs. As with any transfer of European terminology to non-European institutions, this is only partly correct. That southern *gebbar*, as a group, occupied a markedly inferior social position to northern lords is clear. Yet *gebbar* were not legally bound as persons to their lords (as were slaves) nor were they fully bound to the soil. In theory, *gebbar* still owned the plots they farmed. Practice was more complex, and analysts have taken opposing positions on the question of whether southern *gebbar* were tied to the land.[133] Within the smaller local political units ruled by particular *gult* lords, it seems that peasants *were* adscripted to the soil and forced to return to work for their masters if they attempted to flee. But if a *gebbar* managed to cross into the territory of another *gult* lord, he could not legally be forced to return.[134] In such cases, the lord would be allocated another *gebbar* (this was one of the main jobs of the *balabbat*) from the people living on the land – if any surplus existed. As this implies, not all families in an area became *gebbar* at the first introduction of the system. The richest families were naturally chosen first, and as Charles McClellan points out for Gedeo, poorer ones who entered the system later counted as half-*gebbar*.

The proportion of northerners who had been allocated *gebbar* to the number of local families who could be pressed into *gebbar* service was obviously critical for the way the system operated. Areas nearer the centre 'filled up' sooner, and troops were periodically stationed farther afield where more *gebbar* were available.[135] At the very periphery, near the escarpment beyond which the *gebbar* system did not penetrate, perhaps the harshest conditions were found. There, local peoples could escape relatively easily into the lowlands. This sometimes left too few *gebbar* to support the number of northern soldiers; as Peter Garretson shows in his chapter on Maji, spirals of violence then erupted when soldiers demanded the children of *gebbar* as slaves in return for missed tributes. This pattern was aggravated by instability at the centre. As one faction or another gained power in Addis Abeba, and as, therefore, local governors were transferred or lost their positions, soldiers being moved from southern provinces sometimes simply took *gebbar* away as slaves. This decreased the number of possible tribute-givers even further for the next governor and his following, and the whole cycle was repeated in increasingly exaggerated form.

In theory, as I have said, exactly the same relationships were established in the south as previously existed in the north. In fact, the relationship between *gebbar* and *gult*-holders turned out to function differently for two main reasons. First, in the north, both *gebbar* and *gult* lord were members of the same ethnic group, both were Orthodox Christians, and often, as we have seen, the two were united by ties of kinship. This was different in the south. It is difficult to convey the strength of the sense of cultural superiority that northerners brought to the south. Northern colonists viewed southerners as '. . . primitives, without culture and effective government, and as lazy, dirty, and warlike heathen who needed the word of God'.[136] Whatever else they were, a southern *gebbar* and his northern *gult* lord were not kinsmen, at least not in the beginning.

The second difference lay in the relative politicization of the northern as compared to the new southern peasantries. Northern *gebbar* had a hundred ways of resisting 'unreasonable' demands; they spoke the same language as their lords, could use the appropriate ambiguities, could flexibly resist. Most of all, they had learned that their very survival depended upon defending *rist* rights to land. Southerners, in contrast, had not developed these peasant traditions. They had not learned – the hard Abyssinian way – to inspect and to distrust every move of anyone with the least amount of power. It is not then that *rist* guarantees were 'eliminated' in the south; rather, they did not have time to develop.[137]

The *gebbar* system just described functioned in areas that the centre acknowledged as 'settled', *ye-gebbar merēt*, peasant lands, lands that paid tributes. Opposed to this category were 'unsettled' lands known as *ye-nigus merēt*, the emperor's land.[138] Implied in this opposition was the ideology that some lands in the south were not being 'used' and that these could be put to better 'use' by the emperor; this *rationale* was similar to the one used by European settlers in, for example, South Africa and Kenya.

'Unsettled' lands were sold by the government, often to northern settlers.[139] Agents were sent out from the centre in order to survey these lands and to sell them as *ḳelad*, measured land. Again, this process had a definite spatial aspect. It occurred most extensively at or near the centre and faded out southward.[140] Land sales ultimately transformed local class relations, according to the analysis of Charles McClellan below. As a previous no man's land, downslope from Gedeo, was progressively measured and plots of land there sold, and as local Gedeo from the old *gebbar* highlands increasingly settled on these new lands, a new form of landlord–tenant relationship evolved. The new tenants had no legal rights over the land on which they settled; consequently, over time, they lost control over the process of production itself, especially as the demand for coffee increased. By the time of the revolution, a significant portion of southerners found themselves in this new kind of tenancy.

The final denouement for *gebbar* lands was different. As *gult* faded away after the administrative reforms of 1941, old *gebbar* – who as I noted had been richer and traditionally more important families from the beginning – were recognized as the legal owners of the land (as they had been in theory all along). They began to pay taxes directly to the government rather than to the *gult* lord and to receive tax receipts as proof of their ownership. Because their plots were larger than the area they themselves cultivated, they nearly always had others living on their lands. But because these others were often kinsmen or at least members of their own ethnic group, tenancy was less harsh than that described above. The character of the relationship was shaped by local demand for land and for products grown on the land.

In summing up the historical transformations effected by the *gebbar* system,

Markakis and Ayele claim that the 'retreat of feudalism left northern peasants free-holders, southern ones a proletariat'.[141] While this statement captures broadly the contrast between the north and south, it neglects considerable variation in the southern periphery. The extent of the southern proletariat was very small indeed, namely those who were involved in circulating labour migration to a few capitalist agricultural enterprises like the sugar plantations of the Awash valley. In addition, there were sharecropping tenants who lived on measured lands and who paid up to half of their crops as rent. Also, there were 'tenants' on lands owned by former *gebbar*, 'tenants' who sometimes gave only token gifts to their 'landlords'. Finally, there were genuine free-holders, mostly former *gebbar*, and a small landlord élite, generally *balabbat*.

3 Fringe peripheries

I come finally to the third kind of linkage between centre and periphery, that which characterized the lowland fringe included within modern Ethiopia. The *gebbar* system was not instituted in these regions, for a number of reasons. First, the land was not suitable for colonization by highland plough agriculturalists and, secondly, lowland pastoralists were much harder to keep track of and to control than settled horticulturalists. In these areas, then, only *balabbat* were appointed, and a fixed tax, usually on cattle, was demanded. In the early part of the twentieth century, extraction took the form of raids – not only for cattle but also for slaves. Gradually, this was regularized into tax collection, particularly as local leaders were more or less brought into the administration.[142]

All in all, the extent of central control over these regions was probably less than in other areas. As Asmarom Legesse has argued, the presence of the new international border in the south was a distinct advantage for lowlanders, for if Ethiopian officials grew too exploitative, local peoples could simply cross over into the Anglo-Egyptian Sudan, British Kenya, or Italian or British Somaliland.[143] In Borena, for example, Amhara soldiers who manned posts in the lowlands kept slaves from the highlands to cultivate for them (it was impossible to press the surrounding pastoral Borena Oromo into the *gebbar* system). Periodically, these slaves escaped across the border into Kenya, where the British, always willing to make the point that Ethiopians would be better off under Britain, allowed them to settle in Marsabit.[144]

The idea of a delimited border was, in fact, new to Abyssinian notions, and it was one to which governors in peripheral areas adapted only slowly. As Johnson argues below, traditionally there was no idea of a fixed territory in which all the inhabitants could be counted equally as 'citizens'. Abyssinians, that is, those who spoke Semitic languages and who were Orthodox Christians, lived in a certain territory – what I have called the core. But Abyssinian power, and during the twentieth century, Shewan power in particular, was never thought to be limited to that sphere. Rather, it radiated out from the centre. The people who happened to reside in the far peripheries were not Abyssinians, but they were reserved for Abyssinian domination. This whole history appears to be encapsulated in the word that came eventually to mean citizen, *zēga*, 'subdued', 'subject', 'obedient'. Gradually *zēga* came to be applied to anyone within the boundaries of the modern state, under the dominion of the nation.[145]

Whereas most of the highlands experienced a steadily increasing tempo of commercialization during the twentieth century, the fringe lowlands appear to have seen a moderate boom in trade that began in the late nineteenth century and then tapered off. This early expansion was fuelled mainly by the ivory trade. As Douglas Johnson shows below, the trade in ivory reached far beyond the borders of modern Ethiopia, influencing the pattern of leadership among Sudanese peoples, particularly among the Nuer. Following Evans-Pritchard's influential work, anthropologists have thought of the Nuer as the 'type case' of an acephalous segmentary society. Analysing the historical context of Nuer leadership in a way that Evans-Pritchard did not, Johnson argues that the Nuer had many local leaders, leaders who built up followings by exchanging ivory for firearms with merchants from Ethiopia. Moreover, these leaders did not preside over alliances and oppositions predicted only by lineage segmentation. Who sided with whom among border Nilotes had as much to do with the latest actions of British colonial officials on one side of the border and Ethiopian governors and merchants on the other.

The ivory trade also figures prominently in David Turton's analysis of how the Mursi dominated the Kwegu in southern Ethiopia. This kind of partially concealed dominance relationship is found elsewhere in Ethiopia, for example in the Somali lowlands, and it reminds us once again that people in the periphery often developed forms of inequality before their incorporation into imperial Ethiopia, even if these were different in some ways from those of Abyssinian political economy. Because of the relative isolation of the area that Turton describes, the ivory trade began late, toward the end of the nineteenth century, and continued well after elephants in most other areas had been wiped out, indeed until the revolution. Kwegu hunters killed elephants after which most of the ivory was appropriated by their Mursi patrons. Exactly why and how Mursi were able to maintain this kind of domination is an intricate question. Turton shows that a large part of the answer is contained in how Kwegu married.

Marriage also forms the crux of the issue in Wendy James' essay. Like several other chapters, James' is an attempt to place a theory from anthropology – Lévi-Strauss' analysis of forms of marriage exchange – in historical context. As the semi-independent ruler of Gubba in far western Ethiopia was building up his powers through extensive marriage alliances, the surrounding Gumuz – slave-raided by Gubba – resisted. And that resistance was institutionally grounded in the Gumuz system of sister exchange. No Gumuz could marry just because of his wealth; he had to have a 'sister' in order to exchange for a wife. This prevented a build-up of power such as was occurring in Gubba, and it played an important rôle in reconstituting Gumuz society as different sections of the people fled across the Abbay into present-day Wellegga.

THE MAKING OF SOUTHERN HISTORY

This then was the context in which southern peoples made their history during the first three-quarters of the twentieth century, the context in which they struggled, acquiesced, and simply lived their lives. Central institutions and types of centre–periphery linkage provide the background against which southern history becomes intelligible, but they do not comprise the whole story. Local histories were never simply determined by the centre. What happened was also influenced by the organization of local societies and cultures, even the presence of local personalities. This aspect of southern history is perhaps best illustrated by changes in traditional religions.

As already explained, many leaders in the south were made into *balabbat* by the northern administration. What Abyssinians probably never quite understood, however, was that the character of leadership in the south was often different from that of a 'big man' in a peasant political economy. Many southern leaders were essentially religious figures, like the Maale *kati* described below, who, while receiving some tribute, nevertheless had strictly limited political powers. When this kind of leader was made into a representative of the Ethiopian state, the religious and political aspects of local leadership were often split apart. This happened in a variety of ways. If the office had been traditionally inherited by a first son, a second son sometimes took over the rôle of *balabbat* while the first continued to carry out local religious functions. In this way was mediated the contradiction between the old religious rôles of assuring well-being, fertility, and abundance to one's people and the new political task of overseeing tax collection, relaying orders from above, and generally reinforcing the exploitations required by the Ethiopian state.

At other times, the rôle of *balabbat* was carried out by women, widows of local leaders, whose sons then carried out the religious functions. Judith Olmstead has argued that women – traditional mediators in kinship systems dominated by men – were natural choices to act as intermediaries between local political systems of the south and the dominant centre of the north.[146] One of the female chiefs of Gofa became influential enough in this rôle to be listed as a regular guest at Zewditu's state banquets.[147] Finally, at still other times, a northerner who had married into the family of a local leader carried out the functions of *balabbat* while the head of the family retained religious functions. This happened in areas of the Gamo highlands described by Jacques Bureau.[148] In Arsi, too, we are told that the majority of *balabbat* were Amhara by the time of the Italian occupation (though some of these may well have been assimilated Oromo rather than northern settlers).[149]

The division between local religious and political rôles represents the actions of local peoples in dealing with their own situations, 'making their own history'. Division was, evidently, an attempt to resist cultural incorporation, and in particular to draw a boundary around traditional religion. This theme appears clearly in Uri Almagor's chapter on Dassanetch – Amhara relations. In a pattern not unlike the splitting of religious and political rôles that took place in many areas of the highlands, Dassanetch 'Bulls', elders in the age-grade system of this lowland society, kept the real power and legitimacy in the local system, while other men became *balabbat*. The latter were put in a difficult structural position as mediators between the Dassanetch and Amhara, and more than once, they were beaten by peers when they appeared to go against Dassanetch interests.

Division of political and religious rôles did not take place in all southern societies. In Maale, after a period in which political and religious rôles were separated, the two were reunited and the character of local leadership was finally decisively transformed. Maale *balabbat* became very much like their northern counterparts. They began to speak Amharic and to adopt northern customs and dress. They became, essentially, Ethiopian landlords, even though some of the ideology of the old religious rôle remained. Whether political and religious functions remained united or separated depended, as my own chapter attempts to show, on people's actions in the context of particular local conditions and coalitions.

While religious rôles began to change as a response to new political requirements, entirely new religious phenomena also developed. The spread of Islam was an outstanding case. Particularly in areas closer to the Shewan core where traditional religious systems had decayed or had been destroyed, Islam became an attractive way for some southern peoples to re-establish their identities *vis-à-vis* northerners.[150] In other areas, Protestantism offered the same possibility. Foreign missionaries generally were not allowed to work in the Orthodox north, but in the south, strong churches emerged in several places, and non-Orthodox religion began to underline the ethnic differences between northerners and southerners. The Mekane Yesus Church in Wellegga and the Sudan Interior Mission in Welaita are two examples.[151]

More dramatic still was the spread of possession cults. Again, these cults seem generally to have taken root in those areas of the south closer to the Shewan core rather than on the far periphery (where traditional religions remained less challenged). In the Oromo areas just west of Shewa investigated by Karl Knutsson and Herbert Lewis, the *ḳallu*, a person possessed by divine spirits, had begun to fulfil local judicial functions.[152] By passing over their *balabbat* (by then thoroughly Ethiopianized) and by skirting around the local administration (in which delays and the requirement to give bribes had become customary), local Oromo brought their disputes to the spirit medium. Again, a barrier was erected to protect internal social processes from outside domination; local cultures thus showed their creativity in dealing with imperial domination, sometimes in quite unusual ways.

The timing of these heterodox religious developments is an interesting question in itself. More research needs to be done, but it appears that the brief

Italian occupation was a period of great religious transformation for some southern peoples. It has been reported, for example, that the Arsi Oromo finally became committed Muslims only during the occupation, and that before, the presence of Islam had been superficial.[153] The spread of Protestantism in Welaita during the same period (when foreign missionaries had been expelled from the country) was spectacular.[154] And John Hinnant has reported that possession cults began among the Guji Oromo in Sidamo during the Italian occupation.[155] It would seem that southern peoples – suddenly aware that northern domination was not inevitable – began to reassemble and recreate their religious lives.

CONCLUSION

Ideally, the following essays would have been evenly distributed over space and with respect to time. In fact, we have case studies in four of the eight macro-regions of the south – approximately the western half of the south. And most of the essays concentrate on the early twentieth century – roughly up to 1935. What are some of the themes we have thus missed? Let me mention two by focusing briefly on two areas, Harer to the east and Gurage-Kambata close to Shewa.

It is interesting to compare Johnson's analysis of the western frontier with the eastern one that existed just beyond the city of Harer. Johnson argues that the Ethiopian administration in the west was much more successful in adapting to and using local political structures than the Anglo-Egyptian administration in the Sudan. Religious leaders, in particular, did not fit British notions of proper rule, and hence, after some conflict, they were systematically eliminated. Ethiopia, on the other hand, was much less rigid in its expectations and was able to adapt, quite flexibly, to whatever type of local political organization it happened to find (even if local peoples themselves rearranged political and religious rôles as a result).

This type of analysis would hold in a number of macro-regions of the south. But, interestingly, it does not appear to be true of the far eastern frontier dominated by the sub-centre Harer. Most notably, there was strong resistance by the Somali religious leader, the so-called Mad Mullah, Muhammed ibn 'Abd Allah Hasan, beginning in the early years of the twentieth century.[156] In the east, apparently, the Ethiopian administration, along with its British counterpart across the border, failed rather dramatically to adapt to local religion and politics.

There seem to be several reasons for this. First of all, as Peter Garretson has pointed out, the eastern frontier was garrisoned with considerably more soldiers than the west or the south.[157] This, no doubt, was related to the strategic value of the east as the main commercial route from Shewa to the sea. In any case, with such backing, the Ethiopian administration in the area may have taken a more rigid attitude. It may have relied more upon force than flexibility. This speculation, in turn, suggests that the pattern Johnson has analysed for the west may have been based, at least in part, on lack of force. Ethiopian administrators may have had little alternative but to be flexible.

A second reason for the distinctiveness of the eastern frontier was probably religious-cum-political. This involved not just the presence of Islam (the administration got on well with Muslim leaders in the west such as those of Jimma and Bela Shangul). More importantly, the east was the site of a long struggle between cultivators and pastoralists; in the sixteenth century it was the home of Ahmad ibn Ibrahim al-Ghazi, the only invader who had come close to extinguishing the Abyssinian state. The historical memory of this clash – often phrased in terms of a conflict between Islam and Christianity – may have made relations on the eastern frontier more difficult.

Besides the absence of the east from this collection, we have not included studies from the macro-regions that abutted directly on Shewa. Had we been able to add the Gurage–Kambata area, for example, one aspect of centre–periphery relations not covered here, namely labour migration, would have come into focus. As I have pointed out above, the demand for wage labour in twentieth-century Ethiopia was modest. Perhaps it is logical that only the regions closest to Addis Abeba would have been involved. But more was involved than just distance, as in colonial Africa. Gurage and Kambata (the first described in the work of William Shack) were areas of extremely high population density, and as population increased further in the twentieth century, some people were pushed out first into trade, then into migration to Addis Abeba to work as day labourers, and then finally in the 1960s to work in the cane fields of the sugar mills set up in the Awash Valley.[158]

Culturally, too, these regions closer to Shewa seem to have been different from many of the case studies included here. Specifically, the Orthodox church was stronger among local peoples (where Islam had not penetrated before the conquest). In the terms which I have developed above, peoples in these regions were more 'Abyssinianized' than any of the people described below. For example, the extreme polarization between local people and Amhara, such as existed in Dassanetchland, appear not to have existed. What difference common membership in the church made to ethnic categories like 'Gurage' and 'Amhara' is an interesting question; generally, there seems to have been more fluidity in ethnicity in these regions closer to Shewa, at least for non-Islamic peoples.[159]

Despite neglect of these themes, the following essays begin to analyse the history of southern societies in a way not attempted before. They describe both local society and the larger context of imperial domination. The resulting story of state-building – as it is sometimes too blandly called – is hardly unique. England and Russia, to mention only two examples, went through broadly similar phases of development in earlier periods of their history and are still dealing with the residues. Today, Ethiopia is much less advanced along that path, and, in some ways, resembles other post-colonial states in Africa that have had a very different history. Abyssinianization, while successful in holding together a weakly integrated empire in the past, is manifestly maladapted to the later twentieth century, particularly for a socialist Ethiopia. New notions of citizenship are required, new forms of national identity that are not simply extensions of the old, new notions of the worth of different cultures. These processes have perhaps begun. In recalling the history of the south, we hope that the following chapters will make some contribution to their continuation.

II Renegotiating power and authority

2

Neḳempte and Addis Abeba: dilemmas of provincial rule

ALESSANDRO TRIULZI

In this chapter I attempt to describe the relationship between a provincial ruler in Wellegga – Kumsa Moroda – and central authorities in imperial Ethiopia. Specifically, I hope to show that the ties that linked the provincial capital of Neḳemte to the centre of government not only helped to consolidate Shewan–Amhara rule over the western province but also provided new opportunities for Kumsa to expand his own influence. In other words, I intend to show how the periphery (Neḳemte) used the centre (Addis Abeba) to consolidate its own 'periphery', particularly Sibu territory and the so-called 'Arab' land, that is Bela Shangul, to the north-west.

The main source I use in this chapter is the official correspondence exchanged between the Oromo ruler of Neḳemte and the central government between the mid-1890s and the early 1920s. Since this time span includes the reigns of three successive Ethiopian rulers, Menilek II, *lij* Iyasu and *ras* Teferi, the correspondence is of special interest in that it shows the continuity, as well as the complexity, of a particular centre–periphery relationship. Although it would probably be unwise to generalize the results of the present analysis to other annexed regions of the south, I believe the Neḳemte–Addis Abeba case to be significant enough to enable historians to evaluate critically what has been referred to at times as a 'colonial' relationship. Equally, the use of such general terms as 'direct' or 'indirect' rule, the second being the traditional label for Wellegga, proves to be altogether inadequate in the light of the evidence offered by this correspondence. We must therefore inquire in some greater depth into the real nature of a relationship whose origins and motivations are to be found both in local events and in a policy of imperial domination of the annexed provinces.

BACKGROUND TO THE RELATIONSHIP

By the early 1880s, when Gojjamē and Shewan forces made their first inroads west of the Gibe River, the territory lying around Neḳemte in eastern Wellegga was ruled by Moroda, son of Bakare Godana. Bakare was said to be the first 'king' (*moti*) to have united the Leḳa of the Neḳemte region, a subgroup of the Mecha Oromo.[1] This group – usually labelled as Leḳa-Neḳemte to distinguish it from the Leḳa-Ḳelem living north of Tulluu Waalel in the Gidami region – inhabited the area bordered by the Angar River in the north, the Wama River in the south, the Gibe River in the east, and the Diddessa River in the west (see Map 9). This last river, which flows at the bottom of a deep and (in the past) often impassable valley, was also the ethnic border with the neighbouring Sibu, another of the western Mecha sub-groups, who inhabited the territory lying south of the Abbay and east of the Dabus Rivers.

In the past the name Wellegga was applied only to the Sibu-inhabited territory lying west of the Diddessa, while the region situated to the east was called Leḳa.[2] The Leḳa and the Sibu had been traditional rivals since their establishment in the Diddessa area in the mid-eighteenth century when they separated from the main body of the western Mecha in the upper Gibe region. Both groups traditionally participated in the central institution of Oromo society, the *gadaa* system, a ritual and political institution according to which 'holders of the most important political offices were elected for a period of eight years, after which they had to retire and hand over their offices to their successors'.[3]

By the mid-1800s however, parallel to similar processes taking place in the Gibe region, the authority of the traditional *gadaa* officials among the Leḳa-Neḳemte was increasingly challenged by war leaders and other men of influence. One of these, Bakare Godana, managed to build up a position of power around 1851 after his elective period had passed.[4] Bakare, who is remembered in local traditions as a 'man of war',[5] is said to have gradually 'subjected to his rule the many families around Neḳemte, thus unifying the area under a single family'.[6] This was a policy which was strenuously continued by his own son, Moroda, after Bakare died in 1868.

Moroda expanded his father's domains by a blend of diplomacy and conquest until the late 1870s, when he claimed supremacy over vast stretches of territory west of the Diddessa, well beyond the traditional boundary of the Leḳa. Moroda's claims were strongly contested in these new regions, particularly by his Sibu opponents across the Diddessa, by other Leḳa antagonists such as the Nole Kabba, and by the Bera family of the Arjo region to the south-west. This was the situation in the early 1880s when *ras* Gobena arrived in the region at the head of a contingent of well-armed Shewan forces. As it happened, Gobena's arrival presented the Leḳa ruler with an opportunity to consolidate his precarious claims over new territories. This he did by posing as mediator between *ras* Gobena and the other Leḳa rulers of the region whom he seems to have persuaded to submit to the advancing Shewan force. In the process, Moroda's opponents, such as the Nole Kabba and the Arjo people, were soon defeated with the help of Gobena's army, while Sibu resistance was temporarily checked.[7]

It should also be remembered that Moroda, who had previously submitted to *ras* Daraso of Gojjam in the late 1870s, was convinced by Gobena to keep neutral in the territorial dispute between Shewa and Gojjam which ended in

Map 9 The Blue Nile Basin: to illustrate Chapters 2 and 5

2 Women grinding flour at the residence of a *ras*. From the 'Mission Ozil' album of 1908, in the Institute of Ethiopian Studies, Addis Abeba

the Battle of Embabo of 1882.[8] In exchange for his policy of non-alignment, in which he apparently involved several Oromo rulers of the region, Moroda was recognized as sole ruler of his territory and appointed *dejazmach* by Menilek.[9]

From a formal point of view, it seems that the Leḳa territory ruled by Moroda was then declared *madbēt* by Menilek. In the Shewan land tenure system, *madbēt* (from *mad*, table, especially one set for bread) is said to be 'a rural domain whose revenues are especially reserved for the king's mouth'[10] and is considered more generally as 'land which supplied the royal household with grain, pepper, and other goods'.[11] The exact terms of Moroda's appointment, however, are not known. Sources are vague as to what Moroda's appointment entailed as well as to its territorial and administrative implications. In fact, the circumstances of the appointment, which have been narrated by Terrefe Woldetsadik on the basis of *blatta* Derēssa's colourful account, are surrounded by something of the atmosphere of legend. Following the Battle of Embabo, Moroda is reported visiting Menilek upon Gobena's own advice:

> Moroda agreed and took with him a small bag of gold which, asking for a private interview with the king, he emptied on the floor, saying: 'the soil of my father produces this; if you want [it] take me; if you don't, give me to anyone you like and you will get only a quarter of this.' Thereupon the king summoned Gobena and told him that henceforth Moroda's lands should belong directly to his *madbēt* [palace], with no one in between. Thus the chief of Wellegga-Neḳemte secured the direct overlordship of Menilek.[12]

Whether this story is apocryphal or not, the chronicle of Kumsa Moroda (whose Christian name was Gebre Igzīabihēr) makes no mention of it, nor of the fact that Wellegga was made a *madbēt*. The chronicle merely states:

> Two years after the Battle of Embabo *dejazmach* Moroda himself went to Menilek. *Dejazmach* Moroda took with him an uncountable amount of money, ivory, gold, civet, leopard and lion skins as gifts for Menilek. Menilek in return gave Moroda a lot of presents. At that time all the Galla west of Guder submitted. *Dejazmach* Jote also sent his brother with Moroda to Addis Abeba to pay tribute. Within a short time all the Galla who had previously submitted revolted in many places. *Dejazmach* Moroda, *dejazmach* Jote and *abba* Jifar remained loyal. Thus those who revolted lost their lands to the *neftennya* while the territories of these three rulers remained in their hands.[13]

Since political loyalty was just as important as economic wealth to the central government's hold over the western periphery, both sources are probably correct in emphasizing one or the other aspect. There seems to be little doubt, however, as to Menilek's real motive in wanting to establish a direct tie over the gold-producing western district. In the words of a local informant: 'It was because of gold that we became a *madbēt*. It was because he [Moroda] gave gold to Menilek that he made us to be his *madbēt*.'[14]

The economic aspect of subjugation is shown further by another, less considered, aspect of the original agreement between Menilek, Gobena, and Moroda. There was a basic antagonism between Menilek and his general Gobena over the economic resources of the west, and Moroda used that tension to promote his own interests. Sources are altogether silent about any overt antagonism between Gobena and Menilek, but both Cerulli and Atsme make reference to it in their works,[15] and there are definite hints in both Ethiopian and European sources of Menilek's fears of Gobena's growing powers and wealth by the mid-1880s.[16] Wellegga sources substantiate the existence of such conflicts and provide new evidence for their background.

According to *blatta* Derēssa, Moroda extracted, as a condition of his not taking sides in the Shewa–Gojjamē dispute, a formal promise from Gobena that his rule over western Wellegga would not be interfered with: 'So Gobena promised and took an oath (*kaka*) in the name of his king that he [Moroda] should be ruled directly by the king and pay tribute only to him . . . No overlordship except to Menilek was to be recognized.'[17] It seems however that at a later stage, probably around 1888, after Gobena had helped Moroda repel a combined Mahdist–Sibu attack near Nejjo at the battle of Gute Dili, Gobena broke the initial covenant by appointing his own son, Wedajo, as overseer of all market and customs duties in Moroda's land.[18] *Blatta* Derēssa, in relating the event, claims that Moroda 'attempted to object to the [appointment] on the basis of the original *kaka* between Moroda and Gobena. But Gobena pointed out that they had not mentioned this previously. The oath only applied to Moroda's land where he could retain his chieftainship. Moreover, *dejazmach* Wedajo was to rule over Wellegga as Gobena's *inderassē* [representative].'[19]

Gebre Igzīabihēr's chronicle indirectly confirms this when it states that Gobena, after the Anfillo campaign of 1886 that carried his troops to the Sibu and Ḳelem territories north and west of Neḳemte, 'appointed some of his trusted men to rule the newly conquered areas as they were too vast for Moroda to rule.'[20] Following Moroda's protest against Gobena's breach of the original covenant, Menilek is reported to have summoned the Leḳa ruler together with his war general.[21] If we are to believe *blatta* Derēssa, this event eventually led to Menilek's decreeing Moroda's domains as *madbēt*, that is, re-establishing direct overlordship of the central government over the western region.

The chronicle further reveals that, at the death of Moroda in 1889, his son Kumsa (Gebre Igzīabihēr; see Plate 3) was merely authorized by Menilek 'to keep the territories of his father till the next spring when he was expected at court'. During their formal encounter the following year, Menilek confirmed Gobena's appointments in Wellegga. 'There and then', we are told by the chronicler, 'Gebre Igzīabihēr appealed to Menilek to restore to him all the areas taken away by *ras* Gobena and given to his soldiers. Menilek then ordered Sibu Wellegga east of Kujur River to be returned to Gebre Igzīabihēr but that the remaining areas of Nole Kabba, Dapo, Sibu, Gibe and Siba Jorgo were not part of Moroda's domains as they had been conquered by Gobena and given to his soldiers.'[22]

On the basis of the evidence presented by Gebre Igzīabihēr's chronicle, it is possible to make the following points: (1) in assuming the throne, Menilek attempted to delimit the territorial extent of his provincial vassal by recognizing only the latter's hereditary rights over the Leḳa region to the exclusion of all the territories which Gobena had 'helped' Moroda to conquer, that is the Nole Kabba-Arjo region to the south-west, and the Sibu region between the Kujur River and the Dabus. This is consistent with early nineteenth-century Ethiopian and European sources which limit Leḳa proper to the country between the Angar and the Diddessa Rivers.[23] (2) Further, Menilek decreed the administrative organization of the new province. By making it an official *madbēt* for the court's own upkeep, he established direct links between the crown and the western region whose wealth was not to be spoiled by a centrally appointed administration that by its own nature could only 'feed' itself from resources of the assigned territory. (3) Finally, Menilek made his 'royal kitchen' secure by setting up a double structure of political and military checks on his western Oromo vassal. This he did not only by allowing 'Gobena's soldiers' (i.e. central government troops) to maintain strategic strongholds west and south of Neḳemte, but also by retaining control of the Sibu region bordering the yet unconquered 'Arab' territory north-west of Neḳemte.

This compromise was probably accepted by Gebre Igzīabihēr (then only eighteen years old) and by his advisers because it had certain advantages. Being Menilek's *madbēt* meant, at the beginning at least, payment of a fixed tribute in exchange for internal autonomy, while the very location of the

3 *Dejazmach* Gebre Igzīabihēr

Shewan strongholds in the region gave little cause for concern. In effect, both the Sibu in the north-west and the Nole Kabba-Arjo districts in the south-west were 'rebel regions' at the periphery of the provincial capital. Their rulers were traditional rivals of the Bakare ruling family in Neḳemte, and Moroda had made them submit with no little effort using Gobena's help.[24] Therefore the presence of central government troops in these places, though they represented a potential threat to Gebre Igzīabihēr's authority in the region, offered only a minimal degree of interference in his rule over western Wellegga.

The situation was to change in the years to follow, and the precarious nature of the 1889 compromise soon revealed itself. The 1898 expedition of *ras* Mekonnen to Bela Shangul annexed the northwestern corner of present-day Wellegga to Menilek's domains. Coupled with internal changes within the politico-administrative structure of the Ethiopian empire, this created new problems for the crown, which increasingly relied on the western Oromo ruler for the internal administration of the whole western region. At the same time, the heavy load in tributes and taxes, coupled with the settling of northern soldiers in various parts of the province, created new financial and political strains for the Neḳemte ruler. Gebre Igzīabihēr tried to overcome or elude these in a struggle-for-survival policy to which the correspondence with Addis Abeba bears direct evidence. Let me analyse these processes by taking three examples drawn from traditional areas of contention between the local government and central imperial authority: tribute, taxes, and land.

TRIBUTE

According to Mahteme Sellassie Wolde Maskal, Neḳemte was one of the six provinces of the 'reconquered' empire in which 'the Government did not appoint representatives but recognized established local governors who paid to the Government a single fixed tribute for their region'.[25] He also claims that such tribute was paid in kind every year 'according to the agricultural produce derived from each of them'. The Neḳemte rulers were said by Zervos to be quite successful in their bids for autonomy: they paid a fixed tribute in gold and ivory to the central government and thus avoided its interference. 'The treasury of this province is autonomous. It is the governor who has the power to impose and exact tributes and to direct all administrative and military branches of government' (my translation).[26] The statements by Mahteme Sellassie and Zervos are interesting in as much as they reflect the starting point of the original relationship between Neḳemte and Addis Abeba, namely, the payment of a fixed tribute conceived as 'modest' by Richard Pankhurst, in exchange for administrative, financial, judicial and military autonomy.[27] The original relationship was in fact modified several times during Gebre Igzīabihēr's rule (1889–1932), mostly to the benefit of the central government, at times with some gains for the province ruler, but always at the end of a mutual process of adjustment and tug of war.

Gebre-Wold-Ingida Worq states that Wellegga traditionally paid 'a total tax of 1,000 measures of gold yearly'.[28] This is only partly supported by the official correspondence exchanged between Addis Abeba and Neḳemte. It appears from this exchange that, at the beginning, a much smaller tribute was asked from the Oromo ruler. In a letter dated September 1895, Menilek acknowledges having received a tribute of 40 measures (*weḳēt*) of gold, although he seems anxious to receive 'the rest' (an unknown quantity), and complains about the poor quality of a good half of the gold rings, which he sends back.[29] The tribute was gradually raised. It amounted to 300 *wekēt* in 1903 and was pushed to 1,000 by 1905.[30] At the same time, a certain amount of honey and ivory was sent to Addis Abeba yearly; 1,000 thalers 'in lieu of honey' was sent in 1905.[31] The honey tribute was raised to 600 large earthenware pots (*gundo*) by 1906 and increased to 1,000 by 1925. The tribute was often accompanied by 'gifts' (*meteyaya*) ranging from 20 *wekēt* in 1903 to 100 in 1906.[32] Furthermore, after Gebre Igzīabihēr had been charged with the collection of tribute from the 'Arab country' (Bela Shangul) in 1903,[33] he was taxed both in gold (600 *wekēt*) and ivory (100 tusks) on this last territory.[34]

In the exchange of letters, Gebre Igzīabihēr often laments the heavy burden placed on his country's resources. For example, in January 1905 he complains that, as his tribute has doubled, he has been forced to double his people's contribution from the Sibu lower region, the area where the gold-bearing district of Nejjo was located.[35] The following December he writes that, 'since *janhoy* [Menilek] gave me the lands of the Arabs', the demand for tribute from this region has been excessive in view of the fact that Bela Shangul has been 'divided and cut off' by the boundary settlement: 'Those people remaining at present cannot provide the 600 [*wekēt*] to us.'[36] Starting in 1910, when the newly-appointed regent, *ras* Tesemma, added to the existing tribute a sum of 13,000 thalers as provision for the northern troops (*gonderē*) stationed in the region, the burden of these impositions on Gebre Igzīabihēr's financial resources appears to have been heavy indeed. Three years later Nekemte had tribute in arrears of 3,400 measures of gold. A worried Gebre Igzīabihēr appealed to the then ruling *lij* Iyasu in these terms:

> My master, may God show you [the truth]. Formerly the tribute that I paid was 500 *wekēt* of gold. When people told *janhoy* that [my] territory was big, he fixed the tribute by doubling it to 1,000. Because the country was unable to provide these thousand *wekēt*, I started to receive from the [local] inhabitants tributes of two years and have been paying it as an annual tribute. As a result, there is an overdue payment of three years of tribute. I cannot get this from the people because they have already paid and I received [it]. It became overdue because I collected the two-year revenue as a one-year tribute. Concerning this overdue payment of tributes I pleaded to you, my master, while you were here to exempt me as I am in difficulty . . . You, my master, have seen that the country is uncultivated, this being the result of too much tribute, not because of any wrong doing on my part. And now, if I order the people to give the three-year overdue tribute, the country will be completely abandoned.[37]

The exemption seems to have been granted by *lij* Iyasu, but since this is mentioned only once in an undated letter, it may have been repealed later, along with other unorthodox gestures of the short-lived rule of Iyasu.[38] Tribute, however, was soon resumed in the old amount by *ras* Teferi when he rose to power and was kept apparently unchanged in the following years as a stable mark of imperial domination in the region.[39]

TAXES

If one were to take at face value the apparently uncontroversial dictates of the *madbēt* relationship, as expressed by the equation 'payment of fixed tribute in return for financial autonomy', Gebre Igzīabihēr was entitled to an internal right of taxation with no further interference by the central government. Yet this was not so. From 1888 to 1892 Ethiopia was hit by cattle disease and other epidemics that brought the country to the verge of famine.[40] As a consequence of decreased central revenues, a series of new taxes was imposed along with the yearly tribute. A 10 per cent tax on gold was applied, starting in 1901.[41] In 1907 there followed a tax on ivory, while the counting of cattle 'free of disease' for purposes of taxation was started in 1906.[42] A tithe on grain (*asrat*) had been imposed throughout the empire since 1901.[43]

It was probably because of the Great Famine of the mid-1890s that the original tributary relationship was gradually transformed into one of direct domination. This point is brought forward clearly in Gebre Igzīabihēr's chronicle:

> It was a time of great famine. People came to Gebre Igzīabihēr's country from Gojjam, Shewa and from the Galla regions. Bakare Godana and *dejazmach* Moroda had stored grain. So when the famine-stricken people came to him, he fed them for three years. Emperor Menilek also heard about this. Thus he sent 200 *gonderē* to Gebre Igzīabihēr to feed them for at least one rainy season. The following year was not a year of plenty, and Menilek once again asked Gebre Igzīabihēr to feed the *gonderē* for him. This process of 'feed for me' continued until the *gonderē* remained here, planted . . . The famine thus continued for four years. Every living thing suffered. Rats destroyed seeds before they sprouted, and birds destroyed the seeds that escaped from the rats.[44]

The settling of northern soldiers in Gebre Igzīabihēr's domains in the early 1900s was the first signal that things were changing for the worse. Although most *gonderē* troops were quartered away from his personal domains and interfered little in his administration,[45] Gebre Igzīabihēr was asked to pay 10,000 thalers a year for their provisions, a sum which, as we have seen, was later raised to 23,000 thalers.[46] Furthermore, some 1,300 *gonderē* appear to have been quartered in the provincial capital itself and were a source of continuous friction for the Oromo ruler who on several occasions pleaded with the central government to be relieved of their presence.[47] In 1913 Gebre Igzīabihēr lamented:

> Coupled with the country's impoverishment, *ras bitwedded* Tesemma added on me 13,000 thalers to be paid as provision for the *gonderē* . . . for the forthcoming tribute, I have planted plenty of coffee. I have forced the [local] people to plant coffee. As for tributes in the future, I will be able to pay. What worries me is the overdue tributes and the extra 13,000 thalers' worth of provisions for the *gonderē* which *ras bitwedded* Tesemma imposed on me and which *janhoy* had not asked from me.[48]

Furthermore, as the number of *gonderē* was continuously growing, money dried up quickly. In April 1917 Gebre Igzīabihēr wrote to the new regent, *ras* Teferi to warn him that:

> In accordance with *janhoy*'s order, I used to give 10,000 thalers to the *gonderē* for their provisions. Later on, *ras bitwedded* Tesemma added 13,000 thalers on me . . . I have already paid this year's provisions worth 23,000 thalers. The year's pay starts on the 19th of Senē [26 June]. However they [the *gonderē*] came to get their pay before the due date. I told them that I had already paid this year's and that the date for the coming year's pay has not yet approached . . .[49]

At the same time Gebre Igzīabihēr hastened to alert Teferi that, since 'they [the soldiers] might falsely accuse me of having refused to provide food for the campaigners' women', the regent must be informed that the *gonderē* money which Gebre Igzīabihēr provides 'is used up before the end of the year, [because] the men who get provisions at *ras* Demissew's place [Arjo] are many. This *ras* Demissew himself knows . . .' And again in November of the same year (1917), he complained that his own people were leaving his country 'because the tribute was too much and the country [had] turned into a desert'.[50]

In spite of Gebre Igzīabihēr's repeated protests, *ras* Demissew's soldiers remained in the region until the Italian occupation. Gebre Igzīabihēr had no alternative but to bow to the central government on the *gonderē* issue. After all, this was the price for keeping his own people free of the much more exacting *gebbar–neftennya* relationship in which soldiers were fed directly out of peasants' labour. In this respect Gebre Igzīabihēr himself was *ras* Dimessew's own *gebbar*, except that their relationship was basically a financial one. The burden of the central government's impositions thus fell heavily on Gebre Igzīabihēr's own resources.

However much Gebre Igzīabihēr resented taxes and soldiers, the correspondence shows that he was even more disturbed by the presence of Menilek's overseers, judges, and especially customs inspectors in Nekemte. The latter were sent from Addis Abeba allegedly to check 'contraband' but in reality to keep an eye on the region's rule and resources. Menilek tried to reassure Gebre Igzīabihēr of the limited jurisdiction of the central government envoys more than once. In a letter of June 1901 he stated that *neggadras* Yggezu, the central government appointee in Nekemte,

> . . . should not interfere with [Gebre Igzīabihēr's] right of [collecting] customs duties at markets. The taxes are always and ever yours. However, if a person is found having passed through the gates secretly without paying the tax, I have told him [Yggezu] to place men to guard [the gates]. I have told him not to interfere in taxes or customs duties. His jurisdiction over men [traders] who pass the gates without paying the duties depends on your justice. This is not something that should cause any difficulty to you.[51]

Apparently however the presence of central government envoys in the capital did cause difficulty and proved to be a major source of friction between the central government and Gebre Igzīabihēr. For one thing, the Addis Abeba envoys were there to assess the real wealth of the country and thus exercised a direct control on Gebre Igzīabihēr's finances – witness the fact that tribute in gold was raised from 300 *weḳēt* in 1903 to 1,000 in 1905. But above all Menilek's men interfered with the most precious, and apparently lucrative, of Gebre Igzīabihēr's revenues, the taxes on trade that were exacted at the country's customs gates (*kella*) and markets.

The situation seems to have worsened particularly after the official opening, in 1905, of central government customs offices both around Leka proper, at Billo in eastern Wellegga and Mendi in Sibu country, and, what was worse, in the town of Neḳemte itself. Theoretically, the emperor's *neggadras* were only asked to exact a 5 per cent tax on trade on behalf of the central government. At the same time, they were to ensure that traders who had not paid their customs dues at the government's gates situated between Addis Abeba and Neḳemte (Addis Alem, Toki, Chaliya and Billo) would pay in this last locality.[52] It seems however that the imperial *neggadras* often went beyond their assignment and taxed both local and external traders arbitrarily:

> *Janhoy*, earlier a seal had come [from you] stating that *neggadras* Yggezu, by *janhoy*'s order, could supervise the work in my town Neḳemte concerning those who do not bear the seal of the customs office at Billo; *neggadras* Yggezu used to levy customs duties on those [traders] coming through various routes as well as supervising in Neḳemte. Later on, *neggadras* Ṭenna Gashaw, while supervising in Neḳemte, collected duties up to the present. And now, in the town of Neḳemte itself, the men of *neggadras* Haile Gīyorgis are levying duties for a second time on those who had already obtained the seal from *neggadras* Ṭenna Gashaw's man and passed [the gate]. *Neggadras* Ṭenna Gashaw's men are levying five out of a hundred as usual. Again, in Neḳemte itself, on the same day and in the same area the men of *neggadras* Haile Gīyorgis are levying five out of a hundred. Because of this the poor suffer and groan.[53]

The dispute was clearly a major one. As Gebre Igzīabihēr pointed out to the central government several times, it was only through the collection of customs dues that he could pay tribute: 'I pay my tribute by virtue of the money collected as taxes at gates and dues on markets, not because the country is rich enough.'[54] Furthermore, the presence in Neḳemte of imperial agents, who taxed traders the same as Gebre Igzīabihēr's own men, threatened to destroy one of the region's main sources of income. Gebre Igzīabihēr pleaded several times to be allowed to collect dues both for himself and for the central government but to no avail. Although the imperial *neggadras* were ordered eventually to limit taxation to gold and markets, leaving the gates' dues to Gebre Igzīabihēr's own people, the double system of taxation increased the tension between Neḳemte and Addis Abeba. In February 1907 Gebre Igzīabihēr appealed to Empress Ṭaytu in these words:

> *Eteggē*, may God show you [the truth]. When I came last year, I pleaded to you to intercede for me to have *janhoy* agree that no one should interfere with my right of collecting dues at the customs office here and that I would give to *janhoy* the money which I collected from the dues. While I was waiting for a decision, Sarsa Weld came with *janhoy*'s seal instructing me to relinquish the right of collecting dues at markets and on gold, although when the customs office was

> established *janhoy* did not take away [this right] from me. Also, those who purify gold and attend the markets are the [local] inhabitants, not traders coming from another region. And now why should the [local] inhabitants be interfered with to my disadvantage? What did I do wrong? For, when the customs house was established, *janhoy* had allowed me [to be in charge of it].[55]

In October 1907 the Nekemte ruler apparently regained his taxation rights over 'both gates and markets' in his territory, with the exception of the important gate of Mendi in Sibu country. However, the general supervision of the central government's customs office in Nekemte was given to the recently appointed minister of finance, *bejirond* Mulugēta, in 1910. This sealed the right of the centre to fiscal control over Nekemte, a right that Addis Abeba was never to abandon in the years to come.[56]

THE MENDI GATE AND THE SIBU LANDS

The question of the Mendi gate in Sibu country presented Gebre Igzīabihēr with a particularly crucial problem which requires separate treatment. Mendi was the main gate for Sudanese–Ethiopian trade in the west, the gate that connected Oromo traders with the 'land of the Arabs', Bela Shangul. It is no wonder, then, that Mendi was coveted by both Nekemte and Addis Abeba.

In the wave of his initial (but limited) success over the Nekemte customs dues in 1907, Gebre Igzīabihēr did in fact attempt to have his authority extended to the crucial gate of Mendi in Sibu country. That he did not lose time in trying to stretch his authority farther west is shown by a letter to Menilik dated 14 December 1907:

> *Janhoy* . . . You sent me a letter in which you wrote that you had restored the gates and markets to me, as in former times, and I was glad and stationed my men at the markets and gates. Also the gate at Mendi belonged to my father formerly. Believing that, when *Janhoy* restored to me the gates and markets, you did not keep the gate at Mendi away from me, I placed my men there. And now *ato* Sarsa Weld's men refused to leave it to me and are levying taxes [there]. The result is that the poor were hurt. Being at the same gate, they as well as I are levying taxes and the traders are suffering. The routes have been closed. *Janhoy*, may God show you [the truth].[57]

The question of Mendi and its gate was not a new one; it was connected with the recently annexed district of Bela Shangul. After the deportation to Addis Abeba of the three ruling shaykhs of Bela Shangul in 1898, a state of general anarchy was reported in the region. *Ras* Demissew, the over-ruler of this district and the head of the Shewan–Amhara soldiers stationed in Wellegga, had met increasing difficulties both in exacting tribute from the rebellious region and in keeping law and order. Besides, the two small garrisons kept at Afodu and Goha near Dul in Bela Shangul found it difficult to adapt to the torrid climate and seem to have exercised little or no authority over the local Bertha inhabitants. The first five years of Shewan–Amhara direct rule over the region, it was reported, had 'made wilderness out of Beni Shangul'.[58]

In 1903 *ras* Demissew's forces were apparently withdrawn from the district, and he was asked to hand over his authority to Gebre Igzīabihēr. The administration of Bela Shangul between 1903 and 1908 by a peripheral Oromo vassal is an interesting case of 'indirect rule' where the so-called *pax amharica* was in fact mediated through what one may call *pax oromonica*. The topic is of interest in itself and would require a detailed treatment which goes beyond the scope of this paper. Since my aim here is to focus on the basic Neḳemte–Addis Abeba relationship, I want simply to stress the consequences of this form of 'indirect rule' on the bargaining position of the Neḳemte ruler *vis-à-vis* the central government.

After Gebre Igzīabihēr was given control over Bela Shangul in 1903, he was apparently expected to collect a tribute of 600 *wekēt* of gold from the 'Arab' region.[59] He also appears to have been empowered to judge cases and to mediate disputes concerning this region as well as to ensure law and order. Gebre Igzīabihēr made no small use of his powers over his newly acquired 'periphery'. In July 1907 he asked, and was granted, the right 'to till the land in the country of the Arabs'.[60] Previously in November of 1906, he had asked to collect taxes directly[61] and the following month had asked to levy dues at the markets and gates of the northern district.[62] Formally, the *rationale* behind Gebre Igzīabihēr's requests was that he had to send the yearly tribute from Bela Shangul to Addis Abeba. Yet it seems that there was more to it; writing in December 1906 to *ḳennyazmach* Yebesh, perhaps one of his own men at court in Addis Abeba, Gebre Igzīabihēr stated:

> Concerning the collection of taxes in the land of the Arabs, it was my right even in former times. It was from my own hands that *neggadras* Haile Gīyorgis' men took it. And now . . . plead this matter for me to *janhoy* for it would help me cover the expenses for the soldiers' pay. I wrote letters to you as well as to *janhoy* [about it]. I even said that I was willing to collect the dues myself and pay twice as much money to *janhoy*. Since the time that *janhoy* said that they [Haile Gīyorgis' men] should collect the taxes and give me the money, the [Arab] land has been added [to mine] by him. Why should the work [of dues collection] be separated to my disadvantage [from the government of the region]?[63]

It is clear from this letter that Gebre Igzīabihēr was confronting the central government with a basic issue which was at the core of his own 'centre–periphery' relationship with the Arabs' land, namely, his own right to exploit the periphery. In a political reversal of rôles, he asked for those very rights toward his new periphery of which he, in his own rôle as periphery, resented being dispossessed. Thus the question of the Mendi gate became a significant test in this dual set of relationships.

In the end, Mendi was too important to the central government to be relinquished. Although Gebre Igzīabihēr claimed that Addis Abeba had usurped his own hereditary rights in taking over Mendi,[64] his pleas to have the crucial gate fell on deaf ears.[65] In 1907, when Gebre Igzīabihēr realized that he would be unable to win on this issue, he changed tactics and tried to have the central government gate moved out of his territory. 'If we stay at the same gate, and if they collect dues from the same people that we have already taxed, and vice versa, the poor will suffer.' He then continued:

> And now there is in the land of the Arabs [a place] called Egolihan [Agole] which is much more temperate than Mendi. I had a church built [there] and started farming with pairs of oxen. There is not even colds, let alone malaria. Let him [Haile Gīyorgis] go there and collect dues. The gate at Mendi has always been mine.[66]

The Agole shelter, extolled by Gebre Igzīabihēr as being 'better for human habitation than Nejjo', his northern capital, never managed to attract the central government customs people.[67] It was soon to be abandoned, in fact, following the release of the three Bela Shangul rulers in 1908 and their resumption of power. Only then did Gebre Igzīabihēr's insistence on his traditional rights over Mendi and the eastern bank of the Dabus River appear in its full light. He was instantly asked by Addis Abeba to withdraw his own people from the Bela Shangul district and to hand over jurisdiction to the local shaykhs.[68] This was an event the consequences of which the Neḳemte ruler must have anticipated with some anxiety, for he knew that his rule over the Sibu territory east of the Dabus would soon be contested not only by the central government but also by his own ex-periphery, now transformed into a local centre in its own right.

A new diplomatic offensive had to be staged. Shortly after being notified officially that his main rival, Shaykh Khojali (Hojale), had been sent back to Asosa, he wrote a first tentative letter to enquire about his remaining powers over the 'Arabs':

> *Janhoy*. You wrote me that you had restored to *sheh* Hojale his country and that he was going back there. He has accordingly entered his country. Since early times *janhoy* had given me the office of judge in the land of the Arabs. And now, shall I interfere with *sheh* Hojale in matters of justice? Or shall I not? Does the tribute to *janhoy* have to pass through me? Or shall *sheh* Hojale bring it himself?[69]

By December 1908, in answer to Menilek's invitation to mediate in a local feud among Khojali's relatives, Gebre Igzīabihēr wrote back saying that the Bela Shangul rulers were refusing Menilek's orders and that 'besides, the Arabs do not know the regulations of our country'.[70] By January 1909 the scene was set for Gebre Igzīabihēr to plead his case:

> *Janhoy*, may God show you [the truth]. Ever since *janhoy* gave me my father's territory after my father's, *dejazmach* Moroda's, death, I have never quarrelled with my neighbours. Nor have I come to *janhoy* with any serious matter . . . And now the Arabs such as *dejazmach* Abdurrahman and *sheh* Hojale crossed the Dabus and occupied my territory. That [the region] up to Dabus has been tribute-paying [did not begin] in my time. It was colonized (*teḳenna*) by my father, *dejazmach* Moroda, a long time ago. *Dejazmach* Moroda, my father, had gone on a campaign against it in the time of *ras* Gobena for whom he acted as a guide, having crossed the Dabus. That [the region] up to Dabus paid tribute to us and the way was cleared to *ras* Gobena wherever he spent the night, to this all the soldiers who went on a campaign with *ras* Gobena can bear witness.[71]

In a similar letter that Gebre Igzīabihēr sent to Empress Ṭaytu on the same day asking for her intercession, the Neḳemte ruler contended that, although 'Sibu was the old territory of my grandfather', *ras* Gobena had in fact 'sliced off' part of it and 'had given it to his soldiers'. Hence, at a time when the country was to be measured 'by the cord' (*ḳelad*), he asked Ṭaytu's help in having 'his father's property' (*rist*) in Sibu land recognized.[72] Unfortunately, there is no official answer, in the records which I examined, to these two important letters, but from one dated February 1909 it appears that Gebre Igzīabihēr was ordered by Menilek to allow Khojali to settle his people along the eastern bank of the Dabus.[73]

Nor was the Neḳemte ruler able to impress his hereditary rights to Sibu land on Menilek's successors. In September 1913 Gebre Igzīabihēr, who appears in the meantime to have limited his requests, wrote to *lij* Iyasu asking that 'half of Sibu be [his] *rist-gult*', heritable property, and complained that the central government had settled some two hundred soldiers on land he had bought in Sibu country.[74] Similarly, shortly after Teferi's rise to power, he pleaded again that 'the country in the upper part of Dabus has been my father's and mine since the time of the Galla, the time when the land of the Arabs was still unconquered'.[75] A few months later he asked for Empress Zewditu's intercession:

> O Queen. May God show you [the truth]. Sibu has been the *rist* of my grand and great-grandfather. *Ras* Gobena removed me without my doing anything wrong. I have always sought *janhoy*'s permission to have my *rist* restored to me . . . When I say Sibu, I do not mean all of Sibu but only my own *rist*. My *rist* is not even half of Sibu. Besides, the Sibu country is at present full of forests and thickets. There are no people living [there]. You can ask people to ascertain what I am saying.[76]

As in the case of the tax on traders, it appears that Gebre Igzīabihēr was confronted with another refusal by the central government. In a letter he sent to *ras* Teferi in March 1921, in which the Neḳemte ruler officially asked his *siso* holdings to be formally registered by the government, there is no mention of his previous claims over the Sibu territory:[77]

> At the time that the *ḳelad* system was started, I raised my *siso* land according to the regulation. It was not entered [then] into the government [land] register. Although *janhoy* gave me the *shaleḳannet* [rule] when he was well [in health], it was the *siso-gult* upon which the *balabbat* made their living. Men are by nature mortal and demotable. Unless it is entered into the government register now while you [are alive], [especially] if an incapable son succeeds me, my family and relatives might be dispossessed of their *rist*; therefore, let it be entered into the government register. And now, let the town of Neḳemte where I am living as well as the arid region I had bought and the country in the upper part of the Diddessa be reckoned as one out of four according to the number of *ḳelad* and be turned into *gult* for me. Let my *siso* be entered separately into the government register.[78]

Thus, in the rather sad tone of a last will and testament, Gebre Igzīabihēr resorts to the *siso* 'short cut', that is, to have at least a quarter of what remains of his once large territory considered as his successors'. This he does 'according to the regulation', that is, according to the very laws of the centre he had tried to counteract and elude in his struggle for political and economic survival.

SOME PRELIMINARY CONCLUSIONS

From the evidence presented in this paper, we may now reach some tentative conclusions which appear to be of some importance for our discussion. First, the description of Wellegga as one of the regions that paid a fixed tribute and that thereby maintained a modicum of autonomy is inadequate. In fact, Wellegga-Neḳemte fits awkwardly in any of the four regions outlined by J. Mantel-Niećko on the basis of Mahteme Sellassie's original subdivisions.[79] A diachronic analysis of the Neḳemte–Addis Abeba relationship reveals not only that Wellegga-Neḳemte was moved in time from one regional category to another, that is from one relationship to another, but that several types of relationship co-existed at any given period in time within the same territory. Thus Gebre Igzīabihēr's lands were subjected in the beginning to a fixed-tribute status which after 1910 was transformed into a *ḳelad* type of 'region' (i.e. one where land was appropriated by the central government). Within the same territory, and in the same period, we have different types of co-existing 'rules', one beside the other: a basically autonomous local rule in Neḳemte and Nejjo districts; a direct Shewan–Amhara domination that imposed a typical *gebbar-neftennya* relationship over Arjo; and a sort of Addis Abeba-ruled fiscal enclave in the Sibu territory which was entirely surrounded, in one period, by Gebre Igzīabihēr's own land. Western Wellegga proves to be an ideal example of the intricacy of imperial domination in the western region.

Second, the official correspondence exchanged between Neḳemte and Addis Abeba reveals the diplomatic qualities of the Oromo ruler. Gebre Igzīabihēr attempted to limit the damages implicit in his subordinate relationship with the central government by extending, or trying to extend, his own periphery on the outskirts of Wellegga proper. In other words, he posed or tried to pose, as a 'centre' in his own right. Doing so required, of course, a prior degree of local political centralization that other leaders in the south, such as the Maale kings described by Donham in the following chapter, did not enjoy. As we have seen, the imperial government tolerated a degree of local autonomy as long as its basic interests were not affected, and as long as the Neḳemte ruler could be effectively used to mediate the imperial presence in the whole western region. Thus Gebre Igzīabihēr was allowed to rule Bela Shangul after direct domination had failed, but was 'put back in his place', that is in his proper 'peripheral' rôle, when he attempted to derive extra benefits from it, benefits that were to be reserved for the imperial centre.

The ensuing centre–periphery relationship should be graded therefore according to time, space, *and* political convenience. It was a dynamic relationship, the result of a mutual, if unbalanced, process of continuous adjustment to and compromise with the other party's requests. In this respect, changes at the periphery (for example, the annexation of Bela Shangul) as well as changes of regime at the centre of government (the political crises involving the transfer of power from Menilek to Iyasu to Teferi) did affect the interaction between centre and periphery, for the very simple reason that they affected the bargaining position of the respective ends of the relationship.

Thus *ras* Tesemma, during his short-lived regency while Menilek was incapacitated, managed to impose on Gebre Igzīabihēr a heavier tax load than the one assigned by Menilek himself, while *lij* Iyasu's generally lenient policy towards peripheral rulers was reflected in his apparent accession to Gebre Igzīabihēr's requests to decrease the tax. Equally, the frequent appeals by the Neḳemte ruler to the real powers behind the throne (for example, to Ṭaytu before 1910) reflected both Gebre Igzīabihēr's inside knowledge of the decision-making process taking place in Addis Abeba and his attempt to exploit to his own advantage the recurrent political crises occurring at the centre of government. In this respect, the exchange of letters between Neḳemte and Addis Abeba is a further proof that provincial administration of the empire was dominated by the ups and downs of the internal struggle for power taking place at the centre.

Finally, although the official character of this exchange of letters must be borne in mind, it is interesting to note the seemingly ready assimilation by Gebre Igzīabihēr not only of Shewan–Amhara 'rules and regulations' but of the very political language and terminology used by the centre. Only rarely does Gebre Igzīabihēr oppose the term 'my country' (*agerē*) to 'our country' (*agerachin*), the last term prevailing in the exchange and being used by him in the same centralist sense that the Ethiopian crown tended to use. Thus the 'Arabs' were depicted by him as being ignorant of 'the laws of our country', and the Sibu Oromo territory north-west of Neḳemte was claimed by the Leḳa Oromo ruler to have been 'colonized' by his father Moroda – a term (*aḳenna*/*teḳenna*) often employed in Ethiopian sources for processes of expansion among 'wild' tribes at the outskirts of the Christian state.

Equally the 'time of the Galla' or the weight of 'Galla tradition' (the term Oromo never appears in the correspondence) is only evoked sparingly in the exchange and is used by Gebre Igzīabihēr to enhance his own position or his alleged rights rather than as a symbol of differentiation or separate group identity. It must be emphasized, however, that the apparent high degree of co-operation between the Neḳemte ruler and the central government must be assessed against the imbalance between them. In objective terms, the authority and power of Addis Abeba increasingly came to dominate that of Nekemte.

3

From ritual kings to Ethiopian landlords in Maale

DONALD DONHAM

Most social and cultural anthropologists begin their ethnographies with a chapter on history.[1] But such chapters rarely provide more than a background, an array of useful but unconnected information, that introduces the real subject: an analysis of social structures and cultural patterns. Exactly how such long-lasting structures and patterns are inferred from information collected over (at most) a few years is often something of a mystery but is apparently related to the types of societies that anthropologists have generally studied – 'traditional', 'cold', 'tribal'. In these sorts of societies, so the theory goes, structures are more visible, more easily separated from their historical integuments than in more dynamic ones.

This, at least, was how I understood the matter when I began field research in Ethiopia. The decisive event that forced me to see Maale differently was the revolution in 1974. In September of that year, four months after I had arrived in Maale, Haile Selassie was deposed. The events in Addis Abeba were quickly felt in Maale. By November an odd coalition of disaffected Maale had formed and accused the king's son (the heir apparent), the richest Maale chief, and northern landlords living in Maale, of misdeeds and of 'oppression'. (The Amharic word for oppressor, *akorkwaj*, was immediately adopted into the Maale vocabulary from radio broadcasts from Addis Abeba.) Their accusation to the sub-provincial court was dated 21 November 1974 and reads in part as follows:

> During the time Haile Selassie was emperor of Ethiopia, there were rich and powerful people who lived in many places in our country. They were the *balabbat*, *chikashum*, and *grazmach* appointed by Haile Selassie. Most of these people did us much damage: the *balabbat* whose name is Tinke Bailo has done many bad deeds at market and elsewhere. When we bring our things to market to sell them, he forces us to sell them to him at a very low price. Because we are poor people, we sell in the market to earn money. But he upsets the market and makes the country poor by buying something worth five dollars for two, something worth ten dollars for five. If anyone argues with him about the price, then that man is sent away from the marketplace, and his goods are simply confiscated . . . In addition, the *balabbat* has taken away land from Maale people who have paid their land taxes since 1950. He has taken these lands for himself,

> his relatives, and for northerners living in Maale. He has conspired with one of the *chikashum*, Babo Gudari, and the two of them together have instigated quarrels among the people about land. Since Tinke and Babo are *balabbat* and *chikashum*, they force the people to elect their relatives to government positions. The people would like to elect someone else but they cannot . . .[2]

Suddenly, political cleavages were a great deal more apparent. The 'king' of Maale began to look much more like a rich Ethiopian landlord. The history of the conquest of the south and its subsequent administration by Addis Abeba became a more obviously important issue. Instead of being marginal outsiders, landlords from the north and Muslim traders living in Maale began to appear as integral parts of the Maale social system. Instead of being a 'traditional' society, a fairly bounded, self-contained social unit where primordial sentiments survived into the present, Maale was arguably a sub-unit of a larger stratified society. In short, rather than furnishing a simple background, history began to appear to hold many of the analytical answers.

This was nowhere more true than in the problem of analysing pre-revolutionary politics in Maale, and – the subject of the present essay – of understanding the social processes that produced a local élite in Maale of a very special character. During 1974–5, an ideology of divine kingship close to Sir James Frazer's famous description remained alive, at least for sections of the Maale. When the office of king or *kati* was abolished in mid-1975, traditionalist elders informed the new government that without a *kati*, Maale women would not bear children, cows would not calve, and goats would not kid. Even bees have a king, they said. (Maale call queen bees 'king' bees.) While the old ideology remained alive, it is equally clear that the *kati*'s power in the recent period was derived mainly from his rôle in the Ethiopian administration, was backed by the coercive power of the imperial state, and was rewarded by the privilege of land ownership. It is this transformation of the rôle of *kati* from ritual king to Ethiopian landlord that I want to focus on here.

The change was not a smooth and continuous one, and I want to begin to locate the major twists and turns of the story. As I argue below, the major discontinuities in the formation of the Maale élite appear to result from long-term shifts of power in the hierarchy that went from Maale commoners to chiefs to kings to Ethiopian provincial governors to emperors.

POLITICAL CULTURE IN NINETEENTH-CENTURY MAALE

In the late nineteenth century the Maale political hierarchy was composed of three types of office.[3] At the top was the king or *kati*. Located a step below in status were thirteen chiefs or *goda*. Each chief presided over his own territory so that Maale was divided into thirteen chiefdoms. The king had no particular area of his own but lived in the centre of Maale in Bola chiefdom. Below each chief were a varying number of sub-chiefs or *gatta*. Depending on how large the chiefdom was, the number of sub-chiefs varied from none to four.

Of all these offices, indeed of all Maale institutions, kingship was culturally the most elaborated. A veritable halo of mythical charters and dramatic rituals set off the king from the more mundane aspects of everyday life. How the Maale – or at least the dominant strata of Maale – saw kingship will provide an introduction to the ways in which ideas were translated into social action, to the economic and political powers the Maale king and chiefs actually wielded, and finally to the manner in which particular features of Maale economic and political organization were related to the overarching patterns in the historical development of wider Ethiopia.

To summarize, three major notions express the Maale conception of kingship: first, what I will call the doctrine of the original life-giving king; second, the concept of the unbroken but perilous transmission of his vital force; and third, the idea of politics as the orderly union of hierarchical status groups.[4]

The first notion, hardly unusual among African kingdoms, is a kind of colonial myth of the origin of culture. As Maale elders tell the story, kingship was established in Maale at the same time that people learned how to control fire and cook their food. During the time that the Maale were still ignorant of fire, four brothers arrived one day from Bussa to the east. The eldest took up his fire drill, but when he attempted to make fire, taro instead of fire sprang forth. The eldest brother then went to the high country and became the king of Bako, the country just to the west of Maale. Then the next eldest brother tried to make fire but ensete sprang forth. He went away to become the king of Shangama, just to the north-west. Again, the next brother tried and he too failed. When he took up the fire drill, a cow sprang forth and he went to become king of Banna, just south of Maale. Finally, the youngest brother, Maaleka (the name appears to be a contraction of 'Maale *kati*'), took the fire drill, and he, after all of the others had failed, produced fire.

Maaleka then gave coals to the autochthonous people, but because they did not know how to handle fire, the whole countryside was blackened. After the original inhabitants of Maale had cooked their food and slept, they hid the coals in the thatch of their house as they went out to work in the fields. The fire burned the house and all of Maale territory. That, Maale explain, was how the moiety system began. The autochthonous clans became the *raggi* moiety while the king and his followers became the *karazi* moiety. Ideally from that point onward, *karazi* married only *raggi* and *raggi* only *karazi*.

As the elders tell the story even today, it is almost as if the original fire had made all of Maale into Maaleka's field, and henceforth Maale's production and prosperity would depend on Maaleka's cultivation. (Firing, of course, is one of the first steps in making a swidden field in Maale, and it establishes the boundaries of one's plot.) Every year before the time for burning new fields, each of the thirteen chiefs came to the king's compound in prescribed order with tribute and asked his permission to begin burning their fields. Having first burned his own field, the king gave his blessing. Then the chiefs fired their fields, to be followed by the sub-chiefs and then by the common people. This ritual ordering of Maale horticulture was re-enacted at the time of planting. First the king planted and prayed for rain, then the chiefs, then the sub-chiefs, then the common people. The fertility and prosperity of the land in all of its aspects – the ripening of the crops, the fecundity of men and women, and the reproduction of cattle and goats – were said to flow from the energizing and seminal presence of the king.

With so much dependent on the king's powers, succession was perhaps more than usually problematic. What I have called the unbroken but perilous transmission of Maaleka's fertilizing force was expressed and enacted in a Wagnerian cycle of installation rituals that lasted over the whole lifetime of the king. When an old king died, his death was not publicly acknowledged until one of his sons had been chosen as successor. The old king's body was dried and preserved, and his ritual functions were taken over by a non-royal stand-in for the duration of the inter-regnum, which could last for years. The first stages of the installation cycle focused on rituals of epiphany, as Eike Haberland has called them, or rituals designed to confirm the charisma of the new king.[5] On the day that the dead king's body was finally buried, a 'king' bee from a hive brought from Bussa was placed on the big toe of the son who was to succeed. If indeed he was the king, the bee climbed up the son's leg of its own accord, the Maale maintained, to his chest, and to his forehead, where it danced about in circles and then flew off back to Bussa.

Later rituals, still part of the cycle which made the successor into a king, focused on magnifying and enlarging royal potency and power, with mock cattle raids against neighbouring peoples and with the ritually-required slaying of enemies and taking of their genitals as trophies. A king never finally became king, however, until after he had died, his son had succeeded, and (in the middle of his son's installation cycle) those vital parts of his body not buried – fingernails, toenails, teeth, tongue, and genitals – were mixed with the similar remains of all past kings in a special quiver in Maale's *sanctum sanctorum*. Then he had 'met his fathers'. Then he had actually become king, and the line which began with Maaleka was extended yet another generation in a perfect chain of interconnecting father–son links.

With the life-giving, superior force of Maaleka preserved through his descendants, politics in the present was looked upon as the harmonious and fertile union of unequals. Best expressive of this idea was the layout of the royal compound, what the Maale called the 'lion house' (*zobi mari*). From archaeological remains of the lion house built in the early part of this century and from informants' reports, I was able to reconstruct, as shown in Figure 1, the royal compound as it probably existed in the nineteenth century.

In its entirety, the compound was grand by Maale standards, and the lion house, its roof rising to about 35 feet, could be seen from great distances. With two stories, the house was built around a cedar centre post, the uncut top of which extended through the roof as a spire ten to fifteen feet in the air. The whole compound was overwhelmingly a male preserve (the main exception being the king's mother who had her own house to one side of the lion house),

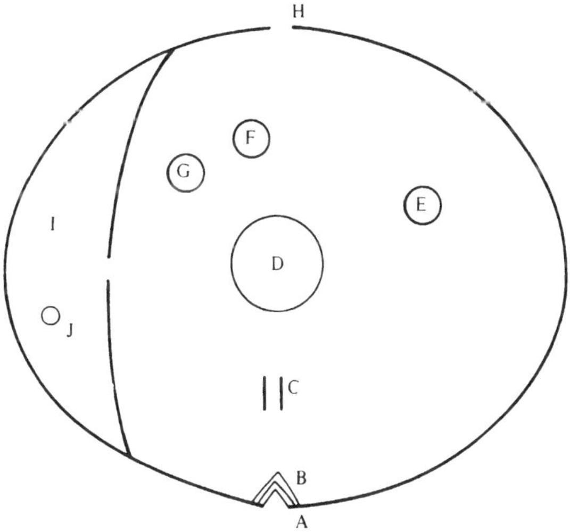

Fig. 1 The royal compound of Maale

A: place outside the compound where the chief of Makana sat when he visited the king (the chief could not enter the lion house, nor could he be allowed to see the king). B: *doddi* or 'union', the main gate through which all Maale men entered. C: *ko'bo basso* (other meaning unknown), the second gate through which only men of the *karazi* moiety went. D: *zobi mari* or 'lion house', the ritual centre of Maale where the king prayed. E: Queen mother's house where she and her guests feasted. F: *merto* or 'song' house where *karazi* men feasted. G: *raggi* house where men of that moiety feasted. H: *pulto karro* or 'small gate' through which *məni* potters and tanners and women past menopause entered. I: cattle corral of the king. J: *ts'osi*, literally 'god', a low house in which was suspended the quiver containing the remains of all the past kings of Maale.

and it was taboo for a woman of childbearing years even to enter. Grinding in the compound was done by male transvestites (*ashtime*) or by elderly women past menopause.

Behind the configuration of houses, gates, and fences in the *zobi mari* lay a particular conception of politics as at once the hierarchical separation and the harmonious joining together of social orders. The name for the main gate, 'union', expresses the idea well. It was the union, almost the sexual union, of the king with his people, *karazi* with *raggi*, Maale with specialist castes, and men with women, that produced political tranquillity and economic abundance. Equality between the elements of these dualities was an alien philosophy; such an arrangement, according to the dominant Maale way of thinking, could lead only to chaos and anarchy. As I noted above, these same ideas were echoed almost a century later when the Maale kingship was abolished by the revolutionary government in 1975. The conservative faction of elders who opposed the change asked rhetorically, 'How can we live without a king? Bees have a king. Termites have a king. Cattle follow a leader. How can we survive without a king? We will kill each other off.'

POLITICAL ECONOMY OF NINETEENTH-CENTURY MAALE

The three notions discussed above formed the dominant framework in which politics and especially kingship were conceived, talked about, and argued over; they constituted the outlines of what might be called Maale political culture. Given the structure of the ideology of power, how was it translated into social action? In practice, what were the powers of the king and the chiefs, and on what economic base did they rest? And finally, how did Maale economics and politics relate to the wider Ethiopian economy?

I have noted that the political hierarchy in Maale was composed of three levels: at the lowest rung were the sub-chiefs (*gatta*), next there were chiefs (*goda*), and last there was the king (*kati*). At the heart of the kingdom, politics was dominated by three office-holders – the king, the chief of Makana, and the chief of Bola. Of all the chiefs in Maale, the latter two lived closest to the king and were the most powerful. They, along with elders who lived in the vicinity of the lion house in Bola, determined succession to the kingship, and they inherited their offices while all the other chiefs (theoretically at least) were appointed by the king.

The coalitions and cleavages in the triangle formed by the king, the chief of Makana, and the chief of Bola shaped the dynamics of Maale politics. Two of the three were apparently often in alliance against the third. If the king grew especially strong, the two chiefs were likely to unite against him, and their opposition could vary from passive measures like delaying prescribed rituals in the king's installation cycle to razing the king's lion house.[6] Similarly, if one of the chiefs grew especially powerful and rich, he invited a coalition of the king and the other chief against him.

During an inter-regnum, the triangular order at the heart of Maale politics broke down. With two instead of three dominant sides, it was a more complicated task to engineer a consensus. And since the power of the chiefs of Makana and Bola often waxed strong while the king was dead (but said to reign), they sometimes had little incentive to install a successor. Consequently, an inter-regnum could often last for several years. As the Maale tell the story, disasters invariably intervened – crops failed or enemies raided Maale or epidemics struck – and elders from all over the land called for a new king.

The eleven chiefs located in more peripheral areas had much less influence on royal politics. Conversely, they seemed to have had more autonomy in their own districts. An elder in an outlying chiefdom told me that since the king did not leave the lion house in former times and since few of them went to Bola, his people did not know much about the king. Only a few of the wealthy and influential elders from the area kept contact with Bola and were known to the king. The local chief, in contrast, was much more involved in and conversant with the affairs of his people, and, within his own boundaries, was likely to become a miniature king.

From sub-chiefs to chiefs to king, the Maale political hierarchy formed an unstable and wobbly pyramid. The position of each block, or each office-holder, depended on the pushes and pulls of those about him, and even the king at the apex had rather limited resources with which to enforce unpopular decisions. The rich and elaborate ideological forms surrounding kingship, rather than reflecting the despotic power of the king, seemed almost designed to conceal his weaknesses. When adjudicating disputes, for instance, the king's was not the last court of appeal. In the exceptional cases in which the king could not use his position and influence to effect a settlement, the affair could be taken to the chief of Makana. Also, apparently, the king sometimes could not prevent blood feuds from establishing their own version of local justice. If the murderer managed to flee to the royal compound and to pass through the second gate, he came under the protection of the king who was then in a good position to settle the case and ritually to reconcile the two warring families by washing their hands together. Otherwise, the murderer or one of his close kinsmen was likely to be killed in vengeance.

Supporting (and in turn supported by) this delicately balanced hierarchy of political power was an array of economic privileges and prerogatives. The king and the chiefs all enjoyed labour tribute, *haile*, and none cultivated his own fields.[7] To call people from various parts of the kingdom to come and work, the king first sent messengers to the chiefs, the chiefs informed their sub-chiefs, and on the appointed day the sub-chiefs, blowing antelope horns, summoned their people to Bola to work on the king's field. There were three large areas in Bola that the kings cultivated (the name of one of the fields was *warshabashe*, 'too much for a multitude'), and the grain from these fields allowed the king to entertain guests in the lion house with open-handed generosity. A famous king named Sago had, at least according to the Maale today, 28 granaries. 'In our forefathers' day, they were always eating and drinking beer in the lion house.'

Besides labour tribute, tribute in kind also upheld the Maale system of political stratification. For all of the sacrifices that he made, the king sent messengers to the chiefs, who informed their sub-chiefs, who in turn decided whose cattle or goats should be sent to Bola. (The power of sub-chiefs to decide exactly whose cattle would be taken must have been a strong sanction for tneir authority in other local matters and in organizing labour tribute.) After the king had passed a certain point in the cycle of his installation, he could legitimately send for goats and cattle not for public sacrifice but for his own use and that of guests at the lion house. Honey in particular was a royal prerogative, and only the king and a few others whom he permitted (most notably the chiefs of Makana and Bola) could brew honey wine.

Both labour tribute and tribute in cattle and honey played an important rôle in Maale political economy, but neither had the internal significance nor the external connections that tribute from hunting had. When anyone killed a buffalo or leopard or elephant, he was required to present the skins or the ivory to the king, unless he happened to belong to the lineage of one of a few important men, like the chiefs of Makana and Bola (in which case the chiefs in question appropriated the skins or ivory). First the killer took a trophy from the animal – a tail or a leg, or, in the case of the enemy man, his genitals – to his minimal lineage head who ritually re-enacted the kill, apparently drawing some of the original killer's power and charisma to himself. The same was repeated by the killer's sub-chief, then by his chief, and finally by the king, who took possession of the animal hide or ivory. Only the king, and, as exceptions, the chiefs of Makana and Bola along with a few others, could sell these items, and in exchange they obtained iron, finely crafted spear heads, beads, perhaps cattle, a very few slaves, and (toward the end of the nineteenth century) guns from foreign traders who visited Maale.

To sum up, political stratification in late nineteenth-century Maale was the result of the interaction of a number of factors – an ideology of kingship, a differential and limited access to coercion, and an array of economic privileges and prerogatives. What then was the effect on the Maale political system of its encapsulation and domination by imperial Ethiopia in the twentieth century? What were the historical factors that led up to the events of 1974 and 1975 that I mentioned at the beginning – the accusation against the king's son, finally his arrest, and the dispossession of all landlords in Maale?

AN OVERVIEW OF THE TWENTIETH CENTURY

In general terms, twentieth-century Maale economic and political history was dominated by two developments: first was the transformation of the Maale king and many of the chiefs into landlords and representatives of the imperial administration. Even more than Western colonial governments, the Ethiopian state had limited resources with which to penetrate local politics and usually had to rely on some form of indirect rule. The Maale king was recognized as *balabbat*, the authority responsible for collecting tribute and for settling local disputes. Maale chiefs were recognized as lower-ranking officials, *chiḳashum*, literally 'mud chiefs'. In return for their services, the king and chiefs – like other such officials in the conquered territories – were given economic privileges (a portion of the tribute they collected as well as tracts of land in the new land tenure system) and political power (backed by northern soldiers). According to John Markakis, 'Ethiopian rule in the south reinforced the pattern of stratification where it existed, and introduced it where it did not.'[8]

The other major twentieth-century process that I want to highlight is the settlement of northern soldiers in Maale. These northern soldier-settlers, *neftennya* or gunmen, were the other group on which the Ethiopian administration of conquered territories rested. During the early part of the century, gunmen in Maale served in official posts of the administration. After the Italian occupation and the ensuing reorganization of government, that rôle came to an end, but northern settlers continued as the richest landowners in Maale until the time of the revolution.

Over the twentieth century, these two groups – on the one hand, northern settlers and, on the other, the Maale king and the richest chiefs – developed into a fairly distinct class *vis-à-vis* surrounding Maale peasants. Northerners, the king, and the richest chiefs lived in the only tin-roofed houses in Maale; they began to send their children to school years before ordinary Maale; they were adept at dealing with local courts; and they could afford, for example, to fly to Addis Abeba to consult a doctor. In sum, their style of life was different, and even the Maale members of this group, the king and some of the chiefs, were beginning to assimilate themselves to national Ethiopian culture.

If this small group of northerners and Maale was developing into a class, it was not always a solidary class. Over the twentieth century the two segments, Maale and northern landlords, came into collision more than once. In fact, the fortunes of northern landlords and of the Maale political élite apparently waxed and waned in inverse proportion. In simplified form, Table 1 illustrates a hypothesis that I will develop below:

Table 1. *The changing balance of power over Maale in the twentieth century*

Ethiopian Emperor	Ethiopian Emperor	Ethiopian Emperor
		Provincial Governor
Provincial Governor	Provincial Governor	Sub-provincial Governor
Maale Political Elite	Maale Political Elite	Maale Political Elite
1894–1911	1911–36	1941–75

Perhaps the single most important variable as far as Maale was concerned was the degree of central control that Ethiopian emperors managed to exert over local governors. On that count, there have been three fairly distinct periods in twentieth-century Ethiopia. The first period, the formation of imperial Ethiopia, began in the late nineteenth century. In the 1880s, the emperor Menilek II managed to reunite the northern kingdoms of Ethiopia and to bring the provincial nobility who had dominated the country in the eighteenth and early nineteenth centuries under his rule. Menilek established postal and telegraph services to the provinces, chartered a national bank, and contracted for the building of a railroad from Addis Abeba to the coast. The decade from 1896, when Menilek defeated the Italians at the Battle of Adwa, to 1906, when he was taken seriously ill, saw the zenith of the emperor's power and the final expansion of Ethiopia to its present borders.[9]

The centralization of government that was effected in this first period did not last. After a long illness, Menilek died in 1913. A combination of circumstances – the lack of a living son to succeed and the reluctance of the nobility to support any strong successor – led to a devolution of power. After the abortive reign of one of Menilek's daughter's sons, *lij* Iyasu, power was divided between Menilek's daughter, Zewditu, and Teferi Mekonnen, later to be known as Haile Selassie I. With government in Addis Abeba immobilized by mutual suspicion between its top leaders, provincialism re-emerged in full force in Ethiopia with powerful governors ruling their provinces like autocrats. It was not until 1930 that Teferi gained the upper hand and finally declared himself emperor or king of kings. Five years later by the time of the Italian invasion, Haile Selassie had only begun to recentralize the government and to reverse the flow of power from the provinces back to Addis Abeba.

This middle period was therefore marked by several features as a distinctive phase in Ethiopian historical development: central authority was weak and provincial governors strong, especially those in the newly conquered territories. As power flowed to the peripheries of the Ethiopian system, people followed, and provincial governors in the south attracted large followings of northern immigrants out to seek their fortune. These followers, *neftennya* or gunmen, entered service in provincial armies, took up lower-level administrative positions, and became clergy in the newly established Orthodox churches in the south. Many bought or were given land in the area.

After the Italian occupation in the late 1930s, Haile Selassie was returned to power in 1941. From then until the revolution in 1974, first with British, and then with American aid, Haile Selassie recentralized and modernized the government. In general he pursued a delicately balanced policy of restoring and supporting the old stratification systems in the north and south and, at the same time, undermining them when they interfered with his own power and that of the central government. In the south, Haile Selassie took away the temporary land grants or fiefs that had traditionally supported provincial governors and others and substituted a salary from the treasury in Addis Abeba. In the north, he weakened the power of the nobility by supporting and promoting a new group of younger, educated men, often from poor backgrounds, to governmental positions. According to Christopher Clapham, the proportion of nobles in the central government dropped from 53 per cent in 1948 to 13 per cent in 1966.[10] Because the new educated élite had no source of power except through their relationship to the emperor, Haile Selassie was able to take on more and more power at the centre. His ascendancy lasted until the revolution in 1974.

How did these phases of Ethiopian political development affect Maale? In the three periods which I have just described, the power of provincial governors in Bako waxed and waned inversely as the power of Ethiopian emperors fell and rose. From the point of view of local Maale history, that oscillation can be most simply indicated by the average time governors of Bako province, the province that included Maale, spent in office. During the first period, Bako governors spent an average of four years in office; in the second period, almost six years; and in the third (when the Bako governorship had been demoted to sub-provincial or *awraja* level and incorporated into the large province of Gamo-Gofa), less than three years. Strong Ethiopian emperors used the classical technique of quickly re-appointing officials to prevent their building up local power bases, so that the shortest terms of office, during the first and third periods, naturally occurred during the phases of strongest central authority.

The Maale remembrance of these periods is also quite different. Most elders could recount only the succession of Bako governors during the middle phase, the period during which governors were relatively powerful. In fact, it is interesting that Maale elders tended to use the idiom of divine kingship when they recalled the rôle of the governor who stayed longest in Bako, *dejazmach* Merid Habte Mariam. After describing the lavishness of Merid's feasts, elders would often say something to the effect, 'He was a real *kati*. The cattle lived many years then and multiplied. People prospered.'

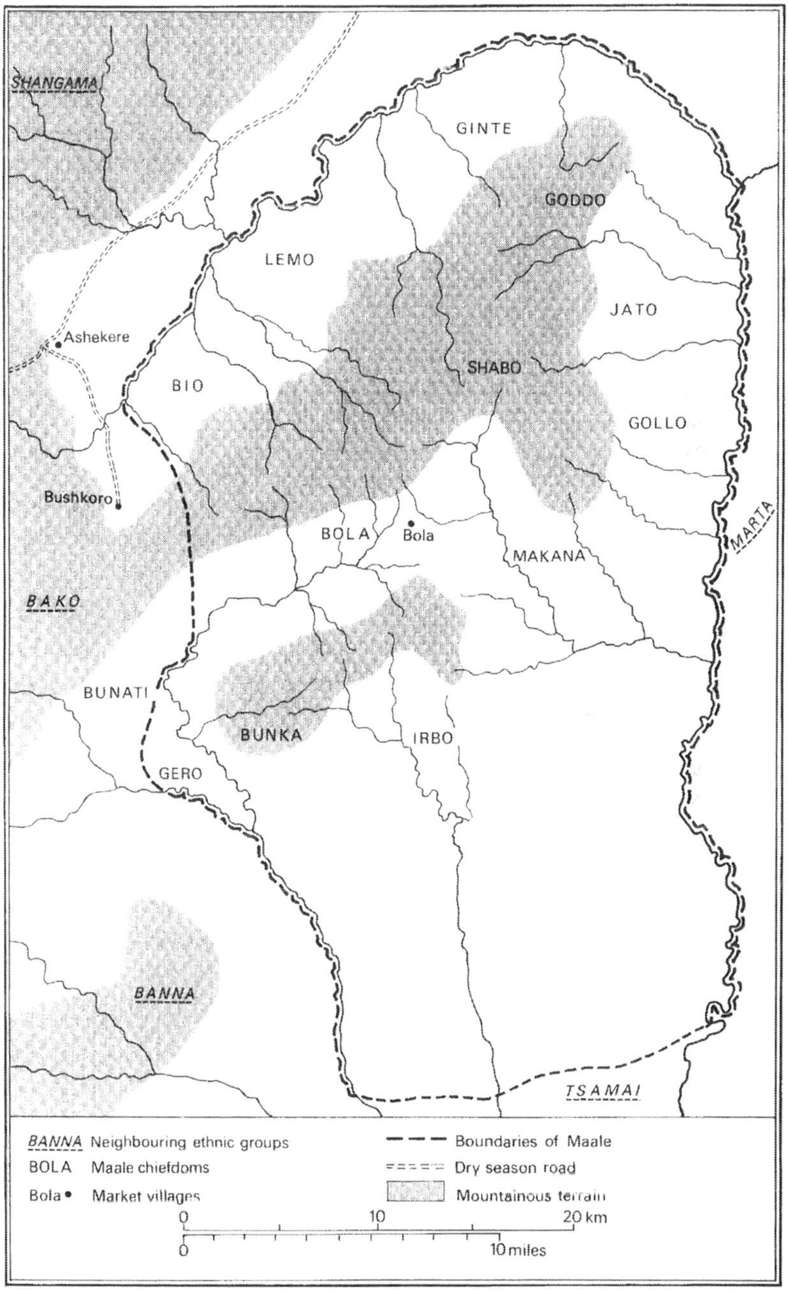

Map 10 Maale and its surroundings

As the power of the imperial centre declined, then, the power of the provincial governor in Bako apparently strengthened. But this result should not be seen purely as a mechanism. The disarray at the political centre of Ethiopia during the middle period did not simply cause the rise in influence of Bako governors. Indeed, the rise of Bako had everything to do with the person who happened to dominate the governorship during the whole of the middle period: *dejazmach* Merid Habte Mariam.

Unfortunately, we know little about Merid. He was a Shewan and, according to Mahteme Sellassie Wolde Mesqel, first served as Menilek's palace official, *agafari*.[11] According to oral information, he was appointed to Bako and Gofa provinces by *lij* Iyasu, and he stayed in office there for almost the next two decades until his death in 1930, after which his son, Beyene, who had married a daughter of Haile Selassie, succeeded.[12] Given the changes in political leadership at the centre (and given the rapidity with which governors in other provinces were changed, even in the middle period), Merid's tenure at Bako was remarkably long-lived. One infers that he must have been exceptionally talented at aligning himself with the 'right' faction at the right moment, from Menilek to Iyasu to Haile Selassie. Also, it may have been easier for him to stay in office because Bako and Gofa were small and out of the way provinces.

In any case, the changing balance of power between Addis Abeba and Bako formed the wider field in which the Maale king and chiefs functioned in the twentieth century. To simplify, the power of the Maale political élite tended to rise as that of their immediate superior, the governor, fell. The political strength of governors, as we have seen, depended in turn upon the degree of central control which Ethiopian emperors could exert. During times of strength, the emperor's power to appoint and reappoint reached all the way down the political hierarchy to the governors over Maale. At other times, those governors – far removed from Addis Abeba – became virtually independent of central control, at least in local matters.

It is this pattern of relationships, I contend, that must be taken into account if we are to understand Maale politics. Again, I want to state the matter carefully: a weak Bako governor did not simply cause a rise in power for the Maale political élite. Rather, we might say that a weak Bako governor was a necessary condition, not a sufficient cause. Given the right external conditions, the Maale king's rise to power always depended further on internal policies and personalities, local economic and political structures. The crux of the matter is the complex way in which conditions imposed by larger, encapsulating social units combine with local events to yield a characteristic pattern of outcomes.[13]

THE STRONG ROLE OF THE MAALE KING AND CHIEFS, 1894–1911

In the late nineteenth century, Maale submitted peacefully to the army of *ras* Welde Gĩyorgis, which had just demolished Welaita and was continuing south-westward establishing forts in Dorze, Kamba, and Gofa. The Maale who had recently lost considerable territory in a war with their neighbours, the Bako, invited the intervention of the northerners. The chief of Makana sent two messengers to Gofa to guide northern gunmen to Maale. The army came, and as one elderly Orthodox priest in Maale told me, 'There were so many young men with spears and guns they were like locusts.' Accompanied by Maale, the Ethiopian army pushed the Bako out of Maale territory (except for one chiefdom which the Maale ceded to Bako), a peace was decreed, and a fortified garrison built on a strategic mountain top in Bako. The fort in Bako became the provincial capital of the surrounding territory, Maale included. A subsidiary and smaller settlement, surrounded by trenches, was established in the Maale highlands at Goddo, and there the governor of the sub-province of Maale was stationed along with his soldiers.

For the first few years the rule of these fortified settlements of soldiers was limited, but strong enough, apparently, to protect themselves. In about 1896 the Bako, after having given tribute for two years, rebelled. The king of Bako is reported to have said, 'Why should a man give tribute? I'll give my spear as tribute. Oxen and honey I won't give.' But spears could provide no match for guns, and the king was killed, beheaded, and his necklace – the insignia of royal office – confiscated.

By 1900 the colonization effort had begun in earnest when Menilek, then at his height of power, appointed trusted relatives to the governorships of Bako and Gofa (the latter province bordering Bako to the north). Both governors established churches and encouraged the formation of periodic markets. By 1905 European travellers who found their way through the south-west reported market towns in Bako, Uba, Gofa, and Maale.[14] All of these towns, as they moved from the mountain tops to lower-lying plains (except for the original market in Maale) continued to be major marketing centres in 1974. Finally, both governors brought retinues of soldier-settlers from their home bases in the north. Because they were among the first arrivals in the area, these immigrants and their children became dominant in local affairs. Until the revolution in 1974, the wealthiest and most influential northerners living in Maale were the descendants of this first wave of northern settlers.

The northern presence in Bako and in Maale was still small enough and provincial governors were changed often enough to necessitate relatively greater reliance upon a policy of indirect rule through the Maale king and chiefs. As I have mentioned, it was the chief of Makana who took the initiative in guiding the northern army to Maale. Arregude, the Maale king who succeeded to power in about 1903 (see Table 2 for the genealogy of the Maale kings), had by that time acquired a gun, and he accompanied and assisted northern soldiers on several campaigns to subjugate peoples to the south of Bako. After he became king, Arregude was held responsible for collecting tribute. If he could not give ivory, then Arregude was required to give children as slaves. The Maale of course hated the enslavement of their children; Arregude's rôle in it, even under the coercion of imprisonment, must have

Table 2. *Succession to the kingship in Maale (all dates are approximate and names have been changed)*

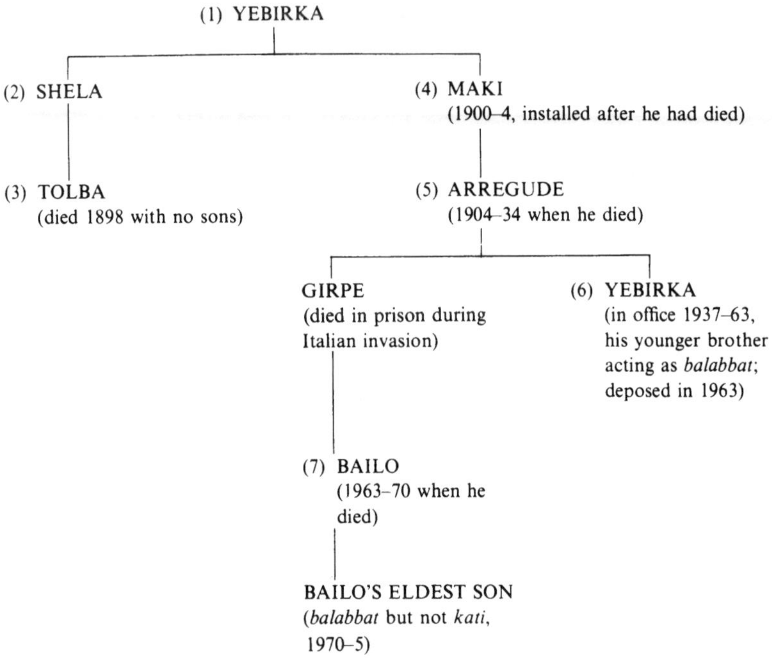

threatened to undermine his political position in Maale. In a daring and successful journey in about 1906, Arregude travelled to the north all the way to Menilek's court to protest against the taking of Maale children. According to the story Maale elders still tell, Arregude told Menilek that he would give ivory, honey, cattle, and goats. Menilek assented and Arregude took a letter from the emperor to the governor of Bako instructing the latter not to take slaves from Maale. Although a few slaves continued to be taken from time to time, their number was slight compared to those from neighbouring countries like Bako and Shangama, where cattle, for instance, were in far fewer numbers.

Arregude's new-found power as intermediary between Maale and the northern administration invited the local opposition of the Makana and Bola chiefs. Arregude, in what was perhaps a piece of bravado, chose to build his lion house on the site of the house of Maale's most famous and powerful king, Sago. Fearing that Arregude would thereby become as powerful (and exploitative) as Sago had been, the chiefs and elders united and in a plain warning they uprooted the centre-post of the partially-built lion house during one of Arregude's absences from Maale. Arregude retaliated by refusing to live in Bola, the traditional residence of Maale kings. During the next few years, according to the elders, a near-famine hit Maale and did not end until the house had been rebuilt and Arregude installed in Bola. God, as he often appears to be, was evidently on the side of the politically dominant.

THE RISE OF PROVINCIAL GOVERNORS AND THE ECLIPSE OF THE MAALE ELITE, 1911–36

By about 1911 the governor of Bako was becoming more and more powerful as his rule spread farther into the surrounding countryside and as central authority in Ethiopia decayed. That year, *dejazmach* Merid (who was to stay in office for the next nineteen years) took up the governorship of the province. One of his first moves in respect to Maale was to establish a second settlement of soldiers at Bunka south of Goddo, the sub-provincial governor's residence. The Bunka site was unfortified and was situated in the valley lying in the heart of Maale territory. The change in type of site signalled the growing penetration of northern power. With a police force stationed in the centre of Maale with about six officers, each of whom had six or seven ordinary soldiers serving beneath him, Merid had a great deal of control over Maale affairs. The Bunka soldiers, although the personal retainers of Merid (*karami*, literally 'servants'), were under the nominal authority of the sub-provincial governor who lived four hours away at Goddo.

At about the same time that Merid was appointed governor, three *gult* fiefs were carved out of Maale territory, corresponding to the three western chiefdoms of Bio, Lemo, and Ginte. The northern fief holders who took up residence there, each of whom kept a retinue of ten to twenty northern soldiers, oversaw public order in their areas, settled local disputes, and completely replaced the local Maale chiefs, who never recovered their influence and prestige. Holders of *gult* fiefs were not answerable to the sub-provincial governor of Maale; instead they were under the formal authority of the provincial governor in Bako. Since both of the latter, however, were personal appointees of the emperor, *gult* holders' political influence in practice sometimes approached that of provincial governors.

The resulting hierarchy of administrative officials over Maale was, therefore, unstable at best, and held room for considerable manoeuvre. Fief holders could use their personal relationship to the emperor to go over the head of the provincial governor, their nominal superior; Bunka soldiers through their personal ties to the governor of Bako probably did the same in regard to the sub-provincial governor of Maale. The room for manoeuvre evidently widened still further during the period of weak central authority in Ethiopia. In Maale, a rough version of frontier justice held sway: northerners sometimes seized Maale land, converted temporary tenures into permanent ones, and sold indigent *gebbar* into slavery.

From the provincial governor downwards, all of these officials, along with their retinues of ordinary soldiers, were supported by the services of Maale *gebbar*. The Maale inhabitants of the chiefdoms of Bio, Lemo, and Ginte all became the *gebbar* of the fief holders of these districts. The sub-provincial governor of Maale was given rights over the inhabitants of Gollo chiefdom, while Bunka soldiers took *gebbar* in Irbo and Bunka. Makana residents came under the control of one of Merid's sons, while those in Gero came under the control of the wife of another of Merid's sons – a daughter of Haile Selassie. Maale living in Jato, Goddo, and Shabo (the area closest to the residence of the sub-provincial governor) were divided among Merid's retainers who lived in Bako. Finally, most of Bola was left to the Maale king (now designated *balabbat*) who was given the right to appropriate goods and services just as the other masters of *gebbar* were.

One Maale elder who was about five years old when his father became a *gebbar* to one of the soldiers in Bunka recalled the system in the following way:

> An Amhara [northerner] took a *gebbar* first of all by getting *dejazmach* Merid's permission. Then he scouted out possible Maale families, asking people who lived in what house and writing down people's names. By bribing the Maale man's neighbours, the Amhara sneaked up on the man at night, captured him, and took him to Bunka where he remained a prisoner until a Maale they already knew and trusted – a chief or another *gebbar* – stepped forward as the man's guarantor. Then he was permitted to go free and then he began his work as a *gebbar*. Any time an Amhara met a Maale on the path, he would ask, 'Whose *gebbar* are you?' If the Maale said nothing, the Amhara would beat him; if he named his master, the Amhara said 'All right,' and let him pass.

According to the same informant, the load on *gebbar* was a heavy one. For a week at a time, the *gebbar* lived in his master's house, cut firewood, brought water, farmed his master's fields, and cared for his mule. He had to cook his own food and to sleep outside on straw. At the end of the week, another *gebbar* arrived and the first left – carrying a sack of grain that his wife would grind and that he would return when he came for the next week of service. In addition, he had to pay four Maria Theresa thalers a year for his master's 'salary' (*demoz*), a large gourd of honey worth approximately three thalers twice a year on holidays, and five thalers whenever his master went on a long journey. Not surprisingly, many Maale chose to move away rather than endure such extractions. And they were able to do so because Maale, situated at the edge of the high plateau where it sloped down to the drier pastoral lands, was apparently at the southern limit of the *gebbar* system. Many Maale, including chiefs, simply moved to Tsemai, which was to the south and across the provincial boundary. Northern rule there was less firmly established and tribute was exacted by periodic forays to seize cattle rather than to impress *gebbar* into service.

Maale who stayed in their ancestral homes and who became *gebbar* had to have cash, and with the need for cash went increased trade and the settlement of Muslim traders from Jimma in Maale. The fief holder of Bio, *fītawrarī*

Turunih, encouraged the settlement of traders by taxing them lightly and protecting them from other northerners. By about 1915 a village of Muslims had established itself on his fief in Bio and, according to one of my Muslim informants who moved there in about 1925, the village had grown to about fifty-six households by that time: 'Those were good days. We grew fat then. A huge gourd of honey could be bought for three thalers. What did the Maale know about prices? We really ate in those days.' A smaller settlement of traders from Jimma who specialized in ivory grew up later in Samworo near the residence of the provincial governor in Goddo. All of these traders bought products in Maale and other peripheral areas and sold them in the marketing centres then growing up in the south-west or to more distant higher-level centres like Jimma and Addis Abeba.

As the commercial and political hold of the empire over Maale tightened, the old rôle of Maale kings and chiefs as intermediaries became more and more anachronistic. At the same time, more and more Maale *gebbar* were needed to support the increasing numbers of northern soldiers in Maale. At first, *gebbar* were not taken from the immediate vicinity of the king, or of most chiefs, the families living in those areas being left to perform the services on which the Maale élite traditionally depended. As the demand for *gebbar* grew, however, the governor of Bako in the early 1930s decreed that all Maale – even those previously serving the king and the chiefs – should become *gebbar*.

The Maale élite reacted in various ways: Arregude, the king or *balabbat* as he was then designated, had recently died, and since a successor had not been installed, the office was at a low ebb in any case.[15] The chief of Bunka simply left Maale and went to live in Tsemai. The chief of Irbo, enraged when one of the Bunka soldiers claimed his neighbours as *gebbar*, attempted to shoot the man. The bullet grazed the soldier's arm, maiming him, and killed his servant sitting nearby.

It was the double effect of the progressive undermining of the power of the Maale élite along with the increasing exploitation of ordinary *gebbar* that seems to account for the Maale reaction to the Italian occupation in 1936. In many ways Italian rule was not easy. The Maale recount, for example, forced labour to build the road from Gofa to Bako and taxes taken in cattle, grain, and honey. Despite all that, Maale still remember the Italians as liberators, and many of them in telling their history made comments like, 'When the Italians came, we became people again' and 'We got back our lives.'

Had the Italians stayed longer, perhaps the Maale would have retained less positive memories. In any case, the Italian interlude from 1936 to 1941 ended one phase in Maale history and prepared the way for the next. Many of the northerners living in Maale died when the sub-provincial governor of Maale led the Bunka soldiers to the battle front. As I pointed out earlier, Haile Selassie took advantage of the losses and disarray caused by the war to institute reforms and to recentralize the government after 1941.

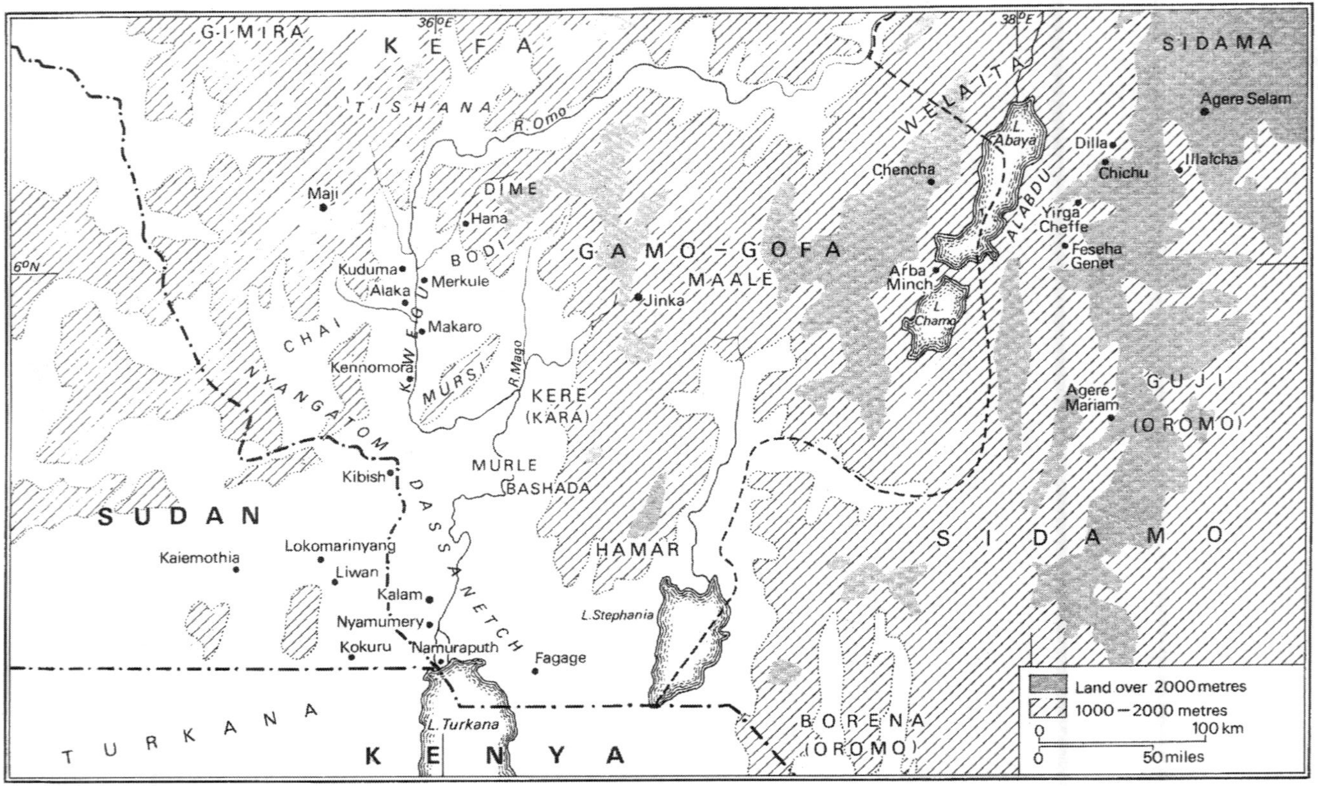

Map 11 The Omo Basin: to illustrate Chapters 3, 4, 6 and 7

REVITALIZATION OF THE MAALE POLITICAL ELITE, 1941–75

Among the first reforms that Haile Selassie promulgated was the abolition of the *gebbar* system. Henceforth, administrative officials were supported by salaries from Addis Abeba, and the old rôle of soldier-settlers was given to a new semi-professionalized police force. Both governors and policemen now circulated from post to post, usually staying in one place only a few years at most.

It would seem that these changes, by separating the northerners remaining in Maale from their former place in the state apparatus, would have ended their economic and political superiority over Maale peasants. Such was not the case, however, for most of the northerners above the rank of ordinary soldier had bought measured land (*ḳelad*) in Maale, which they retained after the occupation. The entire lowland plain which surrounded the mountainous heart of Maale territory (see Map 10) had been declared government land and had been sold to northern settlers, often at low prices, from about 1911 onwards. In some cases, simply paying the land tax was enough to institute a claim to a plot of land. When, for instance, the sub-provincial governor of Maale sent soldiers to the southern plain to guard Maale against northern hunters from the adjacent province, he claimed the land as his own, and began paying taxes on it and taking rents. As it turned out, these low-lying lands were perhaps the most valuable in Maale from the point of view of collecting rents from tenants. The production of all of the most valuable Maale products – cattle, goats, and honey – depended on the grazing areas and flowering thorn trees found in the lowland plains. Few Maale lived there, but most grazed their cattle and tended beehives there. Thus, the number of 'tenants' who could be tapped for rent was comparatively great, and northerners who could sustain any kind of claim to these lands had a lucrative source of income.

Sustaining land claims nearly always meant bringing, and defending oneself in, court cases in Bako, then the sub-provincial capital. The boundaries of plots were poorly defined at best, and because of its lack of resources, the provincial administration had little independent check on the extent of plots located far from the capital. There was then considerable latitude for manipulating land claims, and wealthy and powerful landowners were often able to expand their holdings, sometimes by less than legitimate means. Landowners who lived too far away from the administrative centres to play the political game often found their plots progressively whittled away. Whereas before the occupation the personal supervision of *gebbar* focused settlers' attention locally on Maale, afterwards, the pull of land cases prompted many to build second houses in Bako. There they spent large portions of the year currying the favour of officials who came and went every year or two, and keeping abreast of the latest cliques and coalitions. In addition, the town was the site of the modern educational and medical services that Haile Selassie's government was developing. Rents from Maale could be collected in a two- or three-month stay in the countryside.

With settlers living most of the year outside Maale and with their old function of keeping order taken over by a police station of only three or four men, indirect rule through Maale chiefs and the king once again became a useful policy of local government. By the early 1940s, the royal family had adapted to its revived rôle in the administration remarkably efficiently. One of Arregude's sons, Yebirka, had become king in about 1937. He carried out the traditional rôles of the king as sacrificer and bringer of rains, while his younger brother Hilla assumed all of the duties relating to government work.[16] It was as if Yebirka became *kati* while Hilla played the rôle of *balabbat*.[17]

The chiefs and the king collected government taxes from the Maale through the first decade of the post-Italian period. In the highland centre of the country, there were no northern landlords left. The three grants of *gult* fiefs made by Menilek in Bio, Lemo, and Ginte, had all expired when their owners died. The money that *gebbar* formerly gave to soldier-settlers, or at least a major portion of it, now went to the government through the chiefs and the king. And it was partly from these revenues, apparently, that the government paid out salaries to officials and policemen.

In 1951 tax collection was regularized by dividing the ownership of the highlands into plots of *gebbar rist* assigned to individual Maale. The king, or rather his brother, Hilla, along with a representative of the government, played a major rôle in setting up boundaries and assigning ownership. The final division of land reflected a rather complex interaction of Maale and government expectations and understandings of who should get land. Traditionally the Maale land tenure system had assigned plots (*deni*) to individuals, and the owners of the largest numbers of plots tended to be 'big men', often wealthy heads of large and ramified lineages; when Hilla met with the chiefs and elders of each area in Maale to decide who should get land, it was generally the chiefs and big men who were given precedence. From the government point of view, land was being assigned to former *gebbar* who now would give their taxes directly to the government instead of to soldiers and officials stationed in Maale. The two views more or less coincided in practice, for in creating the *gebbar* system northern settlers had naturally tended to choose the wealthiest Maale as *gebbar*.[18]

While the *gebbar* system, in its last years of operation, worked to undermine the Maale political élite, the post-Italian land division had the opposite effect: the Maale stratification system was strengthened. The king and chiefs (who, of course, were never *gebbar*) now controlled comparatively large plots of land, and the king and some of the more powerful chiefs required (even up until 1975) the traditional forms of labour tribute from tenants as well as rents. The rest of the new Maale landlords – big men and notables such as sub-chiefs – lacked the sanction of custom in requiring labour tribute, but none the less the authority to collect taxes from tenants added to their local status and influence.

With their positions reinforced, the king and the chiefs began more and more to take on the character of northern landlords. Most grew visibly wealthier, and a few, most notably the chief of Bunka, became adept at dealing with provincial courts and influencing local officials. The Bunka chief, for example, threatened to sue the richest northern landlord in Maale, Abebe, for false land claims in his district. (Abebe was the son of the former sub-provincial governor of Maale who had claimed land in the southern lowlands without ever paying for it.) Rather than expose the weakness of his title to the land, Abebe agreed to share half of the proceeds from tenants' rent with the chief. The two then worked together to extract high rents from the many Maale who grazed cattle on their land, the chief using his traditional status and influence in Maale and the northerner his connections with local officials. The land in question contained the only dry-season watering hole for the entire plain to the south of Maale so that almost all Maale with cattle there were subject to payments. According to informants, the amount of rent that the chief and his northern partner took varied: for Maale on good terms with the two, the yearly amount (in the early 1970s) could be as low as 30 or 40 Ethiopian dollars (the price of a young ox). For tenants who had somehow alienated the two landlords, the amount could reach over 100 Ethiopian dollars. Rents were, therefore, not only a rich source of income but a keen instrument of political control.

The structural transformations that dominated this period are perhaps best analysed in relation to one event which, more than any other, dominated recent Maale politics. Yebirka and his brother Hilla were deposed from power in 1963. The story – Maale's social drama *par excellence* – illustrates both the complexities, the apparently accidental details, and what I take to be the bedrock economic and political realities of recent times.

A FINAL PHASE IN THE MAKING OF MAALE LANDLORDS

To pick up the threads of the story, I begin with the last years of Arregude's reign, in the early 1930s. Arregude had four wives and ten children who lived to have children of their own. His first son (by his first wife), a handsome, forceful, and at times violent man named Girpe, was expected to inherit the kingship. In about 1933, however, he was accused (falsely, it seems) of murdering a northerner. He was finally imprisoned in Addis Abeba and, apparently, killed during the Italian invasion. How and why Girpe met this end is a complicated and revealing bit of history in its own right; for my purposes here, let me simply note his disappearance and presumed death.

After Girpe was taken to prison in Addis Abeba, Arregude, according to the Maale, died of grief for his son. And when the Italians arrived in the south in 1936, they found no king in Maale. Pressed to name a successor, the traditional kingmakers, the Bola elders (who had suffered under Girpe's oppression) and the chiefs of Bola and Makana (who probably hoped that good-natured Yebirka would sit lightly on the throne) chose Arregude's first son by his second wife – Yebirka. Meanwhile, Girpe had left four wives and many young sons in Maale.

4 *Grazmach* Hilla in 1951 (from A. E. Jensen, editor, *Altvölker Süd-Äthiopens*)

If Yebirka had personally taken on the rôle of *balabbat*, perhaps the chiefs' expectation of a weak rule would have been borne out. As it happened, Yebirka delegated those political duties to his younger brother Hilla (see Plate 4). And Hilla proved to be as powerful a figure as his brother Girpe. To illustrate Hilla's character, a man who had served him told me the following story:

> One day while I was going to Çhencha [the provincial capital of Gamo Gofa at that time] with Hilla, we almost met our end. God must have helped us. We had a mule loaded with money, taxes that we were transporting to Çhencha. We came up to someone's house, and the mule was just about to die. Hilla ordered me to turn the mule into the yard. (Whoever lived there had a small garden in the yard.) The wife came out of the house and started yelling for help. Her husband, a big man,

came running along with the neighbours and cried, 'By the law, stop! By the law, stop!' By that time Hilla had already taken over the house and laid down. When the husband began chasing the mule out of the garden, Hilla shot out of the house and pulled his gun. We all ran for cover, and the man asked, 'Is he crazy?' I said, 'He's the king of Maale. Haven't you ever heard of Hilla, king of Maale?' 'Oh, my God', he said, 'I'm going to get myself killed for this little garden?' And he went up to Hilla, flattened himself on the ground and said, 'Oh, king, I've erred. I've erred.' Hilla said, 'If I burned your house down now, what could you do in Çhencha?' The man gave us a big pot of beer and a sheep to slaughter. We spent the night there, and in the morning when we were leaving, he gave me five dollars and the boy who was leading the mule two dollars. That was Hilla for you – turning his mule into people's crops. A person can be powerful in his own country, but to do something like that in another country . . . Only now that Hilla is dead do people think he was an ordinary person.

With Hilla gathering power into his own hands, conflicts began to develop – as they were wont to do under strong kings – between the kingship (both Hilla and Yebirka) and the chiefs of Makana and Bola. According to Yebirka, who was still alive at the time of my field work, friction developed between Hilla and the chiefs because Hilla monopolized the government of Maale; he heard all the court cases and therefore enjoyed all the gifts and bribes that this political office entailed. The chiefs were jealous. 'My brother was a little crooked', Yebirka admitted, 'but at least he didn't send cases outside Maale to Bako' (where, he implied, there was still more crookedness).

Only accidentally related to the developing structural tensions at the centre of Maale politics was another incident that widened still further the rift between the royal family and the chiefs. As it turned out, the real murderer of the man whom Girpe had been imprisoned for killing was the brother of the Bola chief. After Yebirka had become king, the Bola chief asked his mother's brother, the chief of Makana, to intercede with Yebirka and to reconcile the two families by washing their hands together – the customary ritual of reconciliation for the families of a murderer and a murder victim. (In effect, the Bola chief's brother had caused the death of Girpe, Yebirka's brother.) Yebirka adamantly refused the Makana's chief's mediation and tried to exile the Bola chief's brother. The dispute rankled and was still unsettled even in 1975. 'The chiefs have destroyed Maale,' Yebirka said; 'They're liars and thieves.'

Yebirka and Hilla probably would have weathered these disagreements and dissensions without much difficulty, but the combination of the deepening cleavage between the royal family and the chiefs of Makana and Bola along with another that developed between Hilla and the northern landlords in Maale proved fatal in the end. Hilla began his political career during the Italian occupation when the Maale were being encouraged to unite against northerners (and, therefore, not against the Italians). From those years, Hilla seems to have developed a heightened sensitivity to the exploitations practised by northern landlords, for after 1951 when some of the owners of *kelad* in the lowlands began to make claims extending farther and farther toward the mountains and into plots held by Maale, Hilla took the lead in opposing them. He argued court cases, appealed against decisions, even going to Addis Abeba, and often he won. Perhaps Hilla opposed the northern landlords because he saw them as a threat to his own power (as they were), or perhaps he had other reasons. In any case, he came into direct and unyielding confrontation with Abebe, a northerner who had apparently tried to ally himself with Hilla by entering an informal union (according to Christian custom) with the latter's daughter. Abebe was the son of the sub-provincial governor of Maale before the Italians, and the landlord with whom the chief of Bunka had developed such an accommodating relationship.

The factions opposing Yebirka and Hilla, after they had been in office for about 25 years, finally went to court in order to depose them and to install Girpe's eldest son, Bailo, then in his late thirties. The chiefs of Bola and Makana both went to the Bako court and testified that Yebirka was not the first-born son of Arregude and that a mistake had been made: Yebirka was not the true king, for people were not prospering, cattle were dying, and the bees did not make honey. The chief of Bunka joined in the accusation and, combining court savvy with the idiom of Maale divine kingship, wrote the judge a list of Maale who had died during Yebirka's reign (augmented, some said, by fictitious names made up from Maale words for tree species).

The main mover behind the court accusation, however, was Abebe, the northern landlord. When I talked to him in 1975, he said, not boastingly, just matter-of-factly, 'What do I have to hide? I was the one who deposed Yebirka. His brother, Hilla, kept testifying against me in court, trying to take away land that belonged to my father. I asked him to stop. I didn't want to quarrel. But he wouldn't stop.' Abebe guided the case through the courts and made the requisite gifts and bribes to judges and officials. As the case moved slowly to a close, Bailo, the pretender, in a politically adroit move, went to the provincial tax collection office and pointed out that Hilla had divided Maale land into plots three or four times too large. The government was being cheated. In 1962, then, Bailo along with a government representative redivided Maale lands. Many of Bailo's supporters were rewarded with plots and, at the same time, the government officials increased their tax rolls.

The resulting coalition of chiefs, northern landlords, and government officials in Bako was simply overwhelming. Yebirka's only supporters were the elders in Bola and many of the outlying common people. I asked an elderly man in the south of Maale how they felt when Yebirka was deposed and he said, 'We just cried. All of our children had been born during Yebirka's time. We had built up our herds during his time. We just cried.' But Bola elders and commoners elsewhere had almost no access or influence in the courts of Bako, and Yebirka was finally deposed in about 1963. Policemen took Yebirka and the master of royal rituals, the *gojo*, to the sacred forest called Dufa. They ordered the *gojo* to break Yebirka's necklace. The old man said, 'Ah! How can I do that? We have never taken the king's necklace before his eyes were darkened.' A policeman kicked the *gojo* toward Yebirka, and finally he broke the necklace. Yebirka told me, 'My neck was sore for months afterwards.'

The events that led up to Bailo's accession in about 1963, although finally the result of many complex and heterogeneous causes, nevertheless lay bare, I think, the major structural transformations in Maale political economy that dominated the post-Italian period: the Maale political élite were no longer really kings and chiefs but Ethiopian landlords. Differences in power no longer rested so much on the ideology of divine kingship, customary forms of labour tribute, and control over valuable trade goods as upon assimilation to northern culture, the ability to use and to influence the imperial state apparatus, and, above all, the ownership of land – an institution backed and regulated by the power of the state.

All of the changes that Bailo's accession heralded proceeded at an accelerated pace after 1963. In Jinka, the sub-provincial capital, Bailo bought a house and spent much of his time there in the courts and with officials. Along with the chiefs of Gero and Bunka, he enrolled his sons in school in Jinka. And he scandalized Maale elders by removing his necklace when he went to Jinka. In Maale, the necklace was the most sacred insignia of kingship; in town, it merely identified Bailo as pagan and provincial. Henceforth, he would live as an 'Amhara', he proclaimed; he would not observe old Maale taboos.

The transformation of the Maale élite would have seemed complete had not Bailo suddenly died in the summer of 1970. His early death, which opponents naturally saw as a sign that he had not been meant to hold office, reopened the issue of succession. Yebirka was still alive. Bailo's eldest son, an educated young man of about twenty, was also a strong contender. From the point of view of the government, there was no question of who should be *balabbat*: Bailo's son was called back from school and given authority over Maale, and for the next five years the young man continued the strong rule that his father had begun. The Maale, however, could not agree upon who should be *kati*. For five years, the Bola elders and the chiefs of Makana and Bola were deadlocked. The Bola elders tacitly supported Yebirka, but, afraid of alienating a future king, they did not openly oppose Bailo's son. The Makana chief was a strong supporter of the son. The Bola chief, finally, had taken offence at the young man's strong rule and refused to back either candidate. During the entire time, Bailo was said still to reign as *kati*, and his body lay in a special house in the sacred forest of Dufa. The question of the succession which had previously seemed so important became irrelevant as the revolution reached Maale in 1975: the kingship was abolished.

CONCLUSION

I began this essay with a note on the connection between anthropological and historical modes of analysis. I hope that by now it will be clear that Maale political structures were embedded in time – not the abstract time of endlessly repeating developmental cycles, but the particular time defined by fluctuations in the imperial Ethiopian state during the twentieth century. Disentangling Maale political structures from their particular temporal integument would have destroyed my whole analytical point.

A similar argument could be made with respect to space. The Maale polity was nested within the provincial domain of Bako, which was, in turn, nested within the imperial domain of Addis Abeba. Analysing the smallest unit, Maale, has required some reference to the structures and rhythms of these larger, encapsulating political units. For example, the two segments of the developing landlord class in Maale – northerners along with the Maale king and some of the chiefs – often came into conflict as one segment became more useful to the imperial administration than the other. This friction between élite segments, if not actually encouraged by government officials, served imperial interests in Bako and Addis Abeba by keeping each segment responsive and ready to please.

The significance of both time and space to social analysis has come to the fore in a number of recent theoretical discussions.[19] As interest has developed in analysing larger-scale structures over longer periods of time, however, there has been a tendency to assume that the only social unit worth analysing is the largest: in Immanuel Wallerstein's phrase, 'the world capitalist system'.[20] The details of what happened in one small community – only a minute and incomplete part of a complex whole – have begun to look increasingly beside the point.

This belief betrays, I think, a misunderstanding of historical causation, for, as I have argued above, local events in Maale were never simply determined by imperial politics. Certainly, the imperial state set limits and conditions, but to use Marx's words, the Maale made their own history, even if not exactly as they pleased. If this be granted, then intensive analyses of small-scale social units becomes all the more necessary. The smallest details of out of the way places can be made to illuminate something as large and complex as an imperial state and *vice versa*.

I can illustrate this two-way process with aspects of the analysis above. First, I have tried to show how local politics in Maale can be understood only in the context of the changing configuration of power in the Ethiopian state. To reiterate, during the twentieth century Maale politicians operated within a wider environment of changing economic and political relationships – an environment now relatively rich, now relatively poor, in available resources. Without understanding the conditions and limits which this environment placed upon political actors in Maale, we would undoubtedly have misunderstood Maale politics. Arregude would have appeared only as a 'great man', Yebirka as only politically incompetent.

But a second point is equally valid: an understanding of local social units illuminates the workings of the Ethiopian state and its central institutions. And perhaps the most interesting aspect of the present case is that it suggests that phases of centralization – when Ethiopian emperors took on 'autocratic' powers – were just the times of greatest autonomy for indigenous officials in some peripheral areas like Maale. This reinforces the argument made by

Douglas Johnson in this volume that the Ethiopian state was different from most modern states. Instead of an administrative staff with a relatively clear chain of command and differentiated offices, the Ethiopian state consisted of an uneasy hierarchy of individuals, each with the same type but different degrees of power, each momentarily subordinated to others by personal ties. This 'patrimonial' state floated on top of local communities, and its power to intervene in local affairs – other than by brute force, which was costly – was limited. It is only since the Ethiopian revolution that a new and strengthened form of the state has evolved – one developing the capacity, however uneven, for more radically transforming local social units.

4

Institutionalizing a fringe periphery: Dassanetch–Amhara relations

URI ALMAGOR

The Dassanetch, located at the northern end of Lake Turkana, were formally incorporated into the Ethiopian empire during the last decade of the nineteenth century. By 1970, however, they did not speak Amharic or practise any of the so-called 'Amharic' customs. They retained their own socio-political and cultural order, maintaining themselves for the most part by using the resources available in their own territory – principally cattle and crops grown on fields periodically flooded by the Omo River.

In 1968–70 during the time of my field work, almost the only visible sign that the Dassanetch were part of Ethiopia was a series of garrisons manned by approximately one hundred and fifty 'Amhara' soldiers (there were no northern civilians in the area).[1] But the Amhara soldiers and the Dassanetch had little direct interaction. In fact, both sides were notably reluctant to develop social relations. The Amhara governor, officers, and soldiers knew almost nothing about Dassanetch social organization, customs, or cosmology, and the Dassanetch knew virtually nothing about the country, people, ruling centre, and institutions of Ethiopia.

The overall picture was one in which the Dassanetch – while ruled over by a network of military garrisons – had developed little orientation, let alone commitment, to the Ethiopian centre. Within certain limits the Dassanetch had even retained a large degree of local autonomy. The question is: how did this state of affairs come to pass? How did relations between the Dassanetch and Amhara develop (or perhaps more accurately, fail to develop) over the little more than seventy years of imperial history?

Perhaps the first aspect of the question that has to be understood involves the nature of the polity that incorporated the Dassanetch. Ethiopian conquest of the far south created an extended political unit whose nature suggests, at least to my mind, the imperialism practised in the ancient world – especially in the Middle East – rather than other forms of colonization. S. N. Eisenstadt has analysed this kind of imperialism and the various ways in which new political units are created by it.[2] In particular, he points out two ideal–typical modes of restructuring conquered populations: one entails little change in the basic structural and cultural premises of the conquered populations, and, over time, 'little restructuring of the relation between center and periphery in the new unit'; the other 'is characterized by the tendency for ecological and political changes to be combined with far-reaching change in the structural characteristics of the populations, and, especially, with a restructuring of the center–periphery relations and types of strata-formation.'[3]

Both modes and various mixtures of the two can be found in early twentieth-century Ethiopia, as other chapters in this volume show.[4] Dassanetch society, by comparison with the Leka Oromo and the Maale, described in Chapters 2 and 3, is interesting for it represents an extreme case of Eisenstadt's first ideal type. Indeed, it is tempting to describe centre–periphery relations between the Dassanetch and the Amhara as having been institutionalized at a relatively low – and finally hostile – level of interaction.

My aim in this chapter is to show how this developed, by examining three aspects emphasized by Eisenstadt. The first concerns local ecological and environmental conditions as they relate to population and territorial social structure. The second focuses on the institutionalized basis of interaction between the two political orders and the individuals who were their main social actors. Finally, the third involves the symbolic dimension of these relations, mainly the selective expression by both groups of the cultural differences between them. Before examining each of these in turn, I will present a very brief overview of late nineteenth- and early twentieth-century developments in Dassanetchland.

AN OUTLINE OF RECENT DASSANETCH HISTORY

The first contact of the Dassanetch with northern Ethiopians was not with Menilek's armies in 1898 but with the small bands of northern hunters who had infiltrated the south some years before. These free-wheeling hunters (known among the Borena as 'Tigre') are remembered today by the Dassanetch as 'Shubatari', according to Neil Sobania.[5] The Shubatari and the Dassanetch appear to have developed relatively harmonious relationships based upon mutual interests. In contrast to the strict boundary and the tension that later developed between Amhara and Dassanetch, some of the early hunters were even incorporated into local society as bond partners. According to an oral text recently collected by Sobania in Dassanetchland, 'People cooked for them [the Shubatari] . . . people put fat in their millet . . . They ate from our bowls; they were our people.'[6]

No such memories exist of Menilek's armies who came later, for the Dassanetch were confronted then with a clearly superior military force. The conquest of the area in 1898 and later forays into the region caused much destruction of people and livestock (even if the destruction was perhaps exaggerated by certain travellers at the time).[7]

From records one cannot reconstruct a clear picture of the events immediately following the conquest. The Ethiopian troops stayed in Dassanetchland for only a short time, after which there was no official Ethiopian presence on the Lower Omo for several years. Dassanetchland was formally included in Ethiopia by the Anglo-Ethiopian treaty of 1907, which demarcated the borders between Ethiopia and British East Africa. When Gwynn and Stigand visited the area in 1909, they found Ethiopian posts with a total strength of about forty troops.[8] About this time the Dassanetch began acquiring arms from traders and from Ethiopian army deserters.[9] Shortly afterwards a Kenyan intelligence report (1917) stated that the Dassanetch had become 'so wealthy and powerful that they threw off the Abyssinian yoke and raided neighbouring tribes on their own'.[10]

The introduction of firearms radically changed the pattern of inter-tribal warfare and raids. The number of casualties rose, livestock was looted in large numbers and small rifle-armed parties could, and frequently did, massacre whole unarmed villages. In particular the introduction of firearms caused what had been local clashes to escalate into serious threats to large sections of neighbouring tribes. Warriors armed with rifles became so powerful that they dominated the military arena during the 1920s and '30s, even though they were puny compared to Turkana and Kenyan forces.

In 1937 Dassanetchland was occupied by an Italian force, which remained until 1941. The Italians rearmed the Dassanetch with new rifles and trained them in modern guerrilla warfare. At the end of 1941 the British army forced the Italians out and defeated the Dassanetch in battle. The British administration concluded that the establishment of a no man's land around the Dassanetch was essential if tribal warfare was to be stopped, and they set up a *cordon sanitaire* to the west in the area known as the Ilemi Appendix. A series of police posts was set up in the Appendix along the Ethiopian border (at Kokuru, Liwan, Lokomarinyang, Kaiemothia and Kibish: see Map 11), which deprived the Dassanetch of their western pastures. The pastures of the Appendix, especially those in the Lorienatom Range, had been crucial to the pastoral economy since they mitigated the severe dry-season pressure on the small homeland pastures. At the end of World War II when the Ethiopians returned to the Lower Omo, the Dassanetch were faced with a *fait accompli* and were unable to regain the lost western grazing grounds. From time to time they tried to force their way into the Appendix, but they were repulsed in several serious armed clashes with the Kenyan police.

By 1970 the Ethiopian presence in the Lower Omo area consisted of only a few scattered police stations in Kalam, Namuraputh, Kibish, and Fagage. During the rainy season the posts were sometimes cut off from the rest of the country for months at a time. There were no all-weather roads. And, as I have pointed out, contact between tribesmen and the police, who for the most part stayed in their posts, was limited, confined mainly to a little barter of coffee beans and clothes in exchange for sheep, goats, and grain. As far as I could tell, no sexual relationships of any kind developed between the policemen and Dassanetch women.

THE SOCIAL AND ENVIRONMENTAL SETTING

As Eisenstadt emphasized, the way in which local populations are incorporated into empires is often influenced by local ecology and social organization. Below, I will present the major features of Dassanetch ecology and society. There are two main points to be emphasized. First, ecology and location made Dassanetchland a relatively favourable place for the Dassanetch themselves (compared to their immediate neighbours) but a very difficult place to control for northern soldiers. Second, Dassanetch social organization presented its own barriers. As I have argued at length elsewhere, Dassanetch society is best seen as a complex of overlapping networks rather than a collection of corporate groups – individuals building up 'social credit' and influence through various sorts of social ties.[11]

Dassanetchland is a semi-arid plain which stretches across the area north of Lake Turkana in southern Ethiopia. The economy of the Dassanetch is based on a balance between pastoralism and flood-retreat cultivation. The Omo River, which crosses the plain and flows into Lake Turkana, inundates the low-lying areas each year, permitting the Dassanetch to cultivate the river banks as well as to raise cattle and small stock.

Changes in the distribution of cultivable land among households are a recurring element in the transhumant way of life practised by every household. When the flood waters recede, the Dassanetch are concentrated near the river and the lake, in settlements or in cultivators' camps. Each year, a man and his household make seven or eight changes of residence, including short periods in cattle camps in the western grazing grounds.

Resources of livestock and land in Dassanetchland are not scarce, irregular, or unstable enough to justify their control by large, localized corporate groups. The basic social and economic units are households, which split up and move about according to seasonal demands. The life cycle of a household is shorter than that of an individual. With no more than its own manpower, clan affiliation, or cognatic ties, a household cannot secure access to land, labour or stock. These resources must be attained via the social networks that a man manages to erect through a continuous process which is affected by changes over the life cycle. The various forms of co-operation with other individuals serve not only to give access to necessary resources but simultaneously provide a means by which to build up social status and brokerage power.

The Dassanetch are divided into eight tribal sections (*en*) and, with the exception of two, each section is seen as co-terminous with a territorial division. Tribal sections differ in population size and territory. The largest is the Inkabelo, whose members account for about half the Dassanetch population and occupy the broadest territory which spreads over both banks of the river and contains the greatest diversity of pasture and arable land. The remaining tribal sections are the Inkoria and the Naritch (both located on the east bank of the Omo River) and the Elele, Randal, and Riele (who inhabit the west bank). Finally, the Oro and the Koro have no land of their own and are scattered over Inkabelo territory.

Each tribal section has a clan system which is a loose structure of exogamous units controlling no resources, having no territorial bounds and with no internal organization or common ceremonies. In fact, members of any given clan are distributed among numerous settlements and camps and live in independent small households that constitute the main units of production and consumption. The solidarity which a man feels for clan members other than his immediate circle of agnates is patently weak.

The main social and political organization of the Dassanetch is the generation-set system which encompasses all the Dassanetch people. Each tribal section has its own generation-set system, and while there are similarities in structures and names, each system functions fairly independently. I shall describe the Inkabelo system, which is based on six named sets divided into three pairs, as follows:

NUMOR	NILIMETO	NIGABITE
NYOGOLOMOGEN	NIKORIO	NILIMKORIO

Each pair of generation-sets forms a line through which a man and his descendants pass. A person's generation-set affiliation is determined at birth since he joins the set of the pair which is counterpart to his father's set. For example, the son of a man affiliated to NUMOR will be NYOGOLOMOGEN, and his sons will be NUMOR, etc.

Since generation-sets recruit members simultaneously and independently of each other, there is considerable overlapping of ages across generation-sets, and there may be quite large age differences between the oldest and youngest members of any given generation-set. This results from the regular staggering of each generation-set's opening and closure of recruitment. This is a complex issue and not immediately relevant here; however, the slight but pervasive age differences between generation-sets are the basis of their hierarchical order of seniority. For example, in the grouping given above the order of seniority runs NUMOR – NILIMETO – NIGABITE – NYOGOLOMOGEN – NIKORIO – NILIMKORIO and back to NUMOR to start a new cycle. This is the sequence through which the generation-sets come to power. Power is vested in the most senior surviving generation-set whose members elect about 30 of their fellows to serve as 'bulls' (*ara*), here termed Bulls.

In 1968–70, it was the NILIMKORIO generation-set which provided the Bulls. The Bulls were the representatives of their own generation-set and of the age-system as a whole; they were also considered as religious and political leaders of their tribal section (some of them filled judicial roles when necessary). Since the Inkabelo was the dominant tribal section, their Bulls were, in effect, leaders of all the Dassanetch. Apart from structural position, the essence of Bulls' power rested in the mystical notion that they alone mediated the divine gifts of children and cattle and thus controlled the fertility of both humans and livestock.

How did aspects of the ecology and social organization just described affect centre–periphery relations in Dassanetchland? I shall concentrate on three points.

First, the occupation by Menilek's troops in 1898 had a very strong impact on the Dassanetch. As the Dassanetch put it, their encounter with Menilek's armies almost ended in the destruction of their society and culture. The fear that the Amhara might one day inflict a similar blow continued to be an integral element in Dassanetch life and influenced and guided many aspects of their relations with their rulers.

Second, for various reasons, the imperial centre did not attempt to impose its own cultural system or the mainly Christian symbols of Amhara identity on the 'pagan' Dassanetch. The policy implemented by the imperial centre in dealing with the new periphery in the distant south was based on retaining a balance of physical force. As I have noted, several military garrisons were set up, and these became instruments for exercising force whenever the balance of power in the area was disrupted, either as a result of resistance against northern rule or because of clashes between rival local groups. However, it should be noted that attempts at such control were not always effective.

There were a number of reasons for this. One has to do with firearms; like other groups in southern Ethiopia, the Dassanetch acquired firearms and continued to possess a considerable number of rifles in spite of several partially successful attempts to disarm them. They were considered as a fighting force to be reckoned with. The second reason why attempts at control failed was environmental. Access to the Lower Omo was difficult and transportation within the area no less so. The transfer of troops from other stations to the Lower Omo and their deployment between the area's various garrisons was slow and difficult to execute. Furthermore, because of the variations in the timing of the rainy season in the highlands and in the Lower Omo (as distinct from inundations), Dassanetchland was often cut off from the highlands for many months at a time.

All told, the Lower Omo basin remained one of the most isolated and least accessible areas in southern Ethiopia. No markets were established in the area — the closest ones were in Jinka and Maji which were separated from Dassanetchland by intervening hostile groups. The size of the Amhara force stationed in Dassanetchland varied over the years, depending on the need to use force. According to my Dassanetch informants, the peak was just after World War II, when several hundred soldiers were stationed in the area; later, in the 1950s and '60s, the number dwindled to about 150.

The third aspect of centre–periphery relations which I want to stress involves local political organization. When the Amhara established their foothold in Dassanetchland at the beginning of this century, they nominated several individuals as headmen or 'spokesmen' for the rest of the Dassanetch – mainly for purposes of tax collection. These people were called *balabbat* by the Amhara, and the Dassanetch called them *kansitch ochumba* ('leaders for the foreigners' or 'leaders of the foreigners').[12] They were often referred to by both

Amhara and Dassanetch as 'chiefs' – suggesting some Kenyan influence. The Amhara themselves observed that *balabbat* was not an appropriate term for the appointed Dassanetch headmen, since none of them owned any land. I, too, shall refer to them as 'chiefs'. The original chiefs represented the various tribal sections, and most of the chiefs in 1970 were descendants or kinsmen of the original appointees.[13]

BULLS VERSUS CHIEFS

It is difficult to assess exactly when chiefs were first nominated. It was probably just after the establishment of imperial control when northern conquerors asked the Dassanetch to appoint their own spokesmen. Their rôle was not very clearly defined at the start; the general idea was that someone should represent the major Dassanetch social units in dealing with the occupying power, and criteria of size (tribal section) and internal divisions (generation-sets) were central in the Dassanetch choice of appointees.[14]

Becoming the main intermediary link between their own people and the administration gave the chiefs potential power and resources which they exploited in due course. However, the extent to which they could use their power and resources was limited by the manner in which they could perform functions as intermediaries and by the ambivalence of their own people's regard for them. Certain patterns and specific instances of interaction reveal the spheres in which the chiefs' functions as intermediaries could be manifested.

The first was tax collection. Among pastoralists this is always a problem, since a man's property cannot always be reliably assessed in terms of his herd. Some of a man's beasts are not really 'his' – being held in trust for others and redeemable at any time. Conversely, part of the herd belonging to any particular man may be dispersed among the herds of others. Furthermore, a sizeable share of a man's livestock may already have been disposed of in the process of creating social ties.

The chiefs were instructed to collect taxes only from the 'rich', but the complexities described above demonstrate that it was no easy matter to settle on a definition of 'rich'. A Dassanetch man's wealth was closely tied up with his stage in the life cycle: upon marrying he withdrew the beasts in which he had rights from his father's herd and – in the process of establishing his own household – he gradually pared down his initially fairly large herd in order to cement various social contracts and fulfil certain obligatory ritual functions. In so doing he acquired a claim in the herds of others, as well as social ties that were major resources in their own right. Thus, a young man could not be 'wealthy' no matter how large his herd was, nor could an elder who had drastically cut down the size of his herd by undergoing the *dimi* ceremony be deemed 'poorer' than someone who still possessed a sizeable herd because he had yet to undergo that ritual.[15] Nevertheless, some elders were considered 'wealthy', and these were supposed to be the target for tax collection.

The Dassanetch were fully aware that any refusal to pay taxes would provoke a strong reaction from the Amhara. Taxes were thus regarded as a burden that could not be escaped, and Dassanetch paid, under protest. On the other hand, the Amhara governor realized that he could neither press the Dassanetch too hard nor exert undue force in executing tax collection. Any attempt to expropriate livestock forcibly would have invited resistance, my informants said, so as to jeopardize the already precarious relations between the Amhara and the Dassanetch. As a matter of fact, in 1970 the governor had no information about the distribution of livestock resources among the Dassanetch, nor had he the administrative capacity to collect taxes regularly on his own. Instead, he had to rely on the chiefs for information and collection. This illustrates one of the constraints on the chiefs' intermediary rôle and can be exemplified in more detail.

The chiefs were asked to present the governor with a list of those persons who were wealthy and hence liable to taxation.[16] This list was to be based on the Dassanetch people's own consensus on the definition of 'wealthy'. It is important to note that in cases of disagreement, where individuals claimed that they should not be on the list or refused to pay, both the chiefs and the disputants appealed to the Bulls for support, and the Bulls' decision was regarded as final and binding. The governor did not know about the rôle played by the Bulls; displeased with the list, he accused the chiefs of cheating him by under-representing the true number of men wealthy enough to be taxed. Furthermore, delays in payments were a major source of trouble for which the governor blamed the chiefs. The latter argued that circumstances such as drought, disease, and demands of the *dimi* ceremony had reduced the ability of the Dassanetch to pay.

The governor often called the chiefs liars, claimed that it was impossible to work with them, and threatened to dismiss them. In the meetings I witnessed the chiefs were carefully circumspect in what they said; they did not mention the Bulls, and, when referring to individuals in whom the governor displayed an interest, used names other than those by which the persons were commonly known.[17] The governor was reluctant to admit his ignorance of these and other details related by the chiefs and thus could usually do very little but accept whatever the chiefs chose to disclose. He told me that the entire situation, with all its constraints on his freedom of action, was disagreeable to him. Such taxes as were in fact collected, were used to finance the governor's own salary and that of some assistants, with the balance being forwarded to Jinka.[18] Ultimately the governor had to settle for a smaller tax revenue than had been expected, and the chiefs were unable to exploit fully the power vested in them as middlemen, because of the decisions made by the Bulls.

A second area of difficulty for the chiefs was that the Dassanetch identified them with Amhara attempts to deprive the Dassanetch of the firearms that they had been using since the beginning of the twentieth century. Firearms, as I have mentioned, were crucial in maintaining the power of the Dassanetch in relation to neighbouring groups.[19]

As representatives of the Dassanetch responsible for public order, the chiefs were required by the governor to turn over any firearms or inform him of their whereabouts.[20] But the chiefs vehemently denied any knowledge of the possession of such arms, whereupon the governor accused them once again of being unreliable liars. Oddly enough, the chiefs' lack of co-operation with the Amhara over the firearms issue brought them no credit among their own people. Young men in particular were suspicious of the chiefs' intentions and avoided informing them about their weapons. The reason for this was that in one way or another the chiefs had unintentionally become involved in Amhara operations directed at collecting and confiscating firearms.

At the end of the 1950s, after some serious clashes with the Turkana, the chiefs were required to accompany Amhara officers in rifle searches. They were supposed to supervise the searches to ensure that nothing else was taken besides firearms; but the Dassanetch later said that the chiefs had helped the Amhara. I even heard rumours accusing the chiefs of having brought in the soldiers in the first place. Chief Irgudo was beaten by members of his generation-set as punishment for this alleged collaboration. But the worst incident occurred in March 1965, during another search operation. The chiefs were asked to persuade the people to turn over their old rifles in return for new ones. The chiefs claimed they had been deceived by the governor and his Amhara soldiers and had believed that modern rifles would have helped them resist outsiders from Kenya. However, once a couple of dozen rifles were confiscated by the Amhara, the Dassanetch accused the chiefs of having tricked them into co-operating with the authorities; and even though the operation as a whole failed, chief Anokhosia and chief Yerar were severely beaten by members of their own generation-sets. Another incident took place in 1969. Chief Irgudo was attacked while sleeping. The reason given for this was that he had informed the Amhara officers in Kalam about three traders who had come from Maji. Prompt action by the Amhara led to the seizure of rifles and ammunition and the capture of the traders. Irgudo told me later that he had not known the traders were dealing in arms. When I asked provocatively how it was possible for a chief to be beaten up, he replied: 'I am not a *kansitch* [chief] of the *ochumba* [Amhara] but of my *hari* [generation-set]. If my *hari* wants to replace me, it can do so. I am *kansitch* of my *hari*. When they beat me, it is bad, very bad. The *kabana* [men of the generation-set] say they hate what I did.' It is interesting that Irgudo in some sense justified the attack made on him.

Some informants told me that although the *hari* could replace a chief, they never did so because no one wanted to be *kansitch ochumba*; thus, chiefs were said to inherit the office from a family member since no one else sought the appointment. I am not sure just how accurate this claim was. At the end of 1969 the governor quarrelled with chief Anokhosia and ordered him not to return to Kalam. He asked the other chiefs to arrange a replacement for Anokhosia. Once this became known, assistants and close associates of Anokhosia, called *kansitch ninika* ('little chiefs') by the Dassanetch, went to many NUMOR elders to persuade them not to elect a substitute but to leave Anokhosia in office as he was the right person to defend the interests of the Dassanetch.[21] Eventually the governor relented and Anokhosia was reinstated.

This brings us to the third sphere – maintaining law and order – which the Amhara regarded as the responsibility of the chiefs. The governor told me that he viewed the hostilities between the Dassanetch and neighbouring peoples as the main problem at hand. The Dassanetch presented him few internal problems, and he found them surprisingly peaceful among themselves. To make this point, the governor stressed the fact that during his two years in Kalam not a single case had been brought before him as local judge. The governor viewed law and order mainly in terms of bloodshed and killings. He contrasted the relatively high rate of intertribal killings with the absence of such violence among the Dassanetch themselves. This impression was, in fact, accurate. But the governor did not realize that the Dassanetch were careful to prevent their internal conflicts from reaching his attention.

It was almost unthinkable among the Dassanetch for someone to take his grievances to the Amhara to seek justice, and such an action would probably have resulted in severe condemnation and sanctions on the part of the people. Even the chiefs who were beaten did not complain to the Amhara. The norm that developed among the Dassanetch was that internal disputes should be internally resolved through meetings, compromises, or judgment before Dassanetch judges. The chiefs were left to handle anything involving relations with other peoples. These ranged from issues such as intertribal marriages and the transfer of bridewealth, divorce, abduction of girls, theft, and compensation, to graver issues such as loss of life in raids, the looting of cattle, and the escalation of hostilities. In their dealings with such problems the chiefs became known beyond the borders of Dassanetchland.[22] It was the chiefs who went to make peace or to negotiate with representatives of other groups, and it was they whom the governor consulted and warned about the scale of intertribal hostilities.

The fourth issue involved the chiefs' mediating rôle whenever Dassanetch or Amhara individuals needed something the other could provide. While this might appear to have been only a matter of doing small favours, it formed an important source in building up a chief's personal power base. Being far removed from the administrative centres and markets of Maji and Jinka, the Amhara soldiers stationed in Dassanetchland were dependent on supplies shipped in by truck from the army centre in Jinka. But in some years the road was not passable during the rainy season, and the soldiers were cut off from their supplies for months at a time. They had to find an alternative source through exchange with the Dassanetch. Mostly they exchanged coffee beans and cloth for Dassanetch sheep, goats, and sorghum. The chiefs were usually the first to be approached for such exchanges. Therefore, chiefs often had coffee when other Dassanetch had none. Their ability to serve coffee at home during informal meetings, as well as to slaughter small stock for hospitality, made chiefs' homesteads important social centres. In addition, the regular salary they commanded, their frequent trips to Jinka for meetings with the district governor, and their acquaintance with Amhara officials and officers, all put them in a position to help their followers. Indeed, these sources of power aided the chiefs in their construction of useful social networks.

Although much of this power was derived from and at least partly dependent upon external sources (the Amhara), the chiefs managed to some extent, by co-operating with one another, to establish an influential power base to rival that of the Bulls. However, the power of two of the chiefs, Atol and Lumuromoi, was based primarily on their wealth in livestock and on the ties they had made by converting livestock into binding social relationships. This alone would have made them prominent figures in Dassanetch society. In fact, on close examination, it appears that the power of the other chiefs did not approach the level one might have expected from the potential inherent in their rôles as middlemen. In other words, in spite of their control over the channels of communication between the two groups and their potential to achieve dominance by 'manipulating the goals, the resources and restrictions of both groups', they did not attain such predominance.[23]

The question is, why not? Perhaps chiefs' attempts were curtailed by a Dassanetch 'strategy of containment'. But this could have been effective only with the help of concurrent attempts to delegitimize Amhara culture. This will be examined in detail in the following section.

INCLUSION AND EXCLUSION IN DASSANETCH–AMHARA RELATIONS

The Bulls formed the centre of Dassanetch society and were an ascribed élite based on their affiliation to the senior generation-set of the age-system. Alongside this ascriptive élite, which symbolized the relations between the social and cosmic orders, there was another élite that consisted of individual elders from various generation-sets who had managed to accumulate sufficient power to become patrons and brokers for others.[24] This was not a homogeneous or bounded group; men could achieve prominence through using resources and social relationships which they had built up over the years or by mediating resources and social ties between others. But no matter how powerful and prominent a man became, he could not join the Bulls unless he was affiliated to the senior generation-set. Considering that the Bulls controlled no resources and that individuals were free to achieve power through the culturally legitimate mediation of resources, one wonders why the chiefs did not co-operate more closely with Amhara officialdom. Arguably, chiefs could have become the main political power and a spearhead for change, leaving the Bulls to play a traditional–religious rôle devoid of power. Such a development has been observed in other societies in Southern Ethiopia (as perhaps with the Maji *kure* as described by Garretson in Chapter 8) but it did not happen among the Dassanetch. Not only were Bulls not relegated to a secondary symbolic position, they remained very much the main repository of power dominating the local political arena.

The Bulls were unable to prevent chiefs from accumulating some power, but this power was so restricted that chiefs frequently had to act against their own personal interests. We do not know much about the power relations between Bulls and chiefs in the past, but it seems obvious that from the outset chiefs accepted the rules of the game of Dassanetch society. This meant, among other things, that they subjected themselves to the authority of the Bulls and could not co-operate with the Amhara against the Bulls. Furthermore, since Bulls were symbolically associated with the well-being and the very continuation of Dassanetch society, no information about the Bulls themselves or about their functions could be allowed to reach the governor.

At the same time, Amhara officers and soldiers were quite unenthusiastic about engaging in closer relations with the Dassanetch.[25] It seems that a form of mutual exclusion developed between the two groups, each closing itself off from the other, each leaving open only those few channels of contact that were deemed necessary for maintaining co-existence.

This process can be analysed better in the context of the symbolic level of interactions between the two groups. I refer mainly to concepts and images that each group evolved regarding the culture and characteristics of the other. It was through these images that each group attributed negative qualities to the other, presenting the other as essentially non-human and dangerous. The negation of the Amhara by the Dassanetch reinforced the position of the Bulls and generated increasing emphasis on the sacred values which they represented. Similarly, the negation of Dassanetch culture by the Amhara constituted an essential element of the barrier separating the two groups and undermined any prospect that an individual Amhara might have had of successfully initiating a closer relationship with a Dassanetch.

From the side of the Amhara, what officers resented most was not the physical inconvenience of being stationed in Dassanetchland but being cut off from their families, communities, and cultural milieu. This isolation was difficult to bear for extended periods. We may assume that the frequency among the Amhara of drunken behaviour, violence, apathy, depression, and even suicide, was directly associated with the soldiers' loneliness.[26] The Amhara took no interest in Dassanetch culture and even viewed it with contempt. They despised the Dassanetch as savages, and the terms they sometimes used expressed their image of the Dassanetch – 'slaves' (*bariawoch*), 'cheats' (*ḳeṭafīwoch*), and 'robbers' (*shifta*), as well as people with no respect for others (*balegē*).

Four images were resorted to repeatedly. First, the Dassanetch were 'pagans' who worshipped animals and trees. Here the Amhara were referring to the leopard skins worn by 'men of *dimi*', to the skins of the Colobus monkey worn by their wives, and to the *miede* branches planted at the centre of the *dimi* village.[27] I recall a situation in which Amhara soldiers watching the *dimi* ceremony jocularly explained to a newcomer that the ceremony was 'their Epiphany' (*ṭimḳet*) and that the *digatch* sticks carried by the girls as a symbol of their future fertility represented a cross (*mesḳel*); these 'explanations' were accompanied by hearty laughter.

Second, the Dassanetch were associated with cannibals (*sew belawoch*).[28]

When I told the governor and some Amhara officers that I had heard this tale before and that it was not true, they insisted that the Dassanetch were indeed cannibals who practised in secret, citing the fact that they did not have a cemetery (*meḳabir*) as proof. Third was the Dassanetch practice of bleeding cattle and drinking the blood during the dry season. The Amhara found this a savage practice and often said the Dassanetch behaved like animals. The fourth image common among the Amhara was that the Dassanetch were 'like women' (*sētasētoch*). They referred mainly to the wearing of bead necklaces and arm bands by Dassanetch men.

On the other side, there were four specific spheres in which Dassanetch images of the Amhara were developed and stressed. First, the few Dassanetch who were recruited as soldiers (*labania*) in Dassanetchland and who had learned a little Amharic served as a source of information about some of the concepts and religious practices of the Amhara. One concept which made a great impression and terrified the Dassanetch was that of the resurrection. For the Dassanetch, the notion that 'the spirits of the dead' (*garam*) would assume flesh and blood was almost inconceivable. They developed an image of the Amhara as *garam*, and often used the term in referring to them derogatorily. A second image was of the Amhara as 'people who eat raw meat' (*gal qom daf gayokha*). This was often brought up when the Dassanetch were eating their roasted meat in communal and ritual meals. A third image concerned the Amhara practice of drinking honey wine (*ṭej*) and especially the drunkenness which occasionally ensued. In Dassanetch culture, intoxication was associated with death and misfortune. Once a year the Dassanetch became intoxicated at the *dimi* ceremony, but they despised the frequent drinking of *ṭej* by the Amhara and associated it with a culture that emphasizes death and disaster. Fourth, the Dassanetch employed references to femininity to derogate Amhara men, just as they did for the Kere, Murle, Nyangatom, Turkana and Bashada. For example, when asked something by an Amhara soldier, a Dassanetch would ask 'What did she want?' They explained this use of the feminine form by saying that 'these people do not know how to fight – like women'. This usage contrasted with that for the Hamar and the Borena, for whom the Dassanetch used the masculine form in appreciation of their fighting skills.

It is striking that the negation of the other culture by both Dassanetch and Amhara centred on similar spheres and used similar images and idioms. This is not unusual in cases of cross-cultural conflict. There were several factors connected with the image-forming process: the minimal knowledge which each group had about the complexities of the other's culture and society; the mutual fear of sudden attack; the proverbs and sayings used in informal social exchanges and handed down from parent to child. All of these may have contributed, and deserve elaboration, but are not immediately relevant to the present discussion. Nor is the question of whether a particular image developed independently in each group, or whether one group created corresponding images as a reaction to the images of the other. Of greater importance here are two other aspects.

First, while each group was aware of the images the other held, neither attempted to change the other's perceptions. It was as though each group accepted a situation in which the other had a partial, selective, negatively-stereotyped picture. Secondly, the images described above were concerned with basic dimensions of human existence – supernatural powers, life and death, collective identity, and nature and culture. In fact, the notions are almost structured into binary oppositions of positive and negative elements in which, needless to add, the negative properties were ascribed to others. Thus, one's own supernatural power was compared with others' 'inferior' deities of nature (animals and trees) or of the underworld (spirits of the dead); the cultural order of the other group was compared to undomesticated nature (eating raw meat, drinking blood); death was seen as a central *leitmotif* of the other culture (cannibalism or drunkenness); and each group saw its own identity as based on masculinity and the other as unmanly (decorated 'like women' or incapable of fighting).

One important aspect of the sexual overtones of identity was related to the mutual fear of attack. The Dassanetch were afraid the Amhara might one day attack them and shave off their *shurte shushulish*, their hair-dress daubed with ochre mud with four phallic protrusions, symbolizing, among other things, manhood and virility. The Amhara, for their part, feared that the Dassanetch would attack them and cut off their penises 'as they do with other tribes'. When I told the Amhara in Kalam that to the best of my knowledge it was the Borena who practised such mutilation, and not the Dassanetch, they responded: 'They are all *shanḳilla*, and don't they do it to their enemies?'

Such reciprocal, opposing imagery dramatized cultural differences to such a degree that both groups were highly aware of the cleavage that separated them. The images so strengthened the mutual exclusion of the other, that any possibility of overtures on the part of one side to enter into exchange relations with the other was precluded. This brought about a double impasse: on the one hand, one group's total rejection of the other meant that it was extremely difficult to render the other group's cultural ideas acceptable; and on the other hand, sanctions were employed (mostly by the Dassanetch) to deter anyone from attempting to bridge the gap or mitigate the cultural cleavage. Such sanctions were justified on physical as well as on moral grounds designed to protect the survival of the people and their culture. Dassanetch elders often expressed the fear that 'the *ochumba* will steal our customs'.

This protection of cultural integrity illustrates the relations between Bulls and chiefs from another angle. The delegitimization of Amhara cultural features by means of derogatory images had the effect of extending this negation to Amhara culture as a whole, making anything Amharic automatically suspect. In a situation of fear, suspicion, and the exclusion of the other group from cultural exchange, each group reverted more and more to its own images and symbols. Thus, the contrast of each of the symbolic spheres in which the other was negated served to reaffirm important cultural themes in each group, such as the relation between the cosmic and the social orders and their continuity. For the Dassanetch, the opposites of misfortune, death, nature, and womanhood were fertility, growth, and a social order based on an age-system which was 'the world of men.' Hence, any action that tended to undermine the position of the Bulls at the apex of the age-system was seen as jeopardizing the sacred foundations of Dassanetch existence and continuity.

This sheds some light on the restricted position in which the chiefs found themselves as middlemen. The Bulls created an effective cultural *cordon sanitaire* around themselves and confined the chiefs to the rôle of one-sided 'go-betweens' – to use Paine's distinction.[29] In order to protect the Dassanetch, the Bulls insisted that all orders and information from the Amhara were to be faithfully transmitted to them without alteration or manipulation; they then instructed the chiefs on what to say and do in dealing with the Amhara. In this sense, by being agents of control, the Bulls became 'joint' brokers limiting the exposure of Dassanetch culture to the Amhara and defending its boundaries from Amharic influences. This was done in informal meetings and gatherings at which, in addition to reiterating images that negated Amhara culture, the Bulls often condemned the chiefs or even denounced them to the people whenever the chiefs had done something which the Bulls considered culturally deviationary or threatening. For example, in a speech held at one such meeting, a Bull berated chief Anokhosia for drinking honey wine in Kalam, thereby bringing down misfortune on the land. He asked: 'What will become of us if we take this?' On another occasion of ritual meat-eating, one of the Bulls teased chief Irgudo for not having a *shurte shushulish* hair-style for fear of the Amhara shaving it off.

Nyamumery settlement, which was my main area of research, was also Anokhosia's home, and not a week passed without a messenger arriving to summon him to the Bulls in order to relate his most recent conversation with an Amhara officer. The chiefs found that their scope of action was severely limited not only because of the Bulls' restrictions but mainly because the Bulls knew almost everything they did or said. This information was elicited by the Bulls from young Dassanetch men affiliated to the chiefs' alternate generation-sets. The Bulls encouraged the feeling among these young men that the chiefs could not be trusted with knowledge about possession of firearms. When two Dassanetch soldiers deserted with their rifles, the chiefs reported to the Bulls that the Amhara officers had asked them to return the rifles and turn in the deserters for punishment.[30] The Bulls not only refused to hand over the two young men, they were angry at the chiefs for even considering such an absurd Amhara request. This was only one instance when the Bulls supported cheating and stealing from the alien *ochumba*. The chiefs often protested that doing so was wrong – at least in Amhara eyes – but this immediately put them in the position of potential collaborators who were biased in favour of the Amhara.

Generally speaking, the dilemma of the chiefs in their struggle with the Bulls was that the chiefs were unable to do anything to improve their image as perceived by their own people. If they praised or defended the Amhara, such behaviour would damage their own position, unless, of course, some large-

5 Emperor Haile Selassie visits the Dassanetch. The Governor of Gamo-Gofa presents a girl with candy, while the Emperor looks on

scale government-sponsored improvement project was under way, such as food distribution in times of famine, amnesty for tax evaders, or setting up a ferry across the Omo River during a visit by Haile Selassie (see Plate 5).[31] In such cases, some of the credit would devolve on the chiefs as well. Should the chiefs choose to denounce the Amhara, it would only serve to enhance the position of the Bulls as leaders of the Dassanetch and defenders of their social order and culture.

This dilemma of the chiefs also highlights the two different levels of relations between Dassanetch and Amhara. The Dassanetch did not consider it incongruous or incompatible to accept food, be exempt from tax, or use the Omo ferry, while at the same time excluding the Amhara on a symbolic and ideological level. When I pointed out to some Dassanetch elders that recent Amhara actions made life easier for the Dassanetch themselves, one of the elders replied: 'All these are nothing; the *ochumba* gave us taxes (*gusatch*) and now they take them.' He admitted the ferry was good, but added that before it existed the Amhara had used Dassanetch dugouts to cross the river.

The direct interaction that did take place between the two groups led each to realize that some of their practices had a great deal in common. For example, when the Dassanetch first observed the Amhara fashion of slaughtering sheep, noting that they butchered the carcass so as to preserve the skin intact, they commented that it was 'similar to the way we do it'; or a newly-arrived Amhara soldier would comment that the Dassanetch stool (*kara*) 'is just like our *barchuma*'. Similar observations were made about other items, such as robes, cooking pots, and fireplaces. Direct exchange also brought about reciprocal influences and borrowing of techniques, such as erecting huts and fences, fishing, storage, picking wild fruit, and so forth. Of particular mutual interest was the awareness that both groups were dependent on and subject to the same external factors. When an epidemic, whose symptoms were diarrhoea and fever, hit the Dassanetch people, the chiefs were told that their meeting with the governor would have to be postponed because they – and many soldiers besides – were taken ill. The chiefs replied that the Dassanetch too were ill, and that it was because of the water. An Amhara responded: 'Yes, we drink the same water.' Another way in which similarities were acknowledged was by reference to firearms and thereby to the dependence of both groups on foreign sources of supply. The Dassanetch commented that the Amhara did not produce rifles or ammunition, and 'like us, they received them from the Italians'.

All these instances are part of what might be called a process of inclusion in the interactions taking place among people living in close proximity for many years. Although there were controls, at least on the Dassanetch side, over the form and extent of such interaction, it was inevitable that individuals from either side would engage in some exchange and would hence realize, through first-hand experience, that some of the things done by the other group were not entirely different from those done by his own group, that both groups lived under comparable conditions, shared the same frailties and needs, and were subject to similar forces.

All told, this process of inclusion asserted that, at least in some areas, the differences between the groups were not as profound as they appeared. While each group had to live alongside the other, engaging in interaction and exchange while at the same time portraying the other in some ways as 'non-human', it is perhaps understandable that each group should also select certain familiar 'human' attributes of the other on which to base the limited form of interaction and exchange that did occur. Perhaps because there was no flow of resources from outside, these attributes were often derived from the technical and subsistence levels.

CONCLUSION

The forms of exchange relations established between the Dassanetch and the Amhara did not develop accidentally. They underwent a structured process which can be called an institutionalization, through which frames of reference and norms were crystallized for the regulation of exchange relations. But like any process of institutionalization, local socio-economic and environmental conditions contributed greatly to the form that the new relations took.[32] First, being remote and inaccessible and notorious for malaria, the Lower Omo region was not an attractive area for colonization. Secondly, the system of flood-retreat cultivation which was based on small mobile household units holding only temporary rights to the land was not conducive to the control of large tracts of cultivable land by a small number of Amhara; in other words, it was not compatible with the *gebbar* system instituted in other areas of southern Ethiopia. Thirdly, a pastoral and semi-nomadic population, based on the movement of small (often fragmented) households across different pastures and between settlements and various camps, was difficult to control and to administer. The large kin and territorial units (clans and tribal sections) had no 'heads', and the heads of the small household units of production were too numerous to deal with. Fourthly, besides this 'acephalous' structure of households, the Dassanetch had a central hierarchical structure, the generation-set system, that embraced everyone. The top of this ladder was occupied by the senior group of elders, the Bulls, who were the political and religious leaders of the Dassanetch. The Amhara military commanders were not aware of this hierarchical structure and were certainly unaware that the Bulls represented a strong centre in their own right.

Against such a background, the ability of the Amhara to exercise effective control was hampered from the outset. They appointed men as 'chiefs' whose local influence they hoped to use to control the people, as *balabbat* were appointed and used in other areas. Although chiefs gained some control over resources and some power as well as limited cultural legitimation of their endeavours, they could not undermine the position of the Bulls. In fact, despite the brokerage power that the chiefs gradually came to wield, their powers never came close to balancing those of the Bulls, and it may be assumed that even if the Amhara had become aware of the position and power of the Bulls, they would probably have failed to manipulate rivalries successfully enough to break in and regulate internal power relations.

Shils points out that the most peripheral sectors are those which 'for most of the time and in most spheres of action and belief, lie outside the radius of effectiveness of the centre'.[33] The Dassanetch, then, appear to fit a description as 'the outermost fringe of the periphery', but their particular relation to the centre requires further explanation. Their alienation and hostility towards the Amhara, their lack of any orientation or commitment to Ethiopia, their reluctance to co-operate and to enter into exchange relations with the local representatives of central power all indicate a *hostile* periphery. There seem to be four factors worth examining in the search for an understanding of how this hostile periphery came into being.

First, the Lower Omo was, and has remained, an area of great cultural diversity with much hostility and violent clashes between its various inhabitants. Secondly, the Amhara neither tried to unify the different peoples of the region nor did they offer much ideological or symbolic justification for the conquest and incorporation of the subjected peoples into Ethiopia. This is a crucial point, for the conquest did not change or even mitigate the conflict-fraught relations that prevailed among the various peoples of the Lower Omo. The regulation of this periphery was, then, necessarily based on force of arms, a force that was limited in its effectiveness and that merely continued the existing pattern of intertribal relationships.[34] Thirdly, the first encounter of the Dassanetch with the Amhara was violent and traumatic; troops brought destruction and death to people who were powerless to retaliate. Fourthly, within two decades of occupation, the Dassanetch were equipped with firearms and soon emerged as a dominant fighting force.

These factors influenced Dassanetch–Amhara relations from the beginning. The occupation began violently and was sustained through fear. Each side regarded the other as a threat. In an area where violence was commonly resorted to in intertribal power struggles, it is not surprising that the Dassanetch fully expected the Amhara to extend their political control through force. At the same time, the Amhara observed the Dassanetch growing into a formidable force in comparison with other local groups and feared that the Dassanetch would attack them as well. The rumours circulating about the cruelty and aggression of Dassanetch raids terrified Amhara soldiers.

This mutual fear of confrontation formed the basis for an uneasy balance of power. Both sides realized that they were more or less evenly matched and that any attempt at using force would be met with resistance. This realization served as a means of control, for it implied a rule of deterrence. Slight deviations from this rule (arms searches, the Dassanetch breaking into a military depot in Kalam to steal food, arms, and ammunition) were condemned by the injured parties, but were also tolerated as part of the game, as an acceptable show of force. Such tacit agreement was exemplified in the way taxes were collected. The Dassanetch knew that tax evasion could provoke violent counter-measures; on the other hand, Amhara officers knew that punitive action would only invite violent resistance. Therefore, both sides had to come to terms. The Dassanetch paid less taxes than the Amhara had expected to collect and employed delaying tactics that drew out payments for years on end; the Amhara governor accepted whatever payments were made and refrained from resorting to force in order to increase his revenues.

The mutual fears of potential violence, the uneasy *modus vivendi* practised between two armed groups, the transmission of images from father to son and from veteran soldier to raw recruit, all tended to be self-perpetuating because they relied on stereotypes – on selected images of reality – that were easily reinforced over time by rumours and occasional physical clashes between the groups. One of the properties of institutionalized relations is, of course, their rigid resistance to attempts at normative and structural change. It is not that change was impossible, but it would have required a radical transformation of the power relations between the two groups, an erosion of the means of cultural regeneration, an alteration of the basic production relationships, and a revision of the Dassanetch structure of élites. No such changes occurred.[35] Not only was there no cultural erosion or change in the Dassanetch élite – on the contrary, the position of the Bulls increased in strength. The growing importance of the Bulls as guardians of Dassanetch cultural values in the face of Amhara interests further stiffened the already rigid norms and framework of exchange characterizing Dassanetch–Amhara relations.[36]

The existence of a strong centre among the Dassanetch themselves was of prime importance in the process of institutionalizing the Dassanetch as a periphery. The Bulls were able to regulate intra-group relations by taking advantage of the pattern of symbolic exclusion and by undermining the chiefs' credibility as political brokers whenever the chiefs seemed to deviate from the pursuit of Dassanetch interests.

In summary, this essay reveals that some of the features common to present theoretical formulations of centre–periphery relations do not form an appropriate basis for the analysis of all cases. Notions such as the dependence of the periphery on the centre, the processes of integrating the various different peoples in the periphery, the meaning, for the periphery, of the centre as infused with a 'metaphysical essence', and the growth of 'civility' in Shils' phrase would not have helped in the case presented here.[37] The Dassanetch used violence in their relations with the centre and with other peoples in the area, and were relatively detached from bonds with the country in which they were located. In these ways they resembled fringe peripheries in the empires of the ancient world that were 'left alone'. But a fringe periphery, as the case of the Dassanetch shows, is not necessarily passive, reacting to radiations from the centre, but can actively engage in institutionalizing its connections with the centre.

III Reorienting kinship and identity

5

Lifelines: exchange marriage among the Gumuz

WENDY JAMES

My opening motif is drawn from James Bruce's description of the southern hinterland of Gonder in the early 1770s.[1] This region, now central and south-western Gojjam, was the home of a substantial Gumuz-speaking population, ancestors to many of the present-day Gumuz of the Blue Nile valley in Wellegga, on whom this chapter focuses (see Map 9). Then as now – or at least to 1975 when my field work was carried out in the Blue Nile valley – the Gumuz speakers were known to the highland Ethiopians simply by a variant of the derogatory term *shankilla*. Bruce describes the productive country of the Agaw, supplying the capital of Gonder with cattle, honey, butter, wheat, hides, and wax.[2] The Agaw also sell many of these commodities, together with other goods from the capital, to 'the neighbouring black savages, the woolly-headed Shangalla'. They receive in exchange 'elephants-teeth, rhinoceros-horns, gold in small pellets, and a quantity of very fine cotton'. However, Bruce tells us, they might receive more if they cultivated trade in a fair way, 'without making inroads upon those savages for the sake of slaves'. Bruce explains how the trade is secured in these conditions by the making of special bonds between the trading families on each side, bonds sealed by an exchange of children:

> The way this trade, though very much limited, is established, is by two nations sending their children mutually to each other; there is then peace between these two families which have such hostages; these children often intermarry; after which that family is understood to be protected, and at peace, perhaps for a generation: but such instances are rare, the natural propensity of both nations being to theft and plunder; into these they always relapse; mutual enmity follows in consequence.[3]

This motif, of the making of reciprocal pledges over future kin ties in the face of great insecurity, is echoed widely in the western Ethiopian periphery. It lends a sharp focus, particularly, to the analysis of the 'archaic' institution of exchange marriage among several communities in the region.

Exchange marriage has too often been interpreted as an institution in isolation, as a set of marriage rules and practices defined as belonging to a 'tribe' but frequently detached from other evident features of a society or its historical and political setting. In western Ethiopia, Grottanelli has treated it as a paleo-Sudanese survival.[4] With more far-reaching implications, Lévi-Strauss has touched on a few African cases in his survey of the underlying principles of exchange which govern marriage systems in general, but without considering local contextual roots.[5] I return to a brief critique of these approaches in the concluding section of this paper.

The work of earlier historians of the Sudan and Ethiopia, focusing on the border regions only as far as this formed a part of the politics and international relations at the 'centre', has been followed in recent years by studies of the border region itself.[6] But inevitably, as historical accounts drawing mainly on documentary sources, the new works focus on the story of the struggle for political power and control by the rising centres of the frontier region itself: the struggle between emerging chiefs, merchants, and frontier administrators. The encroachment of the Ethiopian state since the later nineteenth century opened up new opportunities for the growth of wealth, power and leadership on the frontier, and in the main this is the story being traced by these new historical studies.

But what has happened to the aboriginal peoples, in the face of the encroachment of the state? Here we can draw only on the work of a few anthropologists and administrators, though a fresh approach by such Ethiopian historians as Taddesse Tamrat is being developed.[7] In a few words, one could say that in the period from the 1880s to World War II, gross new stresses developed. Relationships between rulers and ruled, previously contained within a Weberian framework of 'traditional' chieftainship, were ruthlessly transformed into those of exploitation. Pressures of taxation and tribute, as well as those of the long-distance trade in local precious metals, ivory and slaves, rendered the older paternalistic style of rule impossible, and harsh new rulers replaced the old.

In the exaggerated forms of exploitation that developed in the western periphery, the predatory expansion of the state affected particularly the women and children of the subjugated populations. Repeatedly in the sources, it is noted that the demand for *women* slaves was relatively high;[8] and in the system whereby a local population was divided up for allocation to military colonists as *gebbar* there is some evidence that sexual access was among the rights an owner of *gebbar* might expect.[9]

In response, the indigenous population of the new western periphery frequently moved into remoter areas (usually low-lying) of greater safety. In such 'reception areas', newly defensive social systems developed. The south bank of the Blue Nile in Wellegga is such a 'reception area', and within it the immigrant Gumuz have created, partly through the repeated making of exchange marriages among themselves, a distinctive society marked off by defensive political hostility, endogamy, and various barriers to economic penetration by the Oromo highlanders of this province. Wellegga itself was incorporated into Menilek's Ethiopia in the 1890s, a political change which subsequently shaped the relations between highlanders and lowlanders. The

Gumuz of Wellegga have adopted as a self-name the Amharic/Oromo *shankilla*, to refer to all their various sections, as against highland peoples. However, the derogatory overtones of this term (compare the American English 'nigger' or 'darkie'), which have led to its official banning in recent years, are absent for them. Local pronunciation seems best rendered Shankalla rather than Shankilla and as, in a sense, it is a different word, I retain this spelling.

I: GUBBA AND THE SOUTHERN GUMUZ DIASPORA: THE DOCUMENTARY EVIDENCE

Various sources document the story of increasing pressure upon the Gumuz of southern Gojjam since the 1880s. I shall summarize the story by selecting from the writings of some contemporary witnesses, and adding some oral evidence, collected in the Sudan by Peter Garretson, on the history of Gubba.[10] For clarity, I shall use 'Gojjam' throughout to refer to the geographical area of the modern province within its present boundaries.

We know from Bruce, Salt, Beke and others that Gumuz lived in the higher country of what is now central and southern Gojjam in the eighteenth and early nineteenth centuries, although they were exposed to intermittent slave raids and were already beginning to retreat down into the lowlands.[11] We know from Salt that exchange marriage flourished among them in the late eighteenth century in central Gojjam.[12]

Before the era of Menilek's expansion, Gubba was a chiefdom which looked to the Sudanese Nile valley for its economic and political connections rather than to the Ethiopian highlands. It was tributary to the Funj Kingdom of Sennar, and the local chiefly dynasty traced a 'Funj' connection.[13] The indigenous people of the Gubba region, like those in the higher lands to the east, were Gumuz speakers, and partly because of the Gubba–Sennar link, they played a part in the history of the Sennar state.[14] However, with the rather rough treatment it received from the Turco-Egyptian government and during the Mahdiyya, Gubba appears to have entered the Ethiopian orbit towards the end of the nineteenth century.

The population of Gubba was fairly well united under the old regime, but Shaykh Zeggheldu, ruling prior to the 1880s, was the last chief of 'all the Gumuz', according to informants of Zanni.[15] His son Aghib, famous by the name Abu Shok ('The Porcupine'), succeeded about that time, and began to emerge as a strong chief towards the end of the century by taking advantage of his frontier position. In building up his personal power, he managed to divide his own people, and under him and his own son Hamdan, there was a rift between the parties of the 'Funj' (allies of the Gubba chiefs) and the 'Gumuz'. Some of the latter, according to Zanni, decided to leave for the north and north-east in the early years of this century.[16] Our present information can fill in the picture of a movement southwards also. The reasons for these divisions within Gubba, leading to large-scale population movements, are not difficult to find. They are in the main the extra demands made upon the people by their own chiefs as a consequence of Gubba's being found a valuable strategic and economic asset to the new Ethiopian regime in Addis Abeba.

Peter Garretson has suggested that the Sultanate of Gubba really came into its own with the collapse of the Mahdiyya and with Ethiopian expansion and attempts to conquer the lowlands on the frontier in 1898. In that year of great political change, a thousand slaves were sent from Gubba in tribute.[17] This would have entailed widespread raids within Gubba's own territory. By 1902, under Ethiopian pressure, Gubba was demanding tribute from villages beyond its conventional boundary with Fazoghli, villages subsequently included in the Sudan. Tribute, and later commercial trade, took place increasingly in terms of slaves, as the other resources of Gubba were drained away. Gubba placed increasing demands upon its own hinterland, and a rising tide of refugees escaped into the Sudan. In addition to Gubba's own requirements, the Ethiopian overlords in Gojjam would on occasion add their own direct demands, particularly when new appointments caused instability – for example after 1909. Garretson's informants claimed that two thousand slaves were demanded in 1910. The ever-widening circle within which Hamdan raided meant the extension of his political control. Following the 1916 *coup* in Addis Abeba and locally the death of *negus* Welde Gīyorgis, ruler of Gojjam, 1918 was a momentous year: Garretson notes that in this year Hamdan was able to move north and take over Abu Ramleh.[18] Garretson's information also mentions that in the same year Hamdan sacked the southernmost hilly massif of Beri, near the Blue Nile, leaving it quite depopulated.[19] This event occupies a key place in the memories of the Gumuz now in Wellegga, and I return to it in the third part of this paper.

We are fortunate in having a contemporary account of Gubba and its environs for the early 1880s, when the Gumuz were clearly beginning to feel the consequences of Ethiopian expansion. The observant Dutch traveller Juan Maria Schuver spent a total of some twenty months in the Sudan–Ethiopian borderlands during 1881–2.[20] According to him, Gubba already preferred to pay tax to the Ethiopian empire, to the governor of Belia who collected it on behalf of *ras* Adal of Gojjam, rather than to the Turco-Egyptian Sudan via the well-equipped military governor at Famaka. Schuver thought that only preoccupation with other matters, such as conflicts with the Oromo, prevented Ethiopia from annexing Gubba at the time.[21]

Schuver's account divides the Gubba region into five parts.[22] The first was Gubba proper, including the residence of the chief and more than a dozen villages in the plains, with the market town of Ses where Arab merchants and resident Oromo bartered slaves and iron for salt and cotton cloth. Then there was a part of the Gumuz tribe (to the southwest) 'which until recently has been independent and unruly under Jagasien's father Basarote'. Third, there were Bertha living on the hilly massif of Beri to the south, having fled from the Famaka raids across the river; for this reason, we assume, the chief of Gubba had among his titles 'Protector of Beri'. Fourth were the Shinasha, linguistically separate and on their own hill to the east; and fifth, the Kadalo, who spoke a dialect of Gumuz, to the west of Gubba, in an area now included within the Sudan. We are not immediately concerned with the last two groups.

There were still, not far to the east of Gubba, and to the south, independent or semi-dependent Gumuz communities described in some detail by Schuver. As he gives us a picture of south-western Gojjam before the violence which led to wholesale flight of the population upstream and across the river to the new province of Wellegga, I will quote freely from his description.

Schuver saw evidence of pressure on the 'independent Gumuz' from four sources. First was the new presence of imperial Ethiopian control and settlement in this region. He and a companion travelled (without permission) to the Kierien mountains, 45 miles east of Gubba, across a wide and almost uninhabited plain, finding only a few 'independent Gumuz' who had moved from Gubba. He wished to visit the nearest 'Schangalla', whom, significantly, he defined as 'negroes under Abyssinian rule'.

> Towards the close of the third day we struck upon a few Goomoos huts, where we were received with the most delicate hospitality, though we could only communicate with them by signs. Thus is how [they are] found to be up to now, the negroes everywhere, where they have not been vitiated by the contact of Mohamadans or Christians. These people were emigrants from Gooba and live a life of the most absolute republicanism and freedom, every family keeping at a distance of a mile from their nearest neighbours.[23]

He considered that the reason for this lack of population in the plains between Gubba, Kierien, the Blue Nile, and the Dabus was that it was border territory recently devastated by war. At the very time he was making his way to Kierien, in June 1882, Ethiopian soldiers were plundering Wambera and Beri Hill to his south. Beri was an outstanding landmark, an isolated hilly massif that could be seen from miles around. Schuver claimed it had been attacked from Sennar in the early 1800s. In September 1882 he wrote:

> Today, it is three months . . . since the Abyssinians pushed forward their borders considerably to the west, by taking possession of everything which still existed of independent country. For they have not only laid waste and plundered Wumbara and the Berta villages at the Beri hills . . . but they have taken possession of these districts in their usual manner, that is, they have spread a thin net of military colonists throughout the conquered territory.[24]

When Schuver and his companion reached the Kierien mountains, they found these military settlers among the local black population. He considered there were some advantages for the blacks who came under Ethiopian rather than Egyptian rule:

> Those who live under Abyssinian rule are better off than the subjects of Egypt, having to pay only a nominal tribute, but they are more exposed to the exactions of the travelling soldiery, who in their Christian pride tyrannize the heathen considerably. Whenever these unwelcome guests quarter themselves on a negro village, salt and sesame, however distant and rare, has to be provided for them, as they despise the *melach*, a slimy mixture of ground beans, snails and ashes, of

> the natives. Not a goat or sheep can be kept between Gooba and Belia, as the soldiers invariably kill them for their own benefit, nor is tobacco allowed to be grown, as the stringent regulations of Abyssinian bigotry proscribe the use of the evil weed.[25]

The account goes on to give a graphic description of the system of enserfment to an occupying peasant army, commonly known as the *gebbar* system, as it obtained in these regions at the time. Here a very sharp social barrier reinforced the subjugation of the local populace, and intermarriage was rare. Whole families from the highlands were 'billeted' on the Gumuz. This situation is in sharp contrast to that of a century before, when Bruce had observed trading and intermarriage between Agaw and Gumuz.[26] Schuver writes:

> The Abyssinians in these parts have a most excellent system of keeping the conquered negro-tribes in subjection. No garrisons, eating up the produce of the country, are dreamt of, but each time a strip of land is annexed, a certain number of families are told of out of overpopulated Godsham [sic] to settle as colonists in the new tẹrritory. These are judiciously not allowed to herd together in separate villages, but distributed all over the country, so that even the most insignificant negro hamlet shall have its one or two Abyssinian houses. These colonists are liable to be levied 'en masse' at any moment and the system extends so far as to have established before-hand centres of concentration for each well-defined district. Not much persuasion is needed to induce the people to leave their native country, where every inch of land is private property for the half-desert negro-lands where any amount of as good as virgin soil can be had for the taking. They interfere little with the blacks, most seldom intermarry with what they consider a heathen and inferior race, and feel no necessity of propagating Christianity.[27]

In addition to Ethiopian expansion, the Gumuz were facing pressures from the Turco-Egyptian government which sanctioned slave-raids into their hills. Schuver mentions such a raid taking place from the village of the chief Jagasien, only four hours upstream from Famaka. Jagasien he earlier described as living the life of a minor prince under the patronage of Gubba, although under his father Basarote the local Gumuz had been independent. Now, however, they launched their own raids on the still unsubjugated people to their east and south, and on Schuver's second visit to the village, in late 1882, he found them routed.[28]

Finally, as Garretson's informants obviously recall, the greatest source of danger for the people of the region was from their own 'capital', Gubba itself. I shall focus on the relationship which Schuver describes between Gubba and one of the most southerly Gumuz settlements in its orbit, namely the prosperous village of Dasifi, on the way south to Beri.

Presiding over Gubba in Schuver's day was the (approximately) twenty-year-old Shaykh Aghib, already known as Abu Shok ('The Porcupine'), son of Ibrahim (alias Zeggheldu), Hamet, and Mohammed-el-Nur; he was known as the Lord of Monquis (i.e. of the five mountains) and as the 'Protector of Beri'. Although so young, he was undertaking a fourteenth marriage during

Schuver's visit; his harem included three Arab and ten black ladies. He was marrying according to Arab custom in front of a *fakir*, and giving goats, cloth, and salt to the bride's parents. These marriages could not be dissolved. A good number of Aghib's marriages must have been of strategic value, but his powers went beyond what one might expect of a political marriage. During the wedding celebrations at the time of Schuver's visit, one of his wives was surprised with her lover. Both were condemned to death; though 'the intruder into the Scheg's harem was later sold for 30 dollars'.[29] In building up such a large harem, Aghib was following the example of his father, who was said to have had ninety-six children, half of whom were illegitimate. A couple of dozen people boasted to Schuver of this irregular descent, which did not suggest to him any very strict principles of morality in Gubba. But it might remind us that the 'emergence' of a newly important dynasty in north-eastern Africa almost inevitably entails a fan of new strategic marriages, and other alliances. A large number of children is an advantage – particularly children whose loyalty to their *mother*'s people must in some cases be very tenuous. As far as we know, the wives and children of Aghib and his father were all settled near the court and not spread around the realm as were, for example, the Funj princes.[30] Moreover, the authoritarian relationship between the shaykh and his wives was symptomatic of the relationship between ruler and subject population, often also a matter of life or death.

South of Gubba, Schuver wanted to visit Beri and the hill of Abu Danab, on the opposite side of the river. But he managed to get only as far as the Gumuz village called Dasifi. No guides were provided, and so Schuver's little party travelled south on their own. On the way they came across a hamlet whose inhabitants fled in fear, some gold-washers who escaped on sighting them, and a hunter who 'deliberately' misdirected them. They eventually found to their surprise that Dasifi was a very large village, built on a rocky spur, which we can identify as the hill Yaringhe. It was obviously a prosperous community; the people possessed extensive sorghum fields along the river, plenty of pigs, and grew the best tobacco in the region. They were very fond of *merissa* (sorghum beer), and there was a saying: 'Even when there be no more water in the river, there will still be beer in Daseefee.'

Schuver's party found a noisy gathering, apparently a festival, with the whole male population assembled around their two chiefs – an old local dynasty persisted in Dasifi, besides the agent installed from Gubba. However, they were clearly not welcome. 'I was quietly informed that the execution had just taken place of one of the Sheg's own women, who had been caught that morning in the very act of adultery. The lover had been condemned to be sold as a slave, but the female had had her throat cut on the very spot where the mound was raised and her body had been thrown into the river. An empty *angareb* [wooden bed] carried by four men returning from the Nile bore witness to the severe justice of the Goomoos.'[31] There followed a 'passionate war dance' in which the whole population joined.

What was really going on in Dasifi that morning? The execution of women for adultery is so far from modern customary practice among the Gumuz that it is impossible to accept that it was normal justice in the 1880s. It was significantly a 'woman of the Sheg' who had just been killed, and not the wife of an ordinary citizen. Although Schuver does not tell us which of the two chiefs was the principal here, the context suggests strongly that it was the chief appointed by Gubba. The exact parallel with Aghib's own treatment of a wife and her lover, which I have mentioned above, is remarkable. It would appear that in the vassal communities shaykhs appointed by and dependent upon Gubba were themselves building up status and power by similar means. Their marriages, by bridewealth, or other unilaterally-imposed liaisons, offered no protection against harsh treatment of a woman, and allowed no continuing claims over her children. Quite apart from the execution of the woman, the selling of her lover into slavery reflects the extension of Gubba's power into this peripheral community. The very existence of the external demand for slaves (something that was to increase phenomenally) was restructuring relations of power and authority in Dasifi, and was making it easier for petty tyrants to set themselves up in such villages. I have devoted these speculations to Dasifi, not only because of the intrinsic interest of what Schuver has to tell us, but because Yaringhe hill and Beri hill nearby are places mentioned in the oral traditions of the Wellegga Gumuz. They were the last places at which the Wellegga Gumuz had fought the people of Gubba and from which they had fled. Had Schuver witnessed some of the reasons for their retreat to a style of 'republican freedom' like that of the Gumuz settlements he had already seen to the north-east?

Following Schuver's fairly detailed picture of the southern Gumuz of Gojjam in 1882, we have a number of descriptions from 1900 onwards that indicate very large scale disruption of this area and flight either across the Sudan boundary or southwards. I shall select from two accounts, those of Crosby at the turn of the century and Cheesman a generation later.[32]

Oscar T. Crosby passed from the east through southern Gojjam in 1900. This was after the complete incorporation of the region into the new Ethiopian state, and after the eruption and fall of the Mahdist state over the border. There had been destruction of the former homeland of the Gumuz. Crosby found that the country was 'industrially in a very poor position; great areas which a few years ago were said to be covered with fat herds grazing, are now wholly without inhabitants'. There were nevertheless some good cultivations – 'one or two patches hidden in the bottom lands near the river by unsubjected Shankalis, who hide themselves in the valley jungles to escape Abyssinian taxation or servitude. Here they live as best they can, depending, I was told, at the time of my visit, on hippopotamus meat.'[33] After describing the hierarchy of Amhara (there was an imperial outpost at Wambera), Oromo, and Agaw, Crosby gives a useful paragraph on the 'Shankali':

> Beginning at the Durra, and scattered at wide intervals along the route to Wombera, and further westward in the lowlands of the Blue Nile, were found the Shankali, very black, naked save for a string around the loins when living within sight of the Abyssinians, and throwing this aside as cumbersome when free in the

> jungle . . . It is of this material that the Abyssinians have made slaves, and one cannot wonder at it. Those who were seen in servitude to Abyssinian families in and around Markos looked quite as happy and better fed than those who maintained a precarious independence in the bush.[34]

Crosby mentions the village of Gum Gum, poised for safety on the top of a hill up to which water was taken from the Nile, half a mile away. He mentions also that the paths which seemed to have been worked by considerable caravan movements were now overgrown and difficult to follow. 'The few inhabitants who were seen in this region were almost on the point of starvation.' Until Crosby's party found relief from the stores in Famaka, it had been 'a close question' as to supplying his men.

> Perhaps nothing could better indicate the desolation of the country than the fact that for seven or eight days no hyenas were heard around the camp, and further, that the dead bodies of some black fellows, killed in a fight with the Abyssinian garrison at Wombera, were found, three days after the fight, only partially consumed, and that by vultures, not by hyenas, and only one vulture to the body, as far as I could note.[35]

After Crosby, we have a detailed account of journeys in southern Gojjam by Major Cheesman, in the course of his surveys of the Blue Nile undertaken in 1927 and 1929. Cheesman found Gumuz living both in the Dura valley to the east, and Gubba to the west. These Gumuz, not at all 'independent', were on good terms with their local rulers, and at both places, Gumuz musicians were summoned to entertain Cheesman. In the Dura valley, a chief claimed that his father had been given a robe of honour by a European, and the local Ethiopian official from Kolaj was on good terms with the people, even speaking 'Shankalla' as well as Agaw.[36] The Dura valley villages were nevertheless perched on the tops of small hills in the depression. Between the Dura valley and Gubba, Cheesman actually saw no Gumuz villages at all – a distance of some hundred miles. For the better part of this journey he records place after place where the 'Shankalla' used to live and passes through others where we know they used to live, without even mentioning signs of former habitation. Thus, coming down from Wambera via the Shar valley he was puzzled by 'large granite boulders' with 'circular cavities on the top'. They were grinding stones and marked the sites of deserted Shankalla villages. Farther down the valley was an area 'formerly occupied by a negro chief called Egzaw, and the name has been recorded as a place on published maps. He is now dead and his tribe has moved elsewhere'.[37] When Cheesman's party reached the junction of the Bolassa and the Abbay, they turned left, upstream, in order to make observations from the hill of Beri, which they had seen from the Wambera mountains. The way along the river was completely overgrown with unfired long grass, and they had to follow hippopotamus tracks at times. Beri was deserted. It had been sacked by Shaykh Hamdan of Gubba, later known as *dejazmach* Banja. The former Beri chief's name 'Aba Timbaho' means 'father' or 'owner' of tobacco and reminds us that the nearby village of Dasifi too had been tobacco country.

6 This picture, from an album in the Institute of Ethiopian Studies, Addis Abeba, entitled 'Mission Addis Ababa-Roseires 1919–20', is almost certainly of Shaykh Hamdan Abu Shok of Gubba, from the survey expedition of G. W. Grabham and R. P. Black

> The 'city' of the negro chieftain Aba Timbaho [also a name occurring on maps] was on Beri hill. He had been conquered in a local war with Dejazmatch Banja eleven years before, and he and his men had scattered. We saw the remains of his settlement half-way up the hill, marked by much crockery lying on the ground just as they left it when they fled.[38]

Eleven years before takes us to 1918. Peter Garretson's work not only points out the general turmoil of 1918, but an informant of his actually mentioned a raid at this time from Gubba on a place called Bera.[39] It was given as an example of a slave raid by Hamdan Abu Shok and represented as a reprisal for the killing of one of his people. The pressure of long-distance tribute and trade demands for slaves had turned the son of the 'Protector of Beri' into the final destroyer of Beri. Summarizing the evidence so far quoted, we can say that Beri was sacked four times: about 1800 by Sennar, in 1882 by Ethiopian soldiers, in 1898 or so when Hamdan came to power in Gubba, and again by him in 1918. It had provided refuge for a succession of displaced communities up to that date, but nobody settled again after 1918.

The whole region seems to have been emptied. At the crossing point of the Bolassa where Hamdan's men came to meet Cheesman in 1929, they claimed that the nearest village where millet could be obtained was three days away. And as Cheesman proceeded downstream, he camped at a hill called

'Yeringhe', which from geographical indications in the text corresponds to the hill which had formerly sheltered the prosperous village of Dasifi, described by Schuver in 1882. The beer had finally run out in Dasifi, for Cheesman does not even mention signs of a deserted village here. Downstream farther, he mentions that the negroes who had inhabited this part of the country had fled into the Sudan.[40]

THE GUMUZ IN WELLEGGA

Evidence from the south bank of the Blue Nile suggests that there has been a small Gumuz population there at least since the early nineteenth century. In the early period, relations with the Oromo highlanders seem to have been quite good, with tribute being paid by at least some groups and the Oromo providing refuge in time of famine.[41]

However, the wars and disturbances between 1880 and 1920 in southern Gojjam and on the international frontier caused incursions of Gumuz upstream on an unprecedented scale. Some early arrivals had been offered protection by Moroda Bakare, the ruler (*moti*) of northern Wellegga. Moroda had peacefully acceded to Menilek's control in 1882 (see Triulzi's Chapter in this volume, above). But Mahdist incursions reached his domain and were decisively countered at the Battle of Gute Dili near Nejjo in 1886. The army of *ras* Mekonnen passed this way to Bela Shangul in 1897–8.[42] In addition to these events that would have brought increasing pressure on the lowland people, there was increased pressure for tribute payments which encouraged hunters to seek elephants in the valley lowlands, and there was the rapid establishment of gold-mining operations in Menilek's freshly-acquired regions of western Wellegga. Nejjo was the major centre of gold mining and marketing operations, and gold-seekers roamed far and wide in the tributary valleys of the Blue Nile.[43] This alone might have explained the very poor relations between Shankalla of the valley and the highlanders in 1901, when the hill of Tchoki near Nejjo was fortified against attacks from below.

Let me quote the testimony of Hugues le Roux who travelled in 1901 into the gold-bearing areas of western Wellegga with the blessing of Menilek and who described from the vantage point of Tchoki the vast lowland before him. Le Roux's terms are so graphic that one might think he could see with his own eyes the inundation of this lowland by a tide of black immigrants, dangerous, gorilla-like men.

> In fact, through the opening made by the Dabus and the Abbay, the negroes whom the Arabs call Beni Shangul and the Abyssinians, Shankalla, have flooded in. They are extraordinarily wild people. Among all the Nilotic races [*sic*] who have settled between the Blue and White rivers and the sea, they have slipped in through all the valleys. Completely naked men and women, they have sustained harsh wars against the Galla [Oromo]. Still today, the whole of Tchoki mountain is fortified against their attacks. This continuing anxiety is justified: the enormous extent of country [geographical details given] has been invaded by

> these gorilla-men. They alone are capable of living on the mires, which I had seen from the height of the Tchoki mountain, and to which I was to descend.[44]

Having descended to the valley to check the point of confluence between the Blue Nile and the Diddessa, le Roux returned, but followers of his party hopeful of finding gold were attacked on the way back, and some of them killed. Le Roux marched two 'Shanḳalla chiefs' back up to the highlands, and, interestingly, 'delivered them alive' into the hands of the 'Abyssinian' authorities.[45] The new 'colonial' presence in Wellegga cannot have appeared at that time too benign or protective to the valley dwellers. They have managed to keep a certain distance between themselves and the highland authorities ever since.

Patterns of withdrawal and entrenchment are characteristic of the Blue Nile lowlands. For example, there is a very substantial Gumuz population in the tributary Diddessa valley, and in spite of Haberland's assumption that it represents an ancient pre-Oromo survival of aborigines in this region, it is clear from local testimony that these people retain connections with Gojjam.[46] At Dimtu, in a discussion with several elders, I was told that many were living on the other side of the river before the unification of Ethiopia.[47] The king Moroda Bakare of northern Wellegga succeeded in winning the confidence of their forefathers, and they settled between Neḳemte and the Diddessa. There was a pact (*kaka* in Oromo) between Moroda, on behalf of the Bakare line, and the Shanḳalla. They therefore trusted Moroda.[48] But when *dejazmach* Moroda died (probably in 1889), the trouble began. Kumsa, Moroda's son, succeeded him (the Gebre Igzīabihēr of Triulzi's account in Chapter 2, above). During this time, my informants claimed, the pact was broken. Oromo came from Limmu, for example, and captured and sold Shanḳalla at Agaro, in Gore. So the people moved down into the bottom of the Diddessa valley. When the Italians later fought the Bakare chiefs, the Shankalla considered it was a punishment for their having broken the pact.

II: EXCHANGE MARRIAGE IN ABA BULCHO: AS A SYSTEM AND AS A TECHNIQUE

The Gumuz of Wellegga today see their own society as based upon, and bounded by, a *system* of exchange marriage. For them, this system ensures exogamy beyond the immediate circle of close kin and thus the continuation of the generations; it is invested with positive moral virtue on several levels, especially through the promise of peace and security which it offers. Operating endogamously amongst the Gumuz and not extending to the highlanders, it defines and partly constitutes their ethnic distinctiveness. In this context too the system has the effect of shielding lowland society from possible penetration by the highland economy, which could follow from the acceptance of bridewealth in marriage settlements, even among the Gumuz themselves. The Wellegga Gumuz say that they are poor and are therefore obliged to hand over a sister in exchange for a wife, in lieu of the money so readily available to the Oromo.

7 Gumuz women and children

But ironically, partly because of the protection given their social economy by the exchange marriage system itself, the Wellegga Gumuz are rather more prosperous – better-fed, better-dressed on occasion, better-armed – than most local highland peasants. Their image of themselves as poor in a monetary sense is perhaps an analogue in modern idiom of their historical memory of oppression and flight.

I had the opportunity to see something of the marriage system in Aba Bulcho, a substantial village near the Blue Nile in Wellegga, and my account refers primarily to that village.[49] I asked Tilinti Damfa, a well-travelled young man, why his people did not pay bridewealth like the Oromo. He replied:

> The Oromo! They have done it from long ago. We Shanḳalla, we cannot give money, we do not give money. As far as we are concerned, we don't have cattle to farm with. The Oromo have plenty of money. We Shanḳalla, we hoe with our hands, hacking at the ground, *ḳof, ḳof, ḳof*. But the Oromo have everything. Even long ago, they had plenty. The slaves used to do the ploughing, and now the Oromo pay two hundred dollars bridewealth, even six hundred dollars bridewealth. They give [money], the Oromo. But for us, where would we get it

8 A newly married wife of an exchange marriage, still in seclusion and heavily veiled, is led from her hut by a girl of her husband's village

> from? For we Shanḳalla, we Shanḳalla, we marry by exchange; the man who doesn't have a girl to exchange, he elopes with his sweetheart and marries her. He lives with her and builds a house; and he may take a child of theirs and give it back. They marry because they love each other; a girl taken by force will not live with you.[50]

In discussing exchange marriage, elders speak as though they took the initiative in seeking marriageable girls from another 'descent' group, selected girls from their own for the exchange, and then fixed things up with the young men. However, it is admitted that the initiative is usually taken by a young man who has been able to secure a girl to give in exchange, ideally a younger sister.

Real exchange marriage ideally constitutes a long-term pledge between the two sides. The phrase *biyanjigu* means 'they marry by exchange' and shares a root with *fanjela*, the 'brother' and 'sister' thus linked, and also with *anjia*, the word used of the two girls exchanged for one another; each calls the other *anjim*, 'my *anjia*'. The special terminology itself suggests that much more is involved than the crude idea of 'bartering' one woman for another (which is all that survives translation into the Oromo language as *geddara*, trading or barter). Exchange marriage is a long-standing contractual relationship which should last a full generation and is fulfilled by the plentiful birth and survival of children on either side. Many adjustments may be made during the life of such a contract. For example, if one of the women dies, especially with few or no children, her husband's people may request a replacement. The sister or other girl who may be found to take her place is known as *hirba*. And even if a wife who is herself a *hirba* dies, a second *hirba* may be asked for and found. Conversely, if one of the original husbands dies, his widow may be passed on to a brother (usually younger), a brother's son or even a son of the deceased by a different woman. Once an exchange marriage contract is made, the personnel on either side may thus change more than once in the course of its history. If one side is fruitful and the other not, a child may be transferred. To complicate matters further, different generations may be involved on the same level of an exchange contract: a girl may be exchanged by a paternal uncle or even by her own father, if he marries a younger wife late in life.

If a young man has no sister, it is open to him to approach a paternal uncle or other senior man in his group, or even a closely associated group, to 'borrow' a daughter or sister to use as a *fanjela*. If this is agreed, he will promise to give back a future daughter, if one is born to himself and his wife. This returned girl is seen as a direct replacement for her own mother and will be used in a real exchange marriage by her mother's people. It is usually a boy of the next generation who reminds the original borrowers of their debt and requests a girl as his *fanjela*. The return of such a girl is called *sha*, and such *sha* claims take place within groups rather than between them; one borrows or claims back a *fanjela* from those with whom one does not actually intermarry.

Outside the framework of the exchange contract proper, private elopements quite frequently take place, and are known by the ordinary word for 'stealing', *bilokogwa*. After some fuss, especially from the girl's people, the couple will usually be left in peace to live as a married pair. If they have a daughter, they may later be asked to give her back to her mother's people, as restitution for the 'theft' of her mother, and the girl will then be used by her mother's people as a *fanjela* in an exchange contract. This return of the daughter of a stolen woman is also sometimes called *sha*.

Occasionally a woman is kidnapped 'by force', and Gumuz distinguish this from marriage by 'stealing' or voluntary elopement. After a kidnapping, angry demands will be made for the girl's return, and unless the parties live so far apart that the kidnappers get away with it, the rhetoric of outrage may lead to armed conflict.

In the ideally balanced contractual relationship, if all goes well on both sides, if the husbands cultivate and support their wives handsomely, if the wives work hard and bear healthy children, the initial pledge can become a strong and integrating bond – a divinely-sanctioned bond, the Gumuz say, of peace and love. Shavita, an elder visiting Aba Bulcho from another community downstream, explained it in these positive terms:

> This practice is what God gave [the people]. You do not marry your daughter, you do not marry your sister or your father's brother's daughter. God gave people the practice of marrying unrelated persons. You are to give a girl in exchange, and the other will also give you one to marry. To be in-laws, to live in peace and love.

But as in any contract, if one side or the other fails to live up to expectation, the relationship is easily damaged. Exchange marriage in this light is a more fragile bond than bridewealth marriage, since the rights and obligations on either side are supposedly exactly balanced, and defaulting on one side can mean tit-for-tat retaliation. A sanction against the ill-treatment of a wife, for example, is that the husband's own sister is a 'hostage' in the other camp; calling back a sister for any reason will result in the loss of a wife, and one 'divorce' precipitates another. This moral tension between the high ideal of making a bond of peace between brothers-in-law, and the exact measuring of the terms of that peace, gives plenty of scope for rhetoric, as revealed in Tilinti's account below of the strictly balanced exchanges of the marriage ritual and the carefully monitored obligations of those who marry by exchange. If all goes well, which is a difficult feat for both sides, the brothers-in-law can take a gun from each other's hand and sit together in peace.

> Let us suppose I am going to marry a woman. You, my brother-in-law, we must make an appointment. On Friday we will meet at the river. We will exchange women with you on Friday. You must keep your girl on one side of the river and stay with the old men of your country. At the river the girl who is mine must stand on the other side of the river. And you, if you have a belt full of ammunition, you must fire two bullets; and if I have a full belt I must fire two bullets. If you fire more than two, I will also fire more, I will fire four; and in this way we will exchange women. If I give [the escort who brings my wife] a goat and six bottles of araki, also you, brother-in-law, you must give as I do. If you are weak, I will insult you. I will destroy the virginity of your girl, *çet, çet*. If this one of yours is not a virgin, it will be a shame on the daughter of your people. There will be shame on your sister, and my village will refuse her – that's all!
>
> If all goes well, we will have a good name for you; but if your sister is lazy over working in the fields for me, all right! I can do a lot of work. And if mine is lazy, my brother-in-law will tell me. I can beat her. If she steals meat, you must come and tell me – it is a shame upon her. If she steals grain, O brother-in-law, the fault is yours, because of cultivation. You cultivate only a little. If you hoe only a little, brother-in-law, I cannot exchange a woman with you, I cannot marry a woman with you, I cannot marry a woman. As for me, I am not lazy, I can hoe, your sister can live in the proper way with [plenty of] grain and eat well. If we do this, brother-in-law, now that is all right . . . When she goes and brings [some grain] from her parents' home, it is because of the laziness of her husband. But if all is well, brother-in-law, we can sit and cross our legs; we can sit and visit each other. You too, brother-in-law, if you see me – if you see my face like this you must come and take my gun from my hand, you put it down, you make a good place for me, brother-in-law, it is like this, the idea in my heart [literally, 'chest']. I too, if I see you, if I see your face like this, I will take your gun from your hand.

There is one more type of union among the Gumuz, in which a woman is handed over after hostilities to conclude a peace agreement or in compensation for a death. She is known as *nezhokwa* and is married directly without any exchange or reciprocation being required. She embodies the promise of future fertility.

The rhetoric, and positive moral evaluations of exchange marriage as a system, assume the enduring existence of agnatic descent groups. Among the 66 household heads of Aba Bulcho in 1975, a majority claimed to be of the Dukunzilla people, and the village as a whole was regarded as a Dukunzilla settlement. This name has an alternate in Oromo, 'Sese', and Oromo speakers regard the group as an agnatic clan. However, although a good part of the Dukunzilla claim patrilineal descent from a named ancestor, Delisa, I prefer not to beg the question but to refer to the Dukunzilla and like groups as 'sections'. Existing accounts of the Gumuz have tended to accept the rhetorical indications of agnatic descent and to use the terminology of 'clan' and 'lineage'. If we place the *actual practice* of making exchange marriages at the centre of the analysis rather than the people's *representation* of the system as a whole, we can better appreciate the key rôle of this technique in continually recreating and redefining social relations.[51]

A closer examination of Aba Bulcho reveals that there were a number of distinct named groups which could by no means all be regarded as sub-lineages within a system of agnatic descent. They were groups which had not diverged, but rather had come together, over time. This coming together had been characteristically cemented by intermarriage, and the continuing *raison d'être* of the groups lay in their operating as units within the exchange system. That is, within each group, by definition exogamous, a man sought an exchange partner, *fanjela*, in order to facilitate his own marriage. Rather than using 'lineage', I prefer therefore to employ the phrase 'exchange groups'.[52] The relationship between such groups was in some cases close, and in others more distant. But closeness or distance was not represented essentially in terms of descent: it was cast in terms of marriageability.

In addition to the ban on marriage within one's immediate group, there was a prohibition on a man's marriage into his mother's group. This means that an exchange cannot be replicated in successive generations. Where more than one such exchange between groups has taken place in the past, between different individual parties at different times, it seems that a *de facto* recurring practice of shared exogamy has been recast in terms of a general rule, and the relationship represented on the model of common descent. Within the Dukunzilla section, there were two main exchange groups, apparently of equal importance, the Yadija and Jimakila. They were so close that not only was no intermarriage possible between them, but the rule of shared exogamy extended even to the offspring of each other's women. Informants spoke of a common patrilineal ancestor, but not surprisingly, detailed genealogical connections could not be supplied. Another exchange group, Walsa, could not intermarry with actual members of these two first groups, but Walsa men could marry daughters of Yadija and Jimakila women, and arrange reciprocal exchanges. Further exchange groups were Manda and Ambelka, which could marry neither each other's women nor their offspring but could intermarry freely with other Dukunzilla groups, even though they were Dukunzilla themselves. There were various households of most of these groups in Aba Bulcho, and also scattered examples of households headed by men of other (non-Dukunzilla) sections, attached by ties of marriage and said to be living variously with their brothers-in-law or with their mother's or grandmother's people. Rather than being composed of segmenting agnatic lineages, the Dukunzilla were thus a growing assemblage of exchange groups and fragments, forging ties of intermarriage between themselves to the point where the bonds of affinity were recast as those of common descent.

The making of an exchange marriage can reshape the very form of supposedly descent-based kinship. For example, the word *mama* can be glossed 'father's sister'. But it is applied to any woman who may be exchanged by one's father for a wife (one's own mother or another wife), whether she is a 'real' sister of his, a parallel cousin with the exchange group, or – theoretically – no relation at all. Many exchange marriages thus 'rewrite' the application of supposedly consanguineous kinship terms. This gives the practice of making exchanges great flexibility as a political technique, while at the same time preserving a theory of the system as a whole. On more than one level, the making of bonds between unrelated partners through exchange marriage can provide fresh grounds for the rhetoric of relatedness, and ultimately the assertion of common descent where none existed before. The scope for this technique in the context of a disrupted and dispersed society is clearly very wide.

To delve beneath the official representation of exchange marriage among the Gumuz, with its reference to 'descent' groups and the rôle of male elders, is to uncover many different aspects of actual practice, which involves more people than merely elders and many principles besides those of agnatic cohesion. For example, to focus upon the women's part in the operation of exchanges enables us to glimpse the 'system' as a more complex matter and to appreciate its historical resilience in practice. Far from being passive objects through which relations between 'descent' groups are built up, women mediate, modify, and partly control relations between these groups. They participate in the making of exchanges, which they see in many respects as a practice serving their own interests as against, for example, a bridewealth system. Women are moreover not only tokens through which pledges of peace can be made, but they participate in peace-making. In-married women constitute of course nearly half of the adult population of any given settlement; retaining as they do strong ties with their own people, women's very presence modulates the political relation between sections. Women are, moreover, conceptualized as persons above any given conflict. However severe hostilities may become, it is said that women themselves are never attacked and that if a woman were accidentally killed, the bereaved party would demand a girl in restitution rather than kill in reciprocal vengeance. During times of hostility, my assistant Gali Sambato explained, women are 'like the Red Cross and can go from place to place through the fighting without being in danger'. These general moral considerations, as well as the practical circumstances in which women find themselves as go-betweens, give them a good deal of scope in practical political negotiation.

It is true that young people, especially girls, are sometimes married off without having much option and may run away and try to return home; indeed this seems to be expected of them. Alfarse, senior wife of Bosuma, the headman of Aba Bulcho, gave me the following account of her marriage; there was no tone of complaint about her lot, rather some pride that her marriage had counted for so much.

> My *camba* [paternal uncle] exchanged me; they gave me to Dukunzilla. They took me at night and exchanged me. It was dark, and they took my *anjia* there, and brought me here, to Ekotomesha here . . . I stayed here, and then I went back to our house. I got there, they came to look for me, and brought me back. The man made me his wife; I was afraid of the man. I still escaped from time to time, still from time to time. For I was afraid of my husband. At the time I was still escaping, escaping, I became pregnant. So I stayed; it was like this, and I bore my children. Now I stay here; this is how I am living here in Dukunzilla.

A new bride will preserve a formal distance in relation to her parents-in-law for the whole of her life, though the relationship becomes more relaxed as time goes on and as she bears children. There is a range of prohibitions on eating in her husband's village, which seem to hedge in a married woman and which serve as a continual reminder of the fact that she is not a full member of her husband's community but has come from elsewhere.[53]

The bond between the married woman and her people remains strong. Her people, especially the women of her village, try to keep track of her, and although she may be beaten and roughly treated by her husband on occasion (I have even heard of a woman being beaten to death though this was accidental rather than judicial), there is always the possibility that her own people will come to her defence or even ill-treat her opposite number. If she is involved in adultery, as far as my information goes, she will not be formally punished, but her husband and his brothers are likely to fight and even kill an adulterer from their own section and to pursue an adulterer from outside to the point of challenging his section to armed conflict (compare the unfortunate fate of erring wives of the shaykhs of old Gubba and Dasifi, above).

The in-married women of a village draw together with the years, and they play a growing part in the marriage and political affairs of the village. They are increasingly in a position to secure some control over their own children's marriages. It is they, as much as their husband's people, who maintain contact with and try to secure reasonable treatment for their daughters married out. The cultivation of ties with the younger generation of women, even after they marry out, and the refusal to dispose of a daughter without receiving a *quid pro quo* stems as much from the older women as from the men. The general consequences of this marriage system, of the 'conserving' of the womenfolk and the blocking of all routes by which they might be drawn off through slavery, marriage to chiefs, or bridewealth are as much the result of a strong pragmatic sense of community among the women as anything else.[54]

In the Gumuz community I studied, every single marriage, whether of a regular or an irregular kind, could be related to the rules and expectations of the exchange system, and none was justified in relation to any other set of principles. Even in the two cases where money did change hands and the people joked about Oromo-style 'bridewealth', it soon became clear that nothing of the sort was in question. The first case illuminates very clearly not only the high value placed upon marriageable women (higher than Oromo bridewealth in the region) but also their symbolic rôle as life-givers responsible for the next generation and their consequent place in making decisions over marriage.

The case was that of a young man who had sold two guns for $600 to pay over as a kind of bridewealth for his wife. He laughed at my astonishment on hearing this, and said, 'I paid money just like the Oromo!' But it turned out to be quite unlike Oromo custom. The money had gone to the girl's mother, entirely. She had been angry with her husband's people, who had killed a son of hers (I believe spontaneously because of some offence, possibly adultery). Her daughter would have been exchanged by this son, but as he had been killed, she refused to allow any other young man of that section to exchange her. However, she let it be known that she would herself accept money for her daughter. The money thus became simultaneously a kind of blood compensation. It was accepted as appropriate that she should keep it, as she had after all given birth to the young man and his sister.

The retention by a woman of such rights over her own fertility, and over her own offspring, as against those of her husband's people, is ethnographic evidence which raises striking questions about the persisting *rationale* of exchange marriage in previous generations. For women with living experience and shared memories of what may happen to those married for bridewealth to chiefs or merchants, or those dragged off into slavery and forced liaisons, the insistence on a *quid pro quo* for their daughters can be seen as an assertion of their right against the world, in the interest of conserving the future generations of their own community.

To draw attention to the perspective of women is not to provide a complete alternative view of Gumuz exchange marriage; but in lowering the focus to examine cases and actual practice, a level at which women's participation becomes visible, we can also envisage more clearly how the making of exchanges has helped to shape the newly-established society of the Gumuz in Wellegga, a society different in many ways from that of their forebears in Gojjam in the eighteenth and early nineteenth centuries.

III: FLIGHT TO WELLEGGA: MARRIAGE BONDS IN THE RESHAPING OF A COMMUNITY

The immediate history of southerly dispersal from Gubba can be filled in from informants' own accounts. The people of Aba Bulcho, like the majority of

Gumuz on the south bank of the Blue Nile, claim that they or their immediate forebears arrived from across the river in Gojjam, and they also entertain the idea of returning there eventually. All now speak *afan Oromo* as a *lingua franca*, and at the time of my field work accepted 'Shanḳalla' as a general self-designation. 'Gumuz' is a term not well known among them, though it is generally used on the Sudan side.[55]

THE MIGRATION OF THE DUKUNZILLA

Let me give a summary of some oral traditions of arrival from across the Blue Nile, referring mainly to the Dukunzilla section (see Map 9). My oldest informant was Bulti, who was about eighty years old in 1975. He and his father had been born in Wellegga. But he claimed that the Dukunzilla used to live in Gubba, together with the 'Ngaba'. This term refers today to the Sudanese Arabs, but also to the ruling 'Funj' shaykhs of Gubba. In the village I had heard of several named ancestors who used to live at 'Abua', which I take to be Jabal Abur on Gwynn's 1900 map, slightly to the south of 'Abu Shok's village' but north of the present village of Gubba.[56] This according to Bulti was the first place where the Dukunzilla fought the Ngaba. He said that when the people used to live with the Ngaba, the chiefs of those Ngaba used to catch children from the Shanḳalla and sell them. So the Shanḳalla had a meeting, and said to one another, 'Why do these people sell us like this?' And so they fought the Ngaba.

At this time, the chief of the Ngaba was Abu Shok (i.e. Aghib). 'Banja', his son, according to Bulti, was just a little boy. This boy was Hamdan, later *dejazmach* Banja; we can therefore date the period to around 1880. Sometimes there was fighting between Shanḳalla sections. Once for example the Dukunzilla fought the Bugua, and the Ngaba took the side of the Bugua. In some of this fighting Biçad (an ancestor of the Dukunzilla) lost his father; and he avenged his father's death at Dizhangwe.[57] Following this, and fearing reprisals from the Ngaba, Biçad and his brother Zhogwadze led their people to Wellegga. On the way, some of them stopped at 'Erinj', which Bulti named as the second place where the Dukunzilla fought the Ngaba under Abu Shok. We can assume this to be the hill Yaringhe, mentioned by Cheesman, and which marked the site of old Dasifi.[58]

After this fighting, probably not long after 1882, part of the Dukunzilla under the leadership of Gulbak, a son of Biçad, moved to the hill of Beri and settled there for a long period.[59] During this time Banja (Hamdan) succeeded his father in Gubba (we can date this to 1898). During his rule, the Dukunzilla would live peacefully for a period. Then when they were quarrelling among themselves, 'just like the Oromo who rule us today and are our friends but can suddenly turn and fire on us', Banja came in by force with *bazugum* (Gubba chiefs) and 'began to shoot the Dukunzilla, *ruk*, *ruk*, *ruk*, *ruk*, *ruk*' (this could have been the raiding following Hamdan's accession mentioned above). In this war some people were killed and others were taken as slaves, while some remained alive and stayed in the area. But they did not go to the country of

Banja, and Banja did not come to their country. Later their clothes and salt were finished, so the Dukunzilla collected money and a delegation took it to Banja. Then he blew the trumpet and gathered people from far away, and he said, 'These Gumuz came to us for help. What they need is clothes and also salt. Now you see them [addressing his own people]; I am going to leave these 'Gumzu' free. And now you also, you can go to trade in their country.' The Ngaba gave them all *jibba* [Sudanese tunics] and trousers, which they wore to return to their country, and peaceful trade began. 'And they are the ones who trained the Dukunzilla in the use of guns.'

During the time that the party of Gulbak were settled in Beri, their fellow Dukunzilla, led by Bicad and Zhogwadze, were already established to the south in Wellegga. The sons of those who led them there then returned, and found their relatives in Beri. There was a ceremonial reunion, and then the Wellegga party returned, having re-established contact. Bosuma, the headman of Aba Bulcho, was about sixty-five in 1975, and a boy when the major onslaught we can date to 1918 took place. His father had been born in Abua but was among those brought to Beri by Gulbak. When the Ngaba attacked, some of the Beri people (probably Bertha who had settled there for protection) crossed the Nile to Fakoro (a Bertha village name) and some Dukunzilla decided to do the same. But other Dukunzilla informed Banja that they were going, and an ambush was laid. Many were captured, including Bosuma, his mother, and some brothers and sisters. The latter were subsequently taken away, but Bosuma and his mother escaped. The Ngaba set up camp with their captives. Baderg (brother of Bosuma's grandfather) then challenged the Ngaba in charge, for his own mother was in the captured party. The Ngaba said it was the fault of the Dukunzilla themselves, for they had called him in. Baderg wrote letters and went to the highlands, where he stayed for a year at the place of *fītawrarī* Jara (Jara Biftu, the local governor in Wambera), who wrote to the king; and then Baderg returned with mules and slaves from Jara, and ousting the existing chief, Bobo, became a '*negus* of the Shankalla'. His mother was then freed by the Ngaba.

REMAKING MARRIAGE LINKS

This story of one section's move to Wellegga adds an extra dimension to our analysis of exchange marriage, as we can relate it to the evidence of genealogies and specific information on many marriages of the Aba Bulcho people and their forebears. On the basis of this body of evidence (which I cannot give in full here) we can deduce that disruption, flight and isolation can divide sections and lead to smaller exchange groups; these frequently tend to kidnap and 'steal' wives, provoking tit-for-tat retaliation or other reprisals. Such instability, and even hostility, seems to have obtained between the older, long-established settlers of the Wellegga side of the Blue Nile and the various incoming groups, at first, but to have given way to more settled relationships, signalled by the orderly making of 'proper exchanges', at a later date. The widening network of these exchanges, both between immigrants and old settlers and between various immigrant groups themselves, has led to a larger-scale society of Gumuz in Wellegga than there had previously been. Moreover, the coming together of small settler groups, and their mutual intermarriage, has apparently led to their amalgamation into major sections and the consolidation of the collective identity of these supposedly descent-based communities.

In so far as such patterns can be traced, they offer support for the main claim of this study: that is, that an inner connection exists between the history of the Wellegga Gumuz, as sketched in the first part of the paper, and the way in which they practise exchange marriage among themselves today, as described in the second. I will illustrate how, from three different angles, we can trace patterns and interconnections of this kind, by drawing from the detailed evidence.

First, there is plenty of indication that groups have been brought together through intermarriage in Wellegga. Various categorical distinctions are commonly drawn about the origins of the people now in the valley; but these distinctions are in almost all cases now over-ridden by intermarriage. The oldest category of Wellegga settlers were labelled 'Habash' (Abyssinians) because they had associated for so long with the Oromo highlanders. Among these were several groups of the large Jammoa section, about whom I shall say more below. Of more recent incomers, there were Dekereya sections assumed to have come from the Abbay and Dukunza from the Gubba hills. Although these divisions may have been geographically separate in the old days, they are by no means so today, and a good deal of ambiguity surrounds the use of the terms. Fragments of Dukunza sections may be found living with Dekereya, and *vice versa*. In Aba Bulcho, the dominant Dukunzilla section was Dekereya, and people were proud of the civilized ways they had brought with them (as against the rough habits of the hillmen). But at least one group living with them, and spoken of as a component group of the Dukunzilla, was Dukunza by origin. These people could nevertheless still intermarry with the main Dukunzilla groups; perhaps over time, they may come to obliterate the distinction and to share a common exogamic boundary.

In collecting general information about other sections and groups in the region, I noticed that distinctions were frequently made, at either level, between 'Oromo', that is, those who came earlier to Wellegga, and 'Dina', those who followed after.[60] The distinction, always a relative one, was sometimes made between communities who had undoubtedly been closely associated in the past on the far side of the river, and even shared impeccable credentials of common descent; but equally beyond doubt, there were other cases in which the use of these associated labels was a way of knitting together, as complementaries, groups of immigrants of doubtful genealogy and provenance. The claim by one settled group that a new community were 'their Dina' seems to have been a way of integrating them into the society of Wellegga. In some cases, a former distinction of descent between the 'Oromo' and 'Dina' of a given group has been transcended by a sequence of exchange marriages, and a new assumption of shared community.

The theme of migration into Wellegga can also be traced in the successive marriages of particular family lines, if we look at the location of marriages and the relevant section or exchange group. The marriages of four generations ago were mainly in Gojjam, and there are several examples in my notes of marriages at this time with the section Datsipa. This section is said to be found today on the left bank of the Blue Nile, downstream, about half-way to the Sudan border, and there are no representatives upstream as far as I know. The location of the modern Datsipa would appear to be just across the Blue Nile from the old site of Dasifi, the village described as flourishing by Schuver in 1882; it is reasonable, I think, to bracket these names and assume a former association of the Dukunzilla with the people of Dasifi. The headman Bosuma's case was one of those including a link with Datsipa; his father had been born at Abua near Gubba, but he had himself been born near Beri. His father's brother had married a Datsipa woman (and of course old Dasifi was close to Beri). Tilinti's father also had a brother who married a Datsipa woman; it is intriguing to note that his name was 'Hurriya', that is 'freedom' in Arabic. Marriages with Datsipa are very rare at the present time in my notes, but there has been an increasing number of marriages with the Jammoa section over the last two or three generations. I have the impression that some Jammoa were moving south from Gojjam in the same way as the Dukunzilla; it is not unlikely that they were in fact leading the migration, for they already had 'kin' long settled on the south side of the river. Bosuma's own father married a Jammoa woman, near Beri, and so did Tilinti's father, who had himself been born there. These alliances would have stood these Dukunzilla in good stead in their subsequent move south, with their Jammoa affines, to Wellegga.

We can analyse, from a second angle, the pattern of accommodation that appeared to develop between Dukunzilla and various Jammoa groups whom they encountered after arrival in Wellegga, and with whom there was no doubt a good deal of competition over territory and resources in the early decades of the century (relations between sections in the valley are still notoriously fragile). Let me give a brief account of a series of connected marriages between Dukunzilla and Jammoa. Bari was an old man of the Yadija group living in Aba Bulcho with his Jammoa wife (Jaloa group), Eguk. Bari's grandfather had himself crossed the Blue Nile from Gojjam, and fairly soon after, his son Elyas was married by exchange to a woman of the Dembea group of Jammoa. Elyas' eldest daughter was then stolen by the Jaloa group of Jammoa, and when they refused to provide an exchange, he got her back and exchanged her elsewhere. Some time later, the Jaloa killed a Dukunzilla and then handed over a woman in reconciliation, as *nezhokwa*. This was Eguk. Her first husband died, and she was passed on to Bari as his first wife. A younger brother of Bari's then made a proper exchange marriage with the Jaloa, and a daughter of his by a second wife was also exchanged with Jammoa (the

Dishigisha group). Not only the living presence of Eguk but that of two of her married sons by her first Dukunzilla husband, two of her married sons and two married daughters by Bari, and a married son and daughter of Bari's brother by his Jammoa wife, were among the reminders of the accommodation that had been reached between Dukunzilla and Jammoa.

From a third angle, we can see a significant pattern in the internal development of marriage exchanges as practised by the Jammoa themselves. I have only a few independent instances in my notes, but from the connected account of one informant we can conclude that at one time the Wellegga Jammoa were fairly isolated, and that relations with recently-arriving sections were not at first good. There were many instances of hostility and of the 'stealing' or even kidnapping of girls. In one case, reciprocal stealing was later realized as a proper exchange. Esuba was an old Jammoa lady whose father had twice married by exchange into different groups of Dukunzilla at about the turn of the century. She claimed that in the past Jammoa would steal girls from outside and then get themselves killed for it, so their own elders decided that they should marry only from within Jammoa. Thus, quite a large population with (to my knowledge) at least six exchange groups have quite deliberately 'drawn in their horns' and decided on a policy of local endogamy for the sake of their own security and survival. Nowadays (Esuba meant in the course of her own lifetime), they are beginning to make 'proper exchanges' with outsiders again.

A COMMUNITY LEARNS TO PROTECT ITSELF

The geographical retreat from Gojjam was matched by a withdrawal from the newly-instituted chiefs set up among the Gumuz, under the aegis of the new Ethiopian government in the decades following the 1880s. For example, in the story quoted above, appeals from Baderg to the Ethiopian governor in Wambera resulted in his own elevation as chief complete with slaves and mules, and the eclipse of Bobo, the existing Dukunzilla chief, who had so sadly failed to protect the people from the rulers of Gubba. But in finally retreating to Wellegga after 1918 the Dukunzilla were no longer within the reach of the Ethiopian authorities of Gojjam. Their response has been in part to reconstitute their population, both symbolically and demographically, and to reinforce socio-economic systems of circulation among themselves which tend to resist highland penetration and exploitation. I will illustrate these points briefly in so far as they help us to explain the modern strength of exchange marriage.

In the sacking of Beri in 1918, Bosuma lost a number of brothers, sisters, and other relatives. But following the retreat to Wellegga, at least three names of these lost individuals were used again in the next generation. Normally, new personal names are coined for each new child, and names do not recur in genealogies. In this case, it was quite explicit that the loss of persons was being made good, at least symbolically. Opportunities have also been used to reincorporate persons whose status might have become ambiguous. In particular, many former slaves have been reabsorbed as members of the valley communities; here the appellation 'Shanḳalla' has a wide ambivalence which can work to the advantage of the valley people, since a racial category applied by highland society can be read as a social claim, almost a claim of fellow citizenship, on the part of the Gumuz speakers of the valley.

Both escaped slaves and those freed after emancipation during the 1930s have responded to this claim and accepted the opportunity of becoming full members of the society of the Blue Nile Shanḳalla. Some have taken up the Gumuz language, and wherever possible such individuals who have been able to trace some kind of kinship link have been allocated a 'sister' and enabled to marry and found a new household. One old man whom I met at Diddessa Bridge, who spoke only Oromo, had not been able to do this; he had lost touch to the point where he could trace no 'sister' and had never married. But many others had rejoined the valley communities. People from the valley even used to go out searching for lost relatives, and in at least one case, a girl who had passed through many hands as a slave was actually found and bought out of slavery. It was Zajen, an old man, who told me (in my second case of a 'bridewealth' marriage) that his father had bought his mother in this way, for twenty goats and twenty bars of salt. Everyone thought this extremely amusing; the Gumuz were of course beating the Oromo at their own game of 'buying women like packets of soap powder', for this couple were very fruitful, and their children made many fertile exchange marriages which have helped replenish, in the Gumuz view, the ravages of slavery.

The case of my own assistant, Gali Sambato, is a modern example of the capacity of the Gumuz in Wellegga to reabsorb their own. He and some other young children had been taken away virtually as hostages for the good behaviour of the Shanḳalla, following hostilities between them and the Oromo in the Gombo area in 1953. He was educated in Addis Abeba, and after leaving school, instead of taking up such an option as the army, he decided to retrace his origin back in the Blue Nile Valley. He managed to find his relatives and settled down to learn the Gumuz language, having grown up using Amharic. A 'sister' was found for him to exchange, and he was thus able to marry.

Apart from periodic shortages and even famine, the valley is on the whole a productive region where a wide range of crops is grown, complementary to those of the highlands.[61] The valley people have built upon their resources and are reasonably prosperous, though still living basically in a subsistence economy. There would seem at first sight to be plenty of reasons for developing trade with the Wellegga highlands, but in fact trade is not pursued much in that direction. A few things such as cotton are taken up when cash is required, and highland traders do come down to the valley, especially if there is news of a valuable find by hunters. The valley dwellers and highlanders herd each other's cattle at alternate seasons of the year, and most of these activities take place through partnerships of a tenuous sort. But the main trading ventures of the people seem still to be downstream, especially to the Sudan where many young men seek seasonal wage labour in the southern Gezira.

The openness of the valley communities to the north and north-west contrasts with the rather stiff front which they have put up, socially and economically, to the Wallegga highlands. A remarkable feature of their trading relationship, or rather lack of it, with the highlands is that they operate an over-valued currency among themselves. They do not like paper money as the bills are so fragile, and instead prefer the hard fifty-cent piece as their main coin. Known as a shilling, it is of course exchangeable at a rate of two to a dollar in Nejjo. But the Gumuz reckon among themselves, and apparently in relation to highland traders when they wish to do so, three shillings to a dollar. They say, 'Ah. We reckon three shillings to a dollar, a real dollar; of course we know that you only get two shillings for a *paper* dollar.' It is clear that this system represents a deterrent to highland traders wanting to take the cream of the harvested crops in the valley and having to pay in hard shillings; and at the same time it gives a man from the valley who buys an item from the highland market a little extra something for his trouble when he divides it up and sells it to fellow villagers back home. The system is well known to highland traders as the '*shanḳilla* dollar'.

I mention this protective economic barrier set up by the valley people because it is analogous to the social barrier created by their marriage system. Here is another variant on the theme of 'spheres of exchange': in this case, the maintenance of a distinct sphere helps to 'defend' this society from highland encroachment.[62] There is no longer that openness of the Gumuz towards highland peasants which Bruce reported from Gojjam.

Partly because of their consciousness of having other connections of some importance elsewhere, the Wellegga Gumuz have adopted a politically aggressive attitude to their racially defined position as low-status Ethiopians. *Grazmach* Galata Sheshemo, who joined the Sudanese liberating forces in 1940–1, made a journey to Addis Abeba after the war and in an audience with the emperor explained the poor situation of the Shanḳalla and asked for teachers for the Blue Nile valley. He was acutely aware of the older connections of the Wellegga Gumuz and emphasized to me their links with the Funj and with the Sudan where black people were free. He reckoned (in 1975) that the new revolutionary government in Ethiopia would be a good friend to the poor people.

The reaching out of the valley people from what they consciously feel to be a restricted peripheral position, a reaching to the centre of things and to the highest authorities, over the heads of local highland Oromo patrons and *balabbat*, has continued. There was a Messianic movement in the late 1960s which spread from Wambera to the Gumuz in Wellegga, leading them to kill large numbers of their animals in expectation of Christ's coming.[63] This was the background to a renewed demand by the valley people for missionaries and teachers to come to their area. They approached the Evangelical Church of Mekana Yesus (ECMY) run in the highlands partly by Swedish missionaries. The Swedes had carried out brief forays into the valley but had not started systematic work there and did not have the resources to take on the valley in the late 1960s. So the ECMY called in missionaries of the Norwegian Mission Society (NMS) based in Stavanger to take on the work in the Blue Nile valley.[64] This was proceeding apace in 1975, with the Shankalla often pushing initiatives and putting great pressure on the organization for even development, especially of schools, throughout the valley. At one point a number of armed Gumuz briefly took hostage a Mission Aviation Fellowship pilot and others, to press home a demand about schools. There was a sense of euphoria which fed also on the revolutionary fervours of 1974. Gali Sambato, whose main function as I saw it was to be my guide and help in the Gumuz language, was seized upon by the villagers, who pleaded with him to teach their boys Amharic. Although this was the very farthest periphery of Ethiopian society, these people were moulding their own relationship directly with the centre, and demanding to be its citizens, something which they felt they could also be in the Sudanese or old Gubba contexts but not in the local circumstances of Wellegga.

CONCLUSION

I believe the evidence I have offered here counters in the first place Grottanelli's notion that exchange marriage is a passive survival from an ancient cultural tradition. It is true that it is found in predominantly remote areas, but this is not merely because of inertia. Those who practise this kind of marriage are among those who have experienced 'change' most directly, and have actively found responses to it.

Structuralist analysis seeks even wider horizons than culture history. By and large, African exchange marriage falls into the category of short-cycle reciprocity in Lévi-Strauss' terms.[65] That is, the debt incurred in the transfer of a woman in marriage is specifically and fully repaid, either in the form of the immediate exchange of a sister or other girl relative or in the form of the transferred woman's daughter in the next generation (the notorious and possibly hypothetical 'father's sister's daughter' marriage). This return 'completes the cycle', leaving no continuing links of relationship between the parties or binding them into a wider structure of patterned circulation. The contrast is drawn with long-cycle reciprocity, such as that resulting from a general rule of classificatory mother's brother's daughter marriage, which replicates links of obligation between groups and is a part of enduring relationships of 'alliance' across the generations between these groups. The structure of these ideal relationships may itself define the discriminations made between kin. Lévi-Strauss has drawn an explicit connection between such long-cycle reciprocity in marriage and large-scale economic structures based on capital, cash, and extended credit; and analogously between short-cycle, *quid pro quo* marriage exchange and subsistence economies based on barter. He has moreover suggested that whereas the long-cycle structures, in marriage exchange and in economy, are 'better integrated' (almost suggesting they are more successful systems in an evolutionary sense), the short-cycle structures are fragile, a 'precarious edifice'.

Lévi-Strauss does not have much to say on the topic of *quid pro quo* sister-exchange marriage, although it is substitutable for, or even logically prior to, the short cycle of patrilateral cross-cousin marriage.[66] Nor does he use African material in any detail. But in so far as exchange marriage is found in Africa, it has on the whole the short-cycle form of the direct exchange of sisters or other female relatives on a one-to-one basis; and the striking aspect of this institution is that in practice it is surprisingly robust and resilient from the historical point of view. It has survived well into recent times in areas of the African continent that have been exposed to a great deal of historical buffeting, along with patterns of production for subsistence and barter that form the (equally robust) economic base in these areas.[67]

Bruce's account of Gumuz and Agaw trading partners giving each other their children to establish a bond of peace cannot easily be accommodated into Grottanelli's listing of the culture traits of the one group or the other. Nor can it find a ready-made place in Lévi-Strauss' systematic classification of modes of marriage exchange (though I should not have been alerted to its intriguing possibilities without the inspiration of Lévi-Strauss' wider vision). In establishing a short-cycle reciprocal bond, Gumuz and Agaw partners surely found in a mutual pledge the only possible 'stability' between themselves, and thereby survived in a sea of dangers. Some might say that Bruce's report was of an *ad hoc* arrangement to do with economic interest and trade development rather than with the ethnography of marriage and kinship systems. But the making of marriages by whatever means is a way of changing the world, and its analysis cannot be separated from history. Across the boundary between Gumuz and Agaw in old Gojjam, exchanged children intermarried and thus modified the ethnic and cultural scene. Interchange of this egalitarian kind is not found today between Gumuz and Oromo in Wellegga. Because of the formation of the imperial Ethiopian state, a new *shanḳilla* fringe has been created in Wellegga, a racially low-status and (to 1975) largely endogamous and separate society, seeking its security within its own borders.

Henry Salt is the author usually credited with having first recorded the customary institution of exchange marriage among the Gumuz. I believe Bruce was reporting a particularly significant variation of essentially the same bond, in this instance between Agaw and Gumuz trading partners at a time of increasing pressure on the Gojjam lowlands from slave raids. If the former topic is the province of the anthropologist and the latter of the historian, then our academic boundaries must be redrawn.

6

A problem of domination at the periphery: the Kwegu and the Mursi

DAVID TURTON

The Kwegu live on the banks of the River Omo in south-western Ethiopia. They depend for their subsistence mainly on cultivation, but are also expert hunters and fishermen. This chapter is about their relationship with a neighbouring group of cattle herders, the Mursi.[1] There are between 4,000 and 5,000 Mursi and the Kwegu I am concerned with in this chapter do not exceed 200.[2] The relationship between the two groups is, I argue, one of domination. The Kwegu provide the Mursi with various goods and services but do not receive equivalent goods and services in return. Neither side, however, sees this economic imbalance as the defining feature of the relationship. Indeed, in a sense, the Kwegu see themselves as gaining most from a relationship that places them in a socially inferior position, which, to the outside observer, results in their economic exploitation and which is kept in being, in the last resort, by Mursi command of superior physical force.

If the interpretation which I present below is correct, this is a case of the successful domination and incorporation of a peripheral group by a 'centre' which, in relation to the rest of imperial Ethiopia, was itself highly peripheral. Both the Mursi and Kwegu were less affected than other groups by the extension of military and administrative control to the south at the turn of the last century. Lying between two rivers, the Omo and its tributary the Mago, which are difficult to cross for at least half the year, Mursiland was literally bypassed by explorers and military campaigners alike during the twenty years which saw the 'pacification' of the Lower Omo valley by Menilek's forces.[3] No garrison was set up in Mursiland during this period, and the only military 'invasion' subsequently experienced by the Mursi was by a small Italian force which briefly occupied a fort on the east bank of the Omo in 1940. It was not until 1970 that the existence of the Mursi was officially recognized by the creation of a new *wereda* called Mursi-Bodi in Hamar-Bako *awraja*, Gamo Gofa Province. The administrative centre of the new *wereda* was at Hana which is sixty-five kilometres north of the Mursi, in the territory of their neighbours the Bodi. There remains to this day no police post or other administrative centre in Mursiland itself (see Map 11).[4]

I do not wish to claim that the Mursi and Kwegu were unaffected by the process of imperial expansion that more directly affected their neighbours, both in the Omo Valley itself and in the highlands to the west and east. On the contrary, one purpose of this paper is to suggest that Mursi domination of the Kwegu was shaped and conditioned by the growing demand for ivory, which, during the late nineteenth and early twentieth centuries, played such an important part in the domination by Shewans of their southern periphery.

THE KWEGU AND THE MURSI

The Kwegu are a river people. Their settlements are found on both banks of the Omo, never far from the river itself. They regard themselves, and are regarded by their neighbours, as the indigenous inhabitants of the Omo forest. During the dry season (November to February) they cultivate small pockets of floodland along the river bank, and, following the first heavy rain in March or April, plant a second crop in forest clearings, farther back from the river. Their principal crop is sorghum, but they also grow maize, cow peas, beans and tobacco. Fishing, by harpoon and hook and line, is confined to the dry season, when the river is low and the water clear. They hunt game animals, using firearms and pit traps. They keep beehives in the tall trees of the Omo forest and gather wild honey by following the honey bird. Living all the year round in close proximity to the Omo, which is flanked on both sides by eight to ten kilometres of dense tsetse-infested bush, the Kwegu keep no domestic animals except dogs. It is their lack of cattle which makes them, in the eyes of the Mursi, an inferior and peripheral group. Indeed, the Mursi name for the Kwegu, *Nyidi* (sing. *Nyidini*), may be translated 'poor [i.e. cattleless] people'.[5] For their part, the Kwegu give great cultural emphasis to their hunting activities – although they appear to have no tradition of having lived by hunting and gathering alone.

Just as the Kwegu depend mainly on cultivation and see themselves as hunters, so the Mursi depend on cultivation but see themselves as herders. Having little more than one head of cattle per head of human population, they cannot fully support themselves on the products of their herds. In fact, they depend for at least 75 per cent of their subsistence on grain (mainly sorghum). Cattle, however, make a vital contribution to the long-term viability of their economy as an insurance against crop failure, when they may be exchanged for grain in the highlands. Because the Omo itself is such an inhospitable environment for cattle, the Mursi keep their herds in the wooded grasslands 10–20 kilometres east of the river and make clearings along the eastern fringes of the Omo bush-belt for rain cultivation. But since rainfall in the Omo lowlands is too erratic for regular reliable cropping, they also depend on flood cultivation along the banks of the Omo.[6] Floodland is a vital and scarce resource for the Mursi.[7] Between October and February, therefore, the Mursi cultivators – mainly women, children and older men – far outnumber Kwegu at the Omo. The cattle, meanwhile, are kept well to the east of the river ('outside', as the Mursi put it), under the care of young men and boys, although they may be brought to the Omo for a few weeks at the height of the dry season, when the harvest is ready and the tsetse flies less troublesome. During February and March, as the rains approach and the Omo begins to rise, the entire Mursi population moves back to the eastern plain, leaving the river, once more, to the sole occupation of the Kwegu.

Although physically indistinguishable, the two groups are clearly distinct in a cultural sense. First, they speak different, though closely related, languages.[8] Very few Mursi are able to speak or understand Kwegu – many, indeed, are unaware of the name Kwegu itself – but the Kwegu are bilingual, speaking their own language only amongst themselves. Secondly, although both Kwegu and Mursi depend overwhelmingly on cultivation, they are, in ideology and sentiment, hunters and herders respectively. Thus Kwegu, unlike Mursi, are fully at home both in the Omo forest and on the river itself. Knowing, for example, how to make a pit trap, a snare or a honey barrel, how to hollow out a tree trunk to make a dugout canoe, or how to take such a canoe across the Omo when it is running high and fast – these are the expected accomplishments of all Kwegu men. The Mursi, on the other hand, have adapted themselves to the Omo environment only to the extent necessary to exploit it for flood cultivation. While they acknowledge (and indeed take full advantage of) the *technical* superiority of the Kwegu as hunters and boatmen, they nevertheless regard these skills as inferior in a *cultural* sense – that is, in so far as they symbolize a way of life. And while the Kwegu take an obvious pride in their hunting and river skills and do not aspire to become herders, they do not publicly contradict the Mursi dogma that herding is the epitome of a 'civilized' way of life.

A third factor which helps to maintain the cultural distinctiveness of the two groups, despite their frequent and regular interaction, is that marriage and sexual relations between them are denounced as dangerous by the Mursi. It is said, for example, that if a Mursi man were to have sexual intercourse with a Kwegu woman, his cattle would die, and, if found out, he would be beaten. A Kwegu man who is discovered to have had sexual intercourse with a Mursi woman will, in theory, be bound and thrown into the Omo, but, in practice, is more likely to be severely beaten. The children of such illegitimate unions will be Kwegu if the father is Kwegu, but the male child of a Kwegu mother and Mursi father will be legitimized as a Mursi through the payment of up to six cattle to the mother's relatives by the father. (Since these cattle cannot be kept by the Omo, they will end up being herded by a Mursi who has a special relationship, to be described later as patronage, with the mother's family.)

Intermarriage, including that of Mursi men with Kwegu women, though strongly disapproved of by the Mursi, does occur, with the result that some men (I know of one case) carry the stigma of being 'sisters' sons' of Kwegu. Another case I was told of concerned a Mursi, now dead, who took a Kwegu woman as his third wife, handing over goats in bridewealth. The woman continued to live at the Omo and when she visited her husband's cattle homestead she slept 'in the bush' – that is, outside the compound fence. She died childless, but had she borne children they would have been regarded as

Mursi. One other case of Kwegu–Mursi intermarriage is worth describing because it is the only one of which I have first hand knowledge.

> On February 23rd 1974 I met a Kwegu, Tongogoloin, who had several nasty cuts across his back. Three days before, he had been beaten up, with duelling poles, by five Mursi, the sister of one of whom was the mother of his child – now a toddler. T. had already handed over, as bridewealth, five cattle (two cows and three calves) obtained with the help of his Mursi patron, but the attack was apparently designed to persuade him to pay more. A month later he was in trouble again. On March 21st I heard that, on the previous day, he and the same girl had been found together in an empty house by a passing Mursi who was seeking shelter from a sudden downpour. T. was again beaten up and left tied to a tree. (This story was told to the accompaniment of much amusement on the part of the newsbringer and his audience.) I met T. again in January 1982. By this time he had increased the bridewealth by an additional twenty-three 'cattle' – obtained in exchange for bullets, which had themselves been obtained in exchange for ivory – and he was living with his Mursi wife and their two surviving children (regarded as Kwegu) at the Omo.

It should be noted that, while the second of these beatings may have been administered because Tongogoloin and the girl were found *in flagrante delicto*, the first, at least, was motivated by the fact that he had got the girl pregnant without paying bridewealth – an offence which would have provoked a similar response from the girl's brother, even if the offender had been a Mursi. Obviously then, this proscription does not prevent, though it may discourage, marriage and sexual relations between Mursi and Kwegu. One thing it does do, as the above examples show, is prevent a Kwegu from acquiring Mursi status through marriage, and, in the case of Kwegu men, this applies also to the offspring of such a marriage.

The denunciation by Mursi of sexual relations and marriage with Kwegu is, from the Mursi point of view, a way of maintaining the 'otherness' of the Kwegu. Seen in this light, it is part of a wider denunciation of close contact with Kwegu as dangerous for Mursi – or rather for their cattle. As with intermarriage and sex, these wider avoidances are said to have been more strictly observed in the past. Thus it is said that, in the past, a Mursi would not drink from the same calabash as a Kwegu, nor sleep on the same sleeping skin, for fear that his cattle would die. In those days, Mursi and Kwegu built their settlements on opposite banks of the Omo, and when a Mursi visited a Kwegu settlement, he would drink from a special calabash and sleep on a special sleeping skin. Some Mursi have told me that they would not allow a Kwegu to enter their cattle compounds unless he wore shoes, since an animal whose dung he trod on with his bare feet would die. The same justification is given (by Mursi) for the fact that Kwegu make only infrequent and brief visits to Mursi cattle camps. And while Mursi and Kwegu cultivate at the same places along the Omo, their houses and strips of cultivation are not randomly intermingled. Kwegu cultivation strips are usually contiguous and their houses, even when part of a settlement which includes Mursi houses, are grouped together. This is illustrated by Figure 2.

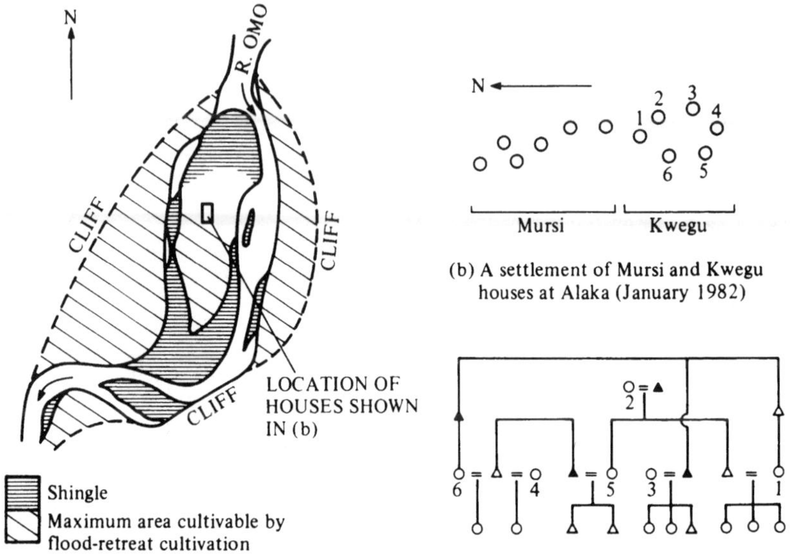

(a) Sketch map of Alaka showing the Omo at its dry-season (January) level

(b) A settlement of Mursi and Kwegu houses at Alaka (January 1982)

(c) Kinship connections of the occupants of the Kwegu houses shown in (b)

Fig. 2 A Mursi–Kwegu settlement

AN EXCHANGE OF GOODS AND SERVICES?

Because of their hunting, bush and river skills, and, as I shall explain, simply because they live at the Omo all the year round, the Kwegu are able to provide important, even vital, goods and services for the Mursi. The Mursi, on the other hand, have little in the way of economic benefits to offer the Kwegu. This suggests, as I shall argue in the following two sections, that the contribution made by the Kwegu to the Mursi economy is more in the nature of tribute than trade. In this section I compare the Mursi and Kwegu from the point of view of the usefulness to each of the specialist skills and services of the other.

The tracking and hunting skills of the Kwegu are valued by the Mursi more as a means of acquiring ivory and leopard skins than as a means of acquiring game meat. Elephants abound in this part of the Omo Valley and appear to migrate in large numbers, during the wet season, between the Mago and Omo rivers. Tracking and shooting elephants in the dense Omo bush is a dangerous activity and a Kwegu accomplishment to which few Mursi aspire. Indeed, many adult Mursi have never seen an elephant despite their abundance in the area. Elephants are stalked by one or two individuals, not attacked 'from all sides' by a large hunting party as Howell describes the Nuer method of elephant hunting.[9] Today, firearms are used, but formerly a spear, with a blade about 35 centimetres long, was planted in the animal's groin while it slept. The hunter then beat a hasty retreat, returning later to follow the tracks of the dying elephant. Leopard are killed by means of a technique designed to minimize damage to the skin. After the tracks of a leopard have been spotted, a piece of game meat is left in a tree close by, as bait. If the leopard returns, the next step is to set a trap. A rifle is lashed horizontally to two forked stakes about two feet from the ground, and a piece of meat tied to the end of the barrel. A string is drawn from the meat to the trigger, so that when the leopard pulls on the meat, it is shot in the mouth.

If it were not for the external demand for ivory and leopard skins, the Mursi would have little use for them (some men wear ivory bracelets, and leopard skins are among the accoutrements worn by contestants in ceremonial duelling).[10] As it is, these products are a highly prized form of wealth, being readily, if secretly, exchanged with highland traders for firearms, ammunition and cattle.[11]

Honey is another specialist product of the Kwegu which is highly valued by the Mursi as a trade good. There is a ready market for honey in the highland towns and villages on both sides of the Omo Valley, mainly, no doubt, because of the enormous popularity of *ṭej* (mead) which is virtually the national drink of highland Ethiopia. Honey is therefore a convenient means of acquiring the cash to buy such relatively small items as axes, hoes, cloth, and goats. If not traded, it may be used to provide mead for an agricultural work-party.

The river skills of the Kwegu include the making and using of fish harpoons and dugout canoes. Fish is regarded by the Mursi as an inferior food to be eaten only out of necessity. During the dry season, however, it can make an important contribution to the diet of those Mursi who are living at the Omo. Harpoon heads are made only by Kwegu (they beat them out of pieces of scrap metal), and few Mursi can match their skills as harpoonists. Making dugout canoes is a traditional Kwegu skill which some Mursi have mastered. Poling and paddling these canoes across the Omo is another traditional Kwegu skill which is shared, to a greater or lesser extent, by some Mursi, who have spent an especially long time at the Omo. But, while it is easy enough to take a canoe across the Omo during the dry season, it is quite a different matter to do so after about March, when its volume and speed increase. Most Mursi then become uneasy crossing the Omo, and very few would attempt a single-handed crossing. The Kwegu, in contrast, pride themselves on being able to take a canoe across the Omo, single-handed, even when it is at its highest, usually in August.

Since the Mursi keep their cattle east of the Omo, they must cross the river in order to take maximum advantage of the available floodland distributed along both banks, especially on the inner bends of meanders. During December and January the Omo can be forded in several places, but preparations for flood-retreat cultivation have to begin in September and October, when the river is still too high to ford. It is therefore vital to the Mursi that, at this critical time, they should have access to dugout canoes, and this means that the canoes must be moored and looked after during the wet season. Thus, it is not so much the skills of the Kwegu as boatmen that are vital to the Mursi, but the fact that the Kwegu live at the Omo throughout the year and are able to watch over the canoes. Since it is the needs of their cattle which prevent the Mursi spending the whole year at the Omo, and since flood cultivation nevertheless makes a vital contribution to their economy, it follows that the Mursi could not sustain a cultural commitment to pastoralism in their present environment without the aid of a people, the Kwegu, who specifically lack such a commitment.[12]

There can be no doubt about the importance of the Kwegu, in an objective economic sense, to the Mursi. It is equally clear that the Mursi have little by way of economic benefits to offer the Kwegu. The only possible economic advantage the Kwegu could derive from the specialist skills of the Mursi would be access to pastoral products. But since, by custom and practice, the Kwegu make only brief and infrequent visits to the Mursi cattle camps and homesteads, it is difficult to see how pastoral products could make a significant contribution to their diet, especially since their hunting and fishing skills ought, anyway, to guarantee them an adequate supply of protein. It is true that cattle could be herded by the Mursi on behalf of the Kwegu, but what would be the economic benefit of such an arrangement to the Kwegu? For the reason just given, they would have little opportunity to make use of such cattle for subsistence purposes, and they would not appear to need them as a form of famine insurance. Hunting provides an alternative food supply, and even if the supply of game meat fails, the Kwegu could use ivory and leopard skins as trade goods to obtain the cash to buy grain in highland markets.[13] We must conclude that there does not exist here the potential for a balanced exchange of economic goods and services.

This being so, the problem for the Mursi is how to *incorporate* the Kwegu while preserving the *otherness* upon which their usefulness as a source of goods and services depends; or in other words, how to engineer an ideological dependence of Kwegu on Mursi which reverses, and, in the eyes of the Kwegu, overshadows the objective economic dependence of Mursi on Kwegu. This is the problem of Mursi domination and Kwegu consent to which I now turn.

THE MEANS OF MURSI DOMINATION

Although I have spoken of the Mursi and Kwegu so far as two separate peoples, and of the relationship between them as an inter-group relationship, this has only been in order to clarify the exposition. In fact, as I hope to show in this and the next section, the Kwegu have been incorporated, as a peripheral and exploited minority, into Mursi society itself: they have been subjected to the political domination of the Mursi 'centre'. The principal means of Mursi domination is an institution which binds individual Kwegu to individual Mursi and which I call clientage (there is no indigenous term for it).[14] Since the Kwegu are few in relation to the Mursi, only a minority of Mursi have Kwegu clients. But each Kwegu man has a relationship of mutual indebtedness with a particular Mursi, whom I call his patron.

The client is expected to perform various services for his patron, based upon the specialist Kwegu skills outlined in the previous section. The patron may, for example, ask his client to kill a game animal to enable him to provide soup for a sick relative (thus avoiding the need to slaughter one of his livestock); he may ask him to kill an elephant or leopard so that he can use the ivory or skin to buy cattle, bullets, or a rifle; he may ask him to collect honey and make mead which he will then use to mobilize a work party to clear a new cultivation site; and he will expect him to be on hand to ferry him and his family across the Omo when it is time to start preparations for planting on the west bank. These are not only valuable economic services, but they also help to further the general social standing and prestige of the patron among his fellow Mursi. He can, for example, use his client's services as boatman to organize the highly important crossing of the Omo at the end of the wet season for other members of his local community. Clients are a political as well as an economic resource.

The jural basis and principal symbolic expression of this relationship (which does not occur between Mursi) is the patron's gift of a large male stock animal to his client at the time of the latter's marriage. If a Kwegu is asked what he receives from his patron, the standard reply is 'He gives me cattle with which to marry.' But the Kwegu do not – indeed, the Mursi specifically say that they should not – use cattle as bridewealth. The animal in question *does* make a contribution to the client's bridewealth, but only indirectly after it has been converted into goats, the conversion being made with the aid of either another Mursi or of a member of a neighbouring group. These goats, which cannot survive long at the Omo because of tsetse flies, will be handed over to various Mursi either as gifts or for safe keeping. The bride's father's patron, for example, will expect to receive part of the bridewealth, which may include ivory, bullets and a firearm, in addition to goats. He bases this expectation on the fact that he, or his father, contributed to the bridewealth of the bride's mother. It is not, however, as a partial contribution to the client's bridewealth that the patron's gift of a stock animal has its greatest importance. Its most significant function by far is symbolic: it symbolizes the interest the patron has in his client's marriage and in the offspring that will result from it. On the strength of his gift, the patron acts on his client's behalf in the bridewealth negotiations, playing the part that would be played by the groom's father in a marriage between two Mursi.

The patron opens the negotiations by asking the bride's father to give him his daughter 'so that she may carry water and collect wood for me', as though he were going to marry her himself. The patron is, indeed, spoken of as 'marrying a wife' for his client, a terminology which implies that he has a kind of proprietory right over his client and over his reproductive potential. By linking this to the reproductive potential of livestock, the patron's gift of a large stock animal, albeit converted into goats, symbolizes the links of indebtedness that will arise out of the marriage for future generations. Thus, the relationship between the patron and his client's children is expressed in the idiom of kinship. He is their 'father' because he 'married' their mother. Not only does the patron receive a share in the bridewealth of his client's daughter, but her marriage cannot proceed without his approval, which is symbolized by his attendance (or by that of a brother or a son), together with the bride's actual father, at the discussions over her bridewealth.

It follows that patron–client links are inherited (the patron's son becoming the patron of the client's son) and that they bind not only individuals but also shallow patrilineal descent groups. So although rights to Kwegu services are individualized in particular patron–client relationships, they are also incorporated in patrilineal descent groups, as are rights to other scarce resources such as women, cattle, and floodland. It may be said that Kwegu marriage is not so much an exchange between two groups of Kwegu in respect of a woman, as an exchange between two groups of Mursi in respect of a Kwegu – or rather, a Kwegu couple. By disposing of the marriages of 'their' Kwegu, the Mursi treat the Kwegu as objects which can be used to set in motion mutually beneficial cycles of reciprocity amongst themselves and which, like cattle, have the added advantage of being able to reproduce themselves.

If, as seems appropriate, we use the term 'ownership' to describe the rights held by a Mursi in his Kwegu client, it is apparent that what is fundamentally owned is not the Kwegu himself but his reproductive potential: he is human capital, in which the patron has a reproductive investment. This is brought out if we consider the way in which a Mursi without a Kwegu client goes about acquiring one. Since by definition there is no such thing as a patronless Kwegu, what such a man has to do is persuade another Mursi who has a client to transfer a share in the reproductive potential of this client to him in exchange for a large stock animal. The clientless Mursi then 'marries' a Kwegu girl, paying all the bridewealth himself and using the Kwegu, in whose reproductive services he now owns a share, to beget children by the girl. The male offspring of this union then become the clients of their Mursi 'father'.

The Mursi, therefore, exercise control over the Kwegu by the same means that, according to Claude Meillassoux, elders exercise control over juniors in subsistence-based societies – by controlling access to marriageable women, the 'producers of the producers'.[15] But there is, of course, a difference. It is precisely by gaining access to marriageable women that juniors free themselves from dependence on the elders and become in due course elders themselves.[16] The Kwegu, on the other hand, are not freed from their dependent status by marriage – even, as was pointed out earlier, by marriage with a Mursi. It is more revealing to compare the status of Kwegu within Mursi society to that of women. For, like women, and unlike juniors, Kwegu remain jural minors in relation to the wider Mursi society even after marriage: they have no legal rights 'against the world' except as clients of Mursi.[17]

The Kwegu express this by saying that they need the protection of their patrons against other Mursi. The following are two standard explanations, given to me by Kwegu, of why they need strong patrons.

> (1) If I didn't have a Mursi [patron] and I killed an elephant in the bush, a Mursi would come and say, 'What have you got there?'
> 'It's ivory.'
> He would say, 'I'm going to take it and, later on, I'll give you an animal to marry

with' [i.e. 'become your patron']. He would just pick up the tusk and take it. If I argued, he would get others, and they would beat me up, tie my feet together tightly and throw me into the Omo. Or else they would hang me from a tree. Back home, my people would say, 'Where is he? He went off into the bush yesterday and must be sleeping out.' Then, when I still didn't return, they would say, 'He must have been gored by a buffalo or a rhino. He must be dead.' If I did not have my Mursi [patron] no-one would worry.

(2) Imagine I had no Mursi and I was clearing here at the Omo while the Mursi were still with their cattle. One of them might come and say, 'This land you have cleared is mine. Why did you clear it?'
'It's mine.'
'It's not yours. Get off into the bush, Nyidini.' I would say to myself, 'If I argue with him, he'll beat me up. What can I do?' So I would go back home and sit down, and people would ask me, 'Why aren't you clearing?'
'My land has been taken by a Mursi.'

If I had a strong Mursi, he would come and find out what was wrong. He would come and find the man who took my land and say, 'Doesn't this man also need to eat? Why just take his land? You should have said to him, "Give me some land so that my wives can plant beans." Then the Kwegu could have marked off a strip for you. Don't Kwegu take you across the Omo? When your children are ill, don't you give them bullets to shoot an animal to make soup? And yet you take their land and chase them off into the bush. I am now going back to the cattle, but if I hear that you have done the same again, I shall come immediately.'

So I would continue clearing. As long as my Mursi is strong, no other Mursi will take my land.

Despite the vividness of these descriptions, my informants were not describing what actually *does* happen. Rather, they were describing what would happen if, *per impossibile*, a Kwegu had no patron. It is not that Mursi never practise violence against Kwegu, as the case of Tongogoloin, described above, illustrates. A certain amount of violence must presumably be experienced by the Kwegu in order to keep alive their alarming vision of what life would be like without their patrons. But such violence is not a normal part of daily life, and Kwegu are not, in fact, bound and thrown into the Omo under any circumstances. These standard, hypothetical descriptions of life without a patron amount to a Kwegu 'state of nature', a myth which legitimizes Mursi domination by showing that a Kwegu without a patron does not count as a legal individual.

The picture I have presented is of a Kwegu dependence on Mursi which has been 'engineered' by the Mursi; an ideological dependence in comparison to which the objective economic dependence of Mursi on Kwegu pales into insignificance. For, according to this picture, the Kwegu depend on Mursi both for their own reproduction and for the means of their subsistence. The goods and services provided by a Kwegu for his Mursi are, from this point of view, tribute extracted in return for the gift of life. But is this the 'point of view' of the Kwegu? Have I succeeded only in presenting a smokescreen of Mursi dogma, behind which the 'real Kwegu' remain as elusive to the Mursi as to the enquiring anthropologist? I have reached a point at which the question of Kwegu 'consent' can be deferred no longer.

KWEGU CONSENT

I have shown that whereas the Mursi depend economically on the Kwegu, the Kwegu gain no significant economic advantage from their association with the Mursi. It is also evident that the willingness of the Kwegu to provide the Mursi with goods and services is not based upon the overt use of physical force by the Mursi. A Kwegu does not say that he accedes to the demands of his patron for fear of physical reprisals, but that he needs his patron to ensure that his rights to property, and therefore to a livelihood, are not over-ridden by other Mursi. I argued in the previous section that this amounts to the acceptance by the Kwegu of the status of jural minors in Mursi society. As women in many societies may depend on their fathers and husbands for legal status in the eyes of the world, so Kwegu depend on their patrons. But what does it mean to say that the Kwegu 'accept' the status of jural minors? By using the term 'domination' in this context I imply that the Kwegu accept the legitimacy of their subordinate status; that they have come to share, in some important respects, a Mursi interpretation of the world. In this section my intention is to defend this argument against the predictable charge of 'Mursi-centred bias'.

The charge is plausible because all my investigations amongst the Kwegu were conducted in Mursi and because, having spent over 90 per cent of my field work living exclusively amongst Mursi, I am certainly closely associated with them in the eyes of the Kwegu. Is it not likely, therefore, that the Kwegu would have given me a Mursi 'version' of their situation on the assumption that this is what I wanted to hear? The answer would be yes *if* a significantly different Kwegu 'version' did indeed exist. What grounds are there for believing that it did, given that my best efforts to discover it did not succeed?[18]

The Kwegu, potentially at least, have considerable bargaining power in their dealings with the Mursi. The services they provide as clients are highly valued, and there is presumably no shortage of would-be patrons vying for the allegiance of Kwegu clients. The dispersed nature of Kwegu settlements along the Omo provides an individual Kwegu with opportunities to change his place of residence by making use of his network of kin and affines. The situation enables him, to some extent, to 'keep his patron guessing' about his present and future whereabouts, and, if he wishes to break off his relationship to his (Mursi) patron altogether, he can go north to live with relatives who are the clients of Bodi and take a Bodi patron himself. Mursi certainly complain about the frequent changes of residence made by the Kwegu, even within the Mursi area of the Omo, from one season to another. Their complaint is the familiar one of those who would control a mobile population (although the Kwegu are in fact less mobile than the Mursi): 'We cannot find them when we want them.' An example of the sort of situation that gives rise to this complaint is provided by the following incident.

> On the 23rd September 1969, the group of Mursi I was living with moved to Makaro, on the Omo, to begin preparations for dry-season planting. At least

> half the cultivable land at Makaro is on an island and, on the date we arrived there, it was impossible to reach the island on foot. The river level was not expected to fall sufficiently to make a foot crossing possible for another three weeks. There was a canoe at Makaro, but it was 'on loan' from its Kwegu owner who lived at Alaka, a few kilometres upstream. Much of the cultivable land at Alaka is also on an island and was also, at that date, inaccessible from the east bank. The Alaka canoe would therefore soon be required, not so much by its Kwegu owner as by his Mursi patron who had a cultivation area on the island at Alaka. It was this man who came to collect the canoe, on September 29th, and before he took it back to Alaka that evening, the first party of cultivators was taken across to the Makaro island, where they were now isolated.
>
> The nearest canoe to the south was a day's walk away, at Kennokora on the west bank. It was owned by an elderly and respected Kwegu, Doki, whose Mursi patron, Aritilohola, cultivated at Makaro. On the same day that the Alaka canoe was returned, I was invited to accompany a party of Mursi who were going south the next day to 'catch hold of' Doki's canoe (as it was called). This was obviously not going to be a straightforward matter. First, the party was divided in half, three of its members (including me) following the east bank and two (including the eldest son of Doki's patron) following the west bank. Secondly, no indication was to be given to people we met on the way of the true purpose of our trip. This was to prevent word of our intentions getting to the Kwegu before us, in which event they might simply take the canoe farther south. Thirdly, my companions intended to use me to add weight to their request for the canoe, since I also needed it (though far from urgently) to get to my supplies, which were on the west bank of the Omo itself.
>
> In fact, it was only my need for the canoe which was mentioned when we reached Doki's settlement on the evening of the 30th. He raised no objection, but said he would accompany us back to Makaro since I would only need the canoe for a few days. Highly vociferous opposition came, however, from the Mursi at Kennokora (who were in roughly the same position as those at Makaro and Alaka) when they realized the next morning what we were about. We eventually got away with Doki and the canoe at about midday after several parties of women and children had been ferried across to the island at Kennokora from the east bank. Doki stayed at Makaro until the 9th of October, taking the canoe back to Kennokora on that day, and the first foot crossing to the Makaro island was made on the 12th.

There are several things to be said about this incident. First, Doki could not, it seems, be ordered to hand over his canoe, even by his patron. Tact and cajolement were necessary. In fact, although Aritilohola's son accompanied us on our journey, he did not spend the night with us at Doki's homestead, perhaps in order to add realism to the deception that it was I who wanted the canoe. A good patron is one who looks after the interests of his client and does not make unreasonable demands upon him, and it is clear from this case that the client has some scope for 'non-co-operation' in order to put pressure on his patron to conform to this model. Secondly, by accompanying us back to Makaro, Doki literally did not let the canoe out of his sight and forced the Makaro people to 'pay' for it by making himself their guest for eight days. It must have been evident to him (a) that it was not my needs (or at least not my needs alone) which had inspired our trip to Kennokora, (b) that the Makaro people intended to keep the canoe for as long as possible, and, therefore, (c) that they did not welcome his decision to accompany us back to Makaro. Third, while Doki made no public show of displeasure at our request (indeed, for all I know, he may have welcomed the opportunity to spend time at Makaro), we were bitterly berated by the Mursi at Kennokora. This was probably where my presence was most important – not, that is, in persuading Doki to agree, but in making it more difficult for the Mursi at Kennokora to disagree. Doki, sitting quietly by while the Makaro and Kennokora Mursi almost came to blows over his canoe, graphically symbolized the potential there is for a Kwegu to play one Mursi, or group of Mursi, off against another.

It is to be expected that the Kwegu would enjoy some room for manoeuvre in their dealing with the Mursi, since a relationship of domination which allowed the dominated no area of choice whatever would amount to bond slavery. But the range of choice available to a Kwegu is not so great as to make his relationship with his patron an entirely voluntary one. A Kwegu *may* be able to choose whom to accept as a patron, but he cannot choose to have no patron at all. The fact that the patron–client link is symbolically expressed by the obligation for the patron to contribute to his client's bridewealth means that the relationship is invested with the quality of kinship: it has a time depth of several generations. But whereas a patron can in theory repudiate an inherited link to a client simply by refusing to contribute to his bridewealth, a client has no such easy option available to him as a means of extricating himself from an unwanted relationship with a patron. He can certainly let it wither, like kinship, with social and geographical distance, by moving outside the orbit of Mursi political control (that is by taking the Bodi option) or he may, at least in theory and by prior agreement with another Mursi whose client he wished to become, refuse to accept the proffered assistance of his patron in arranging a marriage. But in this (entirely hypothetical) case, the issue would resolve itself into a conflict between two Mursi and would be decided by the relative strengths of their respective bargaining positions. Any power a Kwegu might have to affect his own future by transferring his allegiance from one Mursi patron to another, can only derive, therefore, from his skill in playing the two Mursi off against each other, and not from the legally autonomous exercise of his own will.

If the argument against Mursi domination were pursued with comparative evidence, an obvious case would be the relationship between the Mbuti pygmies and the Bantu villagers of the Ituri rain forest of Zaire, described by Colin Turnbull.[19] The Mbuti hunters provide the villagers with various goods and services which are far more important than the goods they receive in return. The Mbuti are at home in their 'forest world', which to the villagers is full of dangers, both real and supernatural. Villagers attempt to control 'their' Mbuti, among other ways by arranging their marriages for them. The 'owner' of the groom pays bridewealth to the 'owner' of the bride.[20] The villagers see themselves as having freed the Mbuti from the necessity of living in the forest 'like animals', and use this to justify their rights to Mbuti goods and services. But the Mbuti enter into this relationship of apparent cultural dependence only out of calculated self-interest and only 'in the village context'. The failure of the villagers to exercise effective control over the Mbuti is explained by the 'constant state of flux' of the nomadic, non-lineal, territorial bands which characterize Mbuti social organization. This enabled them 'to represent to the villagers a structure so fluid that any formal relationship of the kind envisaged by the villagers was impossible'.[21] Fully legitimate marriages for the Mbuti were only those in which they exchanged women among themselves (compare Wendy James' study of this mode of marriage in the previous chapter).

The force of this example is that Turnbull's study was undertaken partly to put to the test of field observation the previously accepted view 'that the Mbuti are subject to village authority, that they are a subordinate people'.[22] What grounds are there then, for believing that a study of Kwegu–Mursi relations which was based on a field investigation of the Kwegu as intensive as Turnbull's of the Mbuti (he spent a full calendar year living with one hunting band of Mbuti) would not similarly undermine the picture of Mursi domination which I have presented in this paper?

The most obvious answer is that while the Mbuti are 'pure' hunters, the Kwegu depend primarily on cultivation and are therefore 'forced' to live in relatively stable local groups. The elusiveness of the Kwegu, although complained of by the Mursi, is very limited indeed when compared with that of a typical Mbuti band, whose whereabouts may be totally unknown until such time as it chooses to 'descend' on its village 'owners'.[23] And yet it may not be physical elusiveness which is the crucial factor. It may be that Mbuti 'social flux' has its most important effect on Mbuti–villager relations not so much by placing physical obstacles in the way of village control as by promoting certain values among the Mbuti themselves. I have in mind here an argument which James Woodburn has presented about the connection between 'immediate-return' economic systems and 'assertive egalitarianism'.[24] Woodburn's point is that the most egalitarian of human societies are hunting and gathering ones, because only this mode of subsistence is compatible with a system in which 'people obtain a direct and immediate return for their labour'. The central feature of the extreme form of egalitarianism which is associated with immediate-return systems is that it 'disengages' people 'from the potentiality in property rights for creating dependency'.[25]

Turnbull sees the fluidity and flux of Mbuti bands as presenting a problem to the villagers in their attempt to exercise political control. But if Woodburn's argument is correct, one would expect the extreme egalitarian values of the Mbuti, rather than their physical elusiveness, to constitute the real obstacle to village control. For such control would depend upon the Mbuti accepting a subordinate position in the social order of the village, not on the basis of calculated self-interest, but on the basis of shared values which legitimize that order. The real problem for the villagers, it therefore appears, is to get the Mbuti to accept, not a particular hierarchy, which may be difficult enough (since the Mbuti would form its lowest level), but the idea of hierarchy itself, which may be impossible.

Turning now to the Kwegu and Mursi, they both have delayed-return systems, so the fundamental prerequisite of successful domination – the acceptance by the dominated of a hierarchical interpretation of the world – can be assumed to be present in this case. The Kwegu accept the legitimacy of subordination itself as a principle of social relatedness, whereas the Mbuti do not. Kwegu 'consent' is, therefore, most fundamentally consent to the idea of hierarchy as a legitimate principle of social organization. But it is, secondly, consent, backed by the threat of violence, to a particular hierarchical system, which places them in an inferior and subordinate position to the Mursi. I suggested earlier that this system is accepted as legitimate by the Kwegu because it makes them 'dependent' on the Mursi, not for goods and services, but for the conditions that make possible the continuation of life itself. In so far as these conditions benefit, in a practical sense, the Mursi at the expense of the Kwegu, the Mursi can be said to have 'engineered' them, and their acceptance by the Kwegu may be described as ideological. It is not that the Kwegu are unaware of the fact that the goods and services which they provide for the Mursi outweigh anything tangible which they receive in return, but that this *economic* imbalance is not for them the defining feature of the relationship. They treat the goods and services which they provide for the Mursi as relatively trivial simply because they *are* goods and services (that is, visible, material, economic realities) rather than the conditions for the continuation of an orderly social life, which is what they receive from the Mursi.[26] I do not claim that Kwegu consent is total and homogeneous; but in fact I have recorded only one negative statement made by a Kwegu about Mursi in general, and this was almost forced out of him by my questioning. He said 'Yes, they are hyenas' (that is, 'they eat us'). Solitary though this statement was, it provides another interesting contrast with the Mbuti/villagers case. For it is the villagers who see the Mbuti as 'parasites' and the Mbuti who see themselves as 'eating' the villagers.

KWEGU IDENTITY: A LONG-TERM VIEW

My account would remain incomplete if it ignored the fact that Mursi–Kwegu relations have developed over time and that Mursi society itself has been affected by, and is partly a product of, external influences. In the final part of this chapter I make some necessarily tentative suggestions about the historical context of Mursi domination.

Let me begin by relating some Kwegu and Mursi oral traditions about the origin of their present relationship. This is how a Kwegu, a man of about sixty, described the first meeting of the two groups, several generations ago.

> The Mursi came from the west and went down to Dole [on the Omo]. They crossed the river there and went on to Moizoi [in the plain, west of the Omo]. They met a Kwegu there, called Gaima, and he brought them, as his guests, to

his home at the Omo. They came with their cattle and the Kwegu had to cut a path for the cattle, through the sorghum, which was nearly ripe, so that they could drink at the river. They made *tishu* ['green' sorghum, lightly toasted] for the Mursi, who sat and ate it in the shade. After the cattle had drunk they were taken back to the plain and returned the next day to drink again.

There were other people in the plain, and the Mursi asked Gaima who they were.

'They are Bodi.'

'Do they keep cattle?'

'Yes.'

So the Mursi said, 'You stay where you are at the Omo. Stay away from the Bodi and we will attack them.' The Mursi fought the Bodi, driving them northwards, all the way to Merkule [the southernmost Bodi cultivation site on the east bank of the Omo, opposite the Mursi cultivation site called Kuduma].

Soon after the Mursi had settled down, the Kuchumba [Amhara] came from many directions. Some came along the river Mui [west], others came from the plain [east], others from Shara [north-west] and others from Buru [north-east]. The latter stole Mursi cattle . . . Later on the Haranchi [Italians] came and fought the Kuchumba. We were already grown up by then.

There is no reason to doubt the broad historical authenticity of this account. The points to note about it are (1) that the Kwegu introduced the Mursi to the Omo environment; (2) that the Mursi came into immediate conflict with the cattle-herding Bodi with whom the Kwegu were presumably already in contact; (3) that the Kwegu were insulated from this conflict because they were not in competition for pastoral resources with the Mursi, with whom they immediately established friendly relations; and (4) that all this happened not long before the turn of the last century, when Menilek's forces first appeared in the Lower Omo region. (The date of the first arrival of the Mursi at the Omo must remain vague, but, from calculations based upon Mursi accounts of the formation of past age sets, I would place it somewhere during the first half of the nineteenth century.)

Mursi accounts of their first contact with the Kwegu tend to be less 'matter of fact' than that just recorded, having the unmistakable purpose of 'mythical charters' justifying present relationships. Both Mursi and Kwegu acknowledge, for example, that some of today's Kwegu are descended from Mursi ancestors. The most commonly told story accounting for this state of affairs concerns an important priestly family, a senior member of which gave me the following version.

Ages ago, when our fathers were on their way to the Omo from the west, there were two brothers. The elder brother's wife was pregnant, and when they got to Dirka [a hill, 30 kilometres west of the Omo] she was ready to give birth. So the younger brother took the cattle on to drink at the hot spring at Dirka, while the elder brother stayed with his wife. After she had given birth, the placenta would not come away. Her husband saw vultures in the sky some way off and said 'I will go and get some meat so that my wife can drink soup.' When he reached the spot where the vultures were, he found some Kwegu eating the meat. He took some of the meat and made soup for his wife, eating the rest himself. It was giraffe meat – something we priests never eat.

> When the younger brother came back with the cattle, the elder brother said 'Don't come near. We have eaten giraffe.' His brother was shocked and said 'Why did you eat it?'
> 'Because my wife was ill. You take the cattle on yourself. I will stay with the Kwegu.'
> So the younger brother went on with the cattle. When he had crossed the Omo and reached the plain on the other side, he built compounds for his cattle and asked whether anyone had seen his brother.
> 'My brother who ate giraffe and joined the Kwegu – where is he?'
> 'He is at a place called Alaka, on the Omo.'
> So the younger brother went to see his elder brother, here at Alaka.
> 'Are you my brother?'
> 'I am he.'
> 'Is this your place now?'
> 'Yes, it has become my place.'
> 'Then let us both eat from it.'
> The elder brother asked how the cattle were and his brother said, 'They are fine.'
> Now I herd the cattle; I am descended from the younger brother. The elder brother's descendants are my Kwegu, so we are brothers.

This story explains the accepted Mursi origins of some Kwegu as a consequence of the incompatibility of Mursi and Kwegu values – in this case the 'laxity' of Kwegu in the matter of food taboos. According to a similar 'mythical charter', Kwegu lack of cattle is explained, not by their occupation of an environment in which cattle cannot survive but by their proven inability to stand up to the rigours of the herding life. The same Mursi informant expressed this as follows.

> Once upon a time the Kwegu had cattle. But they grew tired of them. They just killed them – they speared them and ate them. 'Cattle are bad,' they said. 'One has to herd them all day in the sun. They are a big job. Raiders come and attack us and drive away the cattle. If we had no cattle, we would not be attacked; there would be no hard work; the sun would not beat down on our heads; we could stay in the shade.'
> That is what the Kwegu said long ago. 'We'll be killed if we keep our cattle.'

This 'blaming the victim' is, of course, a familiar device used by dominant groups to justify their positions; one is reminded especially of similar myths about the 'original' control by women of the symbols of male power. Equally familiar is the fact that the myth contains a partial truth which makes assent not entirely unreasonable. For it *is* their lack of cattle which makes the Kwegu immune from attack by their militarily more powerful herding neighbours.

These oral traditions find many echoes in the literature about hunters living in association with herders in East Africa, the most commonly discussed being the Dorobo, or Okiek.[27] Early attempts to account for these 'despised castes' as the 'remnants' of aboriginal hunters, forced into inaccessible forest environments by incoming herders,[28] have now been discarded, a commonly accepted explanation today being that they are made up of more or less temporary refugees from the pastoral economy caught in the 'safety net' of the hunting and gathering mode of subsistence.[29] There are, however, at least two problems with this residue theory. First, it emphasizes the cultural identity of the herders at the expense of that of the hunters, since the latter are defined as would-be or failed herders. A related problem is that the theory cannot take account of the repeated assertions of the historical priority of the hunters, an assertion which, as in the Kwegu–Mursi case, must be treated as reflecting particular historical events, rather than the general chronological priority of hunting as a human adaptation. Two authors who have made intensive field studies of East African hunters living in close association with pastoral neighbours, Blackburn and Harvey, have attempted to account for the distinctive ethnic identity of these groups as a product of their adaptation both to a forest environment *and* to neighbouring groups of non-hunters, and I believe a similar approach may be usefully applied to the question of Kwegu identity.[30]

Although the Kwegu cannot realistically be regarded as a politically independent unit, this should not be allowed to disguise the fact that they have a strong sense of their separate identity, not as a people who lack cattle but as hunters. Their cultural distinctiveness is most evident in their possession of their own language which, although closely related to Mursi, is not mutually intelligible with it and must have begun to differentiate itself from other languages of the Surma group at least several hundred years ago. Their hunting traditions have clearly been long established, and, although their culture has been heavily influenced by their contact with the Mursi, they maintain a vivid and detailed tradition of earlier customs such as the giving of spears, sorghum, and the fatty chest meat of game animals in bridewealth payments to the bride's mother.

Try as I might, I have not been able to find evidence of the assumption of Kwegu identity by Mursi, and *vice versa*, as a simple consequence of change in mode of subsistence. Mursi who, for one reason or another, have few or no cattle, certainly spend long periods at the Omo, and some may never return to full participation in pastoral activities. But mere residence at the Omo, together with Kwegu, does not *ipso facto* lead to the assumption of Kwegu identity. Both Kwegu and Mursi insist that however long a Mursi stays at the Omo, he does not thereby become a Kwegu. Such a change of identity would require the positive assertion of Kwegu values – including, incidentally, the taking of a Mursi patron. As for movement in the other direction, from Kwegu to Mursi, this is even more difficult to envisage because of the operation of the patron–client relationship, which, as described earlier, blocks all exits 'up' for the client, leaving only the 'side' exit to another patron. I have heard of no case of a Kwegu living together with a Mursi in the cattle settlements, let alone of one who has assumed Mursi identity. This is not to deny that this transition is made, in both directions, by the junior generation as a result of intermarriage and sexual relations between Mursi and Kwegu (always remembering that this does not apply to the children of a Kwegu *man*). But this is not what is meant when the proponents of the 'residue' theory speak of the 'permeable membrane' which divides such groups as the Dorobo from their herding neighbours.[31]

Taking all this into consideration, it seems evident that the Kwegu have been occupying their ecological niche along the Omo long enough for this to have given them a distinct cultural identity, and that this identity should be given no less weight than that of their herding neighbours in attempting to understand their present position. Put differently, we should treat as equally problematic the historical permanence and discreteness of both Kwegu and Mursi identity. Who then are the Mursi? Since I have proposed an answer to this question elsewhere, I shall give only the briefest summary of it here.[32]

When viewed over a longer time span than the last two or three generations, Mursi society must be regarded not as an historically permanent and distinct unit, but as a temporary outcome of a vast movement of cattle-herding peoples in the general direction of the Ethiopian highlands. This movement has been generated by the need to reduce the uncertainties of pastoral and agricultural production in an environment in which there is a wide range of fluctuations. The nature of this movement is exemplified by the recent history of the Mursi which has seen them pushing northwards into the territory of the Bodi, and, during the past five years, setting up a permanent agricultural settlement in the Mago Valley. Their advance against the Bodi has been achieved by peaceful infiltration accompanied by periodic wars. These periodic conflicts are publicly resolved by means of peace-making ceremonies which have the effect of giving *de jure* status to what had been the *de facto* occupation by Mursi of formerly Bodi territory. Today's Mursi, in other words, are yesterday's Bodi, while today's Bodi are tomorrow's highland cultivators. For, as herders move into higher, better watered land unsuitable for cattle (because of the tsetse challenge), there takes place a process of cultural and linguistic differentiation which eventually gives rise to new political and ethnic identities. The Mursi think of themselves as having migrated *en masse*, in an anti-clockwise direction, from their homeland somewhere to the south-east. The historical truth of the matter may, I believe, be more accurately summed up by saying that it was not the Mursi who made a journey, but a journey that 'made' them – a journey of cattle-herding peoples going far beyond the present Mursi in both space and time. According to this view, the determining factor in creating and maintaining Mursi identity has been the occupation of and adaptation to a particular environment, whereas Mursi accounts of their own history are based upon the assumption that ethnic groups move about the landscape, pushing each other around like billiard balls across a table and maintaining their distinctiveness as they go.[33] The Kwegu make the same assumption, of course, except that they see themselves as stationary, if not entirely disinterested, spectators as successive groups of herders have shunted their way past.

If this view of Mursi ethnic identity is correct, it illuminates the position of the Kwegu as follows. It shows that Mursi identity is as much the outcome of a process of cultural and linguistic differentiation, generated by ecological and environmental factors, as is their own. Both Kwegu and Mursi identities have been shaped by the same movement of Surma-speaking peoples around the south-western edges of the Ethiopian highlands, the Kwegu having found an ecological niche which provided a perfectly adequate subsistence but which was unsuitable for cattle. It is this fact which has enabled them, as it were, to opt out of the continuing drift, punctuated by periodic wars, into which their herding neighbours have been inexorably locked by their combination of herding and cultivation in a marginal environment. And this, it seems to me, is where we can find the truth in the tradition of Kwegu priority: it is not so much that they were historically prior, as geographically stationary. They remained stationary in their ecological 'trap' as successive groups of herders moved by, not like billiard balls, but like waves, each one overtaking the one in front, as they approached the 'shore' of the Ethiopian highlands. If this is correct, then the Kwegu, far from being a 'residue', do in a sense possess a more permanent cultural identity than their several herding neighbours.

THE CONTEXT OF RECENT IMPERIAL HISTORY

There can be no denying that Kwegu identity has also been shaped by their recent relations with their neighbours. In taking up this second aspect of Kwegu adaptation, I specifically do not assume that they have always been linked to their herding neighbours in the way they are now linked to the Mursi. In fact, I should like to suggest that Mursi domination of the Kwegu, in its present form, is the consequence of a particular series of relatively recent historical events, the most important of which was the penetration by the Ethiopian centre of its south-western periphery, beginning in the late nineteenth century. This suggestion rests upon two assumptions. First, the patron–client link between Mursi and Kwegu, seen as a mechanism of Mursi domination, exists first and foremost to enable the Mursi to exploit the Kwegu as a source of ivory, and, indirectly (that is, through exchange with highland traders), of cattle and guns. Secondly, the trade in ivory, cattle and guns did not begin to have a significant impact upon the Mursi until the late nineteenth century, with Shewan demands for tribute from their recently-conquered southern provinces.

There are several points to make in support of the plausibility of the first of these assumptions. To begin with, there is no doubt that the main value of a Kwegu client, in the eyes of the Mursi, lies in the ivory and leopard skins which he provides for his patron, nor that the main value of ivory lies in its ready convertibility, through external trade, into cattle.[34] Having a Kwegu client is seen as synonymous with having a full cattle compound, and the standard reason given by those Mursi who do not have Kwegu clients for wanting to acquire one is that 'they shoot elephants'. Given the particular rôle of cattle (as a form of famine insurance rather than as a major source of daily subsistence) in the Mursi economy, and considering the social and ecological crises that have drastically affected the Lower Omo region during the past century, it may not be an exaggeration to suggest that the exchange of ivory for cattle has made a vital contribution to the survival of the Mursi as a pastoral people. If the main value of a Kwegu to a Mursi patron is as a source of ivory, it is not surprising that the patron–client relationship begins to appear tailor-made for exploiting Kwegu skills as elephant hunters. The client is obliged to provide his patron with at least one of the tusks of any elephant he kills, in recognition of the contribution made by the patron to his bridewealth. In other words, the Kwegu is 'incorporated', by the link to his patron, into the Mursi system of rights and obligations arising out of the payment of bridewealth, while being permanently confined, by reason of the same links, to the status of jural minor. The productive potential of the Kwegu as providers of ivory so overshadows, in the eyes of the Mursi, their other services, and the link, through bridewealth, between patron and client is so well suited to exploiting this potential, that it is reasonable to assume that the particular shape of the relationship that now exists between Mursi and Kwegu is a consequence of the Mursi demand for ivory.

I come now to the second of the two propositions set out above, that this demand was itself a consequence of imperial Ethiopian domination of the south. While ivory has been exported from the East African coast for at least the last two thousand years, it seems to be agreed by historians that it was only in the nineteenth century, with greatly increased European and American demand, that the interior of the region began to be significantly exploited as a source of these exports.[35] According to Beachey,

> . . . it was in the nineteenth century that the great development of the East African ivory trade took place. An increased demand for ivory in America and Europe coincided with the opening up of East Africa by Arab traders and European explorers, and this led to the intensive exploitation of the ivory resources of the interior. Throughout the nineteenth century, East Africa ranked as the foremost source of ivory in the world; ivory over-topped all rivals, even slaves in export value and it retained its position right up until the end of the century.[36]

Within the East African trading network, Abir distinguishes three caravan trading systems which converged, from different directions, on the interior of East Africa 'about the beginning of the nineteenth century'.

> One system was that of the Khartoum merchants (*Jelaba*), who began to push southwards into the Sudd and along the Bahr al Ghazal following the 'geographical' expeditions sent by Muhammad Ali between 1839 and 1841. The second was the even older system of the Somali merchants from the Banadir coast . . . The third and most important of all to the history of East Africa was the caravan trade of the Arab and Swahili merchants of the East African coast, the so called 'Zanzibari' merchants.[37]

None of these major caravan routes, nor the small trading system of the Kamba in northern Kenya, seems, however, to have made a significant impact on the area north of Lake Turkana.

> As for the areas of the extreme south beyond Lake Margherita (Abbaya) and as far as, and beyond, the Omo river to the west, they escaped to a large extent even the limited social and cultural impact of the Christian north and the Muslim coast in its heyday in the Sidama area. Those areas, where a multitude of

> peoples, cultures and languages existed side by side, was [sic] left in its virginity until the 20th century. We have already seen that the trading systems operating in what is today Kenya only touched on the southern borders of this area at the end of the 19th century. From the little available evidence it also seems that this area was not penetrated by the Somali trading system nor by the north Ethiopian Jabarti trading system and definitely not by the Sudanese Jelaba system.[38]

Assuming these conclusions of Abir are correct, it follows that the peoples of the Lower Omo did not feel the full effect of the nineteenth-century expansion in the ivory trade until the end of the century, as a result of the demands coming from the Ethiopian centre. The Mursi were perhaps the most 'isolated' of these peoples, being hemmed in on three sides by two rivers, the Mago and the Omo. Because of their geographical position, they avoided direct military confrontation with Menilek's forces, and there are no reports of Ethiopian posts being set up, even temporarily, in their territory. There *is* evidence, however, that the Mursi were taking part in the ivory trade by the end of the century. The earliest evidence comes from the first (and only) European expedition to travel through Mursiland during the twenty or so years (1890–1910) which saw the 'opening up' of the Lower Omo, an Italian Geographical Society expedition led by Vittorio Bòttego.[39]

Coming from the north-east, Bòttego's party reached the lowland plains of the Omo in July 1896. Sticking doggedly to the east bank, they then followed the river to Lake Turkana, passing through Mursiland during the first week of August. After making a long detour up the Mago river (which was too full to cross at its junction with the Omo) they reached a Kara settlement just south of the Omo–Mago junction on August 29th. Here they received a friendly welcome which they contrasted with the hostile and unco-operative attitude of the Mursi. They attributed this, no doubt correctly, to the fact that the Kara were 'used to trade'.[40] This trading rôle of the Kara, which is attested to by other visitors to the Lower Omo at this time, is explained by their strategic position on the route from the Ethiopian highlands via the Mago Valley to Lake Turkana – and on the only feasible route (at least in the wet season) from Bako, east of the Omo, to Maji and the southern Sudan to the west. Their main item of trade at the time of Bòttego's visit was ivory, most of which they had obtained from the 'Murzu' (Mursi). Four years later the American explorer, Donaldson Smith, making a second visit to the area north of Lake Turkana, found the people reeling from the combined effects of disease and 'Abyssinian raids'. The Mursi, on the other hand, whom he contacted from the west bank of the Omo in the south of their present territory, appeared to be unaffected by the military turmoil to the south. They were also, it seems, keen to sell ivory:

> The Mursu, whom we found on the banks of the Omo, had escaped the raids of the Abyssinians, and were in a most flourishing condition. After we had shot a couple of hippos for them they became most friendly and brought us much food, consisting of durrha or sorghum, lentils, beans, maize and dried tamarinds. I

> bought a small tusk or two from them at first to start trade; but when I discovered a long line of ebony-like forms bearing about a ton of ivory upon their shoulders to my camp, I had to cry a halt, and it was impossible for me to transport more ivory than I had with me.[41]

It is, of course, impossible to prove that the ivory trade was unknown to the Mursi before the last decade of the nineteenth century. But I think it *is* likely that ivory only then became of major economic importance. This was because a voracious *external* demand, newly created by the energetic collection of tribute by Menilek's governors in the recently-conquered highlands to the west and east of Mursi territory, coincided with an equally voracious and newly created *internal* demand for the products for which ivory could be exchanged – cattle and guns.

Garretson's and Donham's studies in this volume make it clear that the establishment of imperial Ethiopian rule in Maji and Bako respectively imposed heavy demands for tribute on the surrounding population of the highlands, ivory and slaves being the most valued forms of tribute. As for the area farther west, Johnson (also in this volume) writes that, during the first ten years of the twentieth century, 'the Ethiopian demand for ivory outstripped the supply in the immediate frontier area, and it was not long before Ethiopian merchants were being supplied with ivory from deep within the Sudan'.[42] Mursi ivory, therefore, must have found its way eastwards to Bako via the Mago Valley (and the Kara settlement visited by Bòttego's party in 1896) and westwards to Maji which, by 1909 'was being called the "chief market" in south-west Ethiopia for ivory'.[43] This increased demand from the highlands for ivory was experienced by the virtually unadministered Mursi more as an opportunity for trade than as a demand for tribute. One must ask, therefore, what internal needs they sought to satisfy by means of participation in this trade.

The answer is not difficult to find if we assume that during the last twenty years of the nineteenth century the Mursi suffered comparable disasters to those suffered by surrounding groups of pastoralists. For this was a period not only of 'Abyssinian raids', the worst excesses of which the Mursi may have been spared,[44] but of drought, famine, human and animal diseases and intertribal warfare. Since neither Bòttego nor Donaldson Smith makes any mention of the Mursi having cattle, it may be that they met them after their herds had been depleted by rinderpest and/or pleuro-pneumonia and/or raiding, all of which had a devastating, if selective, effect on the pastoralists of northern Kenya during the 1880s.[45] If, as seems likely, the last twenty years of the nineteenth century were a period of ecological crisis for the Mursi followed by relatively rapid human and animal population growth, then the sudden increase in the external demand for ivory that was created by Menilek's southern expansion would have come at a most opportune moment. Apart from trading ivory for cattle (as they have continued to do throughout this century) the Mursi probably also began to trade it for guns and ammunition, the demand for which was both created and supplied by the same process of imperial expansion. This situation would have given the Kwegu a greatly increased, if not an entirely new, importance in the eyes of the Mursi. Through their elephant-hunting skills, the Kwegu were a potential source of the most valued of all Mursi possessions. The institution of clientage enabled the Mursi to exploit the elephant-hunting activities of the Kwegu as a kind of 'commodity production' from which they could cream off a profit in the form of cattle and guns. My suggestion is, therefore, that the incorporation of the Kwegu by the Mursi 'centre' (and therefore the present cultural identity of the Kwegu) was at least partly determined by the incorporation of the Mursi and others into imperial Ethiopia through the expansion of trade at the turn of the century.

IV Expanding tribute and trade

7

Coffee in centre–periphery relations: Gedeo in the early twentieth century

CHARLES W. McCLELLAN

Scholars have recognized the importance of the 'cash crop revolution' in Africa during the forty years following colonial subjugation, the period in which export of commodities such as coffee, cocoa, cotton, and groundnuts expanded tremendously.[1] And a relatively long-standing debate has developed regarding the source of the revolution's initiative and the reasons compelling African producers either to accept or resist cash crop production. In a recent article, for example, John Tosh has suggested that cash cropping was better attuned to the horticultural cycle of the forest zone than to that of the drier savannah. In the savannah, cash crops generally tended to compete with subsistence products both for land and labour. But even in the savannah there were mitigating considerations, such as cash crop prices, access to markets, the consumability of the cash crop, and the availability of a replacement staple.[2] Sufficient incentive was always a factor, and even more important was a need to guarantee basic subsistence before the risks of cash cropping could be taken.

Ethiopia also underwent a cash crop revolution, but – this is perhaps the source of its comparative interest – under quite different economic and political conditions from the rest of Africa. Ethiopia did not come under sustained European colonial control. Yet central rulers did have to adapt to the conditions imposed by the world economy, for their continued political independence was largely dependent upon being able to guide and to take advantage of a successful economic transformation of the periphery. In this process, central rulers had to rely upon agents in the provinces, who, in turn, had to contend with local peoples with ideas of their own. While direction came largely from the centre, social transformations at the periphery were not determined, and they often possessed a dynamic of their own. This chapter is a study of these complex inter-relationships: it examines the case of the Gedeo, speakers of Highland East Cushitic known also as Darasa, who live at the upper reaches of the Rift Valley escarpment in northern Sidamo (see Map 11).

GEDEO IN THE NINETEENTH CENTURY

When incorporated into the Ethiopian empire in the last decade of the nineteenth century, Gedeo was a segmented society of asymmetrical moieties with a strong sense of community. The seven Gedeo clans were territorially defined and apparently combative over available land. Individuals were granted land-use rights by the community based upon economic need and kin and marriage affiliations. Politically, the most significant body was that of the local councils in which all men of majority sat, but in which the voices of the elders were generally decisive. These councils mediated disputes, distributed land, and determined how to meet enemy incursions. If wider co-operation were necessary, it was initiated through tribal councils, of which there were three.

The age and generation system, *gadaa*, provided Gedeo with a more extended sense of ethnic identity and community. The *abba gadaa* (literally 'father of *gadaa*') and his assistant, the *jellaba*, were primarily ritual leaders, their posts shared between two senior and junior clans.[3] Just as clan and lineage affiliation defined a Gedeo's place in space, so *gadaa* marked his place in time and history through its cycle of rituals. By no means egalitarian, Gedeo society seems to have guaranteed at least a minimum subsistence to all.

As a case study in cash cropping the Gedeo most clearly fit Tosh's analysis of the forest zone, although Gedeo by no means typifies true forest conditions ecologically. Their staple, ensete or 'false banana', provided a relatively safe subsistence and was not significantly competitive with coffee for land and labour. To be sure, population and land pressure did exist at the time of the northern conquest, but the land suitable for coffee was downslope, outside direct Gedeo political control. Also, coffee was not new to the Gedeo; it had been harvested wild on a small scale for generations.

By the last decade of the nineteenth century, Gedeo had apparently arrived at a situation in which additional inputs of labour into relatively scarce land were limiting subsistence. A Gedeo shift to coffee production was by no means fore-ordained; downslope areas were equally suitable for ensete production, and had Gedeo remained independent, they probably would have taken advantage of the temporarily weakened position of their Alabdu (Guji Oromo) neighbours to expand ensete. Incorporation into the Ethiopian state helped to settle the issue for Gedeo. First, it militarily secured the land in question, making settlement and cultivation there feasible, accomplishing the task much more quickly and efficiently than the Gedeo themselves could have done. Secondly, the presence of northern settlers intensified pressures on an already heavily burdened subsistence economy. Last, improved transport provided better access to world markets where coffee prices were steadily rising. While the spread of coffee production in downslope areas did restrict the expansion of ensete production, most coffee producers cultivated at least a minimum of ensete and saved space by acquiring their seedlings from upslope producers. Higher prices for coffee helped the community supplement its subsistence in other ways, while also making it better able to meet its tax requirements. Not all Gedeo were able to make the transition however. To do so required sufficient labour, and subsistence had first to be guaranteed.

REGIONAL AND NATIONAL ELITES: BALCHA VERSUS TEFERI

Just as the transition to coffee reflected strains within traditional Gedeo society, it also led to conflicts at the regional and national levels – economic and political struggles to determine not only who would rule but in what manner Ethiopia would respond to the world economy. Pressures on Ethiopia had been growing since the colonial conquest of Africa in the late nineteenth century. Some Ethiopian leaders, portrayed as conservative and isolationist, maintained that Ethiopia could handle any of her European foes, particularly after the victory at Adwa in 1896; others, labelled progressives or modernists, were less confident and argued for a strengthening of the state through modernization.[4] The dichotomy between the two groups is probably too sharply drawn, but the debate between them did bring forth significant changes by the time of the Italian invasion in 1936.

But to view the changes of the 1920s and '30s apart from those earlier in the century would be misleading. The preceding era evidenced both the conditions necessitating later changes and the initial structures that would facilitate the transition. The necessity for change lay primarily in Ethiopia's rapid depletion of the elephant population and in the consequent reduction in ivory exports, trends clearly apparent by about 1910; also involved were a need to support higher settler concentrations in the south and an international pressure to end Ethiopia's involvement in the slave trade.[5] Structures aiding the transition to a coffee economy were being laid – an improved system of roads and bridges, telegraph and telephone, posts, and a railway – all centred upon Addis Abeba. The national administration was clearly seeking tighter and more secure control over southern resources.

The earlier period produced leaders cognizant of Ethiopia's needs and determined to confront them and thereby to ensure their own political power. Undoubtedly, Menilek II, before his death in 1913, foresaw the approaching crisis. His occasional tax breaks to coffee and his promotion of the railway evidence this vision. His successor, *ras* Teferi Mekonnen (regent, 1916–30; emperor as Haile Selassie I, 1930–74) would pursue similar aims. Teferi came to power with administrative experience in both Harergē and Sidamo provinces, the former with an already flourishing coffee economy and the latter with considerable potential in that commodity. He knew the importance that expanded coffee exports could play in modernizing the country and protecting it against both internal and external foes. Although Teferi's position was initially precarious, he strengthened it over time as his access to southern resources improved and as his political opponents were, one by one, neutralized or eliminated.

Teferi's successor as governor of Sidamo was *dejazmach* Balcha, returned to the province for his third tour of duty. Characterized often as a reactionary xenophobe, Balcha, as a Teferi antagonist, was a pious Orthodox Christian convert of Gurage origin, an excellent administrator and soldier, and an Ethiopian nationalist who at heart felt his opponent was selling the country to foreigners. For a brief time, Balcha also had served in the Harergē post, where he and his soldiers both became aware of coffee's potential. The animosity between Teferi and Balcha was thus more than just one over patrimony; it involved control over vital, new resources.[6] If Teferi's endeavour to modernize and centralize the country under his own authority was to succeed, he would have to reduce the power of protegés of Menilek like Balcha whose prime loyalty was to the empress, Menilek's daughter Zewditu. While the potential for coffee in Sidamo provided Teferi with much-needed revenue to achieve his goals, it also opened up new possibilities for insubordination and resistance at the periphery. Teferi had to ensure that the bulk of the new revenues flowed to Addis Abeba and not into the coffers of his political opponents. Balcha, as governor, acted immediately to secure and improve his own position. One of his first acts in 1917 was to construct a new provincial capital, Agere Selam. As its name ('Land of Peace') suggests, its emergence marked the beginning of a new era in Sidamo; peace was now generally secure in the region, and the period of military occupation could be gradually phased out. The centre could thus make its impact more directly felt in the province, regulating both land and labour more firmly. Coffee could be profitably exported only through Addis Abeba.[7] If Balcha were to derive a substantial share of the coffee revenues and counter Teferi's ambitions, he would have to transform Sidamo's political centre into an economic centre as well.[8] Agere Selam's location made it accessible to passing caravans and allowed more room for future growth and expansion; clearly its construction provides evidence that the changes of the 1920s and '30s were not completely directed from Addis Abeba. Other Sidamo towns would follow, better situated to serve the needs of a developing coffee economy. Agere Selam, although militarily well chosen as a mid-point among several ethnic groups, never achieved economic functions; coffee's expansion stimulated conflict among military units in Sidamo, a situation that ultimately served *ras* Teferi rather than *dejazmach* Balcha. Both lack of revenues and military defection were involved in Balcha's ultimate defeat and retirement in 1928.[9]

The transition to coffee was thus under way prior to 1917, but its impetus, at least in Sidamo, was slowed by lack of direction. Mainly, it progressed through an unauthorized, but natural, extension of the *neftennya–gebbar* system into areas suitable for coffee production, as prices for the commodity rose. Consequently, when in the early 1920s, both the national and local administrations determined to direct this expansion for their own purposes, opposition from those with established interests was to be expected.

THE GEBBAR SYSTEM BEFORE 1920

What, then, was the nature of the system that became part of the controversy in the 1920s? The link between *neftennya* and *gebbar* was basically a feudal-like patron–client relationship between northern settlers and indigenous Gedeo farmers, instituted shortly after the area's incorporation into the Ethiopian state.[10] Considering the regime's decentralized structure and the absence of a money economy, the system was well adapted to the nature and needs of the Ethiopian conquest and to provisioning military forces quite distant from the centre, while disrupting local economies and societies as little as possible. As evolved in Sidamo, the system reflected its Shewan origins in both terminology and structure, and the great majority of *neftennya* were Shewans.[11] For forty years (until its formal dissolution in 1941), the *gebbar* system worked quite efficiently, financing the garrisoning and administration of the south in addition to remitting residual revenue to Addis Abeba.[12]

Northern settlers, *neftennya*, mostly soldiers, but sometimes civilians, received usufruct rights over either land or labour as *maderia* (that is in lieu of their government salaries), and utilized these local resources for as long as they remained in government employ. The extent of their privilege depended on their rank, merit and length of service. With government approval, *maderia* of either variety could be passed on to heirs, who also served the administration. The government could also confiscate and reallocate such grants.

At the time of incorporation, the northern administration had, in theory, become the owner of all southern land, with the right to dispose of parcels as it chose. Considering the clear economic impetus behind northern expansion, the administration preferred to disturb indigenous economies as little as possible. Where little resistance was offered, such a policy was beneficial to both sides. Of course, the Ethiopian conquest was in places brutal and devastating.[13] In such cases, change was quite profound from the start. But even where the new Ethiopian rule was not overtly disruptive, long-term changes were often engendered that few could have foreseen.

In the south, new northern settlers were generally faced with two types of land to exploit: (1) inhabited land already under cultivation, from which immediate benefit could be derived, and (2) underdeveloped areas, generally pasture or forest, in the northern Ethiopian perception underpopulated and underutilized. In productive areas like Gedeo, labourers (*gebbar*) were taxed and the land exploited indirectly. In less populated areas, land itself was the taxable unit, measured by the *ḳelad* (a rope or leather thong about 135 cubits or 66–7 metres in length) and organized into *gasha* (in Sidamo, a unit typically eleven by seven *ḳelads*).[14] Measured land might be granted as *maderia* or *rist* (held in perpetuity) or purchased. Since *gebbar* land offered immediate reward to the *maderia* holder with little investment or effort, it was preferred. Along with *gebbar*, some *ḳelad* land was often granted as *maderia* to higher-ranking officials who had the economic and political potential to develop it, but most *ḳelad* land was probably acquired through purchase. Huge areas were offered at ridiculously low prices as an incentive to private development.[15]

Whereas the administration had long-term interests in development, many *maderia* holders did not. They were more interested in immediate reward, and that often meant excessive exploitation of *gebbar* units. Holders of *ḳelad* often did little to improve their land, and its tax base remained low. Most *ḳelad* holders derived their incomes from *gebbar* land, other economic endeavours such as trade or hunting, or land speculation. There was little economic imperative for the development of *ḳelad* lands.

Whether a *nefṭennya* was granted *gebbar* or measured land, his stipend was generally equivalent to a settler of equal rank. Since the quality of all land was not the same, a variable unit and tax rate were used. A *gasha* of poorer quality arid land was larger in extent and taxed at a lower rate than better quality land. Likewise, not all *gebbar* were equally productive. A *nefṭennya* granted ten poor *gebbar* could not expect the same return as one who received an equal number of wealthier ones. Although the term *gebbar*, meaning individual farmer, was utilized in the south, what was really granted to a *nefṭennya* was a *gibir* or tax-paying unit. Each individual peasant family was taxed according to its apparent wealth. Rates ranged from one to five Maria Theresa thalers (MT$) annually. A 'full' *gebbar* was one able to pay the highest amount. Other 'lesser' *gebbar* were grouped together to create 'full' *gebbar* and paid their tax collectively.[16] Thus the tax received by a *nefṭennya* assigned five *gebbar* units was more or less equal to another with an equivalent number. The term *gebbar* was thus used in both the individual and collective senses.[17]

Yet absolute equality among peers was not achievable. There was a general correspondence between the number of a *nefṭennya*'s clients and his rank, but higher-ranking officials tended to have fewer *gebbar* than their status merited. Even among settlers with theoretically equivalent numbers of *gebbar*, some disparity existed. The amount of labour within a particular *gebbar* unit could vary considerably, and, depending on how fully the *nefṭennya* utilized this, incomes for people of equal rank could differ. As for measured land, units might not be exactly equivalent, since measurement was often by eye and frequently prejudiced by pressures from claimants.

Of course, the allocation of either *gebbar* or measured land took time, but *gebbar* were more readily exploitable and thus preferred. Following Gedeo's conquest, a *balabbat* and subordinate *korro* were appointed to mediate contact with the northern administration. They were immediately obliged to organize the requisite labour and resources necessary to erect, fortify and provision a garrison town (*ketema*). Subsistence was thus provided initially on a communal basis, but shortly, individual Gedeo *gebbar* began to be allocated to individual northern *nefṭennya*.

A second task required of the *balabbat* and *korro* was to assign each family a particular level of taxation and to ensure that the assessment was paid. Having thus developed a roster of tax-payers, northern officials proceeded to allocate *gebbar* to settlers on the basis of the latter's merit and rank. *Balabbat* and *korro* leaders themselves were assigned indigenous clients, and their own family estates were exempted from the *gebbar* system.[18] Although many *balabbat* families in later generations would become quite wealthy, indigenous collaborators were initially assigned only minimal rewards, until their loyalty and usefulness could be more fully verified.

Ideally, the MT $5 tax designated in Sidamo was to be in cash so that patrons could purchase their needs, but few Gedeo had access to the money economy, and payment was invariably in kind. For Gedeo, the most convenient tax-fulfilling commodity was their traditional staple, ensete. While some Shewan settlers were willing to accept large amounts of ensete in various forms as payment, many others were not.[19] They encouraged, instead, provision in other commodities. Table 3 is a list of primary products most often presented by Gedeo clients to their patrons.

Table 3. *Primary products used to pay patrons in Gedeo*

Commodity	Percentage of Gedeo reporting payment in:
Coffee	22
Ensete	22
Sheep	13
Cattle	7
Maize	6
Tobacco	3
Ṭēf	fractional
Barley	7
Bole	7
Honey	1

Unfortunately, the table does not demonstrate the great complexity of transactions that was often involved. Nor does it reflect changes in commodity importance over time. In the latter instance, ensete was the commodity most utilized earlier in the century, while coffee gained equal importance by the 1920s.

Ensete as a traditional Gedeo export to surrounding territories continued after the conquest; in fact, Gedeo with surplus time and labour could ease their tax burden by trading their relatively cheap, local commodity for something of higher value. Generally, Gedeo could double the value of ensete by transporting it to neighbouring Guji areas and exchanging it for butter, cotton, livestock or *bole* (an earth salt fed to cattle). These products were then given to *neftennya* or traded further for *wolanticha* (low-grade iron bars), *mesano* (high-grade iron bars), or *boolookos* (a heavy blanket or cloak of wool or cotton).[20]

This trade was attractive only if the *gebbar* could find sufficient labour and time, and much depended on how extensively a *neftennya* utilized his clients at home. Besides the MT $5 tax, *gebbar* were expected to provide a wide range of services for their patrons. Since *neftẹnnya* were technically soldiers and subject to instant military call, and since most early settler households consisted of single males, many of the services were of a domestic nature – grinding grain, cutting and carrying firewood or thatching, and herding livestock. The extent and frequency with which these services were provided varied greatly. Much depended on the number of *gebbar* which a patron possessed, their proximity of residence, and the particular domestic needs of the patron. *Gebbar* who lived close might be called at any time, whereas those at a distance might devote designated periods each year to serving the *neftẹnnya*. Those tasks required of the *gebbar* also bore relation to his particular economic and ethnic background. Gedeo were more likely to perform horticultural tasks while neighbouring pastoral Guji more often herded livestock.[21] In all of these tasks, some effort was made to conserve the *gebbar*'s time and effort. For example, a *gebbar* heading home after a period of service would carry grain for grinding to be returned on his next visit. *Gebbar* who could afford to do so sometimes converted their labour duties into an annual cash payment either in full or in part, but such cases were generally rare. Full dispensation from labour services ranged from MT $10 to $50 per year, a clear indication of their economic importance.[22]

Other assessments were also decreed. *Gebbar* contributed to Christian feast days and to other special occasions such as marriages or christenings involving their patron's household, events to which they were likely to be invited. Each was assessed a few *mahalak* (there were 12–16 per thaler) to be given directly to the patron; alternatively, the *gebbar shum*, one of the *gebbar* chosen to lead the others, might assume responsibility for collecting the donation, and purchasing a sheep or goat for the festivities. If the *neftẹnnya* had his own private estate (*kudad* or *hudad*), *gebbar* were expected to sow and harvest it for him, giving priority to his needs.[23] A soldier on campaign or involved in commerce might require a young *gebbar* to accompany him as a personal servant. Young women might serve directly in the settler household where indiscretions often resulted.

The demands placed upon Gedeo land and labour as a result of the conquest and the subsequent institution of the *gebbar* system exerted great pressures on traditional structures, affecting some Gedeo families more than others. The Gedeo economy was delicately balanced. Land within the traditional core was scarce and fully utilized, fertility being maintained through a system of livestock stalling. Increased concentrations of labour could expand production, but with diminishing returns. Under the *gebbar* system, much labour had to be directed to serving settler needs. Those Gedeo already struggling to maintain subsistence were the hardest hit. Lacking additional land or labour to meet tax payments, they were gradually impoverished, driven into tenancy for northern landlords or forced to flee elsewhere. Thus began a long-term process of proletarianization in the south. While on the surface, little difference existed between labour available to

Table 4. *Gedeo extended-family size correlated with* gibir *payments*

Gibir payment (in MT$):	0	1	2	3	4	5
Extended family size:[24]	7.4	10.0	9.7	10.4	12.0	11.2

poorer Gedeo and to wealthier ones, the small disparity that did exist was apparently crucial. In the labour-intensive Gedeo system, a certain labour minimum was absolutely necessary to maintain subsistence; additional labour could do much to enhance economic security, making possible the clearing of newer, more fertile land, the maintenance of additional livestock, and the export of more ensete. The imposition of *neftennya* demands on both land and labour thus transformed, sometimes devastated, a delicately balanced traditional system.

The effects of the *gebbar* system were experienced in social as well as economic terms. While the rapid movement from a collective to a more individualized tax and tribute system might seem to indicate closer social contacts between Gedeo and their patrons, such was not the case. To be sure, by the turn of the century Gedeo delivered their goods and labour directly to designated northern settlers, but the extent of social interaction remained extremely limited. In cases where a number of adjacent clients made up a tax-paying unit, a *gebbar* chief elected by the clients themselves ensured that each person contributed his assigned share. A *neftennya* with numerous *gebbar* in various locations sometimes employed an agent – a slave or a poorer relative – to supervise *gebbar* services for him. Contact with the *neftennya* was thus often indirect. If a problem developed, the local *korro* or ultimately the *balabbat* might intervene, but only rarely did the *neftennya* punish clients directly. And when he did, tying the recalcitrant taxpayer to the gate post of his compound until requisite services were provided, the experience left vivid impressions of fear and hatred. Relatively few Gedeo travelled with their *neftennya*, and when they did, it was as servants.[25] This was generally a frightening experience since some Gedeo never returned – either taken ill or sold into slavery as most informants suspected. Even when invited to a patron's compound for occasional celebrations, Gedeo interacted with *neftennya* in a very structured and formal manner. Actual Gedeo–settler marriages were uncommon; informal liaisons were more numerous. Although the more human side of the relationship was not absent, *neftennya* clearly viewed Gedeo people as resources to be utilized and exploited for their own benefit. While some *neftennya* did talk of uplifting and Christianizing the indigenous population, their actions frequently spoke otherwise. To have encouraged and promoted assimilation of the Gedeo could only have weakened a structure that benefited northern settlers socially, economically, and politically.

For the most part, northerners in this early period remained isolated in their garrison towns (such as Chichu, Illalcha, Agere Mariam). They ventured out only occasionally, for local military expeditions or campaigns to the north. In slack periods, many were involved in elephant hunting or slave raids directed southward into Borena and ultimately across the border into British East Africa. Since local populations lacked the economic means to acquire firearms, northern possession of guns promoted an impression of invincibility and allowed settlers to exploit the slaves and ivory of the region without indigenous assistance or competition.

Since *gebbar* provided nearly all of a settler's subsistence, northerners had little reason to haggle with their clients in the marketplace. Until the 1920s a kind of dual economy characterized the area. While local markets did develop in the vicinity of many garrison towns, making supervision and tax collection easier, northerners rarely used these markets. These indigenous markets, whether new or traditional, were characterized by bulky agricultural commodities of low value and by the absence of modern monetary relations. Markets within *ketema*, by contrast, dealt with the high-value luxury items that settlers exploited on their own, and transactions were more often in cash.

THE RISE OF COFFEE PRODUCTION

By the 1920s, new patterns of socio-political organization and economic exploitation were apparent. Southern coffee was not a new export, but its expanded scale required a re-allocation and a more extensive use of both land and labour. With the central administration's intensifying interest in coffee production, Gedeo would play a vital rôle in its development but derive proportionately few of the rewards. An export so increasingly vital to the national economy required tight control and close supervision. But before the central government could carry out its objectives, it had to confront jealously-guarded local interests. That necessity engendered more frequent and intimate interaction with the indigenous population, accentuated further acculturation and drew Gedeo slowly into a national money economy.

In Gedeo, the contested land lay directly below the traditional core, on the lower slopes just above the Rift Valley floor, a region for centuries shared and disputed with the Alabdu Guji to the west and the Sidama to the north. Alabdu utilized the region as pasture and as refuge during droughts. Gedeo occasionally cleared plots there, growing maize to supplement their traditional ensete. These areas frequently marked interethnic no man's zones, and, as such, were potentially dangerous and generally unoccupied. Ethnic boundaries were never precisely defined, shifting constantly with the balance of power between peoples. Such zones also provided temporary homes for outcasts, dissidents and refugees in social/ritual transition between societies.

These were also, most importantly, areas of wild coffee, traditionally harvested and traded locally by the indigenous populations. As northerners became more interested in coffee as an export, naturally the desire for land in these areas rose, even if labour problems still existed. In the 1920s when the administration began a concerted effort to measure and distribute land, it found a resident squatter population who considered the area their own; the government effort thus required not only an attempt to promote coffee but to bring its expansion under direct control.

Settlement downslope was already proceeding at the time of the Ethiopian conquest, as the Gedeo were enlarging their homeland by clearing and inhabiting adjacent areas. This expansion probably reflected Gedeo's superior military position *vis-à-vis* their Alabdu neighbours, who had recently been devastated by drought, famine, and animal epidemics. Evident, as well, was a Gedeo population explosion that placed additional pressure on the core area. Peripheral lands were generally assigned by a council of elders to Gedeo families of greatest proven need, and worked by the younger members best able to defend and clear them. Land was occupied as *mura* (messengers of the ruling council) surveyed and demarcated the boundaries of each new plot.

The late nineteenth-century conquest, thus, did not initiate the Gedeo expansion, although it did further stimulate it. By enforcing peace between groups, northern soldiers ultimately made the ethnic buffer zones less dangerous. At the same time, economic pressures engendered by the subsequent institution of the *gebbar* system encouraged continued Gedeo expansion.

As noted, the northern arrival saddled Gedeo with tax and labour requirements at a time when pressure on land was already substantial. Fortunately for the Gedeo, their chief staple, ensete, required little space, but even the paying of the equivalent of MT $5 in tax meant ultimately the maintenance of an additional hundred plants annually, requiring an increased space of up to 50 per cent.[26] Settler demands for *kudad* reduced the amount of already scarce grazing land in Gedeo, which meant heightened pressure on the system of livestock stalling and thus on the ability to maintain soil fertility and, consequently, nutrition. A *neftennya*'s constant labour demands meant less time devoted by Gedeo to the actual care and cultivation of their own traditional staple. Thus, existing economic and demographic pressures, aided by increased security, promoted downslope expansion.

Prior to 1920 this movement took three forms. The first involved individuals who acquired land on the Gedeo periphery assigned to them by traditional authority. When agents of the ruling council demarcated new settlement areas, the location became part of Gedeoland. Secondly, imperial rule caused a certain number of Gedeo to flee the *neftennya–gebbar* arrangement and to take refuge in the forested periphery. Such flight entailed hardship for the abandoned *gibir*-paying units, but was perhaps understandable in cases of over-exploitation or *gebbar* mistreatment. If the missing *gebbar*'s kin could not preserve his estate by paying the required taxes, the land in question was often claimed by the *neftennya* as *kudad* to be worked by the remaining *gebbar*. The chances of the fugitive *gebbar* avoiding detection for long were not good. Since patrons lost valuable labour, they often employed agents to locate escapees, offering rewards for their return. Under such circumstances, informants were always available. Once discovered, an escapee forced to return often attempted flight again, or, increasingly by the

1920s, was permitted to remain on newly-cleared forest lands under new arrangement with the patron.

The third form of expansion also reflected the increasing importance of coffee land. Some *neftennya,* recognizing the potential, encouraged *gebbar* expansion by equipping them with better tools for clearing the area. Since the land involved was unallocated government property, *neftennya* had no legal right to it, but, for them, any measure enhancing the economic possibilities of their clients was to be encouraged. As individual Gedeo moved into coffee areas and developed them, the *neftennya* could demand higher payments, in theory 'creating' new *gibir*-paying units by separating individuals from their larger domestic groups. Encouragement was given to paying tax in coffee rather than in products for local consumption. Increasingly, a few *gebbar* managed to purchase exemption from labour services. Clearly, the *neftennya–gebbar* system was expanding on its own terms to meet new opportunities.

For Gedeo and their leaders, the land in question involved part of the Gedeo homeland. The Gedeo *balabbat* asserted his jurisdiction wherever Gedeo settled; *neftennya* whose *gebbar* were pioneering new areas claimed the same land by right of being 'first settlers'. Yet officially the land remained unallocated. Both the provincial and national administrations were increasingly interested in it, although their objectives concerning the land were not absolutely congruent. As revenues from ivory and slaves fell, both Sidamo's governor, *dejazmach* Balcha, and the imperial regent, *ras* Teferi, struggled to promote the new resource and to garner the lion's share of its revenues.

For the centre, revenue generated from coffee had advantages not afforded by ivory or slaves. Because the latter were luxury items, high in value and relatively easily transported, traders and government agents had long attempted deception. With coffee, such covert activity was more difficult. As a bulk product of relatively low value, it could be moved most profitably by efficient capitalized exporters who shipped to the railhead at Addis Abeba. Government revenues were thus more secure because coffee was more likely to enter the capital. Also, the larger firms involved in coffee export tended to be expatriate operations which the emperor could regulate and with which he himself tended to have close personal connections.

While the export of coffee could be conveniently regulated from the centre, its production at the periphery was dependent upon the co-operation of the administration there. Gradually the centre ensured mutual interest. All three governors appointed to Sidamo after 1917 came from developing coffee regions, and, as a group, reflected steady progress towards centralization of the imperial administration. Despite his personal animosity toward the regent, *dejazmach* Balcha, who governed the province until 1928, encouraged a programme to distribute suitable coffee land and consequently bore the brunt of local opposition from those adversely affected. *Ras* Birru Welde Gebriēl (1928–31), like Balcha a Menilek devotee, was none the less willing to promote government objectives as long as he could enrich himself in the process.[27] *Ras* Desta Damtew his successor, Haile Selassie's own son-in-law, was understandably the most loyal, and involved himself actively and personally in coffee, introducing Sidamo's first lorries for moving the commodity to Addis Abeba.[28]

If coffee production was to be given sufficient impetus, the local administration had to effect certain changes in the economic structure of the south. Suitable land had to be put into cultivation, labour located to work it, and the local people oriented to cash-crop production. As noted, the *neftennya–gebbar* system was already orienting itself to the development of coffee to some extent. Yet, in the process, *neftennya* monopolized both land and labour, leaving little of either for more recent settlers. To have permitted this unauthorized expansion of the *gebbar* system would have jeopardized the government's land allocation prerogative and created an economically powerful southern élite similar to that in the north, whose vitality and influence the emperor sought to diminish. Coffee land in the hands of newer settlers meant a wider distribution of wealth, and guaranteed a heavier settler population in the south, which would enhance security. That security itself was a prerequisite for expanding coffee production.

To ensure the transition to coffee, the administration unquestionably needed the assistance of the local, indigenous population. In contrast to earlier export items, ivory and slaves, which could be exploited most efficiently by small groups of northerners working alone, coffee required larger inputs of labour and considerable organization. Yet in the restructuring of economic relationships, the administration opted for a system of *de facto* tenancy, as opposed to one based on Gedeo free-holding which probably would have been more efficient. An inherent distrust of the colonized was a factor, but one suspects that the chief motivation was a desire to update the basic feudal structure rather than to promote a thoroughly competitive capitalism.[29] Northern landlords who mediated the transfer of coffee from peasants to merchants were mere parasites who contributed little and expropriated a value that might conceivably have been returned to the producer.[30]

A LOCAL CLASH OF INTERESTS

The concerted effort to promote coffee production after 1920 precipitated a struggle for control of the necessary land and labour. At base, it was an economic struggle, but the competing interest groups varied, and some of the motives were personal and political. Present was a basic competition for resources between the centre and periphery. Within the periphery itself, there were conflicts among local groups, struggles that the centre could, if it desired, exploit for its own benefit. Provincial administrators, from the governor to the Gedeo *korro*, had to take sides. Choices were not easy. Hard feelings emerged between two northern settler groups: the early arrivals, tied to the *neftennya–gebbar* system, who had conquered the region and consequently felt deserving of special privilege, versus the later settlers who wanted their own share of economic rewards that they felt their predecessors were monopolizing.[31] Competing too were local Gedeo, who sought to maintain as much control over their own economic future as possible. Coalitions, some peculiar, developed in the struggle, and a broad range of strategies was employed.

The road to conflict was thus set. Some time after 1917 *dejazmach* Balcha ordered surveyors into the areas concerned, to begin measurement and distribution. Conflict was initially minimized as surveyors started their task in downslope locations proceeding only slowly upward towards the more contested regions. Surveyors seem to have avoided at first the more heavily settled areas where anger was likely to be most organized and intense. Since northerners were rarely familiar with the area under survey, they employed local Gedeo assistants, attracted by promises of *ḳelad* land of their own and of escape from *gebbar* status.

How quickly these coffee lands were distributed and became productive is difficult to judge. One traveller in the Sidama area to the north during the 1920s commented upon the rapid deforestation which he witnessed.[32] In Gedeo itself one can get some feeling for the progress of northern settlement by studying the pattern of church building in the region.[33] Ethiopian Orthodox churches were not built for the benefit of local Gedeo; predictably, then, the earliest churches in the region were situated in garrison towns. By the 1920s and 1930s, though, more were being erected in the countryside, still not for Gedeo, but for northern settlers beginning to reside there to keep better watch over their valuable coffee-producing estates. Church building was dependent upon sufficient population and subsequent public pressure, and thus generally followed northern settlement by at least five years. Prior to 1920, present-day Gedeo *awraja* (a sub-provincial political unit) had only three churches, but in the 1920s eight more were constructed, and in the 1930s, nine, despite five years of Italian occupation.[34]

Much *ḳelad* land allocated in the 1920s was given to followers of *dejazmach* Balcha, relative newcomers, many of whom had not seen Sidamo prior to 1917. In the years following, other worthy arrivals were granted *maderia* as they appeared. For Balcha, the distribution solved several problems. A cash crop generated rising revenues for his own and the national administration. Secondly, it won him the favour of his own followers by settling them quickly on valuable land.

But difficulties arose. By exerting the government's claim to the land, Balcha deprived others of it, some of whom had to be evicted. Dispossessed northerners in the affected Gedeo areas were quite often *neftẹnnya* attached to the garrisons at either Bule or Illalcha, many of whom had helped *ras* Lu'ul Seged conquer the region.[35] They felt themselves unfairly deprived of rewards for which they had risked their lives. To them, Balcha appeared selfish and discriminatory. Although they seem not to have obstructed the government's efforts physically, they did encourage their *gebbar* to take such action. They also carried their case to Addis Abeba, hopeful that Empress Zewditu, the daughter of their deceased patron, would rule in their favour. She appears to have done little but listen politely.

To try to defuse the situation, the administration offered to those evicted *ḳelad* elsewhere, often arid land in non-coffee areas, but these proposals were mostly declined. Such individuals retained their *gebbar* in upland areas until the Italian occupation, when that system was officially abolished. But the *gebbar* system had already weakened considerably. Some of the labour previously controlled by *nefṭennya* had been alienated to new patrons. And while some *nefṭennya* successfully persuaded their former clients in coffee areas to continue *gibir*, this illegal remuneration soon came to an end.

Gedeo growing coffee for new patrons were still officially called *gebbar*, but their real position was changing. Many continued to perform a variety of services for their *nefṭennya*, but increasingly patrons preferred their clients to concentrate on coffee production. Land had to be cleared, the wild coffee bushes protected and nurtured, and young seedlings transplanted to more promising locations. It was not that the status of the client had changed, but rather that of the patron; *nefṭennya* took on attributes of quasi-landlords, and their labourers those of tenants. Most of these settlers had been granted *ḳelad* land as *maderia* and thus did not own it, but unlike the case of *gebbar* land, holders had usufruct rights over the land itself, and thus could dictate what was produced on that land and who worked it. In the government's view, the Gedeo had no legitimate right to the land at all. As emergent tenants, they sold a portion of their labour in return for wages, which were granted to them in the form of retention of part of the harvest they produced. They had become a kind of agricultural proletariat, with no land of their own, residing precariously on someone else's land as day labourers.

Yet even in a state of tenancy, some Gedeo preferred the new arrangement to being a *gebbar* on depleted and overpopulated upslope estates. Rising coffee prices offered more opportunity for Gedeo than they could derive from producing ensete. The attraction offered by coffee land is confirmed by the fact that some evicted *nefṭennya* in the area chose to remain as tenants for other northerners allocated land.

Revenues from the commodity eventually permitted a few Gedeo to purchase coffee land in the 1960s and '70s, but initially Gedeo were far from satisfied with the new arrangements. Like evicted *nefṭennya*, they felt unfairly deprived of land they had cleared, and resented having to work it for the primary benefit of someone else. Consequently, Gedeo never really gave up the struggle to regain 'their' land. From the start, physical resistance was one response to their dispossession. Violence in the 1920s was focused against the surveying teams; during the Italian occupation and again in 1960, 1968, and 1974, it was directed against northern settlers and their property.[36] But none of these efforts proved victorious against superior military odds.

Gedeo also attempted to employ legal means. Pooling resources, some Gedeo groups utilized the Ethiopian courts, but with no particular success regarding *ḳelad*. Early in the century, Gedeo had shown remarkable willingness to try Ethiopian justice, winning some cases against unscrupulous *neftennya*.[37] These limited initial victories may have encouraged their efforts against *kelad* in the 1920s and '30s. But, alas, they fell victim to unprincipled lawyers, who protracted cases indefinitely and who laid claim to Gedeo property themselves as payment of fees. Gedeo disillusionment followed, and probably influenced the more violent reactions of the succeeding decades.

The 1920s and '30s were also a time of reckoning for Gedeo leaders, particularly for those serving the northern administration. The Gedeo *balabbat*, Chimburu Shunde, experienced both physical and mental anguish. As an intermediary between his people and the resident administration, he desired to remain true to both. The *kelad* controversy, though, severely tested his loyalties. Chimburu ultimately chose his people's side. He had neither been acculturated nor enjoyed the economic benefits of his position sufficiently, to be completely co-opted. Chimburu's subordinates also faced similar decisions, and, influenced by the Ethiopian administration, some *korro* joined the government side. Chimburu's authority was thus called into question, and the Gedeo divided. Some *korro* clearly hoped to replace Chimburu or at least to be recognized as rival *balabbat*. Financed by his Gedeo supporters, Chimburu travelled to Addis Abeba to present his case. He was kept waiting indefinitely and ultimately returned to Sidamo. Whether the government ever heard his plea is uncertain, but clearly the government's position was never reversed.

Chimburu's resistance continued into the administration of *ras* Birru. In 1928–31 two new issues arose. The first concerned the arrival in Sidamo of numbered tax receipts, and particularly their usage and issuance. With the question of *kelad* still in the courts, Chimburu argued that the names of all claimants to a given piece of land ought to appear on the receipts rather than only that of the responsible tax-payer. Chimburu realized very well that Gedeo peasants without clear records of tax payments could be denied their land claims.

Chimburu's recalcitrance on this issue brought him a public lashing and subsequent imprisonment at the provincial capital, Agere Selam. The *balabbat* instantly became a local Gedeo hero. An appeal to Addis Abeba obtained his quick release, and because *ras* Birru was transferred shortly afterward, Gedeo associated his supposed misadministration with his unjust treatment of Chimburu.[38] While Birru was promoting the centre's objectives in Sidamo, his personal greed and zealousness worked at cross purposes. Certainly the administration did not need a governor who provoked trouble in Sidamo.

The second development of Birru's administration was the imperial decree of September 1930 ordering remeasurement.[39] Since most land had been hurriedly surveyed, often by 'eye' rather than by rope, inaccurate records existed. Some holders possessed lands in excess of those officially registered. Remeasurement promised to locate such disparities, and the excess land was to be reallocated. This decree was a natural extension of efforts in the 1920s that had ensured a wider distribution of *gebbar* labour. In Gedeo some land redistribution did occur and, consequently, some Gedeo received new patrons. But in many instances holders were not forced to give up their land, and instead simply paid additional taxes on their increased acreage.

With regard to official tax receipts and remeasurement, the administration's intentions were clear. It sought tighter control and regulation of a valuable resource and a broadened tax base, by encouraging the development of previously underutilized land and by ensuring that the government got all taxes due it.

THE EFFECT OF LOCAL TRANSFORMATIONS

The victory ultimately achieved by the centre was evident in the fact that by 1935 Gedeo was an important coffee region with local Gedeo as *de facto* tenant producers. The lives of many had changed considerably. These changes ought not be exaggerated; they would be most evident only by the 1950s. In a relative sense, downslope expansion increased geographical distance among Gedeo and, at the same time, promoted a more thorough mixing of clan groups in those areas. Although Gedeo clans had definite localities, residence was never restricted. Traditional Gedeo expansion had had a clear clan focus, but coffee-producing *neftennya* of the 1920s did not recruit on this basis. Downslope locations consequently were characterized by considerable diversity in clan membership.

Relocation of Gedeo families continued through the 1920s and '30s and has been a phenomenon of more recent history as well. Despite precarious tenure arrangements, settlement on coffee land did have its advantages. The need for labour in these areas was constant, and most of it was drawn from the *neftennya–gebbar* system. Coffee brought greater economic benefit for Gedeo than did ensete, and with less effort. Landlords readily accepted the crop and no conversion into other commodities was necessary. Often settlement in the coffee area was part of an extended family decision, with upslope ensete helping to sustain pioneers while they cleared land and gradually brought wild coffee into cultivation. Labour was shared between zones, as were commodities; association with coffee-producing kin made it easier for upslope residents to pay their *gibir*; and a reliable supply of ensete meant that downslope Gedeo could devote more land to coffee. Thus the coffee harvest was vitally important to all Gedeo, whether direct producers of the crop or not, and this fact may help to explain why all Gedeo came to conduct traditional rituals to cure and ward off diseases affecting the crop.[40] The presence of sufficient upslope labour also helps account for the fact that Gedeo, despite its coffee economy, never became an area attracting much migrant labour.[41]

But producing coffee as a tenant also had its limitations. Besides basic insecurity, Gedeo had to face greater interference by northerners in their everyday lives. Holding usufruct rights over land producing a valuable commodity, landlords were more likely to live in the countryside themselves and to have closer personal ties to their clients.[42] Landlords dictated how much of each crop was grown, complained about the general productivity of their tenants, and arrived promptly at harvest time to divide shares.

Trouble also came from another source. Since Gedeo migration downslope continued even after the allocation of the adjacent coffee lands, upslope *neftennya* suffered the loss of *gebbar* labour. As part of a *gibir*-paying unit, *gebbar* owed obligation to the *neftennya*, but as long as the unit met these requirements, the *neftennya* had no legal cause to interfere, even though some of his *gebbar* were now employed full time by downslope landlords. Nonetheless, some did seek to derive extra payments from *gebbar* on coffee land. Not wanting trouble, some Gedeo gave in to these demands and unofficially gave support to both upslope *neftennya* and downslope landlords.

It was this 'interference' in their daily lives that most Gedeo cited as their chief complaint against the tenancy system. When asked their preference between the two systems, most emphatically denied real differences. When forced into a choice, the majority leaned to the *neftennya–gebbar* structure. Those informants who experienced both systems saw the latter in comparatively idyllic terms, partly distorted I suspect by the bitter struggle and disillusionment of more recent years. In that sense, the *gebbar* system represented for them a time when imperial control and influence in the area was indirect and minimal, when their traditional structures and community were still relatively strong, and, most importantly, when they still retained their traditional lands.

Although the central administration did not, in most cases, consciously seek to destroy traditional structures in the south, its presence and the exploitative intentions of its agents often engendered this. Although early downslope migration in Gedeo was carried out under traditional land tenure policy, the imposition of *kelad* erased the old system and created new boundaries and associations. The traditional Gedeo system of land measurement survived somewhat longer in upland areas, and remnants were evident there even in 1975 within particular family plots.[43]

As the size of Gedeoland grew in the twentieth century, geographical distance, in a relative sense, became a factor weakening the communal relations of earlier years. Downslope areas, particularly those not allocated by traditional authority, lay outside clan affiliations. Although the economies of upslope and downslope residents complemented each other, in important aspects they differed, one being devoted to export and the other to local consumption. Coffee producers had more frequent and persistent contact with northern residents, with settler towns, and with the money economy. Their chances of and interest in acculturation were raised. Although receiving some benefit from their association with the downslope areas, the upland ensete areas remained poorer and more traditional and subsequently became sub-peripheries dependent upon the coffee economy. These differences helped to erode further the earlier Gedeo communalism.

The same geographic and economic factors helped weaken the traditional politico-ritual structure. Coffee-producing Gedeo were less inclined to participate in the cycle of ceremonies sustaining the *gadaa* system. Since the traditional ritual sites were in upland locations, downslope residents found it easier to absent themselves. My informants in coffee areas were generally less knowledgeable about their sub-clan affiliations and about the basic functioning and personnel of the *gadaa* system. Such apathy might not have been present had *gadaa* officialdom demonstrated some effectiveness in dealing with the northern administration or in mitigating its impact. The earliest Gedeo *balabbat* had close association with the *abba gadaa* (ritual leader of the *gadaa* system) and, in fact, the *balabbat* drew legitimacy through this connection. But with time, as settler–indigene relations gradually became freer and less impersonal, the *balabbat* became more independent, for he was the only official directed to deal with these matters. For coffee-producing Gedeo in the 1920s and '30s, the *balabbat* was a vital component in their hopes of maintaining rights to their land. The imperial administration helped promote the *balabbat*'s influence by assigning him *gebbar* to supplement income from *kudad*, while the *abba gadaa* himself was denigrated to the status of *gebbar*. Furthermore, many Gedeo found it increasingly difficult and fruitless to channel part of their surplus into a system that, from a religious viewpoint, appeared ineffectual.

But certain elements of the traditional Gedeo structure were retained in the downslope areas, primarily because they served important utilitarian purposes. The men's council continued to meet locally. Since these congregations consisted of all men of majority (those who had reached a specified rank in the *gadaa* structure) without reference to clan affiliation, those in coffee areas, although outside traditional clan jurisdiction, could function without problems. And of course all communities had local issues in need of resolution. Further, the *heiycha*, elders who served as practical ritualists, were still needed for a variety of functions including mediation. Unlike *gadaa* officials, they were not held responsible for the general welfare of the people, and thus their reputations suffered less. Northern officials saw little danger in them, and since the administration did not insist upon the application of northern law except in serious matters, *heiycha* helped preserve order by enforcing the traditional code. But *heiycha*, also dependent in part on contributions for economic subsistence, found the profitability and prestige of their jobs generally reduced.

For northern settlers in the south as well, the 1920s and '30s were times of change. Their greater numbers, the improved security of the region, the rise of coffee as the area's prime agricultural resource, and the emergence of a tenancy system to promote its growth meant new opportunities, freer association with the indigenous population, less stress on the military nature of the southern administration and better access to the material and cultural components of northern society. More churches were built to meet their spiritual needs. Better roads and tightened security meant easier access to the north and to neglected relatives there. New settler towns flourished – Dilla,

Yirga Cheffe, Feseha Gennet – to meet the local and national needs of coffee export. These towns, unlike the *ketema* of an earlier era, were generally easier of access, less fortified, and commercially rather than strategically positioned. Clearly, the period of military occupation was ending. The soldier-farmers of an earlier era were being transformed into farmer-soldiers. Their most important function now was to safeguard Ethiopia's vital new export, to ensure its production and channel it to Addis Abeba. The *nefṭennya* were still expected to fight and did so during the Italian campaign, but their military rôle was gradually being taken over by a professional army.[44] After the war, the transition was fully completed. At that time, settlers in the south were allowed to convert a portion of their *maderia* into *rist*.[45] With this measure, the tenancy system became full-blown: for the first time settlers gained heritable rights to land and thus were free to buy and sell it. This step strengthened the centre's alliance with the southern élite.

CONCLUSION

The changes affecting Sidamo cannot be disassociated from those at the centre. Southern settlers, although they continued to play a vital rôle as a local élite in the 1920s and '30s, were less free than their counterparts two generations earlier. An improved system of transportation and communications gradually brought more direct central influence to bear in the region. Southern landholders could no more step out of line than their Gedeo tenants. Most were expected to supervise the production of coffee, and they had no real choice but to export to Addis Abeba where all the best roads led. Merchants were regulated by the same limitations. A degree of capitalistic competition was permitted and even encouraged, but that was strictly supervised and only served the centre. Profits were possible, but they were in a sense at imperial discretion, 'granted' like a feudal reward, according to how tightly the centre chose to regulate the structure. Profits were generally maximized at the centre, and used by the emperor to promote further centralization and modernization. Capitalism sprang forth where it was most useful and efficient but was utilized within an updated feudal structure.

With the exception of a few state farms, the north lacked those commodities that would bring export revenues, and thus capitalistic development there remained even more retarded. In fact, the north was also peripheralized during the first half of the twentieth century.[46] As the south provided a valuable export, so the north served the centre by channelling its surplus agricultural produce to the capital and to provincial centres to supplement the lifestyles of the emperor's new wage labourers – whether bureaucrats, teachers or soldiers. Even this new and vital élite had to watch its step. It was not totally free to be innovative and individualistic, dependent as it was upon the emperor's approval and support. A bureaucratic feudalism thus persisted until the 1970s. The underdevelopment of the provinces strengthened the power and position of the monarchy and its dependent classes. Foreign-inspired projects for development failed, having been twisted to profit the bureaucratic élite through which they were channelled. Gedeo peasants, subjugated and exploited in the early twentieth century, unwittingly provided the resources to permit subjugation of their northern counterparts several decades later. Ethiopian peasants everywhere thus had a common cause in the revolution of 1974.

8

Vicious cycles: ivory, slaves, and arms on the new Maji frontier

PETER P. GARRETSON

By a little scrap of paper [a treaty]
Many countries have been lost.
In the morning we had nothing to eat,
How can we live if there is no food in the evening also?

From Kaffa to Wallega and Joti's country
And all along the frontier you make treaties.
Why do you do this?
You have us and we are brave soldiers.

From Massowah to Asmara runs the railway
And from Jibuti to Dire Dawa;
From Khartoum runs the boat to Gambela.

Officers let us think this over.
If we do not throw off this load which presses us
In the evening it will be too late.

A song sung by Menilek's soldiers[1]

The idea of a border is perhaps deceptively simple. All too often, borders appear only as blanks in historical writing, a sort of static no man's land, far removed from the momentous happenings located in political centres. And yet the more historians have investigated borders themselves – as for example Lattimore did for imperial China – the more dynamic and indeed crucial for political centres they appear to become.[2]

Such is certainly the case for the area roughly demarcated by the Sudan–Ethiopia border. Here was an old frontier, a changing and ill-defined boundary between empires located on the Nile to the west, Sennar for example, and those located in the highlands to the east, such as Abyssinia. Like most frontiers, this one was a place of refuge for outcasts and the oppressed from both sides. And like the inner Asian frontier of China in particular, this area furnished the launching pad for careers of a significant number of men who were able to capture central power. Emperor Susenyos of Abyssinia and Sultan Muhammad Ablikaylik of Sennar are only two examples.

It is against this long-established background of frontier history with its patterns of interaction between resources from the periphery and power at the centre that I want to place the present study of Maji. Maji was part of a 'new' frontier created by the expansion of Menilek's Shewan domains. It was a fortified town (*ketema*) and provincial capital located in the south-western corner of the new empire. To the west lay the British-administered Sudan, to the south Lake Turkana (formerly Lake Rudolf), and to the east the Omo River. Farther to the south-west lay British East Africa (later Kenya) and farther still was Uganda. From 1898 to 1936 Maji's effective hinterland extended well beyond the international border to include a significant portion of this whole region. Agents financed by Ethiopians in Maji – a ragtag group of 'Abyssinian poachers', 'outlaws', and 'Swahilis' – reached as far as the southern tip of Lake Turkana in British East Africa, as far as Acholiland and Karamojong in Uganda, and as far as Bor on the White Nile in the Sudan (see Map 12).

Two major themes are united in this chapter. The first is a depiction of Maji as an imperial sub-centre, a local provincial capital. Maji's influence on its hinterland appears to have reached out in a series of more or less concentric circles: (1) Dizi-speaking peoples in the highlands immediately around Maji were transformed into *gebbar* or serfs to support northern soldiers, (2) peoples farther afield, particularly in lower and drier areas were subjected to regular tribute collection through local chiefs, and (3) areas still farther away, often well across the formal border, were connected to Maji through trade, raids, and poaching.

The fate of all these zones was intertwined, for all were integrated into a single regional political economy focused on Maji. That is my second major theme: to show how the *gebbar* system in combination with the arms, ivory, and slave trade centred in Maji interacted with politics in Addis Abeba. During the early twentieth century, this interaction produced a pattern of ever-widening cycles of violence, a pattern that was to make Maji notorious.

I: ETHIOPIAN FRONTIER TRADITIONS AND MAJI

To understand the Ethiopians in Maji and their attitude toward neighbouring British colonies, we need to examine two different indigenous concepts of the frontier, one of which grew out of the other. Maji was the end product, the last frontier, of the expanding Shewan state in the late nineteenth century. At the same time, it was related to a much older frontier tradition in northern Ethiopia, one that can be seen, for example, in the province of Ḳwara well before the period under consideration here.

The whole history of Shewa can be seen in terms of a constantly expanding frontier, for the neighbouring peoples that she conquered enabled her to be catapulted into the leadership of the Ethiopian empire at the end of the nineteenth century. The process started in Menz in northern Shewa in the late seventeenth and eighteenth centuries, but expansion to the south and south-west was relatively slow until the reign of Sahle Sillasē who reigned from 1821

Map 12 The Upper Nile Basin: to illustrate Chapters 8 and 9

to 1847. It was during his reign that the Tulema Oromo, or Galla, in the immediate area of the future capital of Addis Abeba were finally absorbed, and parts of the northern Gurage to the south of the Awash River finally submitted.[3]

Menilek, who ruled from 1866 to 1913, supervised a rapid expansion of the Shewan state, giving a free hand to talented generals like *ras* Gobena Dachi to conquer the Oromo people. The first real check to the Shewan conquests in the south-west was presented by Gojjam, a more north-westerly province of the Ethiopian empire, nestled in the great bend of the Blue Nile. Gojjam too had been expanding towards the rich south-west with its traditional exports of gold, ivory and civet. A clash between Gojjam and Shewa was inevitable and took place at the Battle of Embabo in 1882, somewhat south of the Blue Nile. During the next two decades victorious Shewa over-ran Wellegga in the west and Kefa, Welaita, Jimma, Illubabor, Gimira and Maji in the south-west.[4]

Conquests (to oversimplify the actual events) were very differently treated depending on whether the local peoples collaborated with or resisted the Shewan conquerors.[5] Those who collaborated were generally allowed a fair degree of autonomy, like Jimma or the parts of Wellegga ruled by *dejazmach* Joti or *dejazmach* Kumsa (the subject of Triulzi's analysis in Chapter 2), while those areas that resisted, like Kefa, were put under a Shewan general like *ras* Welde Gīyorgis. Maji does not quite fit either of these categories. Maji did not really resist, yet it was given to *ras* Welde Gīyorgis and ruled by his follower *fītawrarī* Demṭē.[6] Like some other areas of the empire there was no strong indigenous centralized government – so a Shewan general was appointed and ruled over the various districts, either directly or sometimes through *balabbat*, the most prominent and/or pliable of local leaders or elders.

Once Welde Gīyorgis' administration was set up in Maji, his ambitious followers looked for new lands to conquer – new provinces that would perhaps be given to them. Some, particularly the imperial troops of Menilek assigned to the province, seemed content to settle as colonists or *nefṭennya*.[7] The Shewan land-tenure system in the south enabled them to take unto themselves, depending on their rank, a number of *gebbar* or peasant serfs to labour for them and give them a percentage of their crop.[8] This whole array of *balabbat*, *nefṭennya* and *gebbar* is generally referred to as the *gebbar* system. In the case of Maji, it seems to have been relatively benign in the early years of imperial rule, but it grew increasingly harsh. By the 1920s and '30s it was perhaps the most notoriously oppressive *gebbar* system within the Ethiopian empire. The individual *gebbar* was initially similar in a very general way to a serf in Eastern Europe, but by the 1930s some districts were reduced virtually to producing slaves, and only after World War II was there a change to a tenant system.

Many of *ras* Welde Gīyorgis' followers were eager to continue the expansion of Shewa, conquer new lands and be given more *gebbar* and new lands of their own – in other words, to continue the process of Shewan expansion set in motion far to the north more than a century before.[9] But two problems stood in their way: a wide expanse of lowlands, where no highlander would ever conceive of living permanently, and the artificial border established by the British.

In contrast to the Shewan frontier was the western Ethiopian frontier to the north, most especially the frontier province of Ḳwara. Ethiopian highland and Blue Nile lowland states had fought over the lowlands west of Ḳwara for centuries, the last Nile states being those ruled by the Funj and the Egyptians.[10] While Shewa had encountered no opponents equal or superior to her in power in her southern expansion, Ḳwara had fought a long struggle, sometimes on the defensive but always raiding and hunting in the lowland areas between the settled valley of the Nile, with its major tributaries, and the Ethiopian highlands.[11] To a new governor appointed to the recently conquered Maji, the neighbouring lowlands of the Sudan and Uganda presented extremely favourable and traditional potential for advancement within Ethiopia's feudal structure. An ambitious young noble could model himself on someone like emperor Tēwodros (1855–68), who had won his spurs on the frontier between Ethiopia and the Sudan. From his base in the province of Ḳwara, Tēwodros had acted as a bandit, poacher and warrior, raiding the lowlands and his neighbours for cattle, loot and slaves. Slowly he built up a faithful band, which, as success crowned success, grew into a veritable army. With this increased strength he was eventually taken seriously at the highest levels of Ethiopia's leadership. He was skilful enough to build the best army in Ethiopia and used it to make himself emperor.[12]

A new governor of Maji could hardly aim so high, but Maji was potentially as advantageous a post as Kwara, Tēwodros' first province. It too could be a stepping stone to swift advancement. There a young noble could build up a powerful following, and perhaps a sizeable army, by several means. First, like Tēwodros he could gain a reputation for bravery and military prowess among the soldiers, poachers and hangers-on at Maji. Then he could attract unattached soldiers by his prestige. If his following became skilful and experienced, they could hope to have success as hunters and raiders. As hunters they could shoot various game for meat, but more especially lion, giraffe, and elephant. Any man who had shot a large game animal was traditionally entitled to certain privileges in Ethiopia. He could then be considered a real leader. *Lij* Iyasu, who replaced Menilek as emperor, travelled to south-western Ethiopia for this very reason. Elephant and their ivory, as well as slaves, held forth even greater rewards. For the governor they provided a painless method of paying tribute, and his remaining share could be sold and the proceeds used for personal use and for distribution among his followers.[13]

However, Ethiopians soon realized Maji was a peripheral, frontier province with a difference. Ivory could not only be collected there in large quantities, but could then be sold for an even larger profit. The slave and gun trade too became increasingly profitable in a greater and greater spiral of violence. A governor could look forward to a lucrative appointment in Maji which would enable him to pay off heavy debts contracted elsewhere and provide capital for political or commercial ambitions.

THE ESTABLISHMENT OF MAJI

Colonists in Maji were inheritors of two different frontier traditions, the northern Tēwodros tradition and the Shewan tradition; in combination they determined the attitude towards the lowlands surrounding Maji. In the Maji highlands themselves the main determinant in establishing a new administration was the Shewan frontier tradition.

When *ras* Welde Gīyorgis had completed the conquest of Kefa shortly after the Battle of Adwa, his next campaign was into the southern reaches of Kefa in late 1897 and early 1898. The only detailed accounts of this campaign, by someone who actually travelled into what was later to be called Maji, were written by a Russian, A. K. Bulatovitch. Only on the Golda/Maji frontier was any resistance encountered, probably primary resistance by peoples whom the conquerors from the north were to call Tishana. The first garrison town was set up in the Maji district of Beru and the whole of the Maji and Boma highlands were occupied, including the Belodiya, Tid, Tirma and highland Boma Murle areas.[14]

Soon the Maji garrison was established further south, near the lands of the most powerful and respected religious figure in the area, the Maji *kure*.[15] Here the traditional Shewan core of provincial administration was set up. Built on a commanding hill were a fortified encampment or *gibbī* (the personal headquarters of the governor), a church and a market. All were carefully observed and guarded by the governor and his retinue of soldiers. Once the garrison was firmly established a constant food supply had to be guaranteed. This was managed in two ways: local tribesmen were directly assigned to soldiers as *gebbar*, or else tribute in kind was obtained through a local leader like the Maji *kure*, usually called a *balabbat*. Initially, the *kure* may have had some power and influence, but by 1909–10 he was a pathetic figure. The initial administration of *ras* Welde Gīyorgis was relatively mild in comparison with what was to follow.[16] From the initial conquest until 1936 the Boma plateau, although it was delineated as part of the Sudan by the treaty of 1907, was considered to be and administered as an integral part of Ethiopia.[17]

MAJI AND THE CRISIS OF 1910–11

The first overlord of Maji, from 1897 to 1910, was *ras* Welde Gīyorgis, and his subordinate in Maji was *fītawrarī* (and later *dejazmach*) Demtc̣. An overlord in a conquered province like Maji usually exercised *ḳurach*, that is to say, he was entitled to tribute, and certain legal cases, particularly those involving murder, had to be referred to him. During this period there is no evidence of a *neggadras*, or head of merchants, having been appointed to Maji proper. This absence, if indeed it was an absence, may be accounted for by the fact that in 1909 *ras* Welde Gīyorgis gave a monopoly of Maji's most lucrative export, ivory, to an Indian, thinking by this means to increase his revenues. This did not happen and the monopoly lapsed. It would have lapsed anyway, since 1910 was a period of considerable political change throughout Ethiopia, and Welde Gīyorgis was transferred to another province.[18]

The change began in the centre and had a direct influence on the periphery throughout the empire. Emperor Menilek had suffered a cerebral haemorrhage and by early 1910 was no longer able to take his usually active part in administration. The empress Ṭaytu tried to fill the power vacuum but was challenged by some of Menilek's generals, prominent among whom was *ras* Tesemma Nado. The empress Ṭaytu did not make any new appointments in the south-west of Ethiopia, as she did elsewhere, but upon her removal from active participation from politics in 1910 it was decided to appoint *ras* Welde Gīyorgis to Begemdir in northern Ethiopia, with *ḳurach* over neighbouring provinces, the core area of Ṭaytu's support.[19]

Dejazmach Birru Haile Mariam was appointed to replace *ras* Welde Gīyorgis in Kefa and Maji; he took up his new post within a month of the departure of Welde Gīyorgis and *dejazmach* Demṭē. The change-over was catastrophic for Maji's people and economy. Maji's whole garrison was withdrawn, and *dejazmach* Demṭē took with him not only his and *ras* Welde Gīyorgis' troops but some of the imperial soldiers as well. These soldiers in turn collected as many of the *gebbar* as they could to take north as slaves, or else raided the neighbourhood – especially the Boma plateau – to get more cattle, sheep, and any other movable booty they could capture. Maji and its immediate surroundings were denuded after Demṭē had left in June 1910. One estimate said that the population of Maji dropped from thousands to a few hundred in 1925.[20]

As the conquerors from the north started to raid preparatory to leaving, resistance among the original inhabitants of Maji and her neighbours began to be organized. This resistance coalesced around two figures, who may have been *balabbat*, and a third, the *balabbat* Debo who had been co-opted by the northern administration. Debo was the *kure* or the major religious figure of the local peoples, and had been made a *fītawrarī*. Although he is said to have resisted *ras* Welde Gīyorgis in the very early days of his rule, he soon became addicted to imported liquor and did what he was told. Further to the north two figures arose to challenge the *gebbar* system more forcefully. The first, Mwanga, was leader of the people of the Boma plateau as well as some within Maji; the second was Serie, leader of the Belodiya, the original inhabitants of Maji province. Mwanga had led resistance in the area for about thirteen years and had a following of 400–500 rifles. His headquarters were on the highland sources of the Akobo river, and he was accepted as the leader of the Tid and highland Murle, as well as some other groups within Maji proper. Serie built his power base in the northern reaches of Maji but also had followers from the neighbouring provinces of Gimira and Golda to the north and west. His following was much larger, estimated at 3,000 by Darley, a former British army officer and then prosperous elephant hunter. None the less, Serie forged a brief alliance among 'all the remaining Shangallas against the Abyssinians', isolating and defeating military posts between the garrisons of Maji and Kefa. He died some time between 1914 and 1918, still resisting the northern conquerors of Maji. Less than a decade later this temporary alliance was renewed and was given the name Tishana by the Ethiopians from the north.[21]

Thus when *dejazmach* Birru arrived in Maji he was faced with some very serious problems. The administration of the province had completely broken down; all that survived was the ivory trade which had been spared due to the efforts of Henry Darley and the Swahili. The *gebbar* system on which he expected his garrison to depend for food was totally disrupted. The only way a major portion of the troops he had brought could be adequately fed was to send them on campaign. Towards the north was his relative *ras* Tesemma (also his main supporter), to the east the Omo River lowlands. Therefore he could not campaign in those directions. But to the south and west were lands not yet extensively explored, let alone raided, and so in 1910 his son Desta was sent out with a large number of troops to reconnoitre. After being turned back by the Didinga, Desta was arrested by the British officer Tanner among the Karamojong.[22]

Dejazmach Birru's resources must have been severely stretched at this time, for not only had Desta been sent far to the south but the resistance of Mwanga to the west and north of Maji and Serie further north would have required large numbers of troops to be contained. Before any kind of order could be brought to the province, *dejazmach* Birru was recalled to Addis Abeba. More important was the fact that his son Desta Birru and the soldiers remained. They were the most powerful, entrenched, stable, and long-lasting factor in Maji's unfortunate history, from 1910 to at least 1936. Even by 1924, out of a total of 66 principal officers in the Maji area, 41 were still surviving officers of *dejazmach* Birru.[23]

John Lamphear has said in a recent article that *dejazmach* Birru was recalled in May 1911 on account of the border violations of his son Desta, and Birru's own claims to the Turkana, Suk, and Karamojong lands. But this was, perhaps, only half the story. For his main supporter within the Byzantine politics of Ethiopia was *ras* Tesemma. *Ras* Tesemma died on 10 April 1911, and Birru could no longer be sure that events would go smoothly at the centre of power at Addis Abeba. However, his wife *weyzero* Sehin was the sister of the new ruler of Ethiopia, *lij* Iyasu, the grandson of emperor Menilek. This assured his remaining in power in Maji for a time, but *dejazmach* Lu'ul Seged replaced him as governor of Kefa by June 1911.[24]

MAJI, 1911–22

After 1912 the regional political situation became confused, and Maji had a rapid succession of different governors and different overlords ruling from

Kefa. It is not clear whether governors from Kefa exercised *ḳurach*, and, if so, what kind. What does stand out is that power in Maji rested firmly in the hands of Birru's soldiers, the *neftennya*. A similar situation existed in other parts of south-west Ethiopia.[25] Kefa and Illubabor had been ruled until 1910 and 1911, respectively, by two of emperor Menilek's most powerful generals. Welde Gīyorgis' transfer to the north, and Tesemma's death, transformed the stable economic and political situation in south-west Ethiopia. *Dejazmach* Birru is but one example of a number of political lightweights who were temporarily given parts of the former generals' dominions. Trade in everything but slaves slumped drastically, and the slave trade came to replace ivory as the basis of the economy of the south-west.[26] The Tishana and Gimira fought bitterly against the new governors, while *lij* Iyasu, still only a boy of sixteen, came to Gimira to assist some of his hard-pressed governors, especially *dejazmach* Mulugēta of Gimira.[27] By 1913 the Tishana and Gimira revolts seem to have largely subsided. Throughout, Desta Birru remained the major local figure in Maji, a position he retained until his death in June 1922.

Desta Birru did not become active again until the next major crisis at the centre, in 1915–19.[28] This was the period when the future emperor Haile Selassie rose to power as regent, removing *lij* Iyasu from the centre of the political stage. It took an inordinate amount of time since Iyasu escaped after the defeat of the major part of his supporters at the Battle of Segale on 22 October 1916.[29] Troops throughout the empire were mobilized to chase him, and major governors of the south-west took large portions of their armies to the north to help hunt Iyasu down.[30] Thus the soldiers who remained in Maji were allowed to have a free rein, with little guidance or control from the centre.

This, then, is the background for the Battle of Kangalla in May 1918, when *dejazmach* Desta's troops were defeated by a combined force of Sudanese troops and King's African Rifles in Sudanese territory north-west of Lake Turkana.[31] The Battle of Kangalla also marked the climax of Ethiopian influence and the last time large numbers of Ethiopian troops were used outside the Maji/Boma highlands. However, the Ethiopians retained complete control of the Boma plateau, still had an official governor for the Turkana, remained a very important influence among the Toposa, and still carried out extensive poaching activities among the Didinga, Murle, Boya, Latuka, and Bari.[32]

The Battle of Kangalla led directly to the recall to Addis Abeba of *dejazmach* Desta Birru, governor of Maji.[33] It was made clear to him that the border would have to be respected in the future, yet he officially remained governor of Maji.[34] His most important follower, *fītawrarī* Meshesha, was a prominent figure at the time of the Battle of Kangalla and was a leader of the local soldier-settlers.[35] No matter what governor was appointed over Maji by Addis Abeba from 1910 onwards, it was the soldiers of *dejazmach* Birru and his son *dejazmach* Desta Birru who were the most consistent and powerful element in the politics of Maji, controlling the majority of the *gebbar*. It was they who insisted on continuing the ivory, arms, and slave trade despite all the pressure applied by the central government in Addis Abeba, by the new governors, special commissioners and slavery department officials, and by British Consuls. The pressure against the soldier-settlers mounted after 1918 and the Battle of Kangalla.

First in January 1919 a special Ethiopian–British commission was sent to Maji under Major Athill and an Ethiopian officer, and a number of Swahili were removed from Ethiopia and repatriated, mostly to Mombasa. Then in 1920 the first British Consul, Major Hawkins, was appointed to Maji. Pressure also came from quite a different source. In 1922 the second Tishana revolt against the northerners began, led by a certain Mirba who eventually controlled some 5,000 square miles in northern Maji, eastern Gimira, and southern Kefa. By mid-1921 the slave trade was on the increase in the south-west, perhaps partly because of the influenza epidemic of 1919–20 that decimated the domestic slave population of Ethiopia. According to some, the increased slave trade in the south-west was a direct result of the need to replenish the depleted stocks of slaves in Shewa and further north.[36]

When *dejazmach* Desta and *fītawrarī* Meshesha were recalled to Addis Abeba in 1922, a brutal looting of Maji took place – by then a usual occurrence whenever a governor was replaced.[37] It was estimated that Maji's population fell to four thousand, having been about forty thousand in 1910.[38] The Tishana, desperate to retrieve some of their enslaved relations, attacked the retreating troops of *fītawrarī* Meshesha and raided peoples farther to the south, so that they could themselves take slaves which they could trade in turn for guns.

MAJI, 1922–36

The new governor appointed after *dejazmach* Desta's death was *dejazmach* Mekuriya, a close relative of the regent *ras* Teferi (the future emperor Haile Selassie). He was supposed to deal with the frontier, arms, and slavery problems but was a hopeless failure in solving all three. Ethiopia's entry into the League of Nations and her promise to eradicate the slave trade within her boundaries put further pressure on the central government to deal with Maji, one of Ethiopia's most intractable slaving provinces. At first there was a good deal of optimism, especially from the new British Consul, Hodson, but the old guard, the soldier-settlers, refused to change their ways and *dejazmach* Mekuriya was soon recalled.[39]

The older pattern was repeated. The departing governor, *dejazmach* Mekuriya, raided Maji and its surroundings and made off with some 18,000 cattle and 50,000 sheep. His wife, *weyzero* Asselefech, carried out at least one raid against the Tishana, obtaining 93 slaves. The Tishana counter-attacked, killing everyone in the military post of Shasha; they were led by Gallajira at the head of some 400–500 rifles.[40] Gallajira, like Serie a decade before, had forged an alliance between men from Gimira, Maji, and even Kefa.

Fītawrarī Wesenē became the new governor in 1925, and Maji was put firmly under the *kurach* of Kefa and its new governor *dejazmach* Habte Mika'ēl.[41] The local settlers still looked to *fītawrarī* Meshesha as their leader. A major attack was launched on the Tishana, the northerners having amassed a six-to-one superiority in arms, and many men, women and children were killed. The Tishana, in retaliation, desperately raided parts of Maji that were relatively undefended, that is, the surroundings south of the garrison of Maji and out to the Boma plateau. By the middle of 1925, when it was clear that the battle had become hopelessly one-sided, resistance broke down.[42] The Maji *kure* played no known rôle in the resistance,[43] and the indigenous peoples of Maji and Boma, the Tid, Tirma, and Murle suffered severely.[44] The Boma plateau was so denuded that an entirely new people, the Kichepo, led by Chief Losanga, appeared and came to settle there.[45] Within a few years Losanga was to provide the main nucleus of opposition to the raids of the northern settlers.

From 1925 to 1932 Maji had at least six different governors, including *ras* Kebbede Mengesha, *ras* Getachchew Abbate, *dejazmach* Asefe, *fītawrarī* Aggedew, *dejazmach* Debbebe and *dejazmach* Mengesha Yilma.[46] Occasionally the British Consuls were optimistic that one or other of the governors would be successful against the entrenched soldier-settlers, but none was. Meanwhile, *dejazmach* Ergetē slowly emerged as the leading settler.[47] Only one element of the trading complex of arms, slaves, and ivory was brought under control during this period. Through the efforts of the British Consuls Hodson and Holland in 1928, most of the Baluchi and Swahili traders were repatriated to India and East Africa, and one of the largest sources of liquid capital in Maji was staunched.[48] What little trade that remained in the Sudanese lowlands was now in the hands of the Toposa.[49] But it should be remembered that the ivory trade had been in steady decline since 1924,[50] and the administration of the Sudan and Kenya governments had been slowly approaching the Ethiopian border, curtailing the trading and poaching activities of Maji.[51]

The period 1932–6 saw an increase in the spiral of violence induced by the internal Ethiopian slave trade and arms trade in combination with the third Tishana revolt. The Tishana refused to submit to the *gebbar* system, and severe intertribal raiding spread throughout Maji and Boma, largely instigated by the administration. But by now the Tishana were in league with the Governor, Ergetē, and with the Maji leader Burji, in the trading of slaves across the Omo to Bonga and then to Jimma. For one section of the Tirma, the depredations were so severe that the whole population took refuge in the Sudanese lowlands around Jabal Kathangor. *Dejazmach* Mengesha Yilma tried in November 1932 to abolish the *gebbar* system, but failed; the resistance of the northern settlers was too strong. The next governor, *ras* Getachchew Abbate, fared no better.[52]

As a last resort emperor Haile Selassie annexed Maji as his personal property (*madbēt*), and appointed *fītawrarī* Zewdē Ayyelle as a governor with Daniel Sandford as his adviser. Maji was declared a model province in 1935, in an attempt to reform and 'modernize' the provincial administration along the lines that had already been attempted in Chercher province. Salaried officials were to be introduced, trade encouraged, and the abuses of the *gebbar* system stamped out. At first, significant progress seemed to be under way. Of particular note was a proclamation once again abolishing the *gebbar* system. This was the second or third such proclamation of the century; none had any real effect. But the emperor's absence from Addis Abeba, as he campaigned against the Italians in the north, and the resistance (once more) of the settlers, were used as excuses to prevent any substantive change. The British occupation of the Boma plateau in June 1936, and the Italian occupation of Maji shortly afterwards, ended the model province experiment. It was the Italians rather than the emperor who drove out the northern soldier-settlers. It might be added that the lot of the original inhabitants of Maji did not improve during the Italian occupation, for the Eritrean troops and low-ranking soldiers who made up the Italian garrison were just as brutal, and raided just as effectively as northern settlers had done before the Italian occupation.[53]

II: TRADERS AND POACHERS

Maji and its hinterland did not only constitute an Ethiopian frontier, be it from the perspective of Shewa or a potential emperor Tēwodros – they also constituted the last frontier of the East African and Sudanese ivory trade. The Sudanese ivory trade, centred on Khartoum, had been sharply curtailed by the Mahdiyya after 1882, making it virtually impossible for the Sudan to export any substantial quantities of ivory.[54] At this time Arabs had only just penetrated into the far reaches of eastern Equatoria among the Latuka and the Toposa.[55] The East African ivory trade had a greater impact on Maji's hinterland, for its influence was continuous from the 1880s onwards. Maji, an extension of the Shewan feudal state, encountered a thriving Zanzibari and Indian capitalized trade and then successfully absorbed it.

Thus Maji became a centre for the export of ivory for an extremely large hinterland stretching deep into Kenya to the west of Lake Turkana (formerly Lake Rudolf), into eastern Uganda, deep into the Sudan across the Bahr-al-Jabal (the White Nile) as far north as Bor, and into the Murle and Anuak lands to its east. The British Consul in Maji, Major Hawkins, estimated the value of ivory taken from the Sudan early in the 1920s as more than £10,000.[56]

A recent authority on the southern Sudan asserts that a regular caravan trade between Maji and Mbale was led by men like Bwangani in the late nineteenth century.[57] This trade, he continues, attracted 'African adventurers – Swahili, Baluchi and others – who were employed to hunt ivory by Ethiopian merchants at Maji'. There are some rather serious errors here. Maji, as we have seen, was not conquered until 1898 by *ras* Welde Gīyorgis' occupying army. Previously no town or people by the name of Maji is known to have existed. Kefa, the neighbouring province to the north, had not been finally conquered and occupied until the late 1890s, and for many decades had fiercely resisted conquest by Ethiopians from the north, thus effectively

9 Weighing of ivory, probably for taxation purposes, at a customs gate outside Addis Abeba. From the 'Mission Ozil' album of 1908, in the Institute of Ethiopian Studies, Addis Abeba

shielding the Maji highlands from Menilek's relentless expansion into the south-west. None of the early travellers indicate an Ethiopian military or commercial presence (some even comment on the lack of it in the plateau or lowland areas).[58] Regular Ethiopian caravans hardly seem possible. It seems much more likely that the first ivory caravans were Swahili-led, as the name Bwangani would seem to indicate.

Thus the East African ivory trade added a new dynamic to a traditional Ethiopian ivory trade. The 'Arab', Ganda, and Baluchi 'poachers' and 'outlaws' were in no way a part of the Ethiopian feudal system but were fairly comfortably absorbed and manipulated by it.[59] Traditionally, Ethiopian governors had supplied especially gifted Ethiopian hunters with guns, so long as they recognized the governor and gave him a specific portion of the ivory taken on the hunt. When exported from the province the ivory would also be taxed at customs posts called *kella*.[60] A Swahili would be regarded in much the same way by an Ethiopian governor. Of course, his caravan would often be on a larger scale, and an investment of more guns, cartridges, and food supplies would be called for. The difference was that a Swahili or Ganda was uninterested in and, of course, incapable of advancing within the Ethiopian political system; his main motive was not political but economic. Furthermore, most of the Swahili had greater experience of hunting and travelling in the Lake Turkana lowland areas, and thus were often more successful hunters than highlanders. Highland Ethiopians had an ingrained fear of the lowlands and its fevers, which were considered to be deadly to one brought up in the highlands.[61]

One of the more curious and fascinating aspects of Maji's history is how it

10 A minor chief of the south-west, out hunting. From the 'Mission Ozil' album of 1908, in the Institute of Ethiopian Studies, Addis Abeba

was able to absorb so successfully the Swahili- and Baluchi-led traders and hunters formerly based in East Africa and, especially after 1904, in Mbale. The first contact between Maji and the East African ivory trade seems to have taken place in 1902. By 1909 Maji was being called the 'chief market' in south-west Ethiopia for ivory. This remarkable growth was due to a complicated combination of circumstances, not the least of which were British regulations in the territories they governed, which sought to control the destruction of elephant herds.[62]

Regulations in the 1890s and after the turn of the century in the Sudan, Uganda and British East Africa, prevented the export through their respective territories of immature or female ivory. Ethiopia had no such regulations and so the only legal export route for these two types of ivory was through Maji. A further spur to the growth of Maji as an ivory centre as opposed to Mbale occurred in February of 1906. A large group of Swahilis raided the Toposa for the first time and looted more than 1,100 cattle, 4,000 sheep, and many donkeys and goats. One informant, 'Karamoja' Bell, arrived shortly afterwards and reported the incident to the government, and many of the Swahili, fearing repercussions, fled. A fair number may very well have ended up in Maji and on the Boma plateau. The best example was Idi Wad Sheru who at that time changed the base of his operations from Mbale to Maji.[63]

One of the main problems inhibiting the growth of trade for Maji was the lack of capital to equip hunting and trading expeditions. This problem was largely solved by three initiatives between 1909 and 1911. In 1909 *ras* Welde Gīyorgis gave a monopoly for the whole of the ivory trade in Kefa and Maji to an Indian firm.[64] Much of the ivory exported from Addis Abeba was in the hands of the Indian company of Mohamedally, one of the largest import/export firms in Ethiopia, and it is safe to say that it was involved in Maji.[65] In the same year, 1909, Allidina Visram, the head of the largest East African company involved in the ivory trade, visited Addis Abeba.[66] It is hard to believe that Maji and its ivory potential was not one of his reasons for travelling the long and difficult caravan route to Addis Abeba (there was no railway at the time), especially since he was involved in the other end of the ivory trade centred at Mbale.

Finally, the Bank of Abyssinia lent some £2,000 to local Maji merchants, round about 1910, as part of its general policy of encouraging small, local Ethiopian traders.[67] Most of the money was quickly funnelled into the hands of local Ethiopian merchants and ivory traders in Maji. They acted as middlemen to the Swahili, Baluchi, and other 'outlaw' types at Maji who did the actual trading and hunting. The money was lent at exorbitant rates of interest and was used to buy ammunition, guns, and supplies for the next hunting and raiding trip.[68] It was the poorest of the traders who suffered most. When a trader had made a substantial profit he rarely went back into the field to take the great risks involved, but lent his capital to a poorer and less fortunate colleague.

On the spot in Maji, Henry Darley invested a similar and probably larger amount of capital in the trade at the same time as the Bank of Abyssinia. The years 1910–11, as we have seen, were the crucial time, when *dejazmach* Demtē and his overlord *ras* Welde Gīyorgis were replaced by *dejazmach* Birru.[69] Darley's £2,000 or more assured not only a handsome profit but also a smooth transition from one provincial government, with its associated merchants, to another. The continuity of the ivory trade and the rôle of the Swahili were maintained.

During this period the arms trade began to play a larger and larger rôle. Arms were increasingly given to Sudanese and Ugandan peoples in exchange for ivory, food, and assistance of all kinds.[70] The slave trade seems to have remained only a minor part of the commerce outside Ethiopia and was rampant only within the empire and on the Boma plateau. Its links were increasingly closer to the *gebbar* system than to the ivory trade of the Maji hinterland in the Sudan.[71] The slave trade seems to have grown within Ethiopia as the ivory trade declined, in effect replacing it.

From 1910 to 1928 several factors affected the ivory and arms trade.[72] The

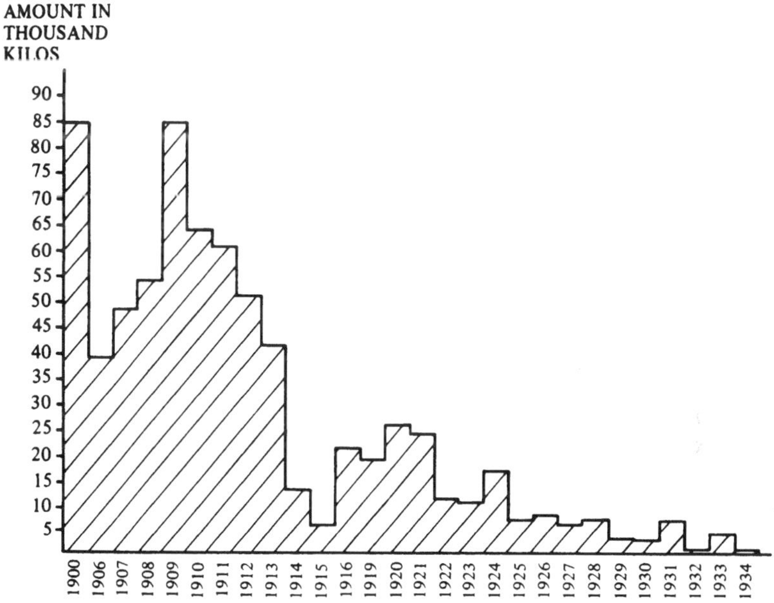

Fig. 3 Ethiopian ivory exports[76]

main one was the slow spread of the administration of the Sudan, Uganda, and British East African governments. The Sudan government took over the Murle (1912), the Latuka (1914), the Boya (1918), the Didinga (1922) and finally the Toposa (1926). Each expansion of the Sudan government administration 'pacified' another portion of Maji's hinterland. Similarly, Uganda moved into Acholiland and then into Karamoja (1910). British East Africa did not establish posts in northern Turkanaland until 1926, although it had a much longer presence among the southern sections of the Turkana. This slow spread of British administration allowed the ivory and arms trade to flourish openly for many years among the Turkana and Toposa and surreptitiously among many other peoples. The bulk of the Swahili, Baluchi, Ganda, and other traders and 'outlaws' were not repatriated until 1928, well after the occupation of Toposaland.[73] Before the late 1920s a good deal of the prosperity of Maji was dependent on the ivory trade, and it in turn was one of the most lucrative of Ethiopian exports.[74] A glance at Figure 3 will show that the trade had been steadily declining in the 1920s throughout Ethiopia. The slave trade within Ethiopia – rather than the arms and ivory trade into the neighbouring colonies – had become the major commercial element at Maji by then.

It seems clear that the slave trade was not only linked closely to the ivory and arms trade, but also to the Tishana revolts, especially during and after the

11 Anuak chief of Gambela, photographed by the Bonchamps Mission, 1897–8; from an album in the Institute of Ethiopian Studies, Addis Abeba

early 1920s. 'The Abyssinians by carrying off the [Tishana] women and children, have made the Tishana their mortal enemies . . . Slave-traders . . . are ever welcome in the country as they purchase captives from the Tishana.' Captive slaves were exchanged for guns so that the Tishana could resist their rulers more effectively. In order to obtain the slaves, the Tishana raided less well-armed peoples far and wide within Maji and out on to the Boma plateau.[75] Thus was the spiral of violence reinforced.

III: MAJI'S IMPACT ON SELECTED SUDANESE PEOPLES

The Boma plateau, as we have seen, experienced the greatest degree of Ethiopian influence radiating from the garrison town of Maji. Nowhere in the lowlands to the north, south, or west of the border was Ethiopia's influence so great or so long-lasting. There is already a growing literature on north-east Uganda and north-west Kenya, pointing out Ethiopia's impact on the Karamojong and the Turkana.[77] But virtually nothing has been written on Maji's parallel and even greater influence on south-eastern Sudan. While Barber and Collins[78] stress the rôle and influence of Ethiopians in northern Uganda, John Lamphear stresses indigenous Turkana leadership assisted by Ethiopian and Swahili individuals or groups.[79] The latter clearly seems to be the pattern among the various peoples of the Sudan that were influenced by Maji.

As one would expect, those peoples closest to Maji tended to experience the greatest influence, but this was not always the case, as, for example, with the Murle. The Toposa and the northern sections of the Turkana were the peoples the most influenced by Ethiopia (apart from the people of the Boma plateau who were virtually a part of the Ethiopian empire until 1936). Only among the Turkana and the Toposa are there specific references to the extraction of tribute and the appointment of Ethiopian 'chiefs'.

Thus the Toposa and the Turkana, along with a few small neighbouring peoples, can be considered as an inner sphere where Ethiopian influence was particularly marked. Farther afield to the north were the Murle and the Anuak, who, although they were close to the Boma plateau to the east, never seem to have paid tribute or had 'chiefs' selected from their midst. None the less, like peoples farther to the west, they provided guides for poachers and traded ivory in return for meat, arms and ammunition. This was also the pattern among the Bari, the Latuka, the Didinga, and the inhabitants of Jabal Lafon. Each will be dealt with in turn.

THE INNER SPHERE OF ETHIOPIAN INFLUENCE IN SOUTH-EASTERN SUDAN

The Turkana and the Toposa were the two main peoples of the inner circle. Both paid tribute and had 'chiefs' appointed from Ethiopia at various times. Other smaller populations nearer the Omo Delta often seem to have been under similar Ethiopian influence, but there is little documentation on them. Also, it is sometimes unclear whether Ethiopian influence in this area came via Maji or Bako, the Ethiopian provincial capital just to the east of Maji.

The northern section of the Turkana was considered an integral part of the hinterland of Maji, although unlike the Boma plateau a garrison town was never built there. Tribute was levied at least half a dozen times between 1900 and 1923, and it was almost certainly collected more times than that. An official Ethiopian governor seems to have been appointed up to 1921, and local elders, already prominent in their communities, were recognized by the Ethiopians as chiefs. Ethiopian relations with the Turkana's neighbours to the north, the Marille and Nyangatom, appear to have been similar in these two respects, as indeed in most others.[80]

But Ethiopia's relations with the Turkana were not merely on a formal political level but involved trade in ivory, arms, cattle, and slaves. Trade and the acquisition of all four of these items were, of course, intimately linked. Very often when the ivory trade had not gone well the 'traders' became 'outlaws' by raiding cattle from neighbouring peoples or from different Turkana sections, in order to make up the difference necessary to pay their loans and debts in Maji. Also, Ethiopian arms could be directly exchanged for cattle and the cattle driven all the way to Maji and be exchanged there.[81] Captives were sometimes taken on the raid, generally women and children (the men were usually killed), and these might be taken to Maji to be sold as slaves. But it should be remembered that slave-raiding was much more widespread within Ethiopia and particularly in south-west Ethiopia; slaving into British territories was insignificant from the Ethiopian perspective – in the dozens rather than in the hundreds.[82]

The other major group of peoples within the inner circle of Ethiopian control were the Toposa. While only a relatively small number of Turkana were to be found in the Sudan and those largely while grazing cattle in the dry season, the majority of the Toposa lived permanently in the Sudan and made up most of the inhabitants of Equatoria Province's Eastern District. There were frequent cases of Ethiopians exacting tribute from the Toposa, and those elders who were popular and highly regarded were often appointed as Toposa chiefs by Ethiopians from Maji.[83] Clearly there are similarities between Turkana and Toposa relations with Maji. However, the Swahili 'outlaws' had a great deal more influence among the Toposa than they did among the Turkana. Intermarriage between Swahili men (they are called Salwahin by the Toposa to this day) and Toposa women was common, and so were Toposa names among the Swahili.[84] In fact, many of the raids and poaching incidents attributed to 'Abyssinian poachers' turned out to have been the deeds of the Toposa.[85]

One of the key differences between the Toposa and the Turkana was that Toposaland lay on the trade route between Maji and Mbale.[86] In fact Toposa was a *lingua franca* throughout most of Eastern Equatoria and west of Lake Rudolf.[87] Toposaland was not really on the shortest route between the two centres but was the only one with dependable year-round sources for water. It is interesting to note that maps still list Ethiopian-language (Amharic and Oromo) place names for many of the water sources along this route.[88] Another major difference between the Turkana and the Toposa is that Toposaland was a source not only of ivory for the visitors from Maji but also of grain and donkeys.[89] It was the only area in the whole region that had donkeys in large supply, donkeys being a necessity particularly in ivory areas where porters were difficult to obtain.

Toposaland then was a centre for Ethiopian, but more especially for Swahili activities in southern Sudan and northern Uganda.[90] There grain supplies and baggage animals could be purchased and guides obtained in exchange for arms or cattle.[91] Ivory, of course, was the greatest lure and Toposaland was regarded as one of the last great frontiers for ivory, complete with an 'elephant cemetery'.[92] The Toposa too were victims of a spiral of violence so often encountered in the ivory trade, but again, as with the Turkana, slave-raiding and -trading did not play such a large rôle as they had within the Sudan in the nineteenth century. The core of the trade involved the exchange of arms and ammunition from Ethiopia for Toposa ivory.[93] Increasingly, however, Swahili combined with the Toposa to raid neighbouring peoples for cattle, which were then traded.[94] This increased intertribal raiding, already exacerbated by droughts within Turkanaland.[95] Maji's influence among the Toposa, though perhaps declining, lasted until 1926, when the Sudan government's administration moved into the area.

THE OUTER SPHERE OF ETHIOPIAN INFLUENCE IN SOUTH-EASTERN SUDAN

North and north-west of the Turkana and Toposa were the Didinga, Latuka, Bari, Päri, and Murle. Each was influenced very much less by Maji than the Turkana or Toposa. But none the less Maji's influence was significant economically if not so much politically.

The Didinga were in the outer ring of Maji's influence in the southern Sudan. Chiefs were not appointed, nor does tribute seem to have been levied from Maji. Until their 'pacification' in 1922, the Didinga were a centre of raids into many of the surrounding tribes, raids that were often blamed on 'Abyssinian poachers'. Many of these so-called 'Abyssinians' were in fact men who had fled or escaped from the Ugandan and British East African administrations, including Ganda, Acholi and other outlaws and malcontents.[96]

However, Ethiopians were involved in Didinga trade, and it was a potential stopping place on the Maji trade route to Mbale, Karamojong, and Acholiland. Moreover, Ethiopians and Swahilis were definitely involved, often in alliance with Toposa, on raids against the Didinga, and on one occasion raided them independently with a force of some 150 rifles. *Dejazmach* Birru in 1910 announced that he would build a capital among the Didinga, but the Didinga defeated his troops. Another threat to take over the Didinga in 1920 was also unsuccessful. The mountainous Didinga highlands must have reminded the Shewan leaders and troops of their own highland climate, for Didingaland was the only Sudanese area (other than the Boma plateau) in which they contemplated building a fortified garrison. The establishment of Sudanese administration among the Didinga in the early 1920s slowly but severely curtailed Maji's activities in the area.[97]

West of the Toposa, the area where the Ethiopians and Swahili were most active was in the Lopit mountains of the Latuka people.[98] They, like the Didinga, were in the outer sphere of Maji's influence. The Uganda government (who had had jurisdiction over the area before the 1914 transfer) had never extended its administration to the Latuka, and the area did not get established government from Khartoum until 1914.[99] Before 1914 the Latuka may have gone to Jabal Lafon to get arms transhipped from Maji, but certainly from 1915 to 1926, and probably both earlier and later, they had many contacts with arms and ivory dealers from Maji.[100] Ethiopia never appointed chiefs or exacted tribute as it did from the inner circle. The arms and ivory trade was concentrated in the northern-most part of Latukaland, the Lopit (or Lafit) mountains, and there is no indication of the trade's having involved cattle-raiding against neighbouring peoples. However, in at least two cases Latuka chiefs were removed for 'complicity' with or involvement in buying arms from 'Abyssinian poachers.'[101] Lopit was a natural stopping-place for any poachers or traders heading west from the Ethiopian borderlands. To the north were the periodic swamps, impassable during the wet season and difficult to cross during the dry season, while to the south was the Latuka mountain range. Furthermore, Lopit had a long tradition in the area for making iron implements used by the Toposa and other neighbouring peoples.[102]

Like the Latuka, the Bari were in the outer sphere of Ethiopian influence, and they too had had a long history of contact with northern Sudanese both before and during the Mahdiyya.[103] But the spiral of violence had affected the Bari, and related Bari-speaking peoples, more severely than any other of the peoples of Equatoria Province. The Ethiopian and other associated 'poachers' exchanged arms and meat for ivory throughout the Bari-speaking areas, from Kajo-Kaji and Yei in the west to Rajaf and Mongalla in the east.[104] Beliniang in the north-east of Bariland seems to have been most persistently involved. In fact, many chiefs there who had been appointed by the Sudan government were deposed and imprisoned for trading with 'Abyssinian poachers'. Evidently the desire for firearms was great.[105]

North-east of Bariland were the Päri of Jabal Lafon – one of the most persistent of the Equatorian peoples trading in firearms.[106] Notable primarily as a possible staging area in the history of the Luo dispersal from the Shilluk/Anuak area to Acholiland, Jabal Lafon continued its trading links in the arms trade into the twentieth century, at least in the early years with the Latuka and Acholi.[107] Never directly under Ethiopian control as regards tribute or the appointment of chiefs, Jabal Lafon nevertheless saw the confluence of two trading routes from the east. The southern one originated at Maji and passed via the Toposa and Lopit hills, while the northern route came from the Boma plateau via the Kangen river (and thus through the Murle) to Jabal Lafon.[108] The trade was confined to arms and ivory, and there is no evidence that it included cattle-raiding or their exchange.

Finally, the case of the Murle should be examined. Although the lowland Murle are closer to the Boma plateau and to Maji than the Toposa, there is no indication that they were within the inner circle of Maji's domination, though it is difficult to be certain, since they were influenced by three other Ethiopian centres on the western frontier (Gurafarda, Gore and Gambela).[109] Also, a section of the Murle lived on the Boma plateau, securely within Maji's inner circle.[110] The lowland Murle seem to have made sure the same did not happen to them. They were disrupted by influence from Maji only some time between 1904 and 1912.[111] The vital element here was the take-over of the Murle by the Sudan government's military administration in 1912, much earlier than had happened anywhere else in the southern Sudan east of the Nile.[112] Constant war was said to have been halted, and there seem to have been only scattered incidents of the exchange of arms, although the Murle were active in helping Ethiopians and 'Abyssinian poachers' to hunt, receiving meat in exchange for their service.[113]

CONCLUSION

In Maji the ivory, slave, and arms traders were intimately connected, and their connections illuminate the basic nature of the *gebbar* system. What is clear for Maji at least is that cycles were created in which violence periodically increased in intensity, particularly when there was a major change of government at the centre. Departing governors taxed heavily and raided for slaves in order to take what wealth they could to their home areas. Local peoples struck back when they were able, often raiding each other for slaves, for that was the only way to get arms. Incoming governors then brutally crushed the rebellion, after which *gebbar* had nothing left, were unable to pay new taxes and were therefore forced to sell their children as slaves. This was a pattern repeated again and again between 1910 and 1936.

One way to interpret this material is to compare Maji with the southern Sudan in the nineteenth century. In the Sudan, the ivory and slave trades of the last century fed each other as violence became more and more intense. In south-west Ethiopia during the early twentieth century there was a similar, but not identical, spiral of violence. The evidence indicates that the ivory trade was declining in actual and perhaps real terms after the mid-1920s. As ivory declined as a source of revenue, slaving became more and more important and finally became the major source of revenue, directly in terms of sales of slaves and indirectly in governors' taxation of slaves exported to provinces in the north.

In the Ethiopian case, the *gebbar* system was at the root of the problem, and the ivory trade initially masked its basic rôle and importance. By the 1930s the *gebbar* system under *balabbat* like the Maji *kure* had become a continuous source of slaves. This was supplemented by raids on peoples who refused to submit to *gebbar* serfdom like the Tishana, and some of these raids spilled over into the Sudan, especially after 1910. British pressure, however, showed finally that easier prey were to be found within Ethiopia itself. Raids into British-administered areas were eventually not worth the trouble they caused.

Thus only the arms and ivory trades continued on a major scale from Maji into the Sudan. It seems that much of this trade used a network that had a long history. The routes stretched from the Maji highlands to the Toposa, Lopit, Jabal Lafon and Jabal Beliniang. It seems clear that in its later stages Ethiopian and even Maji influence in the Sudan was exaggerated; the Toposa and Didinga played a larger rôle than was thought to be the case at the time. Maji's impact on the administration of south-eastern Sudan was significant on the Boma plateau until 1936, because the plateau was within the framework of the *gebbar* system. Farther south and west towards the Turkana and Toposa, Maji's writ was diplomatic rather than administrative, and declined with the approach of British administration. As soon as the various British colonies found enough revenue or sufficient interest to occupy unadministered areas, Maji's rôle rapidly waned.

Like most other areas on the peripheries of imperial Ethiopia, Maji was directly affected by change at the centre in Addis Abeba. And, as in other borderlands to the north and east, the escarpment played an important rôle as a refuge and centre for the restructuring of local political organizations. The arms and slave trade, intimately linked to the *gebbar* system, provided the main spur for Maji's expansion into south-eastern Sudan and for the organization of local Tishana resistance.

9

On the Nilotic frontier: imperial Ethiopia in the southern Sudan, 1898–1936

DOUGLAS H. JOHNSON

South-west Ethiopia and the southern Sudan, despite their contiguity, have yet to be considered by historians and anthropologists as bearing any historical, geographical, political or cultural relationship to each other. As far as historians are concerned, the Ethiopian escarpment contributed to the southern Sudan's general isolation, and highland Ethiopians rarely descended to the plains except for plunder. Historians are in general agreement with Sir Edward Evans-Pritchard's assertions that the Sudanese Nilotes of the border region were protected from Ethiopia either by a 'corridor of death' – malaria in the swamp and tsetse in the highlands – or by the absence, on the Ethiopian side, of any systematic 'civilized' administration.[1]

This chapter will focus on the Anuak and Nuer, who, like other frontier pastoralists such as the Dassanetch, lived in environments uncongenial to highland colonization. They were spared some of the more extreme forms of imperial Ethiopian rule: their territory was not settled by soldier colonists, land was not alienated and appropriated to local *balabbat*, and the people were not reduced to *gebbar* servitude. Yet, for at least the first thirty years of this century Ethiopian influence was felt by Nilotes on the border and was expanded by them to the banks of the White Nile and the Bahr al-Jabal (see Map 12).

Through interwoven systems of tribute and trade, large sections of the southern Sudan, though administered by the Anglo-Egyptian government, were effectively exploited by imperial Ethiopia as part of its hinterland. As both targets and agents of this exploitation the Nilotes were involved in a variety of relations with Ethiopian authorities. Such autonomy as the Nilotes gained on the fringes of the Ethiopian empire was maintained by their geography, their culture, and their ability to manipulate the international border. In the end they were able to achieve far more flexible relations, based on reciprocity, with the Ethiopian border administration than they enjoyed with the Anglo-Egyptian government in the Sudan.

Geographically, it is important to note that the country occupied by the Nilotes changes from upland forests at the foot of the Ethiopian plateau to grasslands on both sides of the international border. Agriculture was supported in both forest and plain, but pastoralism was restricted by tsetse in the wooded uplands and by the erratic water supply in the lower grasslands. The population of the region was and is small, achieving greater concentrations near the forests but becoming more scattered and mobile in the plains.[2] The irregular distribution of water and high land forced a seasonal mingling of populations which transcended both political and social boundaries. A greater mixing of peoples was also produced by the three great Nilotic migrations of the Shilluk and Anuak in the seventeenth century, the Dinka in the eighteenth, and the Nuer in the nineteenth. The broader historical patterns of population movement and the seasonal mobility of the Nilotes spread Nilotic culture to non-Nilotes. Non-Nilotes were brought into Nilotic society with such regularity that adapting to other cultures and to shifts of population became a distinctive Nilotic habit long before the appearance of the Ethiopian empire in the south-west.[3]

INDIGENOUS POLITICS AND RIVAL ADMINISTRATION ALONG THE BORDER

Some Nilotes already had links with highland Ethiopia through trade before the middle of the nineteenth century, but it was the expansion of Shewa into Wellegga, Illubabor and Kefa in the 1880s and '90s that brought the Nilotes into the political orbit of Ethiopia. The early raids into these areas did not immediately lead to conquest and occupation. Shewan authority over Ḳelem, Sayo and Anfillo was established through an alliance with Jote Tullu during the repulse of the Mahdist invasion of Bela Shangul and Wellegga in the 1880s.[4] But it was only with the imminent fall of the Mahdist state and the advance of the Marchand expedition into the Upper Nile basin at the end of the nineteenth century that Menilek was moved to establish 'effective occupation' of the new border.[5] In 1897 *ras* Mekonnen occupied Bela Shangul while *dejazmach* Tesemma was dispatched to the Sobat. Only one detachment of Tesemma's army reached the mouth of the Sobat in May 1898, where it planted its flag and then retreated.[6] The new Anglo-Egyptian government entered the Sobat valley later the same year, and in 1902 the Sudan–Ethiopian border agreement placed the whole of the Sobat and Pibor rivers inside the Sudan. The delimitation of the border did not bring Ethiopian influence in the area to an end. If anything, it was only just beginning.

Both the Sudan and Ethiopian governments gradually consolidated their control over those peoples on the Nilotic plains whom they claimed to rule, but the quality of that control and the ultimate objectives of administration differed. The British administration of the Upper Nile early in this century was marked by a consistency of purpose. It required unanimous submission from all peoples found within the Sudan's borders. It recognized only one type of subject and neither accepted nor recognized any qualifications to submission. All paid tribute, all obeyed the strictures imposed by the government, all accepted the government's right to appoint or confirm leaders. Once this uniformity was established, diversity within the different societies so controlled was allowed: the type of tribute and the manner of its collection varied, differences in customary law used to regulate internal order were recognized, and leaders with differing bases of authority were accepted. But as far as the British administration was concerned, all those peoples within the borders of the Sudan were its subjects, and all subjects were regarded as totally Sudanese, therefore, totally subject to the regulations of the Sudan government. It did not recognize peoples as being partially Sudanese and partially something else, nor did it recognize qualified autonomy for peoples within its territorial jurisdiction.

The administration of the new Ethiopian empire was more flexible and medieval in its recognition of persons who could be regarded as semi-citizens. Within the confines of its territory the empire acknowledged different relationships between subjects and the imperial authority. There were people with whom relations were based almost exclusively on trade; there were those who were obliged to pay tribute and by doing so retained some autonomy; there were some who had rather more onerous obligations and whose own freedom of action was strictly limited; and there were others who were raided. In many ways the degree of 'citizenship' was determined by the degree of exploitation involved and the degree of reciprocity in that exploitation. The degree of exploitation varied not only for those people on the fringes of the empire, but for those in different positions within the hierarchy of the empire. As the political frontier of the empire expanded, the relationship of some peoples to the empire changed.[7] With the introduction of *neftennya* settlers in areas formerly on the frontier, peoples who previously had some political rights of their own could be transformed into *gebbar* and independent leaders into *balabbat*. It was only on the very frontier where political ambiguities existed that subject peoples could exploit those ambiguities to maintain a degree of autonomy usually unavailable to others well behind the frontier.

The Nilotes lived between these two forms of encroaching administration. On the Sudan side of the border the administration advanced through military pressure, tribute and judicial regulation to obtain one goal: political submission. On the Ethiopian side the government's goal was the extraction of local wealth, and it almost revelled in a diversity of means to obtain it. There was for a time a frontier within a frontier; for not only was there the conflicting jurisdiction of Illubabor and Wellegga provinces, but within those provinces there was the rival authority of different rulers. Some local rulers had risen by alliance with the conquering Shewan state, but a growing number of others were imperial agents, appointed to their positions on the frontier by the authorities at the centre. This diversity of power was a political reality along the Nilotic frontier up to the time of the Italian conquest of Ethiopia.

The boundary affecting the Anuak, Nuer and the peoples variously called 'Cai' (by the Nilotes) or 'Burun' (by the Arabs) was agreed in 1902, but some ambiguities remained. From 1903 onward the Koma and other Cai along the Daga, in the region known as Warragarra, officially passed from the control of

Gidami in Ethiopia to the Sudan, but continued to pay tribute, and acknowledged Oromo overlordship as late as 1912.[8] The final boundary running through the Adongo Anuak, along the Oboth and Akobo rivers, was not fixed until 1921. Even within Ethiopia the border was not clear. In the early part of this century the frontier north of the Baro was under the control of *dejazmach* Jote. The Baro separated his province from Illubabor, which was ruled by *ras* Tesemma from Gore, and the rivalry between Jote, a local Oromo leader, and Tesemma, an Amhara conqueror, meant that the Baro region, inhabited by the Anuak, was frequently in dispute. This conflict of jurisdiction was further complicated by the granting of a trade concession to the Baro Syndicate under the Syrian merchant Hassib Ydlibi in 1908–16. The jurisdiction of the Syndicate extended along both banks of the river up to the frontier and it had authority to administer and tax the Anuak living within its territory. Since the Sudan government had been running a trading station at Gambela on the Baro since 1904, the Baro Syndicate became involved with the Sudan as well as with the Ethiopian authorities at Sayo and Bure. The years between 1908 and 1917 were particularly chaotic due to the arrest, reinstatement and final removal of Jote, and the encroachment on Jote's domain by Gore and Khojali al-Hassan of Asosa.[9]

The Sudan government was distressed to be so constantly awash in so fluid a border, though it sometimes took advantage of the lack of frontier enforcement to wade in after fugitive subjects. Until the mid-1930s the border was very much an hypothesis which had yet to be proven. In general the Sudan government sought to bring regularity to the border just as it sought to bring regularity to its own territory. Ethiopia was more willing to accept some flexibility among border peoples. The differences between British and Ethiopian approaches to administration are most clearly seen in their policies towards tribute, trade and local leaders.

TRIBUTE

In Ethiopia tribute was an end in itself, and tribute demands often preceded conquest. We shall see later that tribute was linked to trade, and that demands for tribute expanded the trading network. The two were complementary for they worked towards the same goal: the extraction of local wealth. In the Sudan at the beginning of this century, tribute was a political action aimed at strengthening administrative control through imposing a form of 'discipline' that placed its subjects in the habit of obeying the government. Thus when the activities of the Ethiopians interfered with the collection of government tribute from the Nilotes, the Upper Nile Province government saw the threat more in political than in economic terms.

In the first two decades of this century both British and Ethiopian administration of the Nilotic plains was sporadic and seasonal. The highland Ethiopians were inhibited by their dislike of the lowlands from maintaining a year-round presence. British administration was affected, like the movements of the Nilotes it tried to control, by the seasonal flooding of the plains along the Sobat and its tributaries. Following a transhumance of its own, British administration expanded into the plains during the dry season (November–April) and contracted back to its administrative centres along the rivers during the rains. This made control of the Nilotes very difficult, and the precariousness of the administration's position induced some restraints. Because the government's military power was limited it was vital to obtain submission by peaceful means where possible. It was unwise to make too many demands that would be resented and that could not, in any case, be effectively enforced.

Until 1909 the question of tribute, and therefore of 'effective administration', was not energetically pursued. But Ethiopian success in trading for Nilotic cattle and ivory (see below, pp. 232–7), as much as anything else, forced the Sudan government to adopt a more forceful tribute collection policy, with most unsettling consequences. As early as 1903 the government recognized that most of the Zaraf valley ivory was going to Ethiopia, and by 1904 it began considering means of tapping the ivory at this source as a way of halting the flow into Ethiopia. The establishment of Sudanese trading posts at Itang and Gambela in 1904 was an attempt to divert Sudanese ivory back to the Sudan, an attempt effectively thwarted by Jote and Tesemma. By 1909 the encouragement which the government had given to Sudanese merchants to trade along the border had failed to produce any significant results in diverting the ivory trade.[10]

These developments drove the governor of Upper Nile Province very nearly to distraction. The Sudan received no benefit from Nuer ivory exported to Ethiopia by the Oromo. 'I mean to say', he exclaimed in almost Wodehousian prose, 'that with the dawn of effective administration on the frontier, Ivory should find its way into Abyssinia only upon our conditions, and in settling a local tariff hereafter we should remember that the means to purchase Ivory from the Nuers lies with the Abyssinians, exclusively.' He proposed a 20 per cent export duty on all ivory crossing the border. 'In my opinion, the Nuers will not at first attempt to frustrate us in our determination to exact an export tax from the Abyssinian buyers of their Ivory, and our firm demand for cattle tribute will quickly show them that Government has come to stay.'[11]

The control of the ivory trade thus became linked with tribute and establishing 'effective administration'. Tribute and trade were incorporated into the new administration policy for all Nuer in 1910. Control was to be exerted through administrative patrols which collected tribute and opened up the cattle trade for Sudanese merchants. In this way the government hoped to establish its authority not only through the demonstration of force but through a province-wide regulation of cattle and ivory, the two most important commodities in the Nuer trade with Ethiopia. In the end, no real progress in taxing or diverting the ivory trade was achieved, but there was more success in the collection of tribute. During the years 1910–12 the Jikany and Lou paid tribute willingly to secure government protection against the rifle-armed Anuak.[12]

The government tried to control Anuak raiding, both to reassure the Nuer and to consolidate its authority along the frontier. But the 1912 campaign against the Adongo Anuak was forced to retire after heavy losses, and Anuak raids against the Nuer continued. The Nuer, quite understandably, felt that government protection was not worth the price. The Gaajak were the first to take the opportunity which their trade with Ethiopia offered, arming themselves throughout 1911 and 1912 in the face of severe Anuak and Ethiopian raids. By 1913 they openly declared that as they could now protect themselves, they would pay no more tribute. Elsewhere in the province continued tribute demands which brought little in return were increasingly resented, and the Gaawar, too, resisted the collection of tribute in 1913 and openly rebelled. With these new hostilities the demand for firearms throughout Nuer country greatly accelerated the arms trade. Yet provincial officials were forbidden by Khartoum to take any military action along the border for fear of disturbing the Sudan's relations with Ethiopia.[13]

The outbreak of World War I ended all plans for punitive campaigns against the Nuer. Throughout the war years tribute had to be extracted from the Jikany by force, sometimes as they recrossed into the Sudan at the end of the dry season. The inability of the Sudan government to assert itself along the border in any significant way resulted in the Jikany placing themselves outside the range of effective administration. Fearing that this was having an unsettling effect on more firmly administered peoples, the Sudan government campaigned against the Jikany in 1919–20, as soon after the end of World War I as possible. This patrol was militarily a success and did much to raise provincial morale, but its political effect was much more ambiguous. Throughout the 1920s reliance on military force gave way to closer civil administration among the Nuer along the border.[14]

ANUAK LEADERSHIP

The loss of administrative control and revenue that the failure to collect tribute or to regulate trade implied was only one aspect of the threat of Ethiopian trade to British administration in Upper Nile Province. Another threat was the way that Anuak and Nuer leaders were brought into the Ethiopian orbit, even when settled inside the Sudan. The flexibility of the Ethiopian attitude to these frontiersmen meant that it was possible for them to be incorporated into the Ethiopian administrative system far more easily than into the more rigid hierarchical structure preferred by the British.

Anuak leadership ran along two parallel channels, the village headmen (*kuaari*, sing. *kuaaro*) and the nobles (*nyiye*, sing. *nyiya*). Both forms of leadership were based on a regular and constant transfer of power. Headmen attracted and maintained followings through generosity and by maintaining an equilibrium between the political factions of their villages. Their tenure of office was limited by the *agem*, the village revolution that occurred when a rival for the headmanship raised a sufficient following to seize the drums of office. A deposed headman left his village but could regain the headmanship later through his own revolution.[15]

The parallel institution of kingship was confined to two lineages of nobles, the Nyigoc and the Nyiudola, originally concentrated on the Oboth and upper Akobo. Kingship revolved around the possession of the royal emblems. Any holder of the emblems could be ousted, like the village headmen, by any other rival noble who raised a sufficient following to oppose him. In the past the transfer of kingly emblems was largely ritual, and deposed nobles would frequently hand them over peacefully. The relative ease of this transfer and the fact that only descendants of fully installed nobles could claim the emblems encouraged rapid circulation of the emblems, and by the end of the nineteenth century nobles held them very briefly, though they could hold them more than once. Nobles who did not possess the emblems could still attain power by insinuating themselves into commoner villages through the village revolution. A deposed headman sometimes preferred a challenge from a noble; for a noble, who owned no land in a commoner village, was less entrenched than other potential rivals and could be deposed more easily later.[16]

While nobles entered commoner villages 'through the cracks in their political structure', their entry was frequently resisted.[17] The encroachment of the nobles on commoner territory was one impetus to Anuak expansion north of the Akobo to the Baro and Gila rivers. Opposition to the nobles encouraged some commoner villages, already under pressure since the 1850s from Nuer raids, and more recently from the highland Ethiopians, to abandon their straggling settlements and coalesce into more compact stockaded villages. Villages, originally consisting of one clan or a lineage of a clan, became autonomous political units under their own headmen.[18]

The fact that the international border placed most of the headmen in Ethiopia and most of the nobles in the Sudan did not mean that the nobles were untouched by Ethiopia. In fact it was the nobles who first took advantage of the opportunities offered by the Ethiopian presence and the arms trade which it brought. Udiel-wa-Ngenya, the first noble to receive Ethiopian arms, used his weapons to increase his power among the Anuak, extracting land from commoner villages and also raiding the Gaajak Nuer in 1899–1902. Another Ethiopian-supported noble, Uliimi-war-Agaanya, used his new power to murder rival nobles, and expelled one, Akwei-wa-Cam, from his country. Akwei fled to Ethiopia where he traded skins and ivory for rifles which he brought back to his village north of the Oboth and distributed to young warriors. Then, when Uliimi was in Ethiopia, Akwei attacked his village and captured the royal emblems. Akwei became the most powerful Anuak noble. He attracted various young Anuak, Ethiopian hunters, bandits and Sudanese deserters from the Egyptian army through the lure of plunder and good hunting, and he obtained a virtual monopoly in the firearms and ivory trade throughout south-eastern Anuakland.[19]

The rise of these three nobles through their connections with Ethiopia produced a greater internal mixing of the Anuak population. Various clans were dispersed in their flight from the battles between rival nobles, and several lineages of different clans amalgamated into compact townships for defence against the nobles' new power. At the same time the nobles attracted many persons from all over the country who came either for protection or advancement. By 1910 all the Anuak living on the plain below Gurafarda had fled to the Akobo, where the nobles ruled, to escape being made into *gebbar* by the Ethiopians coming down from the plateau.[20]

The nobles' territorial base was the Sudan, but they extended their influence into commoner territory, which was in Ethiopia,[21] drawing closer to the Ethiopian orbit. There was a reciprocal extension of Ethiopian influence into the Sudan through the nobles. Udiel, Uliimi and Akwei were all, at different times, agents of the administration at Gore, and Akwei, if not the others, was appointed *fītawrarī*, 'leader of the vanguard', by *ras* Tesemma.[22]

In appointing nobles *fītawrarī* the Ethiopians may have recognized their political autonomy, but at some point the vanguard must join the main force, and very soon the governor at Gore tried to control them. Ethiopia countered its support for Udiel by also supporting Uliimi. Udiel and Akwei were both briefly detained in Bure before 1908, and all three were summoned to Bure in 1912. Akwei was never tamed, but Udiel's following was disarmed and his headmen made independent of him by the Ethiopian authorities. Udiel did rearm himself, but he remained dependent on the Ethiopians in his rivalry with Akwei.[23]

Ethiopian efforts to control the Anuak before World War I were largely ineffectual. Being suspicious of British intentions, Ethiopia was reluctant to disarm the Anuak under British pressure. Rivalries within the frontier administration itself hampered any uniformity of action, and the economic advantages of continuing the ivory and arms trade with the Anuak outweighed any other consideration.[24]

When Jote was deposed in 1908, his country passed over into Amhara control. In May–June 1912 the Amhara governor of Gidami marched against the Anuak when they refused to pay his demand for arrears in tax, but meeting the Nuer first he attacked and was repulsed by the Gaajak. The next year the governor of Gore tried to subdue the Anuak on the Baro, but was effectively thwarted by Jote, now reinstated, who quietly supported the Anuak. For the next three years the Anuak, along with the other peoples along the western frontier, faced increased tribute demands, and many Anuak headmen, from whom the tribute was extracted, began to resent Ethiopian extractions. In 1915 Majid Abud, a Syrian, was entrusted with the task of subduing the Anuak along the Baro. He attacked Akwei and others of Udiel's Anuak opponents with a force raised from Gore, Anfillo and the Anuak, but dissensions within his force crippled him, and Akwei and other Anuak leaders escaped into the Sudan. Majid was replaced in June 1916, and the Ethiopians tried a more conciliatory approach.[25]

The Sudan government had more success in controlling the nobles after Akwei died inside the Sudan at the end of 1920. The British commander at Akobo co-opted the institution of kingship by himself investing Akwei's twelve year-old son, Cam-war-Akwei, with the royal emblems early in 1921. The final fixing of the international boundary through Anuak country later that year placed Cam, and the emblems, firmly inside the Sudan, while his main rivals were in Ethiopia. Government control over Anuak kingship was tightened when the emblems were confiscated from Cam in 1927, and the government tried to limit tenure of office of future kings to one year.[26]

The nobles' response to this new restriction was to abscond with the emblems to Ethiopia. Between 1928 and 1934 four out of the six successive kings installed during that time crossed the border. It was only with great difficulty that they were induced to return and the emblems recovered, often piecemeal as they were hidden in different places. Majid Abud's renewed activity in 1933 forced the last absconder back into the Sudan, giving the Sudan government another chance to retain control of the kingship. The tenure of each king was extended at the discretion of the government. A stricter control over the possession of the emblems was maintained – they sometimes rested in the Akobo office safe.[27]

Throughout this time the Sudan government tried to reduce the number of nobles installed, and the Nyiudola lineage, based in the Sudan, was favoured over the Nyigoc, who resided mostly in Ethiopia. This intensified feuds between the Nyiudola and Nyigoc living in Ethiopia during the late 1940s, almost embroiling the Sudan and Ethiopian governments in an international incident. Additional threats to peace on the border came from disgruntled Nyiudola nobles, including one former king, who took to living in Ethiopia, occasionally adopting the traditional life of the aristocratic *shifta*, living with small bands of followers by hunting and brigandage.[28]

The nobles, uncontrolled by Ethiopia and controlled only with difficulty by the Sudan, helped to maintain Anuak autonomy along the border. But most Anuak lived under their headmen, and here again it was the mobility of leadership, through the village revolution, that helped prevent the establishment of a more fixed form of leadership under Ethiopian control. The fact that the Anuak believed that '*nobody* ought to be in office for a very long time'[29] meant that there was already a momentum against allowing any leader, whether arising from within or supported from without, to entrench himself. There was very little chance for the Ethiopian government to select leaders and settle them on land as *balabbat* because eventually they would be deposed and ostracized from their villages. Differences did develop between headmen on either side of the border. The Sudan government at first accepted with surprise, mingled with relief, the fact that with village revolutions headmen could be deposed with ease and would leave with good grace. But as government became more established it was those headmen who insisted on carrying out government orders who tended to be deposed most often, and the Sudan government tried to put an end – unsuccessfully – to the revolutions.[30] Ethiopian headmen seemed to attain slightly more authority over their villages. Because the headmanship was 'an institution based upon Anuak notions of prestige' and was maintained by the generous distribution of goods, the continuation of an ivory trade within Ethiopia gave headmen there greater opportunities to increase both their wealth and their prestige, and so to attract more followers. The continuous flow of Anuak between leaders on either side of the border established a further limitation to Anuak leadership, guaranteeing that it would continue to follow traditional ideals rather than foreign ones.[31]

NUER LEADERSHIP

Ethiopian influence on Nuer leadership was more indirect since most Nuer lived in the Sudan. The main contact the Nuer had with Ethiopia was in trade. Some Nuer leaders took advantage of this trade to expand their power base, but they were not able to do so to the same extent as the Anuak leaders.

One such leader was Gai Jang, a prominent Gaajak Man of Cattle (*wut ghok*) at the turn of the century, with influence among both the Jikany and the Lou, who had further enhanced his spiritual reputation by accumulating magic (*wal*). His cattle camp at Wunakoi, already a focus of attention for Jikany and Lou during the initiation of age-sets, became a major centre in the cattle-ivory-arms trade. In 1911 his own son travelled as interpreter and guide for Oromo merchants from Gidami, trading arms for ivory among the Lou and Dinka. The Lou at this time got most of their guns through Gai Jang's village. His involvement in the trade gave him easier access to rifles than many other Nuer, and, before his death in 1914, he was reported to be one of the early advocates among the Gaajak of resisting by force the collection of tribute.[32]

Living in the Sudan, Gai Jang benefited from the Ethiopian trade without submitting to Ethiopian regulation. Ethiopian traders depended upon him to expand their trade in the Sudan, yet restrictions on Ethiopian activities limited the support they could give (assuming they were inclined to do so) to leaders such as Gai Jang to dominate the trade among the Nuer as the nobles had done among the Anuak. The Nuer trade, as will be shown, was too diverse and individual. No Nuer leader overcame the individualism of his people. At the most they helped to gather together a larger group of persons to trade, increasing the volume of commodities to be traded at any one time, as Macar Diu, the Gaawar leader, did prior to rebelling against the government in 1913.[33]

If no Nuer leader catapulted himself to autocracy through trade, there were a number of Nuer leaders along the frontier who attained influence, not only through the position they held between the rival administrations of Ethiopia and the Sudan, but through their pivotal role in relations between these administrations and other border peoples. They came to prominence during the years of World War I when British administration in the area was virtually moribund and when the rivalries of Ethiopian border officials brought additional uncertainties to the frontier.

In the early part of the century Gaajak relations with Ethiopia were confined to the Oromo at Gidami. With Jote's fall from power in 1908 and the arrival of a quick succession of Amhara governors in his province, trade relations became unsettled, and the Nuer themselves became targets. In 1911 one section of the Nuer moved into the Sudan to avoid paying tribute.[34] In 1912, *ato* Zerefu, the governor of Gidami, attacked some Gaajak villages near the mouth of the Khor Macar but was repulsed with the loss of over a quarter of his force. Zerefu carried away a number of Nuer captives but most were ransomed back to the Nuer. The Ethiopians tried quickly to restore something like the *status quo*, using a Nuer intermediary from Gidami, and reopening the arms trade as soon as possible. This raid created some uncertainty between the Gaajak and the Ethiopians, but it had two other effects: it helped to unite the Gaajak sections against a common threat, and it further strengthened Gaajak–Oromo relations, for the Oromo merchants began to keep the Nuer informed of the movements and intentions of their Amhara masters. The raid also hastened the downfall of *ato* Zerefu and the reinstatement of Jote.[35]

It was at about this time that the activities of Khojali al-Hassan, the semi-autonomous ruler of Asosa in Ethiopia, began to have their effect on the Nuer. His encroachment on Jote's domain in Beggi and on Jote's former preserve along the Daga brought him into conflict with Nuer living near the Koma. But very soon Khojali began wooing the Nuer away from Jote and Gidami. In 1915 he brought eight Nuer to Asosa to act as witnesses for him in a dispute with Jote. Four of them were sent to Addis Abeba, and the other four returned to their homes with cattle, some of which they were to trade on Khojali's behalf. Throughout the next year more Nuer came to visit Khojali, some to trade cattle and some to go on to Addis Abeba to meet the emperor, returning with gifts of rifles and mules. Other Nuer joined Khojali in his open conflict with Jote's people.[36]

Having diverted much of the Gaajak trade to himself and having employed some Nuer in his campaign against Jote, Khojali tried to use the Nuer in his raids against the Koma. One result of Khojali's alliance with *ras* Teferi at the time of *lij* Iyasu's overthrow in 1916 was that Khojali was required to supply *ras* Teferi regularly with 'recruits' for his army. Most of these were captive Koma, but raiding into the Sudan carried increasing risks of retaliation by the Sudan government. In 1918 Khojali tried to persuade the Gaajak to force the Koma into Ethiopia,[37] but Khojali soon found that there were some groups of Koma, Meban and other 'Cai', who enjoyed the protection of the Nuer, especially by the Kaang section of the Gaajak leader Mut Dung.

Mut Dung was another Man of Cattle who had enhanced his power through acquaintance with the Ethiopians. In relation to the Koma he seems to have acted more like an Ethiopian feudal lord than a Nuer chief. When the Ethiopians raided along the Daga in 1917, he went to meet them astride his donkey and persuaded them to retire. The next year, when *fītawrarī* Nagaw Ashana raided the Daga as far as the Gaajak cattle camps at Bar, Mut Dung refused to give up the Koma refugees who had fled to him and again forced the Ethiopians to withdraw. He had enough power, even when pressed by the Sudan government, to bargain with Khojali. During the campaign against the Gaajak in 1920, when Khojali was reluctant to supply him with ammunition, Mut Dung threatened to retaliate by diverting all his grain to the very government he was fighting. It was only his accidental death later that same year that removed Mut Dung as an influence along the frontier.[38]

After 1920 both the Sudan and Ethiopian governments began to tighten their control over their respective sides of the border, but the approaches of the two governments were again drastically dissimilar. The British continued to insist that because most Nuer were settled in the Sudan, all Nuer were Sudanese. Throughout the 1920s the British District Commissioner at Nasir freely crossed the frontier to follow the Jikany to their cattle camps. There was a certain logic in his actions, given the nature of administrative dry-season movements elsewhere in Nuer territory. By 1929 the government in Khartoum prohibited these unauthorized border crossings. In 1931, under Ethiopian pressure, the Sudan government further admitted Ethiopia's right to tax those Nuer settled permanently in Ethiopia, giving up its own claim to do so itself.[39]

A stricter observation of the border was acceptable to the Sudan only if it was followed by a stricter control of border peoples by Ethiopia. After British insistence that Ethiopia restrain its Anuak, Majid Abud was reappointed frontier agent along both banks of the Baro, with jurisdiction in both Wellegga and Illubabor provinces.[40] This jurisdiction included those Nuer in the ambiguous position of living most of the year in the Sudan but grazing part of the year in Ethiopia.

In trying to assert Ethiopian authority over these Nuer, Majid followed the precedent of *dejazmach* Birru, who appointed several Nuer agents in the Sudan in order to assert Ethiopian claims to the Daga valley when he was governor of Sayo in the early 1920s.[41] Majid made at least one Nuer a *fītawrarī*, another one a *kennyazmach*, and handed out Ethiopian clothes to other Nuer chiefs as they came in increasing numbers to settle in Ethiopia. Koryom Tut, the Nuer *fītawrarī* and the most influential Nuer leader permanently settled in Ethiopia, was taken to Addis Abeba in 1935 and presented to the emperor, and returned to his home with presents of money, arms, and ammunition.[42] These activities unsettled the Sudan administration of the Jikany. Having admitted it had no right to tax Nuer living in Ethiopia, the government looked with growing concern as Majid encouraged more and more Nuer to build permanent villages in Ethiopian territory. Many Nuer wished to escape unpopular government-appointed chiefs, and unsuccessful contenders for government appointments went to Ethiopia where their ambitions were satisfied.[43]

The Sudan proposed a grazing rights treaty in 1933, placing all Nuer under Sudanese authority. In the meantime the District Commissioner at Nasir felt compelled to cross the border once to prevent an intersectional fight and once to collect fines. One Nuer chief who had been given clothes by Majid was arrested as he re-entered the Sudan at the end of the 1933 dry season. British authority over the Nuer was re-established when Majid withdrew from the border after being defeated by the Anuak in 1934. In 1936 the grazing rights treaty was ratified, but shortly after that the Italians occupied the entire border. Nuer leaders in Ethiopia, bereft of their ally, immediately made their peace with the Sudan government, handing over their Ethiopian clothes as they did so.[44]

The British attitude towards administration of the Nuer was summarized in 1916 by C. H. Stigand, then inspector at Nasir and later governor of the province. The Nuer, he declared, 'have no paramount chief, no tribal organization of any value and no chief of any authority or influence. If there is to be any order or discipline in the Nuer country the machinery for it must be created by Government.'[45] In effect the government had been unable to co-opt leaders who would collect tribute and impose obedience. There were and had been highly influential leaders: Ngundeng, Deng Lakka, Dual Diu, Guek Ngundeng, Gai Jang and Mut Dung. But these men's secular influence rested on a spiritual authority that the Sudan government did not recognize.[46] During the 1920s such leaders were removed, not because they refused to work with the government, but because they did not fit the government's concept of acceptable figures of authority. The campaign against the Lou and Gaawar in 1928–30 was followed by a steady secularization of Nuer leadership.[47] Anuak leadership, on the other hand, was more successfully co-opted precisely because it did meet the government's criteria of authority in that offices could be transferred according to known and controllable rules.

The Ethiopian authorities recognized that there were in practice no unacceptable forms of leadership on the frontier, only unacceptable leaders. They, too, tried to get rid of leaders who had become too powerful, whether Jote Tullu or Akwei-wa-Cam. Ethiopia recognized the ambiguities of the border and adapted to them; *fītawrarī* appeared among the Nuer and Anuak as well as among the Oromo. As part of the vanguard of empire they existed by definition in opposition to something else – in this case the Sudan government. This mode of political rule was more suitable to Nilotic political life and to the conditions created by the border. It was a response that adapted to, rather than regulated, border movements.

THE TRADE IN IVORY AND FIREARMS

Ivory, taken through trade and tribute, was the foundation of Ethiopian–Nilotic relations. The demand for Sudanese ivory in Ethiopia began with the introduction of tribute in south-western Ethiopia, which seems to have been one of the early objectives of Shewan campaigns.[48] Between 1882 and 1898 all the states from Kefa to Bela Shangul began to pay ivory and gold to Menilek. Gold-poor regions such as Anfillo exchanged coffee and slaves for livestock with Sayo, and then traded the animals to Asosa and Bela Shangul for gold.[49] The gold-producing regions' chronic poverty in cattle ensured that livestock became an important trade commodity in meeting Addis Abeba's tribute demands. It was as suppliers of ivory and livestock that the Nilotes entered the Ethiopian trade.

The first Nilotes involved in the Ethiopian ivory trade were probably the Dinka, who had a long history of exchanges with the Blue Nile. From the

1850s to the mid-1870s traders from Sennar, Fazoghli and Fadasi travelled through the Cai and Dinka lands to the Sobat, exchanging beads for ivory and gold dust. They also raided for slaves, and the Egyptian government station built at Nasir in 1875 was intended to halt such contacts between Fadasi and the Sobat valley. Some of the Dinka living along this route fled for safety to Jote Tullu and the Leḳa Oromo, where Schuver found some 2,000 of them in 1881, employed as Jote's hunters, herders, and shock troops. These Dinka may be the original 'Abigars', an ethnic term now applied to the Nuer, but which can be loosely translated as 'cowboys'. These men seem to have disappeared from Jote's court by the turn of the century, and we do not know if this is because they died in the wars of the 1880s or were sent as tribute to Menilek. It is speculation at this point, but it is possible to suggest that some may have escaped from Jote as he drew closer to imperial Ethiopia, and returned to their old homes, now occupied by the Jikany Nuer, just as many of the Abialang Dinka had already done to escape raids along the White Nile. Certainly we know that at the beginning of this century the Jikany Nuer population living along the Ethiopian border was largely bi-lingual in Nuer and Dinka. If Jote's former Dinka 'cowboys' did join the Nuer, then this would explain the existence of Oromo-speaking 'Abigar' on the Baro as early as 1898. It was these Oromo-speaking 'Nuer' (i.e. Abigar) who were the first agents and intermediaries in the trade between the Nuer and Oromo.[50]

The new political circumstances of the Ethiopian conquest rapidly expanded the trade. The Anuak, squeezed out of some of their land by the Nuer, were driven by extremity to trade ivory to the Ethiopians and soon also traded for firearms to increase their supply of ivory. Since Nuer country contained most of the elephants, the Nuer began trading ivory to Anuak and Arab intermediaries. The constant demand for ivory soon expanded beyond the frontier. In 1903 elephants were abundant on the Bahr al-Zaraf while almost non-existent along the Sobat. The Nuer search for ivory took them not only to the Zaraf valley but to the Khor Adar.[51]

Because of the international boundary, the Jikany Nuer, and more particularly the Gaajak, became the main intermediaries in the supply of ivory to Ethiopia. Both considerably expanded their contacts with other peoples in the process. Jote had been forbidden by Menilek in 1903 to enter the Koma and Meban country of Warragarra on the Daga which he had formerly claimed. Oromo merchants thus were confined to seasonal markets in Gaajak country. Some Nuer intermediaries employed in the annual collection of ivory lived in Gidami itself, but most of the Nuer involved were settled in the Sudan. By 1903 Gaajak parties went on annual visits to the Zaraf valley late in the dry season (March–May), trading bulls, tobacco, and spearheads for ivory. By 1905 Nuer hunting-parties along the Khor Adar were coming into contact with the Meban.[52]

Inside Ethiopia Nilotic trade was divided between *dejazmach* Jote, at Gidami, Sayo and Anfillo, and *ras* Tesemma, at Gore and Bure. Both had ivory monopolies in their own territories, effectively thwarting the attempts of

Sudanese merchants to trade in Sudanese ivory inside Ethiopia. The Baro marked the boundary between their provinces, and for the first decade of this century their rivalry was carried out in Addis Abeba and did not immediately affect the Nilotic trade. Between 1900 and 1909 Ethiopian ivory exports were at their highest, and the rate of exchange of cattle for ivory among the Nuer remained fairly steady, at about one cow for every ten pounds of ivory (see Table 5). But between 1910 and 1911 the Nuer got more for their ivory. Ethiopian ivory exports dropped drastically in 1910 as supplies dwindled, and the Ethiopians increased the supply of firearms to frontier peoples to maintain what supply of ivory remained. However, by this date the frontier had been virtually denuded of elephants. It was at this time that Jote fell from power. Menilek's demands on Jote had increased with his suspicions. In 1908 he began to support Khojali al-Hassan against Jote in the Beggi area, and he transferred the administration of the Anuak and Nuer to *ras* Tesemma. In the same year Jote was imprisoned.[53]

Jote's tribute had risen from 4,000 pounds of ivory, 200 slaves, 500 ounces of gold, and 7,000 thalers in 1903 to 4,000 pounds of ivory, 200 slaves, 1,300 ounces of gold, and 20,000 thalers in 1909. Much of the added gold and currency could be obtained only through increased ivory sales. By 1909 the Oromo began to come into the Sudan in greater numbers to obtain ivory to ransom Jote's freedom. In Gidami itself a rapid succession of governors between 1910 and 1912 plundered the province and its hinterlands along the same pattern then being followed in Maji (see Garretson's account in the previous chapter). Oromo merchants began travelling deep into the Sudan to increase their trade, using Nuer guides to take them as far as the Ghol and Twij Dinka on the Bahr al-Jabal, exchanging rifles for ivory. The Nuer, too, became more aggressive in their trade, taking their ivory by canoe up the Baro into Ethiopia, quickly selling it for cash, then buying rifles or cattle before escaping undetected by the Ethiopian authorities.[54]

This buccaneering in the ivory trade, produced first by Menilek's pressure on Jote, and then by instability in the empire before and after the emperor's death, was followed by an immediate contraction of the activities of Oromo merchants. Jote's release in 1912, the temporary resolution of the political crisis in Addis Abeba, and the Sudan government's vigilance against the Gidami-based merchants, helped to re-establish some control over the frontier ivory trade.[55] But the demand for ivory continued unabated, and with Oromo merchants once again confined to their markets in Gaajak, the Nuer were left in full possession of a flourishing ivory trade network.

The fact that Dinka, Shilluk, and other Nuer frequented Gaajak markets meant that no one group of Nuer could control the distribution of guns, but the significant profits that could be made in the interior were an incentive for those nearer the source of the trade to expand their own operations (compare the price of guns on the frontier with that in the interior during 1912–13, in the Table). The Gaajak used surplus captured Anuak rifles to become the main arms suppliers to the Lou in 1912. The next year the Lou, too, supplied the

Table 5. *Arms, ivory and cattle rates of exchange, 1901–35*[99]

Year	Purchaser	Source	Price	Quantity
1901	E. Jikany	Oromo	1 big tusk	300 beads
			1 med. tusk	200 beads
			1 small tusk	100 beads
			1 cow	40 beads
1903	Nuer	Oromo	10 lb tusk	1 cow
			50 lb tusk	10–15 cow calves
1909	Gaajak	Oromo	*c.* 99 lbs ivory	10–15 cows
1910	Nuer	Oromo	2 bulls	1 calf
			10–15 sheep	1 calf
	Anuak	Anfillo	1 large tusk	10 Gras rifles
1911	Nuer	Greek merchants	£ 2–3	1 Gras rifle
			£ 2	9 rds ammo.
	Nuer	Oromo	78–9 lb tusk	2–3 rifles, 50 rds ammo. each + 15 cow calves
1912				
c. April	Lou	Jikany	1 bull + 3 cows	1 rifle, 20 rds
c. Oct.	Gaajak	Oromo	1 bull + 3 cows	1 rifle, 30 rds
c. Dec.	Anuak		1 large tusk	10 rifles, 40–60 rds
			1 small tusk	70–100 rds
1913				
c. Feb.	Gaawar		2 cows	1 rifle
c. March	Jikany	Ethiopian merchants	1 sheep	12 rds
c. April	Lou	Ethiopian merchants in Jikany	1 cow	1 rifle
	Lak	Lou or Jikany	2 cows + 1 bull	1 rifle
	Gaawar	Lou or Jikany	3 cows	1 rifle
c. July	Anuak	Oromo and Baro Syndicate	1 cow or 1 large bullock	1 rifle
			$MT 8–10	1 rifle
			$MT 1	6 rds ammo.
c. Dec.	Gaawar	Jikany	1 60 lb tusk	2 rifles
1914	Gaajak	Jote	24–30 lbs ivory	1 single-shot rifle
			c. 99 lbs ivory	1 magazine rifle
	Gaajak	Ethiopians	1 bull	30 rds ammo. or less
	Anuak		1 large tusk	10 rifles, 60 rds
			1 med. tusk	8 rifles
			1 small tusk	70–80 rds
			1 large tusk	400 rds
1915	Jikany	Ethiopians	1 bull + 3 cows	1 rifle, 20 rds
			1 bull	60 rds
			1 cow	90 rds

Table 5. (*cont.*)

Years	Purchaser	Source	Price	Quantity
1916	Jikany	Ethiopians near Jokau; market S. of Kurmuk	1 bull + 2 cows 1 bull	1 rifle, 20 rds 20 rds
1917	*Ethiopians Nuer	Nuer and Anuak Ethiopians	$MT 20 2 cows 1 cow 1 large tusk	1 rifle 1 rifle 300 rds 8 rifles
1923	Jikany	*Dejaz.* Birru	37.5 lbs ivory	3 rifles, 30 rds
1925	Dinka, Bor Dist.	Gaajak	1 bull + 1 cow 70 lb tusk	1 rifle, 40 rds 2 rifles, 80 rds
1926	Anuak	Ethiopians	2 bulls + 1 calf 1 50 lb tusk	1 rifle 1 rifle
1927	Lak	Gaajak	2 bulls + 1 cow	1 rifle, 40 rds
c. 1928	Jikany	Ethiopians	1 pregnant cow	1 rifle
1931	Jikany	Ethiopians	1 pregnant cow 1 bull	1 rifle 50 rds
1935	Anuak	Gore and Gambela	$MT 1	3 rds

Note: Unless otherwise identified, 'Nuer' refers to all those different groups of Nuer trading at markets in Gaajak territory, and 'Ethiopian' is used when the source does not specify the origin of the merchants involved.

* In 1917 the Ethiopian need for rifles was so great that they were buying them back from the Nuer and Anuak, who were glad to get the money to buy ammunition, which was then scarce.

Lak and Gaawar, and by the early 1920s the Lou were the main brokers in ivory–rifle transactions between the Gaawar and Jikany. The Jikany went even farther afield. Arabic-speaking Nuer appeared in Talodi in the Nuba mountains in 1913 selling arms for cash. In the early 1920s, as elephant populations receded farther away from the frontier, they began trading rifles to the Twij and Bor Dinka for cattle and ivory, taking the cattle to the Aliab on the west bank of the Bahr al-Jabal and trading them for more ivory.[56]

The Ethiopian ivory trade significantly altered the patterns of ivory distribution among the Nuer from the Bahr al-Zaraf to the Baro. There had been virtually no ivory trade along the Bahr al-Zaraf in the nineteenth century. What ivory was obtained was either cut up for bracelets or given as offerings to shrines, such as the Mound of Ngundeng or the shrine of Deng Lakka. As this ivory belonged to the divinities who spoke through the prophets, the tusks could not be redistributed. Very little ivory seems to have been collected in this way. Ngundeng's Mound accumulated only between 58 and 88 tusks in the first ten years or so of its existence.[57]

The great increase in demand for ivory can be seen clearly even from the fragmentary evidence which we have. In one month in 1903, 275 tusks were taken from the Zaraf to the Gaajak. In 1908, 400 trade calves were found in one Gaajak trading centre, representing 1,333 to 2,000 pounds of ivory at 1903 prices. An estimated 1,600 unlicensed breechloaders had come into Upper Nile Province, mostly through the Nuer in 1910–11, and these represented some 41,599 pounds of ivory at 1911 prices. In 1913 Macar Diu's section of Gaawar bought 57 rifles which would have cost about 3,420 pounds of ivory. Jote's sale of 1,000 rifles to the Nuer in 1913–14 could have bought between 25,000 and 30,000 pounds of ivory. Finally, an average Gaajak party of three to four men each carrying twelve to fifteen rifles trading among the Dinka in 1925 could have expected to collect between 1,260 and 2,100 pounds of ivory at then current prices.[58]

These figures assume that ivory was the main item traded, but indigenous sources suggest that cattle had a much more important rôle than indicated by the official records (compare Turton's analysis in Chapter 6, above). In 1909–10 the Gaajak traded ivory for cattle to rebuild their herds after the 1908 rinderpest epidemic,[59] and they continued to build up their herds by trading rifles for cattle with the Dinka of Upper Nile Province, who lacked the same access to ivory as the Nuer. Cattle was also accepted in exchange for arms from the Gaawar, but only by itinerant Gaajak trading in Gaawar country. The Gaawar took only ivory to the Gaajak trade centres. By the 1920s the Twij Dinka also used ivory to increase their herds, selling ivory to the Gaajak for cash, which was used to purchase cattle in the official markets then being set up by the Sudan government.[60]

The Nuer traded ivory collectively and divided the proceeds from the trade along kinship lines. Among the Zaraf Nuer ivory tusks did not belong to the men deemed to have killed the elephant but to their kin.[61] It was the kin group, not the individual, who traded, and rifles obtained from the exchange of tusks were still, in some cases, distributed along kin lines in the same way that ivory cut up into bracelets was distributed. Ivory continued to be given to spiritual experts who assisted in the hunting of the elephants, but these individuals accrued no great wealth and secured no better trading position than other Nuer since the tusks were given to the divinity, not to men personally.

Still, some figures such as Dual Diu certainly increased their prestige and influence through the rituals which they performed to 'call' elephants to the hunt.[62] The intensified interest in elephant hunting placed them in wider demand. The fact that Guek Ngundeng was unable to accumulate as much ivory around his father's Mound in the 1920s as his father had done in the 1890s is some indication that the material gain of the Ethiopian ivory trade offered a competitive attraction to more spiritual investments.

The Anuak trade network was, by contrast, more restricted. Many Anuak lived in Ethiopia, and much of the trade was directly linked to collection of tribute through village headmen. Those inside Ethiopia were never lost for suppliers; Bure, Sayo, Gidami, Anfillo, and Maji all competed for Anuak trade.[63] Through both Oromo and Amhara traders the Ethiopian Anuak were able to supply the Sudan Anuak at a fairly steady rate. Akwei-wa-Cam established a monopoly over the ivory trade and over the supply of rifles to the two biggest Anuak districts in the Sudan. He also attracted Oromo and Amhara hunters since his district, unlike others on the frontier, still had elephants.[64] It was not so easy for Anuak nobles living closer to Ethiopian authority to maintain a similar monopoly. By 1916 the minor Anuak chiefs under Udiel-wa-Ngenya, who had earlier been made independent of him by the governor of Bure, had begun trading ivory on their own, and Udiel was forced to begin raiding into the Sudan as his own supplies of ivory dwindled.[65] Some Anuak sought other supplies of ivory, trading with the Majangir in the 1920s for ivory and other commodities used in the highland trade.[66] Many Nuer also traded ivory for guns with the Anuak on a casual but constant basis.[67]

The main centres in the supply of firearms shifted with the changing currents of Ethiopian politics. With Khojali al-Hassan's ascendancy after 1908, Asosa and Bela Shangul rivalled Gidami as major sources of arms for the Nuer. For a while the competition between Khojali and Jote escalated the arms trade. Jote flooded the Nuer market with a thousand rifles during and after the rains of 1913–14.[68] Khojali's final domination of Jote and his successors did not diminish the importance of the Nuer trade, since the continuing demands of Addis Abeba remained an incentive. Khojali paid Addis Abeba gold and slaves to maintain his autonomy, and by doing so secured most of the Wellegga trade.[69] Nuer travelled to Asosa and other parts of Khojali's domain to exchange cattle and ivory for guns and ammunition, and it was only with the establishment of a Sudanese police post on the Daga in the late 1920s that the major route of the arms traffic was once again diverted south of the Baro.[70] The disarming of the Lou and Gaawar in 1930 further restricted the arms trade to the frontier. This was not a permanent interruption. After World War II the trade resumed, and by 1949 the Jikany were once again selling rifles to the Nuba Mountains.[71]

The frontier trade was not exclusively confined to cattle, ivory and rifles. Tobacco, grain, seeds, cloth and metalware were also traded,[72] but these items were incidental to the main trade. The main trade was affected in numerous ways by the political relations between the Ethiopian frontier provinces and Addis Abeba. The demand for ivory in tribute was persistent, and cattle and firearms were largely ancillary to obtaining ivory. As supplies of ivory along the frontier declined, the Ethiopian trade network expanded, largely through Gaajak Nuer intermediaries, between the border and the Nile valley. This trade increased contacts between the peoples of the region, affecting not only relations between Nilotes, but between Nilotes and non-Nilotes.

RELATIONS BETWEEN BORDER PEOPLES

Because of the movements in the nineteenth century already mentioned, the Nilotic communities in what was to become the Sudan–Ethiopian borderlands were already intermingled by the turn of the century. The Anuak and Nuer on the Sobat, Baro, and Pibor lived in varying degrees of co-operation and confrontation, with Nuer marrying Anuak girls, Anuak boys being given Nuer initiation marks, Anuak living in Nuer villages or under Nuer leaders, and trading during the dry season when the Nuer and Anuak traded with each other. There was also fighting, and the turning point came in 1911 with four separate Anuak raids against the Lou and Jikany. Akwei-wa-Cam and a number of other Anuak captured many Nuer, and some were even sold to Gidami as slaves. Fighting continued throughout 1912 until the Nuer began to redress the balance through arming themselves.[73]

Despite such large scale hostilities there were still contacts that overcame the new tensions. The Anuak at Itang maintained good relations with the Gaajak, and one headman in 1912 was successful in reducing the level of violence between the Anuak and Nuer in that region. By 1913 renewed Ethiopian activity along the border brought the Nuer and Anuak closer together, until a recognition of the common danger drove them to make peace. This peace extended only to the Anuak on the Baro, and in 1914 the Jikany and Lou combined in a massive pre-emptive raid against the Anuak on the Akobo, that forced the government to intervene on the Anuak side.[74] Throughout the early years of World War I tension still existed. Again, it was the common danger from Ethiopia, with Majid's campaign in 1916, that drew some Anuak and Nuer together. The Anuak on the Baro, Udiel's enemies, received assistance from the Nuer who assembled at Itang to help repel Majid's second advance.[75] This was the area in which intermarriage was most common, and the Nilotes living there combined together when faced with an external threat.

The gradual imposition of peace along the border generally reduced the number and intensity of clashes between Nuer and Anuak. The security that the Sudan government helped to create after World War I increased intermarriage and mixed settlement, with the Nuer settling along the Baro, Gilo, and Makwei by the 1930s.[76] This mingling of Nuer and Anuak had its effect on intersectional relations among the Nuer. In a Lou intersectional fight along the Pibor in 1922 one section approached the Jikany for aid while the other enlisted the Anuak.[77]

If Nilotes were mixing with each other during this period, so were Nilotes with non-Nilotes. Nilotic influence among the Cai peoples dated at least to the days of the Dinka occupation of the White Nile and Sobat. Nilotic elements in the languages of the area are strong enough to suggest either a Nilotic origin of some of these peoples (such as the Meban), or the assimilation of Nilotes into non-Nilotic societies. Even more important is the borrowing from Nilotic culture that has gone into the reconstruction of certain societies in the aftermath of extensive raiding in which the Nilotes participated. This has continued into the present century, as for instance when the Anuak and Koma settlements along the upper Jokau became so mixed as a result of Nuer and Ethiopian raiding that the Anuak became part of the Koma community.[78]

The selectivity of the Nuer in choosing their targets, which we have seen in their relations with the Anuak, is also found in their relations with the Cai. The Kaang section of the Gaajak used to raid the Meban and other peoples north of the Yabus, while the Tar section, which lived in Ethiopia, raided the Koma on the Jokau and Kigille. Yet very early on the Koma were able to seek refuge with the Nuer when raided by the Ethiopians. The Kaang section also had close ties with the Ban Shoa Meban. The Kaang Gaajak traded grain with the Ban Shoa and opposed both Ethiopian and Nuer raids along the Daga. Mut Dung actively intervened to prevent one section of Gaajak raiding the Ban Shoa, an intervention which led to a Nuer intersectional fight. Mut Dung then moved his dry season camps farther away from the rest of the Gaajak and closer to the Koma on the Daga. Even after his death, Mut Dung's section protected the Koma from *dejazmach* Birru's raids when he tried to reassert Sayo's claim to the Daga in the early 1920s.[79]

The Cai chose alternate protectors. The Koma sometimes spied on the Nuer for the Anuak, and in 1917 some fled the Nuer to Khojali. Even the Ban Shoa tried to persuade the government to fight Mut Dung in 1917 if by doing so retribution could also be visited on those other Nuer who had victimized them. Much later other Koma were willing to abandon the protection of the Sudan government, crossing to Ethiopia to avoid paying tribute when encouraged by Koryom Tut, the Nuer *fītawrarī*.[80]

Koma border hopping, which complicated Sudan–Ethiopian relations in the 1960s and '70s, is not a recent development.[81] In an area that has been persistently raided from all sides, people like the Koma find themselves between two fires, and in order to survive they fight fire with fire by seeking protection with one side against the other. The use of one predator against another may have predated Menilek's expansion, but the simultaneous arrival of Menilek's forces and the Sudan government added a new dimension to this pattern. The presence of two governments on the border provided greater scope for manoeuvre and additional restraints on immediate neighbours.

The existence of the international border encouraged the mobility and mingling of societies. The Nuer and Anuak moved their settlements, sometimes to avoid Ethiopian forces, sometimes to avoid each other, and in doing so they moved their settlements closer together in many areas. The non-Nilotes also had to move to avoid raids. The Majangir, living entirely in Ethiopia, were forced, by Anuak and Ethiopian raids north of the Baro, into 'empty' land which in many cases had been formerly settled by Koma, Mao, and Oromo, all peoples who were dislocated by Menilek's expansion. Like the Koma and the Anuak, the Majangir became mixed with those who raided them, many joining their relatives who were captured and raised among the Anuak, even assisting Ethiopian Anuak in raids against Sudan Anuak.[82]

Expanding tribute and trade

The incorporation of captives into Nilotic society not only increased internal mixing and inter-ethnic ties, it inhibited the spread of Ethiopian slaving into the Sudan. The Nuer refused to aid Khojali's raids against the Koma. Only once were they reported to have contemplated selling Meban captives into slavery, and that was after the Sudan government's campaign of 1920 when the Gaajak needed to rearm to defend themselves. Even then many of their Meban captives were assimilated into Nuer society.[83] Among the Anuak both Udiel and Akwei were known to have sold their Anuak and Nuer captives to the Ethiopians, and much later some Anuak sold kinless children to the Murle in the Sudan, but on the whole captives seemed to have been kept or ransomed and exchanged.[84] In many ways, then, it was the internal strength and the external influence of Nilotic societies that both limited the dislocation caused by Ethiopian demands and raids and influenced the reconstruction of societies so dislocated.

CONCLUSION

This examination of relations between the imperial Ethiopian government and the Anuak and Nuer requires some alteration of existing interpretations of Ethiopian frontier administration and of Nilotic societies. Ethiopian political influence cannot be measured solely by a physical presence along the frontier. Compared with the Anglo-Egyptian administration on the Sudan side of the border, Ethiopian administration was extremely flexible, and it was through that flexibility that Ethiopian influence was expanded. The Nilotes were active participants in both the expansion and limitation of that influence.

Ethiopian administration in many parts of southern Ethiopia tended to tie its subjects to the land. Leaders were co-opted as *balabbat* with grants of newly-alienated land, while the labour force was fixed to the locality by the *gebbar* system. The highland hierarchy floated over this fixed base, connected by the individual strands of *neftennya* settlers. This did not happen to either the Nuer or the Anuak, two Nilotic peoples living in different ecologies, with different economies, settlement patterns, and political systems. The Anuak were not, like the Nuer, pastoralists who were hard to tie down, but there were many reasons why *both* peoples escaped the most common forms of Ethiopian colonization. There was, to begin with, the highland distaste for the unruled and unruly lowlands, whether forest, swamp, or desert. The peculiarly intense internal rivalry along this section of the border, of Amhara against Oromo, Asosa against Sayo, Sayo against Gore, Gore and Sayo against the Baro Syndicate, allowed the Nuer and Anuak ample opportunities to slip between the cracks of the Ethiopian political system and to keep the cracks open. There was also the international border, a yawning gap between administrative systems that could never be completely shut. The inhibitions of geography, internal political rivalries, and the international border are not enough, however, to explain the limitations on Ethiopian administration or the directions which it took. For that we must also look at the internal qualities of the Nilotic societies.

Among the Nuer and Anuak, there was a mobility of leadership which the border encouraged. The mobility among the Nuer was essentially physical. Because of the pattern of seasonal movements neither leaders nor followers could be expected to stay in one place on either side of the border for long. Among the Anuak, followers were more stationary while leaders moved among them, funnelled through the Anuak political system by the parallel channels of headmen and nobles. The Nuer and Anuak leaders each, in their own way, responded to the principle that Godfrey Lienhardt recognized for Anuak headmen: 'I must follow them, I am their leader.'[85] With the creation of the border and the alternative attractions of the Sudan and Ethiopian administrations, large numbers of persons moved from side to side, as the opportunity arose or as the occasion demanded. In cross-border rivalries, leaders too could migrate, and there was no great feeling of the permanence of allegiance once given. As one Anuak headman advised his son in the early 1930s, he should give one hand to Ethiopia and the other to the Sudan.[86] With such practised jugglers, any attempt to base local administration solely on local leaders was clearly a precarious operation.

Another factor in the survival of Nilotic autonomy was the habit of assimilation. It was common for Nilotes not only to absorb dislocated persons but to assimilate themselves into other societies as well, as the Nilotes among the Cai, the Anuak and Dinka among the Nuer, and even the Dinka among the Oromo attest. That Nilotes habitually assimilated war captives and welcomed the relatives of such captives meant that participation in Ethiopian slave raids offered little gain or attraction. This inhibited the expansion of slave-raiding and offered a means of reconstruction in the wake of raids. Local communities may have been destroyed or dispersed, but Nilotic societies were not. At most they were rearranged. Their response was flexible and in that flexibility lay their resilience. The habit of assimilation further encouraged mobility of population, and such mobility was inimical to the establishment of the *gebbar* system,[87] as the flight of the Anuak from the plains beneath Gurafarda to the Anuak nobles showed.

In so far as the Ethiopian administration was successful in extending its influence, this too was achieved through flexibility. To a certain extent the internal rivalries within Ethiopia helped to maintain this influence over border peoples because the administration itself did not present an inflexible front that could only be accepted or rejected. There were alternatives within the administration, alternatives entirely lacking in the more uniform British administration of the Sudan. Unlike the British, the Ethiopians could and did incorporate spiritual and ritual leaders. It seems common practice in Ethiopian administration that such men were given exalted titles which left their precise powers, and even their relationship to the administration, undefined.[88] This lack of political, and in the case of the Nuer and Anuak, territorial precision was more in keeping with the fluctuating authority of spiritual and ritual leaders and the migratory habits of their followers. These leaders were Ethiopia's tenuous connection to the moving base of its people.

The relative strengths of Ethiopian administration of the Nilotes are evident when compared with the attempts at closer regulation by British administration in the Sudan. While the Ethiopians were more content to work through things as they were, the British sought to reconstruct Nilotic political structures to fit their own forms of administration. Reliance on tribute patrols in the Sudan produced no links with the Nuer political organization, no links with a structure which the government could use in building its own administration. The Sudan government was more successful in regulating the succession of Anuak royal emblems, but it failed entirely to suppress village revolutions. The Ethiopian trade network, however, did follow the existing political organization of both the Nuer and Anuak, and it linked this organization to the wider Ethiopian trading network and the wider Ethiopian political system. The extensive, if indirect, influence which Ethiopia exerted in the southern Sudan in this way was an important factor in the motivation of the Sudan government to reassert its own control. The presence of Ethiopia and the involvement of the Nilotes in Ethiopian trade and politics had profound consequences on the direction of administration of Upper Nile Province right through the 1930s. The flexibility of Ethiopian administration, and the Nilotes' adaptability to the border, were two reasons why the Nilotes eluded stricter control by the Sudan administration, and why, unlike the pastoralists on the Ethiopia–Kenya border,[89] the Nilotes were never fully divided along tribal lines or restricted in their ability to respond to changes in their environment.

Throughout this period there was a reciprocity in Nilotic–Ethiopian relations which the Nuer, for one, see continuing to the present day. Both the reciprocity and basic equality that developed in Nilotic–Ethiopian relations are encapsulated in a story frequently told among the Lou Nuer, of an Ethiopian visitor to the prophet Ngundeng (*c.* 1845–1906) at the turn of the century. The version given here was told by Gatkek Bol Ngundeng, a grandson of the prophet, in conversation with the late Stephen Ciec Lam, a prominent Lou Nuer politician who had been active in the exile movement in Ethiopia and the bush during the Sudanese civil war.[90]

> *GBN:* It was said that the Ethiopians (*buny*) were rebelling at that time. They rebelled against the Italians (*tilian*).
> *SCL:* The Italians were after we were born.
> *GBN:* They rebelled before. This is not the Italian war after you were born. The Italians drove them into the bush before then.
> *SCL:* Oh. The war before, the war which is called 'Adawi'.
> *GBN:* It was said that the Ethiopians were coming from Fashoda (Paciöt). At the time when they were in Fashoda, they came but they stopped, because it was the rainy season. They went to a place called Jiör. People were dying of starvation, people were suffering from malaria in the water. They did not reach the village, so they went that way. Their leader (*kuar*) came through Jiör and found that the Dinka were coming, they were coming to the cattle byre, they were coming to the Mound [of Ngundeng]. He followed the people until he reached the Mound.
>
> When he arrived, people were surprised. Where did the man come from,

carrying his gun? He sat down. Ngundeng said, 'Why do you look at him? He was brought by Divinity (*kuoth*). What he came for, he will tell us. Give him something to eat.'

A cow was killed, and he was given other things to eat. He spent some days there, but no-one knew who was going to talk to him. Then the Ethiopian came before him [Ngundeng] and he sat in front of Ngundeng. The Ethiopian spoke in his own language, and Ngundeng understood him.

He asked him, 'What do you want?' He replied, 'I am a man who has been walking in the bush, father, I am walking in the bush.' The Ethiopian said, 'Now I have left other people behind, and I will not find them since I left them with nothing to eat. I came here to find something to eat from you, so that I may take it to them.'

Ngundeng said, 'My son, those you left there in the bush will not die, as you saw them, they will not die. There is something back there that will fill them. The thing that was killing them, you will find it is finished. You will find them, they will be satisfied.'

Then Ngundeng told the Lou that the Ethiopian should be given some cattle. He gave him about eight big oxen to feed them. [The Lou said] 'Waa! Son of Nyayiel [Ngundeng's Lou mother], how can we give the Lou's cattle to someone who comes from a place we do not know? He may kill people because of those cattle one day.' 'Sons of my mother's brother,' [Ngundeng replied] 'you will follow those cattle one day. If you give a person a good thing, one day, sons of my mother's brother, if something happens you will join with those people.' They said, 'You are playing with cattle!'

Ngundeng said, 'I will give him the black and white brindled bull (*tut kernyang*) and four other oxen.' People said, 'Yes, if it is the *tut kernyang*, give it to him.' He said, 'Do you know why I give him the *tut kernyang*?' 'No.' 'You will one day follow it.'

He took the *tut kernyang* to his country. Ngundeng told him, 'You! You will go with the *tut kernyang*, and you will have to sharpen its right horn. You must always sharpen it. You will not eat it soon. Graze it until you find what are you searching for. This *tut kernyang*, people objected to my giving it to you, but they will follow it one day.'

So the Ethiopian set out. He went to his people and he found that they were well. He found waterbucks in plenty around their camp. They killed the waterbucks, and every day they increased. That was the leaving of the Ethiopian, until he reached his own country.

The story refers to known historical contacts between the Lou and Ethiopia before the arrival of the Anglo-Egyptian government. The version recorded here seems a clear reference to that small band of *ras* Tesemma's soldiers who tried, but failed to meet Marchand at Fashoda. It certainly agrees with contemporary accounts of the hardships they faced.[91] Yet this is not the only meeting between the Lou and Ethiopia before the beginning of this century. Among the Gaajak it is remembered that at least one Oromo delegation set out from Sayo to seek out Ngundeng at his village of Weideang because of his importance and because of the large concentration of ivory at his Mound.[92] Persistent inquiries among the Lou about Ethiopian visits to Ngundeng, however, elicit only this one story, in one form or another. What is more, the Ethiopian visitor is usually identified as Haile Selassie.[93] The memory of a real encounter has been expanded to include recent experience and to incorporate knowledge of the wider world only recently learned. The relationship between the Nuer and Ethiopia is expressed in a myth of a very recent origin.

The relations are reciprocal, as between equals. Ngundeng the prophet helps to create Haile Selassie's rise to power by foretelling it, the ability of a truly great prophet. The gift of cattle is the gift of life, and certainly from what we now know of the border trade, the Nuer contribution to the border political system through providing the goods on which the system of tribute survived was considerable. Yet this is not the main message of the myth. Ngundeng refers to the time, now come to pass, when the Nuer will follow the cattle given to Haile Selassie, fleeing the civil war in the Sudan. The Nuer helped to establish the Ethiopian state along its farthest borders, and the reward for that is safety during a time of strife. The gift of survival is repaid by survival.

The re-evaluation of British and Ethiopian administrations which this study produces must be accompanied by a re-evaluation of our understanding of Nilotic society. The quality of the Nilotic ethnography has attracted wide attention and discussion, but for many anthropologists, and even some historians, the Nuer do not have history – they have structure. They are 'a text-book example of an "acephalous" society',[94] the archetype of segmentary opposition. This stereotype must now be questioned.

It is an exaggeration to describe the Nuer as acephalous. Far from having no leaders they had many: leaders with extensive spiritual influence and leaders who grasped the opportunities which association with Ethiopia offered. The antagonism of the Sudan government to spiritual leaders, and the strategic threat posed by Ethiopia made these men targets of the Sudan administration, and they were systematically removed. By the 1930s Nuer society was not so much acephalous as decapitated.

Similarly here, as in other parts of Nuer territory, the theory of segmentary opposition works better in principle than in practice.[95] We find Nuer siding with Anuak against Nuer, and, what is more surprising, Nuer siding with Koma against Nuer. Along the border, as elsewhere, Nuer raiding was followed by occupation, and occupation involved intermarriage and mixed settlement, establishing a series of exchanges and reciprocal obligations which modified internal Nuer political groupings.

Another more surprising modification must be made in the interpretation of Nuer political economy. In particular, the assumption that the narrowness of Nuer economic and social horizons inhibited their involvement in trade must be questioned.[96] We find instead that for a period of some thirty years the Nuer were involved in extensive trade in a variety of commodities, and that they took an active rôle in expanding that trade and searching out new markets. Because this trade was based on ivory and firearms and was directed towards Ethiopia, it was suppressed by the Sudan government, who tried to replace it with selectively supported Arab merchants trading in administrative centres rather than in Nuer trade centres. This removal of the Nuer from active participation in trade, and the replacement of the Nuer trading network by a more restricted and less vigorous official network, constituted one of the many inhibiting influences on southern Sudanese economic activity that followed the imposition of the Southern Policy in 1930. Nuer lack of interest in Arab traders in the 1930s and '40s was taken as evidence of their narrow economic interests rather than the restrictiveness of administrative policy. Recent events have shown once again how quickly the Nuer do respond to new economic opportunities, especially those involving periodic movement, as in migrant labour in the building trade in the northern Sudan and more locally the collection and transportation of dried fish all along the Bahr al-Jabal.[97]

Curiously enough, the difficulties which the Sudan government faced in establishing regulated trade through selectively supported Arab merchants illuminate further the different sort of relationship which the Nuer had with Ethiopia. Evans-Pritchard observed that the Nuer regarded purchases as a form of reciprocal obligation. Their idea 'is that you give something to a merchant who is thereby put under an obligation to you. At the same time you ask him for something you need from his shop and he ought to give it to you because, by taking your gift, he has entered into a reciprocal relationship with you.'[98] Misunderstandings naturally arose from these different expectations. It was precisely this expectation of reciprocity which marked Nuer dealings with the highland Ethiopians and with many border peoples, an expectation which was not fulfilled during the early years of Sudan administration. But just this kind of reciprocity is remembered by the Nuer as the essential quality of their historical contacts with Ethiopia.

Epilogue

WENDY JAMES

Sir Edward Evans-Pritchard, the pioneer craftsman of modern social anthropology, saw himself working in the same medium as the historian. Before his time there had been a wealth of broad historical speculation of the long-term, evolutionary kind in anthropology, but it had often approached the remoter 'tribal' cultures as mere specimens or *objets trouvés*. As such, they were evidence for historical processes external to themselves, but without the ability to make their own history or to reflect upon it. Evans-Pritchard's key inspiration for us, I suggest, has been his delineation of autonomous critical consciousness and a will to action within societies formerly supposed passive in this sense. To concede this independent voice and will to the remotest peoples, however circumscribed by environmental constraint or political control, is in a significant way to admit these peoples into the historical arena.

The most expressly historical of Evans-Pritchard's studies was that of the Sanusi Order among the Bedouin of Cyrenaica.[1] This region, although in the African continent, is of course outside Africa in the limited sense, that 'sub-Saharan' sense which has come to define the Africanist field. Perhaps for this reason, the historical implications of Evans-Pritchard's anthropology have often been overlooked by those who have adapted his methods to construct their own models for further research in the Africanist field. The historical elements which are an integral part of his analyses of the social world of Nuer, Azande, Shilluk and Anuak have not always been recognized, and students of other parts of 'Africa south of the Sahara' have tended to pass them over in favour of his representations of cultural form and structural principle.

Perhaps the very definition of Africa in the now out-dated, mid-twentieth century sense, that is virtually 'those areas of the inner African continent under European rule', entrenched the assumption that this broad category of African peoples had no real history. A line across the continent defining what most people mean by 'Africa south of the Sahara' might still be drawn fairly straight through the west and central regions, but would make a large circular detour southwards to exclude Ethiopia. This line is an inherited boundary of the colonial imagination, and it unfortunately inhibits communication not only between those who study Ethiopia on the one hand and those concerned with the rest of Africa on the other, but also between historians and anthropologists.

Ethiopia is one of the most visible regions of 'historical' Africa in the historians' sense, though as Donald Donham has indicated in Chapter 1, that history too often defined itself as the story of the state alone (a familiar theme now in European and American history). By the early 1930s, Evans-Pritchard's work in the Sudan had, however, already been extending the horizons and methods of historical enquiry. It is not often recalled that at that time he was planning a major study in Ethiopia. He had been granted a two-year Leverhulme Fellowship to carry out a study of the Oromo (the 'pagan Galla'), and he was ready to embark on this in 1935. But because of the growing political crisis and the expected Italian invasion of Ethiopia, he was delayed on the border for two and a half months and finally obliged to give up his project. It is interesting to speculate on the form that his account of Oromo society might have taken. Perhaps the very palpable presence of the past in Ethiopia, and its special relevance to the spread of the Oromo language and peoples, their inner diversity, multifold relations with other peoples, and their contribution to the forging of the modern state, would have given Evans-Pritchard's account that fertile historical insight which in the event emerged in his later work on North Africa. A major book by him on the Oromo, as a British social anthropologist strayed beyond territories under British rule, might usefully have opened a conversation between 'Ethiopianist' and 'Africanist' studies a couple of generations ago. It might also have fostered a greater awareness of the historical dimension of even stateless societies among social anthropologists in other parts of Africa, and thus fruitfully have linked the methods of anthropology and history within Africanist academia.

As things in fact developed, the standard monographs and collections of papers which came to define the Africanist field contained very little reference, if any, to Ethiopia; we think immediately, for example, of *African Political Systems*, edited by Evans-Pritchard and Fortes (1940), *African Systems of Kinship and Marriage*, edited by Radcliffe-Brown (1950), and *African Worlds*, edited by Forde (1954). The French studied French Africa, and Ethiopian ethnography was left largely to Italian and German scholars, operating with quasi-racial theories and museum-oriented methods. Malinowskian field work had not yet arrived in Ethiopia. Even the pioneers of African history excluded Ethiopia from their studies. We recall for example Vansina's early classification of African kingdoms which made no reference to imperial Ethiopia, or to the older kingdoms which it had absorbed.[2]

There were earlier periods, from classical times up to the relatively recent explorations of James Bruce, for example, when old Abyssinia was treated for what it was: a complex civilization set within the north-east part of the African continent. It is only since the establishment of the modern Ethiopian state by Menilek II, simultaneously with the successful European scramble for other territories in Africa, that its 'uniqueness' in academic circles has been so emphasized. The Italian occupation, and the subsequent liberation of the country, made Ethiopia a world-wide symbol of African identity, but if anything this intensified the mystique and raised the prestige of scholarly Ethiopian studies high above the (admittedly often pedestrian) village research which was becoming common in colonial Africa. The detailed circumstances even of Ethiopian topography, let alone the life of its rural people, remained obscure, while scholarship within Ethiopia continued to flower largely from the older linguistic, literary and theological traditions.

The 1960s saw the beginnings of a great change in African studies. With the independence of former colonial territories, the vitality of local history came to the fore, not only within social anthropological studies but in the immense expansion of research by professional historians, who began to follow the anthropologists into 'the field'.[3] This body of new historical work was fostered by the African universities. The old disciplinary boundaries were crossed repeatedly, not only by European scholars, but by African colleagues trained both overseas and in Africa; American participation in African research burgeoned; and these developments began to affect Ethiopia also. Even within Ethiopian studies, the 'African' elements in Ethiopian society and civilization were increasingly discussed; and the current re-evaluation of Abyssinian culture in the African as well as the 'Semitic' context surely opens the way for a general return of Ethiopian studies to the African fold.

We offer the present collection of essays on Ethiopia and the wider project it represents, in part as a contribution to the new dialogue between Africanist history and social anthropology. First, we would like to emphasize again the inherent importance of a comparative consideration of Ethiopian institutions and ethnography with those of other African countries. Secondly, we draw attention to the cultural connection and social interaction across international boundaries in the Horn of Africa. Thirdly, on the basis of our consideration of *provincial* Ethiopia, we particularly advocate the advantage of a dual method of approach to the world of peoples caught up in (and contributing to) the process of state formation. There is a double aspect to local society within Ethiopia, illustrated in one form or another in each essay above. The internal patterns of social organization and culture which we have examined are themselves partly shaped by historical processes which have drawn each locality into relationship with the state; conversely, the formation of the state itself has been to some extent a story of negotiation and compromise with such provincial circumstances.

This interweaving of internal and external threads within the texture of local community in Ethiopia, what we can term the 'double-stitching' of provincial society, is particularly striking to observers from another country. By comparison with the former European anthropologists of colonial Africa, they can claim the benefit of a 'seeing eye' in relation to the imperial, as well as the local elements. The very clarity of the distinction between these elements in Ethiopia, particularly in the southern periphery, give analyses such as those above a particular value for those engaged in the study of other regions of modern Africa. The ending of colonial rule in many parts of Africa has revealed the enduring character of older structures of dominance: we are now seeing the strength of old political systems, old élites and trading networks, older patterns of cultural dissemination, and the complexities of peripheral response to all these. A notion of the self-contained society, state or stateless, is no longer plausible. It must surely follow that the old line between the study of Ethiopia and the rest of Africa should finally be breached, and one of the most important centres of economic, political and cultural influence in the continent be drawn into the mainstream of African studies.

Notes

ABBREVIATIONS

AA	*African Affairs*
AEH	*African Economic History*
AP:CR	Accounts and Papers: Commercial Reports (*PP*)
BD	Bor District files (Juba)
BSGI	*Bollettino della Società Geographica Italiana*
Civsec	Civil Secretary's files (Khartoum)
END	Eastern Nuer District files (Juba and Nasir)
ENRC	Eastern Nuer Rural Council files (Nasir)
EP	Equatoria Province files (Juba)
EO	*Ethiopian Observer*
FO	Foreign Office papers (PRO)
GJ	*Geographical Journal*
IJAHS	*International Journal of African Historical Studies*
Intel	Intelligence Department files (Khartoum)
JAH	*Journal of African History*
JES	*Journal of Ethiopian Studies*
Mongalla	Mongalla Province files (Khartoum)
NRO	National Records Office, Khartoum
PP	*Parliamentary Papers* (Great Britain)
PRO	Public Records Office (Kew)
SIR	Sudan Intelligence Report
SMIR	Sudan Monthly Intelligence Report
SMR	Sudan Monthly Record
SNR	*Sudan Notes and Records*
SRO	Southern Records Office, Juba
UJ	*Uganda Journal*
UNP	Upper Nile Province files (Khartoum and Juba)

1. Old Abyssinia and the new Ethiopian empire

1 For comments and criticisms that helped to improve this chapter, I would like to thank the following scholars: Bahru Zewde, Lionel Bender, Jacques Bureau, Jane Collier, John Comaroff, Donald Crummey, Wendy James, Allan Hoben, James McCann, Charles McClellan, and Merid Wolde Aregay. Of course, the following interpretation remains my own. I have neither carried out anthropological field research in northern Ethiopia nor worked with primary historical documents; rather, this first chapter is a synthesis of published

work, an attempt to place materials that already exist in a new framework. I have relied heavily on the analyses of Donald Crummey and Allan Hoben.

2 I follow Crummey in distinguishing between Abyssinia – kingdoms in the north from the thirteenth to the nineteenth centuries – and Ethiopia – the modern state created by Menilek at the end of the nineteenth century. See Donald Crummey, 'Abyssinian Feudalism', *Past and Present* 89 (1980), 115–38.

3 Mordechai Abir, *Ethiopia: The Era of the Princes* (London: Longmans, 1968); Richard A. Caulk, 'The Origins of Development of the Foreign Policy of Menilek II, 1865–1889' (Ph.D. thesis, Department of History, School of Oriental and African Studies, University of London, 1966); R. H. Kofi Darkwah, *Shewa, Menelik, and the Ethiopian Empire, 1813–1889* (London: Heinemann, 1975); Harold G. Marcus, *The Life and Times of Menelik II* (Oxford: Clarendon Press, 1975); Sven Rubenson, *The Survival of Ethiopian Independence* (London: Heinemann, 1976); Zawde Gabra-Sellasse, *Yohannes IV of Ethiopia* (Oxford: Clarendon Press, 1975). Large gaps remain in this literature. We still do not have, for example, a history of the expansion into the south, a chronology of campaigns, much less an analysis of the expansion's causes and consequences.

4 J. Baeteman, *Dictionnaire amarigna–français* (Dire Dawa, Ethiopia: Imprimerie Saint Lazare, 1929), col. 939, translates *dar ager* as frontier countries, particularly those adjoining the Anglo-Egyptian Sudan. This phrase was also used of the new southern frontier: *cf.* Enrico Brotto, *Il regime delle terre nel governo del Harar* (Addis Abeba: Servizio Tipografico Governo Generale Africa Orientale Italiana, n.d.), p. 92, for Arsi. For an analysis of what frontiers meant to the northern highland political economy and how this changed during the twentieth century, see James C. McCann, 'Households, Peasants, and Rural History in Lasta, Northern Ethiopia, 1900–35' (Ph.D. thesis, Department of History, Michigan State University, 1984).

5 In history, Merid Wolde Aregay has been something of an exception to this characterization, in as much as he has analysed the impact of the periphery on the centre. See his 'Southern Ethiopia and the Christian Kingdom, 1508–1708, with Special Reference to the Galla Migrations and their Consequences' (Ph.D. thesis, Department of History, School of Oriental and African Studies, University of London, 1971). Also see the recent work of McCann, 'Households, Peasants, and Rural History' (see Bibliography for details). Finally, for an anthropological work that attempts to link periphery to centre more than most, see William A. Shack, 'Urban Ethnicity and the Cultural Process of Urbanization in Ethiopia', in Aidan Southall, ed., *Urban Anthropology* (New York: Oxford University Press, 1973).

6 The period which I am discussing in regard to Abyssinia is a very rough one, from the late sixteenth to the nineteenth centuries, with occasional glances backward. I am concerned to construct an outline of Abyssinian society from a distance; this undertaking does not mean, of course, that significant changes did not occur during this period.

7 Jack Goody, *Technology, Tradition and the State in Africa* (Oxford: Oxford University Press, 1971); *Production and Reproduction: A Comparative Study of the Domestic Domain* (Cambridge: Cambridge University Press, 1976); *Cooking, Cuisine and Class: A Study in Comparative Sociology* (Cambridge: Cambridge University Press, 1982); *The Development of the Family and Marriage in Europe* (Cambridge: Cambridge University Press, 1983); Jack Goody and S. J. Tambiah, eds., *Bridewealth and Dowry* (Cambridge: Cambridge University Press, 1973).

8 Goody himself (*Technology, Tradition and the State*, pp. 30–1; *Production and Reproduction*, pp. 110–11; *Cooking, Cuisine and Class*, pp. 210–12) has considered Ethiopia in relation to his theories, but since he neglects the most important sources, his conclusions – that Ethiopia fits the 'Eurasian' category — stand in need of reconsideration.

9 The basic work on northern Ethiopian land tenure is Allan Hoben, *Land Tenure Among the Amhara of Ethiopia: the Dynamics of Cognatic Descent* (Chicago: University of Chicago Press, 1973). On the meaning of *chisennya*, see Gebre-Wold-Ingida Worq, 'Ethiopia's Traditional

System of Land Tenure and Taxation', *EO* 5 (1962), p. 313. See also Joanna Mantel-Niećko, *The Role of Land Tenure in the System of Ethiopian Imperial Government in Modern Times* (Warsaw: Wydawnictwa Uniwersytetu Warszawskiego, 1980), p. 117. It should be pointed out that *chisennya* did not mean 'tenant' in all areas. In Begemdir and Menz, it referred simply to a homesteader.

10 Dan Franz Bauer, *Household and Society in Ethiopia: An Economic and Social Analysis of Tigray Social Principles and Household Organization* (East Lansing: African Studies Center, Michigan State University, 1977).

11 Allan Hoben, 'Family, Land, and Class in Northwest Europe and Northern Highland Ethiopia', in Harold G. Marcus, ed., *Proceedings of the First United States Conference on Ethiopian Studies* (East Lansing: African Studies Center, Michigan State University, 1975); Merid Wolde Aregay, 'Society and Technology in Ethiopia, 1500–1800', in Department of History, eds., *Proceedings of the Second Annual Seminar of the Department of History* (Addis Abeba: Addis Abeba University Press, 1984). The lack of differentiation between élite and commoner culture is also noted by Donald Levine, *Wax and Gold: Tradition and Innovation in Ethiopian Culture* (Chicago: University of Chicago Press, 1965), p. 156, by Ronald A. Reminick, 'The Manze Amhara of Ethiopia: A Study of Authority, Masculinity, and Sociality' (Ph.D. thesis, Department of Anthropology, University of Chicago, 1973), p. 35, and by Wolfgang Weissleder, 'The Political Ecology of Amhara Domination' (Ph.D. thesis, Department of Anthropology, University of Chicago, 1965), pp. 230–1.

12 John Markakis, *Ethiopia: Anatomy of a Traditional Polity* (Oxford: Clarendon Press, 1974), p. 91.

13 Levine, *Wax and Gold*, pp. 163–4.

14 On the European notion of orders see Georges Duby, *The Three Orders: Feudal Society Imagined* (Chicago: University of Chicago Press, 1980).

15 Hoben, 'Family, Land, and Class', p. 168.

16 Donald Crummey, 'Society and Ethnicity in the Politics of Christian Ethiopia during the Zamana Masafent', *IJAHS*, 8 (1975), p. 269. However, most present-day Amharic speakers would not be aware of this semantic connection.

17 Berhanou Abbebe, *Evolution de la propriété fonçière au Choa (Ethiopie) du règne de Ménélik à la constitution de 1931* (Paris: Libraire Orientaliste Paul Geuthner, 1971), p. 42.

18 Enrico Cerulli, *Etiopia occidentale (dallo Scioa alla frontiera del Sudan): Note del viaggio 1927–28*, Vol. 1 (Rome: Sindacato Italiano Arti Grafiche, 1933), p. 125.

19 Reminick, 'The Manze Amhara', p. 69. See also Levine, *Wax and Gold*, pp. 80–1, and Allan Hoben, 'Social Stratification in Traditional Amhara Society' in Arthur Tuden and Leonard Plotnicov, eds., *Social Stratification in Africa* (New York: Free Press, 1970), p. 195.

20 Crummey, 'Abyssinian Feudalism', p. 135.

21 Reminick, 'The Manze Amhara', p. 61.

22 Of course, a person's ambitions were related to his or her structural position. People at the very bottom of society probably did not aspire to be regional governors. What a person could hope for was relative. In this sense, the military ethos discussed below was probably stronger the higher one went in the class system.

23 Walter C. Plowden, *Travels in Abyssinia and the Galla Country* (London: Longmans, Green, 1868), p. 137, quoted in Gene Ellis, 'The Feudal Paradigm as a Hindrance to Understanding Ethiopia', *Journal of Modern African Studies* 14 (1976), p. 287.

24 Hoben, 'Social Stratification', p. 212.

25 Levine, *Wax and Gold*, pp. 238–86.

26 Simon D. Messing, 'The Highland–Plateau Amhara of Ethiopia' (Ph.D. thesis, Department of Anthropology, University of Pennsylvania, 1957), p. 575.

27 Hoben seems to see high mobility not only as a 'myth' but also as a reality of Ethiopian society. However, it is not always clear with respect to what number of strata and what size social system his discussion takes place. When Donald Crummey studied regional élites who

occupied provincial governorships over the last two centuries, he found 'marked continuity' ('Abyssinian Feudalism', p. 136). See also Patrick Gilkes, *The Dying Lion: Feudalism and Modernization in Ethiopia* (London: Julian Friedmann, 1975), pp. 32–45. Finally, Weissleder writes, 'At Ankober, at least, I found no evidence for the firm confidence, often expressed by old and young, that any Amhara could rise from humblest beginning to highest office and power by bringing his great feats of military prowess to the attention of his leader or king' ('Amhara Domination', p. 67).

28 Margery Perham, *The Government of Ethiopia*, 2nd ed. (London: Faber and Faber, 1969), p. 164, quoted in Ellis, 'The Feudal Paradigm', p. 287.

29 Crummey, 'Abyssinian Feudalism', p. 137.

30 Levine, *Wax and Gold*, p. 93.

31 Crummey, 'Abyssinian Feudalism', p. 137.

32 *Ibid.*

33 Crummey is apparently alone in maintaining that 'strata had distinct cultures' ('Abyssinian Feudalism', p. 135). However, the evidence that he gives (sumptuary laws and dress patterns) seems more directly related to differential consumption patterns than to actual cultural differences. When Plowden, a man from a society with developed status cultures, visited Ethiopia in the nineteenth century, he wrote, '. . . it must ever be remembered that between the chief and the most ragged of his followers there is no distinction, save that of wealth or good fortune . . . there is none of those real and essential differences of education, of language, or of breeding, and consequently of thought and feeling, that elsewhere prevent the servant and his master, the soldier and his officer, from meeting on a footing of intimacy . . .' (*Travels*, p. 60, quoted in Hoben, 'Social Stratification', pp. 192–3).

34 Marc Bloch, *Feudal Society*, 2nd ed. (London: Routledge and Kegan Paul, 1962), p. 446.

35 Crummey, 'Abyssinian Feudalism', *passim*.

36 Hoben, 'Social Stratification', p. 191.

37 In earlier times, up till the sixteenth century, local governors did not have companies of soldiers. Rather, the emperor at the centre stationed regiments of troops, *chewa*, at strategic points on the frontier. By the seventeenth century, however, emperors had lost control of the *chewa*, and by the nineteenth century, the word *chewa* had changed semantically to mean merely 'gentility'. See Merid Wolde Aregay, 'Southern Ethiopia', Chapter 4.

38 Taddesse Tamrat, *Church and State in Ethiopia, 1270–1527* (Oxford: Clarendon Press, 1972), p. 101.

39 Cerulli, *Etiopia occidentale*, Vol. 1, pp. 128–9.

40 Crummey, 'Abyssinian Feudalism', p. 124.

41 Max Weber, *The Theory of Social and Economic Organization* (New York: Free Press, 1947), pp. 324–85.

42 In the early seventeenth century Almeida reported that the king could not take governorships away from established families in Tigrai, Seraye, Shirē, Temben, and Dembia – C. F. Beckingham and G. W. B. Huntingford, eds., *Some Records of Ethiopia 1593–1646* (London: Hakluyt Society, 1954), p. 72. During the reign of Iyasu II (1730–55), 'The people of Damot rebelled, demanding that they should be given a governor from among the sons of the country, which, they claimed, was by then already the practice in Gojjam, Amhara, Begemdir, and Tigrai' – Richard Pankhurst, *State and Land in Ethiopian History* (Addis Abeba: Institute of Ethiopian Studies, Addis Abeba University, 1966), p. 7. Finally, Svein Ege confirms this general pattern for the kingdom of Shewa in the mid-nineteenth century. The kingdom consisted of three zones, the core area of which was presided over by local hereditary nobles who gave only light tributes to the centre – 'Chiefs and Peasants. The Socio-Political Structure of the Kingdom of Shäwa About 1840' (Hovedoppgave i historie, University of Bergen, 1978), pp. 139, 160.

43 This happened most extensively on the frontier, and it was a process that continued through the early twentieth century. While Teferi Mekonnen, for example, was governor of Harergē,

he transferred much land from *gult* into *rist* tenure. See Tsehay Berhane Sellassie, 'Developments in Land-Tenure in Hararge Province (1887–1935)' (Paper presented at the History and Culture of the Peoples of Harar Conference, Addis Abeba, 1975).

44 Taddesse Tamrat, *Church and State*, p. 99.

45 *Ibid.*, p. 103. See also Carlo Conti Rossini, 'I loggo e la legge dei loggo Sarda', *Giornale della Società Asiatica Italiana* 17 (1904), pp. 33–5.

46. Weissleder, 'Amhara Domination', p. 124.

47 M. L. Bender, 'The Origin of Amharic', *Journal of the Institute of Language Studies* (Addis Abeba University) 1 (1983), pp. 41–2.

48 Christian identity was intimately tied up with the *rist* system. At times, landholders were required to convert to Christianity or to lose their *rist* rights. The equation of Christianity with *rist* appears in the proverb: 'The Muslim has no *rist*. The sky has no pillar.'

49 Merid Wolde Aregay, 'Southern Ethiopia', pp. 104 and 298.

50 Taddesse Tamrat, *Church and State*, p. 173.

51 Donald N. Levine, *Greater Ethiopia: The Evolution of a Multiethnic Society* (Chicago: University of Chicago Press, 1974), p. 149. On the ethnic hierarchy in general, see Messing, 'The Highland–Plateau Amhara', pp. 63–7.

52 Baeteman, *Dictionnaire*, col. 294; Ignazio Guidi, *Vocabolario amarico–italiano* (Rome: Istituto per l'Oriente, 1953), col. 219.

53 There appears to have been a semantic continuum from 'Amhara' with strong overtones of freedom (Weissleder, 'Political Ecology', p. 54) to 'Shanḳilla' with strong overtones of slavery.

54 Guidi, *Vocabolario*, col. 559, cited by Richard Pankhurst, 'The History of the Bareya, Shanqella, and Other Ethiopian slaves from the Borderlands of the Sudan', *SNR*, 59 (1977), pp. 1–43.

55 Galla was the name that Amhara used principally for Oromo ethnic groups, one of the largest congeries of related peoples on the southern frontier.

56 For the meaning of Galla in Tigrinnya as an 'inferior race' see Francesco Da Bassano, *Vocabolario tigray–italiano* (Rome: Casa Editrice Italiana di C. de Luigi, 1918), col. 809. However, Bahrey, a monk who lived on the southern periphery at the end of the sixteenth century and who wrote a history of the Galla, does not refer to racial features in his description (see Beckingham and Huntingford, eds., *Some Records*).

57 Baeteman, *Dictionnaire*, col. 1032.

58 This sentiment is echoed in a proverb about the Agaw: 'An Agaw has nine hearts. Eight he hides. And he chats with one.' See McCann, 'Households, Peasants and Rural History', p. 61.

59 Merid Wolde Aregay, 'Southern Ethiopia', pp. 152–3. See also Crummey, who argues that the application of the term 'Galla' depended not so much on objective facts of descent as on the supposed degree of divergence from central Abyssinian culture ('Society and Ethnicity', p. 278).

60 Perry Anderson, *Lineages of the Absolutist State* (London: New Left Books, 1974), p. 147.

61 Perry Anderson, *Passages from Antiquity to Feudalism* (London: New Left Books, 1974), p. 147.

62 Crummey, 'Abyssinian Feudalism', p. 128–9, emphasizes this in terms of the difference between 'tribute' and 'tax'.

63 This quotation is slightly rephrased from Merid Wolde Aregay, 'Society and Technology', pp. 155–6.

64 Richard A. Caulk, 'Armies as Predators: Soldiers and Peasants in Ethiopia, *c.* 1850–1935', *IJAHS*, 11 (1978), pp. 457–93.

65 Francesco Alvarez, *The Prester John*, Vol. 2, p. 515, cited by Merid Wolde Aregay, 'Society and Technology', p. 168 and note 60; Max Grühl, *The Citadel of Ethiopia* (London: J. Cape, 1932). When Grühl asked a Kefa man why he did not grow more coffee, the man replied,

'Why should we cultivate coffee and obtain more berries than we need for our own use? The Habeshi [Abyssinians] would only take them away from us' (p. 229).

66 Future research may qualify this conclusion, but it is unlikely to alter it dramatically – see Merid Wolde Aregay, 'Society and Technology'.

67 Frederik C. Gamst, 'Peasantries and Elites Without Urbanism: The Civilization of Ethiopia', *Comparative Studies in Society and History* 12 (1970), pp. 373–92.

68 Donald Crummey, 'Towns in Ethiopia: The Eighteenth and Nineteenth Centuries', unpublished manuscript, University of Illinois, Urbana.

69 I am assuming that the nature of basic inequalities – the social relations of production – define the type to which any society belongs. Much of the controversy over whether Abyssinia was feudal has stemmed from different definitions of feudalism rather than different readings of empirical data.

70 Goody, *Production and Reproduction*, p. 113.

71 See James McCann's argument that it was control over capital – particularly oxen – rather than control over land that was the key factor of production in the north: 'Plows, Oxen, and Household Managers: A Reconsideration of the Land Paradigm and the Production Equation in Northeast Africa' (Working Paper No. 95, African Studies Center, Boston University, 1985).

72 Max Gluckman, *The Ideas in Barotse Jurisprudence* (Manchester: Manchester University Press, 1972), p. 79.

73 Hoben, *Land Tenure Among the Amhara*, p. 12.

74 *Ibid.*, p. 9.

75 John Hajnal, 'European Marriage Patterns in Perspective' in David V. Glass and D. E. C. Eversley, eds., *Population in History: Essays in Historical Demography* (Chicago: Aldine, 1965).

76 Hoben, 'Family, Land, and Class'.

77 Jack Goody, 'Marriage Policy and Incorporation in Northern Ghana' in Ronald Cohen and John Middleton, eds., *From Tribe to Nation in Africa: Studies in Incorporation Processes* (Scranton, Pennsylvania: Chandler, 1970) and Max Gluckman, 'The Lozi of Barotseland in North-Western Rhodesia' in Elizabeth Colson and Max Gluckman, eds., *Seven Tribes of Central Africa* (London: Oxford University Press, 1951).

78 *cf.* Lloyd Fallers, 'Are African Cultivators to be Called Peasants?' *Current Anthropology* 2 (1961), pp. 108–10.

79 My conclusion at this point is conditioned by the fact that there are only two categories in Goody's typology – 'African' and 'Eurasian'. Once fundamental kinds of inequality or social relations of production (rather than simply levels of technology) are taken as the defining features of societal types, it seems likely that 'Eurasia' will be broken down into a number of different categories. At that point, it remains to be seen whether Abyssinia, perhaps along with other African empires such as those of northern Nigeria, belong to a 'Middle Eastern' type. In any case, the presence or absence of the plough in itself seems unlikely to be determinative of larger differences in political economy.

80 Volker Stitz, *Studien zur Kulturgeographie Zentraläthiopiens* (Bonn: F. Dümmlers Verlag, 1974).

81 On banditry see: Richard A. Caulk, 'Bad Men of the Borders: Shum and Shefta in Northern Ethiopia in the Nineteenth Century', *Proceedings of the Second Annual Seminar of the Department of History* (Addis Abeba: Addis Abeba University Press, 1985); Donald Crummey, 'Banditry and Resistance: Noble and Peasant in Nineteenth Century Ethiopia' in Sven Rubenson, ed., *Proceedings of the Seventh International Conference of Ethiopian Studies* (East Lansing: African Studies Center, Michigan State University, 1984).

82 Ethiopia is, as it were, an upside-down China. See G. William Skinner, ed., *The City in Late Imperial China* (Stanford: Stanford University Press, 1977). My approach to regional systems is indebted to Skinner and to Carol A. Smith, ed. *Regional Systems Analyses*, Vol. 1

and 2 (New York: Academic Press, 1976).

83 Quoted in J. Spencer Trimingham, *Islam in Ethiopia* (London: Oxford University Press, 1952), p. 2.

84 Taddesse Tamrat, *Church and State*, p. 81.

85 On this development see Trimingham, *Islam in Ethiopia* and Ulrich Braukämper, 'Islamic Principalities in Southeast Ethiopia between the Thirteenth and Sixteenth Centuries', *Ethiopianist Notes* 1, 1 (1977): 17–45 and 1, 2 (1977): 1–43.

86 Taddesse Tamrat, *Church and State*, pp. 203–5.

87 Tigrinnya spilled over into region 3 to some extent, even though the latter was mostly populated by Amharic-speakers; see M. L. Bender, J. D. Bowen, R. L. Cooper, and C. A. Ferguson, eds., *Language in Ethiopia* (London: Oxford University Press, 1976), end maps. Whether other indicators of interaction correlate with linguistic distributions – and whether therefore the boundaries between regions 1 and 3 should be slightly redrawn – is an open question at this point.

88 Volker Stitz, 'The Amhara Resettlement of Northern Shoa during the 18th and 19th Centuries', in Harold G. Marcus and Donald E. Crummey, eds., 'Ethiopia: Land and History', special issue of *Rural Africana* 11 (1970), pp. 70–81. Amhara in Shewa had survived the Oromo invasions in three ecological zones: the highlands surrounded by steep escarpments, the lowland river valleys, and the hills east of the main north–south escarpment. See also Svein Ege, 'Chiefs and Peasants'.

89 On the importance of these three battles, see Addis Hiwet, *Ethiopia: From Autocracy to Revolution* (London: Review of African Political Economy, 1975), pp. 4–14. On Embabo and Chelenko, see Richard A. Caulk, 'Territorial Competition and the Battle of Embabo', *JES* 13, 1 (1975), pp. 65–88, and 'The Occupation of Harar: January 1887', *JES* 9, 2 (1971), pp. 1–20.

90 Markakis, *Ethiopia*, pp. 90–1.

91 Richard Pankhurst, trans., *Tax Records and Inventories of Emperor Tewodros of Ethiopia (1855–1868)* (London: School of Oriental and African Studies, 1978).

92 For the example of Lasta, see McCann, 'Households, Peasants, and Rural History': 'The small amounts of high quality honey and butter and the trickle of talers coming out of Lasta were more symbolic tribute than substantial inputs into the imperial treasury' (p. 95).

93 Bahru Zewde, 'Economic Origins of the Absolutist State in Ethiopia (1916–1935)', in Department of History, eds., *Proceedings of the Second Annual Seminar of the Department of History* (Addis Abeba: Addis Abeba University Press, 1984), pp. 1–5.

94 Besides the argument presented by Bahru in 'The Absolutist State', this is the conclusion of Joanna Mantel-Niećko, *The Rôle of Land Tenure*, Chapter 8.

95 Bahru, 'The Absolutist State'.

96 On the end of Menilek's reign and on Iyasu's short rule see Marcus, *The Life and Times of Menelik*, Chapters 8–9.

97 On the development of the remarkable intellectual circle around the newspaper *Birhanina Selam*, see Addis Hiwet, *Ethiopia*, pp. 68–77 and Richard A. Caulk, 'Dependency, Gebre Heywet Baykedagn, and the Birth of Ethiopian Reformism', in Robert L. Hess, ed., *Proceedings of the Fifth International Conference of Ethiopian Studies* (Chicago: University of Illinois at Chicago Circle, 1982).

98 The symbolic aspects of new institutional arrangements should always be kept in mind, for they often illustrate the mixing of old ideas and new social structures in twentieth-century Ethiopia. For example, the imperial guard, set up in 1929 by a Belgian military mission, included a military band of 'freed negro slaves under a Swiss bandmaster' (Perham, *The Government of Ethiopia*, p. 165). Minstrels had occupied a low-status position in Abyssinian society. The new army, then, symbolically replicated the old Abyssinian hierarchy of highlanders (the rest of the army) over the 'Shankilla' slave-band.

99 Christopher Clapham, *Haile-Selassie's Government* (London: Longmans, 1969), p. 77.

100 This was an estimate by MacGillivray, the first director of the Bank of Abyssinia, cited by Richard Pankhurst, *Economic History of Ethiopia, 1800–1935* (Addis Abeba: Haile Selassie I University Press, 1968), p. 470.

101 Charles McClellan, 'Land, Labor and Coffee: The South's Role in Ethiopian Self-Reliance, 1889–1935', *AEH* 9 (1980), pp. 69–83. See also Jon R. Edwards, 'Slavery, the Slave Trade and the Economic Reorganization of Ethiopia, 1916–1935', *AEH* 11 (1982), pp. 3–14, and McClellan, 'State Transformation and Social Reconstitution in Ethiopia: The Allure of the South', *IJAHS* 17 (1984), pp. 657–75.

102 Pankhurst, *Economic History*, p. 336

103 Gilkes, *The Dying Lion*, p. 145.

104 Markakis, *Ethiopia*, p. 173.

105 Bahru, 'The Absolutist State', p. 4.

106 Gebru Tareke, 'Peasant Resistance in Ethiopia: The Case of *Ẇeyane*', *JAH* 25 (1984), pp. 77–92.

107 Markakis, *Ethiopia*, pp. 257–8. See also Harold G. Marcus, *Ethiopia, Great Britain, and the United States, 1941–1974* (Berkeley: University of California Press, 1983).

108 The first map of early twentieth-century Ethiopian political divisions of which I am aware – in 1906 – is that contained in Carlo Rossetti, *Storia diplomatica dell'Etiopia durante il regno di Menelik II* (Turin: Società Tipografico-Editrice Nazionale, 1910). For the 1930s, see the following sources: Corrado Zoli, *Etiopia d'oggi: con sette grafici e tre travole fuori testo* (Rome: Società Anonima Italiana Arti Grafiche, 1936), p. 270; Adrien Zervos, *L'Empire d'Ethiopie: le miroir de l'Ethiopie moderne, 1906–1935* (Alexandria, Egypt: Imprimerie de l'école professionnelle des frères, 1936); and Perham, *The Government of Ethiopia*, end maps. Map 4 is based upon these last three sources, none of which completely agrees with the others. I have attempted to resolve differences by concentrating on the territories of particular governors, all of whom had the title of *dejazmach* or above, just before the Italian occupation. I have also found useful the maps in two books by Roberto Asinari di San Marzano: *Dal Giuba al Margherita* (Rome: Editrice l'Azione Coloniale, 1935) and *Dalla piana Somalia all'altipiano Etiopico* (Rome: Editrice l'Azione coloniale, 1953).

109 Pankhurst, *Economic History*, p. 497.

110 Bahru Zewde, 'Relations Between Ethiopia and the Sudan on the Western Ethiopian Frontier' (Ph.D. thesis, School of Oriental and African Studies, University of London, 1976), p. 368.

111 *Ibid.*, p. 441.

112 Map 6 and population figures for Ethiopian towns in the pre-Italian period are based upon a remarkable Italian tourist handbook: *Guida dell'Africa Orientale Italiana* (Milan: Consociazione Turistica Italiana, 1938).

113 There was a secondary string of towns on the old north–south axis that led into the Sudan via Metemma and into Eritrea.

114 Population figures for Ethiopian towns in 1973 were taken from *The 1975 Statistical Abstract of Ethiopia* (Addis Abeba: Central Statistical Office, Imperial Ethiopian Government, 1975).

115 Gilkes, *The Dying Lion*, p. 146.

116 Bahru, 'The Absolutist State', pp. 15–21.

117 Gilkes, *The Dying Lion*, p. 78.

118 Markakis, *Ethiopia*, p. 244.

119 Asmarom Legesse, 'Post-Feudal Society, Capitalism, and Revolution: the Case of Ethiopia', *Symposium Leo Frobenius II* (Bonn: Deutsche UNESCO Kommission, 1980), pp. 195–226.

120 *Ibid.*, p. 220.

121 Karl Knutsson, for example, notes the strength of ethnic identification among the pastoral Arsi Oromo compared to Shewan Oromo who migrated to the Arsi highlands. See his

'Dichotomization and Integration: Aspects of Inter-Ethnic Relations in South Ethiopia' in Fredrik Barth, ed., *Ethnic Groups and Boundaries: The Social Organization of Cultural Difference* (London: George Allen & Unwin, 1969). On the northern periphery, the case of the Kunama is instructive. The almost institutionalized raiding back and forth between Tigrai peoples and the Kunama during the mid-nineteenth century must have been accompanied by strongly developed and exclusive ethnic identities – see Mansfield Parkyns, *Life in Abyssinia* (New York: D. Appleton, 1856), Chapter 24.

122 Shack, 'Urban Ethnicity'.

123 Markakis, *Ethiopia*, pp. 178–81.

124 Christopher Clapham, 'Centralization and Local Response in Southern Ethiopia', *AA* 74 (1975), p. 81, and 'The Horn of Africa', in Michael Crowder, ed., *The Cambridge History of Africa*, Vol. 8 (Cambridge: Cambridge University Press, 1984). See also Edmond J. Keller, 'Ethiopia: Revolution, Class, and the National Question', *AA* 80 (1981), pp. 519–49.

125 In broad outline, this kind of typology has had a long existence in Ethiopian scholarship. It appears perhaps first in an Ethiopian source: Mahteme Sellassie Wolde Maskel, *Zikre Neger* (Addis Abeba: Neṭsanet Press, 1942, E.C.). More recently, Mantel-Niećko, *The Role of Land Tenure*, Chapter 5 has analysed and clarified it.

126 Studies of these semi-independent kingdoms include the following: Herbert S. Lewis, *A Galla Monarchy: Jimma Abba Jifar, Ethiopia, 1830–1932* (Madison: University of Wisconsin Press, 1965); Bahru Zewde, 'A Biography of Dejazmach Jote Tulu, Abba Iggu (1885–1918)' (B. A. thesis, Department of History, Haile Selassie I University, 1973); and Peter P. Garretson, 'Shaykh Hamdan Abu Shok (1898–1938) and the Administration of Gubba', in Joseph Tubiana, ed., *Modern Ethiopia From the Accession of Menelik II to the Present* (Rotterdam: A. A. Balkema, 1980).

127 Zervos, *L'Empire d'Ethiopie*, pp. 331, 398, 409.

128 Berhanou Abbebe, *Evolution de la propriété fonçière*, pp. 29ff.

129 Mantel-Niećko, *The Role of Land Tenure*, pp. 82–5. She mentions that the root, *gbr*, has the meaning of 'to force' in three Semitic languages – Tigrinnya, Hararī, and Gurage – and that adscription to the soil may therefore have had an ancient existence in Abyssinia. Merid Wolde Aregay is more specific historically. He locates a major change in the early seventeenth century when peasants were allowed to bear arms; before that, apparently, farmers were adscripted to the soil and only 'free' soldiers bore arms (Merid, 'Southern Ethiopia', pp. 380ff). Finally, it is interesting to note that *gebbar* or its equivalent, *gabaro*, also occurs as an important category in Oromo society. On the Mecha Oromo, see Lambert Bartels, *Oromo Religion: Myths and Rites of the Western Oromo of Ethiopia – An Attempt to Understand* (Berlin: Dietrich Reimer Verlag, 1983), pp. 133–65. As a category, 'gabaro' contrasts with 'borena' – 'pure' Oromo who had the power to bless and curse. By implication, 'gabaro' seems to indicate descendants of those free persons who had been incorporated into Oromo society in the past. This is corroborated by the sixteenth-century monk Bahrey who wrote that an Oromo generation set 'made them [people of Feṭegar] the slaves which they called *gabare*' (Beckingham and Huntingford, eds., *Some Records*, p. 116 note 1). This leads one to wonder whether the early Oromo did not have a '*gebbar* system' of their own that encouraged the rapid extension of Oromo society in the sixteenth century – through incorporation of outsiders.

130 Little systematic work has been done on revolts in the early twentieth century in the south. Bairu Tafla reports that the king of Dawro rebelled in 1895–6 when Welde Gīyorgis was away from his province; see 'Two of the Last Provincial Kings of Ethiopia', *JES* 11, 1 (1973), p. 51. Also, when troops were withdrawn from the Rift Valley lakes region in 1916 to fight *lij* Iyasu's father in Shewa, local people rebelled and order was not re-established until 1919 (Ulrich Braukämper, *Geschichte der Hadiya Süd-Äthiopiens* (Wiesbaden: franz Steiner Verlag, 1980), pp. 326–32).

131 Martino Mario Moreno, 'Il regime terriero abissino nel Galla-Sidama', *Rassegna economica*

Africa Italiana 25 (1937), p. 1502.

132 The translation that occurs at the beginning of this volume is a slightly modified version of that contained in Addis Hiwet, *Ethiopia*, p. 72. For the Amharic original see Asbe Hailu, *Birhanina Selam* 3, 29 (1927), pp. 225–7.

133 Berhanou, *Evolution de la propriété fonçière*, p. 103, maintains that serfdom did not exist in Ethiopia. However, Mantel-Niećko presents evidence to the contrary in *The Role of Land Tenure*, p. 84.

134 Cerulli, *Etiopia occidentale*, Vol. 2, pp. 206–7.

135 Cerulli, *Etiopia occidentale*, Vol. 1, p. 136.

136 Harold G. Marcus, 'Some Reflections on the Development of Government and Taxation in Southern Ethiopia Around the Turn of the Century', in *IV Congresso Internazionale di Studi Etiopici*, Vol. 1 (Rome: Accademia Nazionale dei Lincei, 1974), p. 637.

137 In this respect John Markakis and Nega Ayele's analysis is misleading – see *Class and Revolution in Ethiopia* (London: Review of African Political Economy, 1978), p. 25.

138 Moreno, 'Il regime', p. 1497.

139 'Unsettled' lands could also be granted as *gult*. At first glance, such grants would appear to be worthless without control over labour. A number of ways existed, however, to attract tenants. In Kefa, holders of *gult* on unsettled lands attracted *gebbar* who fled oppressive conditions in nearby areas to come to their lands as tenants, *çhisennya*. See Cerulli, *Etiopia occidentale*, Vol. 2, pp. 205–6, and F. de Halpert quoted in Perham, *The Government of Ethiopia*, p. 320. Holders of *gult* in Arsi often sold lands to immigrants from Shewa – both Oromo and Amhara who were being pushed out of the area around Addis Abeba by commercial developments. Buyers received *rist* rights and became *gebbar* for the *gult*-holders. These sales of land had drastic effects on the traditional pastoral economy of the Arsi Oromo. Without adequate lands for their cattle, many were forced into cultivation. See Brotto, *Il regime della terra*, pp. 92–7.

140 Allan Hoben, 'Social Soundness Analysis of Agrarian Reform in Ethiopia' (Washington: United States Assistance for International Development Report PN AAE–958, 1976), p. 35.

141 Markakis and Nega, *Class and Revolution*, p. 41.

142 Two historical studies of the far Ethiopian peripheries have been done recently: Neil W. Sobania, 'The Historical Tradition of the Peoples of the Eastern Lake Turkana Basin, c. 1840–1925' (Ph.D. dissertation, School of Oriental and African Studies, University of London, 1980) and Dennis Hickey, 'Ethiopia and Great Britain: Political Conflict in the Southern Borderlands, 1916–1935' (Ph.D. thesis, Department of History, Northwestern University, 1984).

143 Asmarom Legesse, 'Ethiopian Colonists and Frontier Peoples: The Boran Case' (Paper presented at the Society and History of Imperial Ethiopia Conference, Monterey, California, 1982).

144 Perham, *The Government of Ethiopia*, p. 313.

145 Aleme Eshete has called attention to this semantic transformation in 'General Examination on Ethiopian Feudalism' (Paper presented at the Ethiopian Feudalism Conference, Addis Abeba, Ethiopia, 1976). The transformation can be seen in a comparison of Baeteman, who translates *zēga* simply as dependent subject in the 1920s (*Dictionnaire*, col. 858), with Leslau, who by the 1970s lists 'citizen' as one of its meanings – Wolf Leslau, *English–Amharic Context Dictionary* (Wiesbaden: Otto Harrassowitz, 1973), p. 193.

146 Judith Olmstead, 'A Woman in Imperial Ethiopia: Seventy Years of Gamo Highland Factional Politics' (Paper presented at the Society and History of Imperial Ethiopia Conference, Monterey, California, 1982).

147 Kebbeda Tessema, *Ye-Tarik Mastawsha* (Addis Abeba: Artistic Printing Press, 1962, E.C.), p. 106–7.

148 Jacques Bureau, 'Etude diachronique de deux titres gamo', *Cahiers d'études africaines* 18 (1971), pp. 279–91.

149 Brotto, *Il regime delle terre*, p. 94.
150 According to Trimingham, *Islam in Ethiopia*, pp. 101–2, Islam served a similiar function in the seventeenth century in establishing and maintaining a non-Abyssinian identity.
151 On the Sudan Interior Mission in Welaita, see Raymond J. Davis, *Fire on the Mountains: The Story of a Miracle – the Church in Ethiopia* (Grand Rapids, Michigan: Zondervan Publishing House, 1966); on the Mekane Yesus Church, see Gustav Aven, *Evangelical Pioneers in Ethiopia* (Stockholm: IFS Forlaget, 1978).
152 Karl E. Knutsson, *Authority and Change: A Study of the Kallu Institution Among the Macha Galla of Ethiopia* (Goteborg: Etnografiska Museet, 1967); Herbert S. Lewis, 'Gada, Big Man, K'allu: Political Succession among the Eastern Mech'a' (Paper presented at the Society and History of Imperial Ethiopia Conference, Monterey, California, 1982). See also Lewis, 'Spirit Possession in Ethiopia: An Essay in Interpretation', in S. Segert, ed., *Ethiopian Studies Dedicated to Wolf Leslau* (Weisbaden: Otto Harrassowitz, 1984).
153 Abas Haji, 'The History of Arssi (1880–1935)' (B. A. dissertation, Department of History, Addis Abeba University, 1982), p. 72.
154 Davis, *Fire on the Mountains*.
155 John Hinnant, 'Guji Trance and Social Change: Symbolic Responses to Domination' (Paper presented at the Society and History of Imperial Ethiopia Conference, Monterey, California, 1982).
156 Said S. Samatar, *Oral Poetry and Somali Nationalism: The Case of Sayyid Mahammad 'Abdille Hasan* (Cambridge: Cambridge University Press, 1982).
157 Peter P. Garretson, 'Ethiopia and Garrison Government in the Ogadeen, 1887–*c*.1930' (Paper presented at the Society and History of Imperial Ethiopia Conference, Monterey, California, 1982).
158 William A. Shack, *The Gurage: A People of the Ensete Culture* (Oxford: Oxford University Press, 1966), and 'Some Aspects of Ecology and Social Structure in the Ensete Complex in South-West Ethiopia' *Journal of the Royal Anthropological Institute* 93 (1963), pp. 72–9.
159 Fecadu Gadamu, 'Ethnic Associations in Ethiopia and the Maintenance of Urban/Rural Relationships, with Special Reference to the Alemgana-Walamo Road Construction Association' (Ph.D. thesis, University of London, 1972).

2 Neḳemte and Addis Abeba

1 Abebe Ambatchew *et al*., 'Field-Trip to Näqämte', *Bulletin of the Ethnological Society* [University College of Addis Abeba] 6 (1957), p. 15. On Bakare's rise to power see especially Tasama Ta'a, 'Administration in Leqa Neqemte between 1850–1923' (B. A. thesis, Department of History, Addis Abeba University, 1976), pp. 3–8, and 'The Oromo of Wollega: A Historical Survey to 1910' (M. A. thesis, Department of History, Addis Abeba University, 1980), pp. 37–45.
2 Abebe Ambatchew *et al*., 'Näqämte', p. 6.
3 Jan Hultin, 'Political Structure and the Development of Inequality Among the Macha Oromo', in *Pastoral Production and Society*, ed. Equipe écologie et anthropologie des sociétés pastorales (Cambridge: Maison des sciences de l'homme and Cambridge University Press, 1979), p. 284.
4 Bairu Tafla, 'Four Ethiopian Biographies', *JES* 7, 2, (1969), p. 11. The process is also described in Lambert Bartels, 'Studies of the Galla in Wällägga', *JES* 8 (1970), pp. 149–54.
5 Bartels, 'Studies of the Galla', p. 151.
6 Terrefe Woldetsadik, 'The Unification of Ethiopia (1880–1935): Wälläga', *JES* 6 (1969), p. 74.
7 *Ibid*., pp. 73–9. See also Enrico Cerulli, 'The Folk-Literature of the Galla of Southern Abyssinia', *Harvard African Studies* 3 (1922), pp. 74–82, and Alessandro Triulzi, 'The Background to Ras Gobäna's Expeditions to Western Wällägga in 1886–1888: A Review of

the Evidence', in *Proceedings of the First United States Conference in Ethiopian Studies, 1973*, ed. Harold G. Marcus (East Lansing, Michigan: African Studies Center, Michigan State University, 1975), pp. 148–56. For a detailed account of Moroda's dealings with early Shewan encroachments in Wellegga, see Tasama Ta'a, 'Administration', pp. 15–23, and 'The Oromo', pp. 69–77.

8 On the Battle of Embabo, and the territorial competition between Shewa and Gojjam, see R. A. Caulk, 'Territorial Competition and the Battle of Embabo', *JES* 13 (1975), pp. 65–88.

9 Gebre Igzīabihēr family papers, chronicle of the Bakare family of Neḳemte, Amharic ms., n.d. (hereafter cited as Gebre Igzīabihēr chronicle), fols. 30–32 (I am indebted to *weyzero* Atsede Habte Mariam, a great-grand-daughter of Bakare, for a copy of this ms). See also Bairu Tafla, 'Four Ethiopian Biographies', p. 12, and *blatta* Derēssa Amante (interviewed by Baissa Lemmu, Addis Abeba, April–December 1962, typescript, 25 pp.), p. 9.

10 Berhanou Abbebe, *Evolution de la propriété fonçière au Choa (Ethiopie) du règne de Ménélik à la constitution de 1931* (Paris: Imprimerie Nationale, Librairie Orientaliste Paul Geuthner, 1971), p. 12.

11 Richard Pankhurst, *State and Land in Ethiopian History* (Addis Abeba: Institute of Ethiopian Studies, 1966), p. 107.

12 Terrefe Woldetsadik, 'The Unification of Ethiopia', p. 82.

13 Gebre Igzīabihēr chronicle, fol. 33. The absence of an armed intervention is the alleged reason for Mahteme Sellassie's inclusion of Wellegga-Neḳemte among the six regions which paid fixed tribute to the central government. See Mahteme Sellassie Wolde Maskal, 'The Land System of Ethiopia', *EO* 1 (1957), p. 288, and J. Mantel-Niećko, 'The Division of Ethiopia into regions According to the Native Land Typology in Use at the Turn of the XIXth and XXth Centuries', in *Modern Ethiopia from the Accession of Menilek II to the Present*, ed. Joseph Tubiana (Rotterdam: A. A. Balkema, 1980), p. 475.

14 Informant: *ḳennyazmach* Abdisa Musa, interviewed in Neḳemte on 3 August 1972. See my *Field-Notes* deposited in the Institute of Ethiopian Studies, Addis Abeba, LN–10, p. 33.

15 Aṭsme Gīyorgis, 'Ye-Galla Tarik' (Institute of Ethiopian Studies, ms. 173, fol. 94). See also Cerulli, 'Folk-Literature', p. 72.

16 Jules Borelli, *Ethiopie Meridionale* (Paris: Ancienne Maison Quantin, 1890), p. 150; see also Aṭsme, 'Ye-Galla Tarik', fol. 94. A summary of the evidence is in Triulzi, 'Background', pp. 143–5.

17 *Blatta* Derēssa interview, p. 9.

18 On the Battle of Gute Dili see Alessandro Triulzi, *Salt, Gold and Legitimacy: Prelude to the History of a No-Man's Land, Belā Shangul, Wallaggā, Ethiopia (ca. 1800–1898)* (Naples: Istituto Universitario Orientale, 1981), pp. 156–67.

19 *Blatta* Derēssa interview, p. 9.

20 Gebre Igzīabihēr chronicle, fol. 36.

21 *Ibid.*

22 *Ibid.*, fol. 40. It was on this occasion that Kumsa was baptized with the Christian name of Gebre Igzīabihēr and was appointed *dejazmach* by Menilek.

23 Abebe Ambatchew *et al.*, 'Näqämte', p. 6.

24 Resistance to the expansion of the Bakare ruling family of Neḳemte is recorded in Gebre Igzīabihēr chronicle, fols. 23–4. See also Bartels, 'Studies of the Galla', pp. 149–54.

25 Three out of the six provinces were situated in today's Wellegga (Neḳemte, Ḳelem and Bela Shangul); the others were Jimma, Gubba and Aussa. See Mahteme Sellassie Wolde Maskal, *Zekire Neger*, 2nd ed. (Addis Abeba: Neṭsenet Press, 1970), p. 74; partial translation into English is in Mahteme Sellassie, 'The Land System', p. 288. See also Pankhurst, *Land and State*, p. 136.

26 Adrian Zervos, *L'Empire d'Ethiopie, le miroir de l'Ethiopie moderne 1906–1935* (Alexandria, Egypt: Imprimerie de l'école professionelle des frères, 1936), p. 398.

27 Pankhurst, *State and Land*, p. 136.

28 Gebre-Wold-Ingida Worq, 'Ethiopia's Traditional System of Land Tenure and Taxation', *EO* 5 (1962), p. 321. Tasama Ta'a, 'Administration', pp. 28–9, claims Moroda was subjected to a tribute of 500 *weḳēt* of gold and 100 *feresula* of ivory, but that the amount of gold was doubled during Gebre Igzīabihēr's time. Unfortunately I was able to consult Tasama's study of Neḳemte administration, based partly on the same correspondence which I use here, only after I had written my paper. I refer the reader to Tasama's very interesting work for more detailed background information on Neḳemte that could not be included in this text.

29 Menilek to Gebre Igzīabihēr, 2 Pagumē 1887 Ethiopian Calendar (hereafter E.C.)/6 September 1895. Gebre Igzīabihēr family papers, correspondence with the central government. I am indebted to *weyzero* Atsede Habte Mariam for allowing me to consult Gebre Igzīabihēr's official correspondence with Addis Abeba (all letters quoted hereafter come from the same source). The full text of this letter illustrates the style of the correspondence and reads as follows:

> The conquering Lion of Judah, Menilek II, Elect of God, King of Kings of Ethiopia. Let it [this letter] reach *dejazmach* Gebre Igzīabihēr. How have you been? I, thanks to God, am well. I have received the forty *weḳēt* of gold that you sent as tribute, but I have written [sent] to you the other day swearing and saying that because I was in difficulty I gave my arm bracelet to a smith and had it made [melted]. And now let the rest [of the gold tribute] follow quickly and come to me. Also, the gold handle that came was found to be an alloy [mixed with iron] and worthless. And although I had told you to stop [bringing] gold lumps and bring me rings instead, you started bringing them [in lumps] and had them moulded into rings here. Is this good? Now also I have sent back to you twenty *weḳēt* of gold which were [found to be] of poor quality and worthless. If you bring such kind of gold next time it will not be [received]. Check it by melting and bring the good one. Written on the 2nd day of Pagumē in the town of Addis Abeba, the Year of Mercy 1887 [6 September 1895].

30 Menilek to Gebre Igzīabihēr, 23 Hamlē 1895 E.C./29 July 1903, and same, 10 Nehasē 1897 E.C./15 August 1905.

31 Menilek to Gebre Igzīabihēr, same date.

32 1 *gundo* is about 4.5 kilogrammes. See Menilek to Gebre Igzīabihēr, 17 Meggabit 1898 E.C./25 March 1906, and Zewditu to Gebre Igzīabihēr, 22 Hamlē 1917 E.C./29 July 1925. It is interesting to note that the official correspondence exchanged between Neḳemte and Addis Abeba contains no explicit reference to slaves being sent as tribute to the centre of government. Most Wellegga slaves in fact came either from the Baro region farther west or from the Bela Shangul border district. Statistical data on the slave trade in Ethiopia during this period are to be found in Richard Pankhurst, 'The Ethiopian Slave Trade in the Nineteenth and early Twentieth Centuries: a Statistical Inquiry', *Journal of Semitic Studies* 9 (1964), pp. 220–8. See also Chapter 9 in this volume.

33 See, for instance, the letter of acknowledgement by Menilek dated 17 Meggabit 1898 E.C./25 March 1906.

34 In 1903 Gebre Igzīabihēr had been entrusted by Menilek with the administration of the newly-conquered Bela Shangul district. See Menilek to Gebre Igzīabihēr, 3 Meggabit 1899 E.C./11 March 1907, and same, 1 Nehasē 1899 E.C./7 August 1907.

35 Gebre Igzīabihēr to Menilek, 28 Tahsas 1898 E.C./6 January 1906.

36 Gebre Igzīabihēr to Menilek, 20 Tahsas 1899 E.C./29 December 1906.

37 Gebre Igzīabihēr to *lij* Iyasu, 2 Meggabit 1905 E.C./11 March 1913. It appears from the tone of this letter that Gebre Igzīabihēr is trying to exploit *lij* Iyasu's benevolent policy towards peripheral rulers, particularly after the harsh period of *ras* Tesemma's regency and his exploitative rule over western Ethiopia.

38 Gebre Igzīabihēr to *lij* Iyasu, n.d., but probably 1906 E.C./1913–1914.

39 Gebre Igzīabihēr to *ras* Teferi, n.d., but probably Hidar 1910 E.C./November–December 1917, and same, 27 Ṭir 1913 E.C./4 January 1921.

40 On the famine, see Richard Pankhurst, 'The Great Ethiopian Famine of 1888–1892: A New

Assessment', *Journal of the History of Medicine and Allied Sciences* 21 (1966), pp. 95–124, and pp. 271–94.

41 Gebre Igzīabihēr to Menilek, 4 Nehasē 1893 E.C./9 August 1901.

42 Gebre Igzīabihēr to Menilek, 3 Meggabit 1899 E.C./11 March 1907. Cattle was taxed at the rate of one head out of 40 castrated oxen, and one thaler for every ten sheep or goats. See Menilek to Gebre Igzīabihēr, 13 Nehasē 1898 E.C./18 August 1906.

43 Mahteme Sellassie, 'The Land-System', p. 295.

44 Gebre Igzīabihēr chronicle, fols. 42–3.

45 Shewan-Amhara soldiers' garrisons (*ketema*) were established in north-eastern Wellegga, particularly in the Horro-Gudru and Limmu regions bordering the Abbay, in the region of Arjo south-west of Neḳemte, and, after Jote's fall in 1908, in the Ḳelem and Sayo regions around Dembidollo. Scattered garrisons were kept in the Bela Shangul district after its annexation in 1898 until 1903. The commander in chief of Shewan-Amhara soldiers in Wellegga, known locally as *gonderē*, was *ras* Demissew, while Ḳelem was placed under *ras* Tesemma until the latter's death in 1911. See Terrefe Woldetsadik, 'The Unification of Ethiopia', pp. 84–5, and Bahru Zewde, 'Dejazmach Jote Tulu (1855–1918)' (B. A. thesis, Department of History, Addis Abeba University, 1970), pp. 48–51. See also Tasama Ta'a, 'Administration', pp. 32–4.

46 Gebre Igzīabihēr to *lij* Iyasu, 2 Meggabit 1905 E.C./11 March 1913.

47 Gebre Igzīabihēr to Menilek, 21 Tahsas 1899 E.C./30 December 1906 and same, n.d., but probably before 20 Ginbot 1899 E.C./27 May 1907.

48 Gebre Igzīabihēr to *lij* Iyasu, 2 Meggabit 1905 E.C./11 March 1913. According to oral information gathered by Tasama Ta'a, the Neḳemte-based *gonderē* were, according to Gebre Igzīabihēr's wishes, eventually moved to Arjo, *ras* Demissew's headquarters, by order of *lij* Iyasu. See Tasama Ta'a 'Administration', p. 33.

49 Gebre Igzīabihēr to *ras* Teferi, 18 Miazia 1909 E.C./26 April 1917.

50 Gebre Igzīabihēr to *ras* Teferi, n.d., but probably between 4 and 15 Hidar 1910 E.C./13–24 November 1917.

51 Menilek to Gebre Igzīabihēr, 26 Ginbot 1893 E.C./2 June 1901. On the rôle of the *neggadras* in imperial Ethiopia, see Peter Garretson, 'The *Naggadras*, Trade, and Selected Towns in Nineteenth and Early Twentieth Century Ethiopia', *IJAHS* 12, 3 (1979), pp. 416–39.

52 Gebre Igzīabihēr to *ras* Teferi, n.d., but probably Ṭiḳimt 1912 E.C./October–November 1919.

53 Gebre Igzīabihēr to Menilek, 2 Tahsas 1898 E.C./11 December 1905. The mixed rôle of the imperial *neggadras* based in Neḳemte is well illustrated in Tasama Ta'a, 'Administration', pp. 27–30.

54 Gebre Igzīabihēr to *ras* Teferi.

55 Gebre Igzīabihēr to Ṭaytu, n.d., but probably Yekatit 1899 E.C./16 February 1907.

56 *bejirond* Mulugēta to Gebre Igzīabihēr, 23 Hidar 1903 E.C./2 December 1910.

57 Gebre Igzīabihēr to Menilek, 4 Tahsas 1900 E.C./14 December 1907.

58 SIR 190 (May 1910), Appendix A. Gebre Igzīabihēr's rôle in the annexation of Bela Shangul is shown in Tasama Ta'a, 'Administration', pp. 30–2.

59 Gebre Igzīabihēr to Menilek, 10 Hidar 1899 E.C./19 November 1906.

60 Menilek to Gebre Igzīabihēr, 22 Hamlē 1899 E.C./28 July 1907.

61 Gebre Igzīabihēr to Menilek, 10 Hidar 1899 E.C./19 November 1906.

62 Gebre Igzīabihēr to *ḳennyazmach* Yebesh, 16 Tahsas 1899 E.C./25 December 1906.

63 *Ibid.*

64 Gebre Igzīabihēr to Menilek, 20 Tahsas 1899 E.C./29 December 1906.

65 Gebre Igzīabihēr to Menilek, 20 Ginbot 1899 E.C./27 May 1907.

66 *Ibid.*

67 Gebre Igzīabihēr to Menilek, 6 Ṭiḳimt 1900 E.C./17 October 1907.

68 Menilek to Gebre Igzīabihēr, 7 Miazia 1900 E.C./14 April 1908.

69 Gebre Igzīabihēr to Menilek, 8 Yekatit 1900 E.C./15 February 1908.
70 Gebre Igzīabihēr to Menilek, 18 Tahsas 1901 E.C./27 December 1908.
71 Gebre Igzīabihēr to Menilek, 16 Ṭir 1901 E.C./29 January 1909.
72 Gebre Igzīabihēr to Ṭaytu, 16 Ṭir 1901 E.C./29 January 1909.
73 Gebre Igzīabihēr to Menilek, 9 Yekatit 1901 E.C./16 February 1909.
74 Gebre Igzīabihēr to *lij* Iyasu, 11 Meskerem 1906 E.C./21 September 1913.
75 Gebre Igzīabihēr to *ras* Teferi, 10 Tahsas 1909 E.C./16 August 1917.
76 Gebre Igzīabihēr to Zewditu, 15 Hidar 1910 E.C./24 November 1917.
77 In 1902 E.C./1909–10 the central government proclaimed that all land in Ethiopia should be measured by a special type of cord (*ḳelad*) and divided into units of about 40 hectares each (*gasha*). After land was measured, about two-thirds of it was confiscated by the state while about one-third (*siso*) was left to the original inhabitants or land-holding groups. In Wellegga, in actual fact, *siso* meant rather one-quarter of the original land. On this see Tasama Ta'a, 'The Oromo', pp. 88–90.
78 Gebre Igzīabihēr to *ras* Teferi, 2 Meggabit 1913 E.C./11 March 1921.
79 *cf.* Mantel-Niećko, 'The Division of Ethiopia', p. 470, and Mahteme Sellassie, *Zekire Neger*, p. 164.

3. From ritual kings to Ethiopian landlords in Maale

1 The field work on which this chapter is based was supported by National Science Foundation Grant GS-41672. The support of the Foundation is gratefully acknowledged, as is the affiliation as Visiting Scholar given me by the Institute of Ethiopian Studies of Addis Abeba University. I want particularly to acknowledge the contribution of my Maale research assistant, *ato* Yekade Kelibo.
2 Individual names have been changed in this document, as well as in the rest of the chapter. Names of villages in which I did field research have also been changed.
3 To begin, I have to establish a base line in the late nineteenth century before Maale was incorporated into the Ethiopian empire. In the 1890s the northern empire not only defeated the Italians at the Battle of Adwa but expanded into the south and west to ward off encircling colonial powers. During this expansion, Maale was incorporated into Ethiopia. Inevitably, beginning at this point introduces distortions. It tends to imply that before the 1880s, Maale was unaffected by northern Ethiopia, that the 1890s was a great watershed between the time when Maale existed as a free, independent, traditional polity and the time when it was colonized, dominated, and therefore changed by northern Ethiopia. Let me simply say that Maale was probably conquered by the north once before in the fifteenth century and, more than that, Maale was an economic component of the vast and complex trading network that covered all of Ethiopia for centuries. If the 1890s are one historical breaking point, then, it is not as if there is no history of interaction between Maale and the north.
4 These three aspects of Maale divine kingship are discussed more fully in Chapter 2 of Donald L. Donham, *Work and Power in Maale, Ethiopia* (Ann Arbor, Michigan: UMI Research Press, 1985). In particular, the full text of the myth about the first Maale king is given there.
5 Eike Haberland, *Untersuchungen zum Äthiopischen Königtum* (Wiesbaden: Franz Steiner Verlag, 1965).
6 See Theodore Caplow, *Two against One: Coalitions in Triads* (Englewood Cliffs, New Jersey: Prentice Hall, 1968).
7 The Maale word, *haile*, is remarkably similar to the Amharic, *hail*, 'power'.
8 John Markakis, *Ethiopia: Anatomy of a Traditional Polity* (Oxford: Clarendon Press, 1974), p. 108.
9 Harold G. Marcus, *The Life and Times of Menelik II: Ethiopia 1844–1913* (Oxford: Clarendon Press, 1975), pp. 174–213. For the immediately preceding period, see R. H. Kofi

Darkwah, *Shewa, Menilek and the Ethiopian Empire, 1813–1889* (London: Heinemann, 1975).

10 Christopher Clapham, *Haile-Selassie's Government* (New York: Praeger, 1969), p. 68.

11 Mahteme Sellassie Wolde Mesqel, *Che Belew* (Addis Abeba: Commercial Printing Press, 1961 E.C.), p. 19.

12 Interview by the author and Alexander Naty of a servant of *dejazmach* Merid, Addis Abeba, 1983.

13 Unfortunately, documentary sources for Maale history, even in the early twentieth century, are extremely limited. What is perhaps the first mention of Maale occurs in Jules Borelli, *Ethiopie méridionale* (Paris: Ancienne Maison Quantin, 1890), pp. 334 and 439. Borelli evidently interviewed Gofa traders about this area while he was in Jimma. Because Maale was off the beaten track for travellers, not much else is recorded. The fullest mention of Maale, such as it is, occurs in Oscar Neumann, 'From Somali Coast Through Southern Ethiopia to the Sudan', *GJ* 20 (1902), pp. 373–401. He writes on p. 386:

> After two days' marching we came to a river called Shambala [the major river between Marta and Maale on the accompanying map] by the Abyssinians of our escort. On the other side we saw natives running away from their cotton-fields in terrible fright. We were here in the country of the Male, which may be identical with the Mela mentioned by Donaldson Smith. The Male are not yet absolutely subjected by the Abyssinians. I gave presents to some old men and women, who were not quick enough to run away, and sent them back to their fellows, but I was not able to have any intercourse with the people, as the next day nobody appeared.

Maale is listed on a map but not mentioned by C. H. Stigand, *To Abyssinia Through an Unknown Land* (London: Seeley, 1910) and only mentioned by Arnold Hodson, *Seven Years in Southern Abyssinia* (London: Fisher Unwin, 1927), p. 269.

I am aware that it is a difficult task to establish from ethnohistorical data rises and falls in power of the Maale king. I have, for example, fairly extensive case material on various kinds of political contests in the twentieth century – conflicts between the king and governor and between the king and chiefs, cases involving succession to the kingship, and so forth. Below I shall present some of this material and try to show how it exemplifies the overall pattern briefly outlined so far.

14 Fernand Maurette, 'Etat de nos connaissances sur le nord-est africain', *Annales de géographie* 14 (1905), p. 450.

15 A. E. Jensen, 'Die Male', in *Altvölker Süd-Äthiopiens: Ergebnisse der Frobenius-Expeditionen 1950–52 und 1954–56*, ed. A. E. Jensen (Stuttgart: W. Kohlhammer, 1951), p. 268.

16 The division between the elder and younger brothers of ritual and political duties respectively seems to have occurred very early. Father Gabriele da Casotto visited Maale briefly in the early 1940s during the Italian occupation, and he refers to Hilla as *balabbat* and *as a ḳennyazmach* in 'Note sulle popolazioni dell'alto e medio Galana', in *Studi etiopici*, ed. C. Conti Rossini (Rome: Istituto per l'Oriente, 1945), pp. 150–81. On p. 153 he writes, 'The political constitution of the Acia [Maale] is similar to that of the Are of Bacco, the only difference being that the regal and religious powers, instead of being united in the king, are divided between two members of the same family, usually between two brothers' (my translation). This arrangement was confirmed by Jensen and his team when they visited Maale in early 1951 for three months. On p. 268 of 'Die Malle' Jensen writes:

> In 1950 he [Yebirka] was a man of about 40 years, very good looking, racially a Nilotic type, of strong intelligence but quite well-meaning and agreeable. Against the Amharas he followed a policy of passivity. The undergovernor of Bako prefers not to have anything to do with him and prefers his brothers Grasmatsch . . . [Hilla], on whom the Amhara generally rely in administrative matters. There was however no official political

policy, as perhaps was the case among the Tsamako or among the Konso, that brothers should divide responsibilities, that . . . [Yebirka] should be the religious and . . . [Hilla] the political master of Male . . . [Hilla] acted at times only under the instructions of . . . [Yebirka] or, as it is handled in the case of primitive cultures, under the instructions of old and respected men (my translation).

17 The split between religious and political rôles occurred extensively in the south during the twentieth century. The most obvious 'head' of local peoples was often an essentially religious figure; when these men were made *balabbat* by the imperial administration, it was apparently difficult for them to maintain old religious and ritual powers – tied up as they were with notions of fertility and well-being – and at the same time to fulfil the rougher rôle of intermediary with the Amhara. Younger brothers, and most strikingly, mothers often played the rôle of *balabbat*, while elder brothers and sons inherited ritual positions. See Jacques Bureau, *Les Gamo d'Ethiopie; étude du système politique* (Paris: Société d'Ethnographie, 1981), pp. 227–49, and Judith Olmstead, 'The Woman who Governed: Factional Politics in the Gamo Highlands' (Paper presented at Society and History of Imperial Ethiopia Conference, Monterey, California, 1982). In this volume, see Chapter 4 by Uri Almagor.

18 This is also reported for the Gedeo by Charles McClellan, in Chapter 7 of this volume.

19 Dependency theory, regional systems analyses, and peasant studies all exemplify this trend. For dependency theory, see Immanuel Wallerstein's influential work, *The Modern World-System: Capitalist Agriculture and the Origins of the European World-Economy in the Sixteenth Century* (New York: Academic Press, 1974). Regional systems analyses have been influenced by G. William Skinner's work on marketing and urban system in China; in particular, see his essay, 'Regional Urbanization in Nineteenth-Century China', in *The City in Late Imperial China*, ed. G. W. Skinner (Stanford: Stanford University Press, 1977). The field of peasant studies originated in American cultural anthropology, and is perhaps best represented at present by the British periodical, *Journal of Peasant Studies*.

20 Immanuel Wallerstein, 'The Rise and Future Demise of the World Capitalist System', *Comparative Studies in Society and History* 16 (1974), pp. 387–415.

4. Institutionalizing a fringe periphery

1 This chapter is based on data which I collected during field work among the Dassanetch of south-west Ethiopia during 1968–70. My field work was carried out mainly among the Inkabelo, the largest tribal section. I use the category 'Amhara' to refer to anyone from the central highlands of Ethiopia, whose mother tongue is Amharic and who practises, at least nominally, Orthodox Christianity.

2 S. N. Eisenstadt, 'Sociological Aspects of Imperialism in the Ancient World', *Jerusalem Journal of International Relations* 3 (1978), pp. 94–106.

3 *Ibid.*, p. 95.

4 *cf.* Donald N. Levine, *Greater Ethiopia: The Evolution of a Multiethnic Society* (Chicago: University of Chicago Press, 1974), pp. 174–5. His analysis of the Ethiopian empire in terms of the transition from a patrimonial system to a bureaucratic empire is based on S. N. Eisenstadt's study, *The Political System of Empires* (London: Collier-Macmillan, 1963). See also E. J. Keller, 'The Revolutionary Transformation of Ethiopia's Twentieth-Century Bureaucratic Empire', *Journal of Modern African Studies* 19 (1981), pp. 307–36.

5 Niel Sobania, 'Neighbors and Strangers: Networks in the Eastern Lake Turkana Basin at the Turn of the Century'. (Paper presented at the conference, Society and History of Imperial Ethiopia, Monterey, California, 1982).

6 *Ibid.*, p. 27.

7 A. Donaldson Smith, *Through Unknown African Countries* (London: Collier-Macmillan,

1897), p. 294, and J. J. Harrison, 'A Journey from Zeila to Lake Rudolf', *GJ* 18 (1901), p. 272.

8 C. W. Gwynn, 'A Journey in Southern Abyssinia', *GJ* 38 (1911), p. 124, and C. H. Stigand, *To Abyssinia Through an Unknown Land* (Philadelphia: J. B. Lippincott, 1910), pp. 215–26.

9 For an interesting account of the acquisition of firearms by tribesmen, their raids into British East Africa, and a punitive expedition (1918) against them, see J. Yardley, *Parergon or Eddies in Equatoria* (London: J. M. Dent, n.d.), R. O. Collins, 'The Turkana Patrol, 1918', *UJ* 25 (1961), pp. 16–33, and J. Barber, *Imperial Frontier* (Nairobi: East African Publishing House, 1968), Chapters 14 and 15.

10 See J. K. R. Thorp, 'The Geluba', Administrative Notes, Marsabit, 1942, p. 17, Kenya National Archives.

11 Uri Almagor, *Pastoral Partners* (Manchester: Manchester University Press, 1978).

12 The Dassanetch word *ochumba* has two meanings; one is 'strangers with cloth', which is how the Amhara were first described; the other is 'people without *shurte shushulish*' (i.e. without the Dassanetch men's hairdressing).

13 My informants also told me that the number of chiefs in the past was less than in 1968–70. The kinship relation of the chiefs mentioned here to those who served in the past is as follows: Irgudo was the brother's son of Hamunyabuk, whom he succeeded; Korugur was the son of Atomosia, who was chief before Lockwaria. Lockwaria was the brother's son of Atomosia, and Korugur succeeded chief Lockwaria. Lumuromoi was the son of Dabo, who was chief before him. Yerar was the brother's son of Koriko, who was chief before he was succeeded by his son Loluk. After Loluk's death, Yerar became chief. Anokhosia was not a descendant of any chief. He was *kansitch ninika*, assistant and messenger, of chief Hamunyabuk, and was nominated as chief in 1942.

14 There was a division between the chiefs. I shall not refer to those who represented the Inkoria and Naritch tribal sections located east of the Omo River and administratively affiliated to Turmi in Hamarland. In my description, the other six chiefs, who are more relevant here, represent tribal sections located west of the river when I was in the field. Yerar represented the Oro tribal section; Korugur, the Elele; and Lumuromoi, the Randal. The remaining three chiefs, Anokhosia, Atol, and Irgudo, all belonged to the dominant Inkabelo tribal section. The latter three were affiliated to different generation-sets, and each represented his own set as well as its alternate counterpart. Thus, Anokhosia was chief for NUMOR–NYOGOLOMOGEN; Atol represented the NILIMETO–NIKORIO generation-sets, and Irgudo was chief for NIGABITE–NILIMKORIO. NUMOR–NYOGOLOMOGEN and NIGABITE–NILIMKORIO were numerically the largest generation-sets, and Anokhosia and Irgudo functioned in addition as chiefs for the two small tribal sections of Riele and Koro respectively.

15 The *dimi* ceremony is the major ceremony that a man is expected to undergo. A man 'goes to *dimi*' about eight to ten years after having fathered a daughter, so that all his daughters will receive a blessing for future marriage and fertility. The ceremony lasts about six weeks, during which time he is expected to slaughter much stock for ritual purposes, as well as for entertaining guests.

16 It is interesting to note that Amhara authorities accepted the Dassanetch concept that 'it is the cattle that are important and not land'. The Amhara governor admitted to me that he had no idea how the Dassanetch agricultural system worked. For more details on that system see Almagor, *Pastoral Partners*, pp. 38–45.

17 On naming see Almagor, 'Name Oxen and Ox-names Among the Dassanetch of South West Ethiopia', *Paideuma* 18 (1972), pp. 79–96.

18 The Dassanetch say that they have been required to pay their taxes in money only since the end of the 1950s. The tax, from whomever it was taken, was Ethiopian $0.25 per head of cattle and $0.10 per head of small stock (Ethiopian $2.50 = US $1.00). The money collected by the chiefs in 1969 (after the emperor waived past unpaid taxes) totalled, for the west bank

of the river only: Anokhosia, $700; Irgudo, $900; 'Atol, $570; Yerar, $500; Lumuromoi, $500; Korugur, $400.

19 See the essays by Serge Tornay, 'Armed Conflicts in the Lower Omo Valley, 1970–76: An Analysis From Within Nyangatom Society', and Uri Almagor, 'Raiders and Elders: A Confrontation of Generations Among the Dassanetch', in *Warfare Among East African Herders*, ed. Katsuyoshi Fukui and David Turton, Senri Ethnological Studies No. 3 (Osaka: National Museum of Ethnology, 1979).

20 Dassanetch obtained firearms from Maji or from Amhara soldiers stationed in Dassanetchland. Buying rifles in Maji was no simple matter. Dassanetch had to drive a small herd through the territories of hostile groups and sell the cattle in Maji for Ethiopian $120 per head. Each rifle cost from $250 to $400. Rifles and ammunition sold to the Dassanetch by Amhara soldiers were not the weapons with which those soldiers had been issued nor those kept in the Kalam army depot. They were purchased in Jinka and elsewhere and smuggled into Dassanetchland on army trucks. The sale of arms was mediated through Dassanetch soldiers (*labania*) and not through the chiefs.

21 Anokhosia was held by the Dassanetch to be a 'friend of Haile Selassie'. This was because he went to Addis Abeba on the emperor's return to Ethiopia after the Italian defeat in the Second World War. The story is told that Anokhosia met the emperor, who appointed him chief. He returned to Dassanetchland with the army, and it was often said that he had 'brought the *ochumba* to Dassanetchland'.

22 In colonial reports (*cf.* Thorp, 'The Geluba', and R. G. Turnbull, 'Turkana Frontier Affairs', Administrative Memorandum, Lodwar, 1944, Kenya National Archives) only the names of the chiefs are mentioned, as if they were the only leaders of the Dassanetch.

23 R. Paine, *Patrons and Brokers in the East Arctic* (Newfoundland: St. John's Institute of Social and Economic Research, Memorial University of New Foundland, 1971).

24 For more details, see Almagor, 'Gerontocracy, Polygyny, and Scarce Resources', in *Sex and Age as Principles of Social Differentiation*, ed. J. S. La Fontaine (London: Academic Press, 1978).

25 The Amhara who returned to the Lower Omo after the Italian defeat in World War II were compared unfavourably to the Italians by the Dassanetch, who often said that 'the Amhara were bad and the Italians were good'. The Italians, I was told, 'did not collect taxes [some elders admitted that they gave the Italians cattle and small stock as 'gifts'] while the Amhara ask for taxes all the time and make our life difficult'. Also the Italians 'gave the Dassanetch firearms, while the Amhara try to confiscate them'. Generally, the Dassanetch maintained that 'the Italians liked us and we liked them, but the Amhara hate us and we hate them'.

26 During eighteen months of my field work there were three cases of suicide among the Amhara soldiers. There were some doubts about one of the cases – it could have been a case of accidental drowning because of drunkenness.

27 For more details on the symbolism of various clothes and acts appearing during the *dimi* ceremony, see Almagor, 'Colours that Match and Clash: The Explication of Meaning in a Pastoral Society', *Res – Anthropology and Aesthetics* 5 (1983), pp. 46–73.

28 There are widespread rumours in south-west Ethiopia that the Dassanetch 'eat their dead' or 'eat human flesh'. I heard such stories in Jinka before arriving in Dassanetchland.

29 Paine, *Patrons and Brokers in the East Arctic*, p. 6.

30 The replacement of the Dassanetch soldiers (*labania*) was high. Most of them were under pressure from thier age-mates to desert after a short period of service, and indeed they often did so – taking their weapons with them. Only a few *labania* who spoke a bit of Amharic and who worked as translators served for longer periods.

31 The ferry was brought to the Omo River and the amnesty for tax evaders was granted at the end of 1968 when the emperor visited Dassanetchland for one day. The impact of the emperor's visit was to intensify the power struggle between chiefs and Bulls that was connected with a possible change-over in the Dassanetch generation-set system. See Uri

Almagor, 'The Year of the Emperor and the Elephant among the Dassanetch of Ethiopia', *Northeast African Studies* 7 (1985), pp. 1–22.

32 S. N. Eisenstadt, 'Social Institutions', *The International Encyclopedia of the Social Sciences* 14 (1968), p. 415.

33 E. Shils, 'Society and Societies: The Macrosociological View' in E. Shils, *Center and Periphery* (Chicago: University of Chicago Press, 1975), p. 40.

34 Katsuyoshi Fukui and David Turton, eds., *Warfare, passim.*

35 At the beginning of the 1970s the Amhara authorities introduced development projects for irrigation in an attempt to change the production system in the direction of permanent cultivation (see Almagor, *Pastoral Partners*, p. 8). However, at the same time a series of outbreaks of violence occurred between the Dassanetch and the Nyangatom (see Tornay, 'Armed Conflict') that lasted several years.

36 In 1969 the Dassanetch were asked to vote for Amhara candidates to the House of Representatives. However, the whole election campaign among the Dassanetch turned into another facet of the struggle for a change-over between generation-sets and of the rivalry between the Bulls and the chiefs (see note 31). The episode took a form which had nothing to do with access or commitment to the Ethiopian national framework.

37 E. Shils, 'Society and Societies', pp. 42–6.

5 Lifelines

1 This chapter draws upon research conducted in Ethiopia over a period of nine months in 1974 and 1975, most of which was spent in western Wallegga. This research was funded by a grant from the SSRC in London, and during my time in Ethiopia I was attached as a Visiting Scholar to the Institute of Ethiopian Studies in Addis Abeba. I would like to acknowledge the invaluable assistance of Mr Gali Sambato and Miss Rahel Mammo. I was grateful for the general support and facilities offered me by the ECMY. Pastor Jan Ulveseth, at Nejjo, was particularly helpful in making my field research possible, in the Blue Nile Valley. Mr Karl Erik Lundgren, who has an intimate knowledge of the region, kindly read and commented on a draft of this chapter.

2 James Bruce, *Travels to Discover the Sources of the Nile, in the Years 1768–1773*, 2nd revised edition, by Alexander Murray (Edinburgh: Constable and Manners and Miller, 1804), Vol. 3, p. 455, and Vol. 5, pp. 399–402.

3 *Ibid.*, Vol. 5, p. 401. Slaves at that time were not a part of the tribute; they were 'reserved for presents to the king, and great men' (p. 402).

4 Vinigi L. Grottanelli, *I Mao: missione etnografica nell'Uollega occidentale*, Vol. 1 (Rome: Reale Accademia d'Italia, 1940). See also the same author's article, 'I Pre-Niloti: Un'arcaica provincia culturale in Africa', *Annali Laterenansi* 12 (1948), pp. 281–326, in which he introduced the term 'Pre-Nilotes'. Grottanelli regarded exchange marriage as a diagnostic feature which these peoples shared with the south-eastern paleo-Sudanese culture ('I Pre-Niloti', p. 323). He is the only ethnographer to have made an intensive study of this institution in the field, specifically from the 'northern Mao' of the Dabus basin. These were regarded as an older survival, by comparison with the 'southern Mao' of Anfillo, who had apparently lost exchange marriage through acculturation to their Busase (Kefa) overlords.

5 Claude Lévi-Strauss, *The Elementary Structures of Kinship*, trans. James Harle Bell and John Richard von Sturner, ed. Rodney Needham (London: Eyre and Spottiswoode, 1969); see especially Chapter 28.

6 Alessandro Triulzi, *Salt, Gold and Legitimacy: prelude to the History of a No-Man's Land, Belā Shangul, Wallaggā, c. 1800–1898* (Naples: Istituto Universitario Orientale, 1981), and 'Trade, Islam and the Mahdia in Northwestern Wallaggā, Ethiopia', *JAH* 16 (1975), pp. 55–71; Peter P. Garretson, '*Shaykh* Hamdan Abu Shok and the Administration of Gubba, 1898 to 1937' in *Modern Ethiopia from the Accession of Menilek II to the Present*, ed. Joseph

Tubiana (Rotterdam: A. A. Balkema, 1980); Bahru Zewde, 'Relations between Ethiopia and the Sudan on the Western Ethiopian Frontier, 1898–1935' (Ph.D. thesis, Department of History, School of African and Oriental Studies, University of London, 1976), and 'A Biography of Dejazmach Jote Tulu, Abba Iggu (1885–1918)' (B. A. thesis, Department of History, Addis Abeba University, 1973); Atieb Ahmed Dafalla, 'Sheikh Khojele al-Hassan and Bela-Shangul (1825–1938)' (B. A. thesis, Department of History, Addis Abeba University, 1973); Girma Mengistu, 'The Busase of Anfillo, Quellam, Wallaga (A Historical Study)' (B. A. thesis, Department of History, Addis Abeba University, 1973).

7 The main publications here are Vinigi L. Grottanelli, 'The Vanishing Prenilotes Revisited', *Bulletin of the International Committee on Urgent Anthropological and Ethnological Research* (Austria) 8 (1966), pp. 23–36, as well as his book *I Mao*; Frederick D. Corfield, 'The Koma', *SNR* 21 (1938), pp. 122–65; Jack Stauder, *The Majangir: Ecology and Society of a Southwest Ethiopian People* (Cambridge: Cambridge University Press, 1971); Wendy James, '*Kwanim Pa: the Making of the Uduk People. An Ethnographic Study of Survival in the Sudan–Ethiopian Borderlands* (Oxford: Clarendon Press, 1979). Dr Taddesse Tamrat has recently led a team of historical researchers among the Gumuz of Gojjam; I have had the opportunity of seeing a paper presented by him to the International Symposium on History and Ethnography in Ethiopian Studies, Addis Abeba, 1982, 'Early Trends of Feudal Superimposition on Gumuz Society in Western Gojjam'.

8 Leone Zanni, 'La tribù dei Gumus: note etnografiche', *La Nigrizia* 57, 8 (1939), pp. 156–9, makes specific reference to the Agaw from Dongur taking women and girls as slaves from the Gumuz.

9 This was confirmed to me by Tsehai Berhane Selassie.

10 Peter P. Garretson, Department of History, Florida State University, ms. notes.

11 Bruce, *Travels*, Vol. 3, pp. 455, 512; Vol. 4, pp. 27–8, 45, 443; Vol. 5, pp. 399–402; Henry Salt, *A Voyage to Abyssinia and Travels into the Interior of that Country, Executed under the Orders of the British Government in the Years 1809–1810* (London: Frank Cass, 1967 [1814]), pp. 380–2; Charles T. Beke, 'Abyssinia – Being a Continuation of Routes in that Country', *Journal of the Royal Geographical Society* 14 (1844), p. 9; Taddesse Tamrat, 'Early Trends'.

12 Salt's account, based on information from Omazena, a slave at Chelicut whom he met in 1810. Omazena had been many years away from his homeland, Dabanja, and so his account can be taken to refer to the late eighteenth century. Dabanja was 'three days' journey beyond the Nile', and we can identify it as the place already named by Bruce as Banja, with the common Gumuz prefix Da-. The name occurs on modern maps, and is indeed about three days' journey beyond the Blue Nile, if one were travelling from the direction of Gonder by the east side of Lake Tana and crossing just below the river's exit. Omazena gave a very lively account of his people, mentioning among other things the general equality and the absence of priests and rulers, as well as the exchange of sisters in marriage. The Dizzela, Omazena's own people, are continually engaged in war with the people of Metikul and Banja (i.e. the Agaw of these centres) who 'frequently invade the country for the express purpose of procuring slaves'. However, the Dizzela themselves take prisoners, and either set them to work making cloth or iron, or kill them. When pressed, his people retire to a certain mountain.

13 R. S. O'Fahey and J. L. Spaulding, *Kingdoms of the Sudan* (London: Methuen, 1972); Wendy James, 'The Funj Mystique: Approaches to a Problem of Sudan History' in *Text and Context: the Social Anthropology of Tradition*, ed. R. K. Jain (Philadelphia: ISHI, 1977).

14 James, 'The Funj Mystique', pp. 126–7.

15 Zanni, 'La tribù dei Gumus'.

16 *Ibid.*

17 Garretson, '*Shaykh* Hamdan Abu Shok', p. 8.

18 *Ibid.*, pp. 7–8.

19 Peter P. Garretson, ms. notes on interviews in Damazin, near Roseires, Sudan, kindly shown to me.

20 Juan Maria Schuver, *Reisen im Oberen Nilgebiet*, Supplement No. 72 to *Petermanns Geographische Mitteilungen* (Gotha: Justus Perthes, 1883). The final section of this account is devoted to the region of Gubba (pp. 70–91). The English versions used here are drawn from Schuver's own manuscript notes, which were used for the preparation of the published German text. The notes, in various languages, were recently discovered in Holland by Dr Gerhard Baumann, and we plan to make them available in due course.

21 *Ibid.*, p. 71.

22 *Ibid.*, p. 77.

23 *Ibid.*, p. 83 (from the corresponding English ms.).

24 *Ibid.*, p. 88 (translated from the published German). For Sennar raid see English ms.

25 *Ibid.*, p. 83 (from the English ms.).

26 Bruce, *Travels*, Vol 5, pp. 399–402; see above, opening paragraphs of this chapter.

27 Schuver, *Reisen*, p. 83 (from the English ms.).

28 *Ibid.*, pp. 84 and 90.

29 *Ibid.*, p. 82.

30 J. L. Spaulding, 'The Government of Sinnār', *IJAHS* 6 (1973), pp. 19–35.

31 Schuver, *Reisen*, p. 80 (from the English ms). It is interesting to note that in the ms. notes, Schuver admits that if he had arrived earlier he would not only have saved a life, but 'acquired a grateful and trustworthy servant' (a detail omitted from the published German text).

32 Oscar T. Crosby, 'Notes on a Journey from Zeila to Khartoum', *GJ* 18 (1909), pp. 46–61. R. E. Cheesman, *Lake Tana and the Blue Nile* (London: Macmillan, 1936).

33 Crosby, 'Notes', pp. 50–1.

34 *Ibid.*, p. 54.

35 *Ibid.*, p. 57.

36 Cheesman, *Lake Tana*, pp. 336–7.

37 *Ibid.*, p. 353.

38 *Ibid.*, p. 359. Cheesman includes a photograph of *dejazmach* Banja, opposite p. 356.

39 Garretson, ms. notes.

40 Cheesman, *Lake Tana*, p. 361.

41 There is evidence that in the pre-Menilek era, there were a few Gumuz communities in the Blue Nile lowlands, on the left bank, and upstream of the Dabus confluence. They seem to have lived on stable terms with the Oromo highlanders. For example, d'Abbadie, following his travels of the 1840s in western Shewa, mentions that beyond the Limmu (Oromo) there are Naga blacks who pay tribute, are never attacked by the Limmu and in years of famine take refuge with them. 'They occupy a vast *kolla* near us and are not enemies. Their chiefs speak Oromo. In their language 'water' is *haya*, 'cow' is *tanga*.' This linguistic detail confirms the identity of the 'Naga'as Gumuz speakers (Antoine d'Abbadie, *Géographie d'Ethiopie* (Paris: Mesnil, 1890), p. 75). In an article of 1859 d'Abbadie refers to 'Guinza' as Negroes living on the banks (plural) of the Abbay, though without linking them with the 'Naga'. (Antoine d'Abbadie, 'Notes sur les nègres d'Ethiopie', *Bulletin de la société de géographie* 17 (1859), p. 172.) Other sources referring to Gumuz on the left bank in the pre-Menilek period include Lejean, who writes in 1865 of seven big tribes of the Goumouz or Gubba on the Blue Nile, four to the right and three to the left (Guillaume Lejean, 'Note sur les Fougn et leur idiome', p. 242). Marno, from observations in 1870, writes of 'Gumuz' living in the mountains south and east of Fazoghli and on both banks of the Blue Nile, and when he is travelling in Bela Shangul, he notes that 'Dar el Gumus' lies partly on the west bank of the Blue Nile (E. Marno *Reisen im Gebiete des blauen und weissen Nil, im Egyptischen Sudan, und den angrenzenden Negerländern* (Vienna: C. Gerold, 1874), p. 29). Schuver also heard, while in Gubba and Dasifi, of small states of the Gumuz on the left bank, between the

Dabus and the Diddessa, which were sometimes ruled by an Oromo aristocracy but at other times were independent and at war with the yellow-skinned people (which appears to be a reference to the Shinasha). The Gumuz in Dasifi told Schuver that beyond the Oromo, there were yet other Gumuz (Schuver, *Reisen*, p. 87).

42 A. Triulzi, 'Trade, Islam and the Mahdia'; Terrefe Woldetsadik, 'The Unification of Ethiopia (1880–1935): Wälläga', *JES* 6 (1968), pp. 73–86.

43 L. Vannutelli, 'L'Uallega e l'industria mineraria', *BSGI* 4 (1903), pp. 561–75. A. Weld Blundell suggests a figure of 80,000 for the annual export of Nejjo in his article, 'Exploration in the Abai Basin, Abyssinia', *GJ* 27 (1906), pp. 529–53.

44 Hugues le Roux, 'Voyage au Ouallega: Itinéraire d'Addis-Ababâ au Nil Bleu', *La géographie* 4 (1901), p. 228.

45 *Ibid.*, p. 230.

46 E. Haberland, 'Über einen unbekannten Gunza-Stamm in Wällägga', *Rassegna di studi etiopici* 12 (1953), pp. 139–48.

47 Rahel Mammo was my assistant and interpreter on this occasion in 1974.

48 Terrefe Woldetsadik, 'Unification', mentions that Moroda extended his power with the help of 'some devoted vassals', p. 74.

49 I spent ten weeks in Aba Bulcho, June–September, 1975, and also made some inquiries in the settlements near Diddessa Bridge in the course of my work in western Wellegga in 1974 and 1975.

50 This and subsequent texts used in this account were tape-recorded in Aba Bulcho, 1975, and transcribed and translated in collaboration with Gali Sambato. In my work with the Gumuz language I have been greatly helped by the loan of ms. notes from M. L. Bender, and his article, 'Gumuz, a Sketch of Grammar and Lexicon', *Afrika und Übersee* 62 (1979), pp. 38–69.

51 Lee Irwin, 'Some Notes on Saysay Culture', *JES* 6 (1968), pp. 131–9; Patrick Wallmark, 'The Bega (Gumuz) of Wällägga: Agriculture and Subsistence', in *Peoples and Cultures of the Ethio-Sudan Borderlands*, ed. M. L. Bender (East Lansing, Michigan: African Studies Center, Michigan State University, 1981), p. 79. I used 'lineage' terminology in my own earlier references to the Gumuz, for example in *'Kwanim Pa*, pp. 242–3, but on reflection consider that the 'descent principle' in Gumuz society does not take precedence in the way that the terminology of 'segmentary lineages' would imply. The writings of Pierre Bourdieu have been a valuable guide in rethinking Gumuz marriage; see especially his *Outline of a Theory of Practice*, trans. R. Nice, (Cambridge: Cambridge University Press, 1977).

52 There are many analogous features between the present Gumuz system and the traditional marriage system of the Tiv of Nigeria. I have found the Bohannans' work on the Tiv illuminating in my study of Gumuz marriage, as well as the autobiographical account of Tiv society by Akiga: R. East, ed., *Akiga's Story: The Tiv Tribe, as seen by One of its Members* (London: Oxford University Press for the International African Institute, 1939); Paul and Laura Bohannan, *The Tiv of Central Nigeria*, Ethnographic Survey of Africa, Western Africa, Part 8 (London: International African Institute, 1953), *Tiv Economy* (Evanston: Northwestern University Press, 1968) and *A Source Notebook on the Tiv Life-Cycle* (New Haven: Human Relations Area Files, 1966).

53 Among the prohibitions are for example those on eating chickens and eggs, or even taking food or drink from pans which might have been used for eggs. This appeared at first to be a blanket prohibition on all women at all times, but on further enquiry, appeared to apply only to women living in their husbands' villages, and not to the chickens and eggs of their own village; *cf.* Wallmark, 'The Bega (Gumuz)', pp. 110–11.

54 There are elaborate ceremonies, songs and rites which are the exclusive province of women among the Wellegga Gumuz. The younger women of a village are educated into this women's culture by the older generation. During my short stay in the village, I was only able to glimpse something of this field, which remains undescribed.

55 In Wellegga, apart from using the blanket term 'Shankalla', the Gumuz speakers refer to themselves by section names, such as Dukunzilla (or the Oromo equivalent Sese), Agalo (Oromo, Ebanja) and so forth. Wallmark has adopted *bega* 'people' as an ethnic self-name (Wallmark, 'The Bega (Gumuz)', p. 79); the stress is on the second syllable. However, 'Gumuz' occurs at least as far back as 1822 in the written sources (Frederic Cailliaud, *Voyage à Méroé, au Fleuve Blanc, au delà de Fâzoql dans le midi du royaume de Sennâr*, 4 vols. (Paris: L'Imprimerie royale, 1823–7) where he refers to 'Dar el Goumousse'), and is accepted today by the majority of speakers of various closely-related dialects of the Gumuz language both in Sudan and in Ethiopia.

56 C. W. Gwynn, 'Surveys on the Proposed Sudan–Abyssinian Frontier', *GJ* 18 (1901), pp. 562–73.

57 The Bugua and Dizhangwe sections were said by my informants to be now in the Sudan.

58 Cheesman, *Lake Tana*, p. 360. Erring, as a settlement, and Iaringhe, as a hill, both appear on immediate post-war maps, scale 1 = 100,000, Asosa sheet.

59 Taddesse Tamrat's research has revealed that 'Gulbak' occurs as a topographical name in western Gojjam as far back as the seventeenth century – 'Early Trends', p. 12, and p. 19 note 43.

60 I am aware that the distinction *Oromo/dina* can be used in various ways. Here, *dina* carries the implication of 'stranger from the wilderness', rather than 'enemy'.

61 Wallmark, 'The Bega (Gumuz)', pp. 109–10 and *passim*.

62 P. J. and L. Bohannan, *Tiv Economy*; M. Douglas, 'Primitive Rationing', in *Themes in Economic Anthropology*, ed. Raymond Firth (London: Tavistock, 1967).

63 Wallmark, 'The Bega (Gumuz)', pp. 99–100.

64 Successive reports chronicle the efforts of the Norwegian Missionary Society in their magazine *Norsk Misjonstidende* (Stavanger), from 1979 onwards.

65 Lévi-Strauss, *Elementary Structures*, Chapter 27.

66 *Ibid.*, pp. 448–9.

67 Wendy James, 'Sister-Exchange Marriage', *Scientific American* 233 (1975), pp. 84–94.

6. A problem of domination at the periphery

1 I should like to record my gratitude to Dr James Woodburn, Professor Eike Haberland and the Rev. W. F. Muldrow for their help and encouragement when I was planning my first field trip to the Omo valley, with the intention of studying the Kwegu, in 1968. Bill Muldrow gave me invaluable practical assistance when I was setting out from Maji to make my first contact with a group of Kwegu whom he had visited a few months earlier. I am also grateful to James Woodburn, Dr Paul Baxter, Dr John Comaroff, and to participants in the Monterey Conference (particularly Dr Wendy James), for their helpful comments. The weaknesses that remain in the chapter are, of course, my own responsibility.

2 The Kwegu described here are only part of the Kwegu population of the Lower Omo valley. Others live farther upstream, in association with the Bodi (see W. F. Muldrow, 'Languages of the Maji Area', in *The Non-Semitic Languages of Ethiopia*, ed. M. L. Bender (East Lansing, Michigan: African Studies Center, Michigan State University, 1976), p. 606), and yet another group of Kwegu lives south of Mursi territory, just south of the junction of the Omo and the Mago. The latter, whom I have never visited, and who are known as Muguji to their southern neighbours, the Kara and the Hamar (Jean Lydall, 'Hamer', *The Non-Semitic Languages of Ethiopia*, ed. M. L. Bender (East Lansing, Michigan: African Studies Center, Michigan State University), p. 394), do not, as far as I know, have a special relationship with the Mursi. They certainly have no regular contact with the Kwegu described here, who barely know of their existence. (This need cause no surprise. Blackburn says of the Okiek (Dorobo) hunters of the highland forest region of south-western Kenya that 'many Okiek local groups are so distant from each other that they have no knowledge of each other' – R.

H. Blackburn, 'In the Land of Milk and Honey: Okiek Adaptations to their Forest and Neighbors', in *Politics and History in Band Societies*, ed. E. Leacock and R. Lee (Cambridge: Cambridge University Press, 1982), p. 285). The northern Kwegu, on the other hand, do have close and regular relations, notably ones based on intermarriage. Muldrow puts the total population of the northern Kwegu at 600, which is probably an over- rather than an underestimate.

3 The only exception was the Bòttego expedition, which, following the left bank of the Omo, travelled through Mursiland in August 1896 – L. Vannutelli and C. Citerni, *Seconda spedizione Bòttego: l'Omo viaggio d'esplorazione nell'Africa orientale* (Milan: Hoepli, 1899). On Menilek's campaigns in the Lower Omo area see Chapters 4 and 8 of this volume.

4 The most direct involvement of the Mursi with the Ethiopian centre has come during the past ten years, as a result of the famine relief operations of the Ethiopian Government's Relief and Rehabilitation Commission. During the early 1970s the Mursi suffered their worst period of drought and hunger in living memory and conditions were again very bad at the end of the decade. One result of this has been a spontaneous migration, beginning in 1979 and now accounting for about 20 per cent of the entire population, from Mursiland proper to higher, better watered land in the Mago Valley. Having set up a permanent agricultural settlement within three hours' walk of a highland market in an area unsuitable, because of tsetse flies, for cattle, the migrants are in the process of becoming sedentary agriculturalists, like their highland neighbours, with whom they are developing close economic ties (D. A. and P. Turton, 'Spontaneous Resettlement after Drought: An Ethiopian Example', *Disasters* 8 (1984), pp. 178–89).

5 On one occasion, when I was pressing a Mursi on the relationship between the two groups, he asked, in some exasperation, 'Don't you English have Nyidi?'

6 Butzer estimates that the 'upland plains of the Lower Omo Basin' receive a mean annual rainfall of about 480 millimetres, but adds that 'year-to-year variability is very great as is the concentration of the rains in the several rainy spells within the year' (K. W. Butzer, *Recent History of an Ethiopian Delta: The Omo River and the Level of Lake Rudolf*, (Chicago: University of Chicago Department of Geography Research Paper No. 136, 1971), p. 26).

7 At this latitude, the topography of the Omo banks does not allow thé creation of extensive flooded flats such as release the Dassanetch, farther south, from reliance on rain-fed cultivation (*cf.* Almagor in Chapter 4 of this volume).

8 Both languages are members of the Didinga-Murle or Surma groups. See A. Tucker and M. Bryan, *Linguistic Analysis: The Non-Bantu Languages of North-East Africa* (Oxford: Oxford University Press, 1966), pp. 370–91, and M. L. Bender, 'The Languages of Ethiopia: A New Lexicostatistical Classification and Some Problems of Diffusion', *Anthropological Linguistics* 13 (1971), pp. 165–288; M. L. Bender, 'Nilo-Saharan Overview' in *The Non-Semitic Languages of Ethiopia*, ed. M. L. Bender (East Lansing, Michigan: African Studies Center, Michigan State University, 1976), pp. 467–72. See also Eike Haberland, 'Zur Sprache der Bodi, Mursi, und Yidenic in Südwest Äthiopien' in *Neue Afrikanistische Studien*, ed. J. Lukas (Hamburg: Deutsches Institut für Afrika Forschung, 1966).

9 P. P. Howell, 'A Note on Elephants and Elephant Hunting among the Nuer', *SNR* 26 (1945), p. 95.

10 D. A. Turton, 'Territorial Organisation and Age among the Mursi', in *Age, Generation and Time: Some Features of East African Age Organisations*, ed. P. T. W. Baxter and U. Almagor (London: Hurst, 1978), p. 110.

11 Two types of firearms are used by the Mursi: the 6.5 millimetre Italian Manlicher Carcano carbine and the 8 millimetre Austro-Hungarian Manlicher rifle.

12 This point is brought home by the recent migration of Mursi to the Mago valley (see above, note 4). These are now the only Mursi who do not make use of floodland at the Omo, but, in cutting their dependence on this resource, they have moved into an area of high tsetse challenge where successful cattle herding is impossible.

13 My impression is that the Kwegu have fared better than the Mursi during the recent years of drought.

14 There is no equivalent in Mursi (nor, as far as I know, in Kwegu) for the English terms 'patron' and 'client'. A Mursi refers to his client as *Nyidini a-nano* ('my Kwegu') and a Kwegu refers to his patron as *Muni a-nano* ('my Mursi', *Muni* being the self name of the Mursi).

15 Claude Meillassoux, 'The Economy in Agricultural Self-Sustaining Societies: A Preliminary Analysis', in *Relations of Production: Marxist Approaches to Economic Anthropology*, ed. D. Seddon (London: Frank Cass, 1978), pp. 127–57, and *Maidens, Meals and Money* (Cambridge: Cambridge University Press, 1981). See also Emmanuel Terray, *Marxism and 'Primitive' Societies* (New York: Monthly Review Press, 1972).

16 According to Meillassoux, 'It is through women that the elders maintain authority over the juniors, it is also through women that the latter emancipate themselves from the elders' (*Maidens*, p. 78).

17 Like women, therefore, Kwegu approach more closely than juniors in Meillassoux's model the position of an exploited social class. Indeed, according to Meillassoux's usage, they approach it more closely than women:

> Class relations are created, not out of *categories* like 'elders' and 'juniors' but through the dominance of entire, organically constituted communities which endow *all their members*, irrespective of age or sex, with prerogatives and privileges, over *all* the members of the dominated communities. In fact, classes cannot be reduced to categories of age and sex. They are organic social groups operating in functional relations dependent one upon the other, and each possessing their own mode of reproduction (*Maidens*, p. 81; italics in the original).

18 When I first visited the Lower Omo valley, in 1968, I intended to study hunter/non-hunter relationships and was well aware of the importance of conducting such a study from the vantage point of the hunters. The Kwegu were therefore the first people I contacted in the area. Rightly or wrongly (probably, I now think, wrongly) I gave up my plan to focus my research on them because they were so few and because they were not the 'pure' hunters which, as a callow graduate student, I was hoping to find. In turning my attention to the Mursi I maintained a strong interest in the Kwegu and went out of my way to cultivate particular friendships among them. My principal Kwegu informant worked for me for several short periods during my first field trip – he was then a boy of about fifteen and is now married with two wives and (in 1982) two children – and I believe I have as close a relationship with him as I have with any Mursi. In my (private) conversations with him and other Kwegu I have tried to elicit an assessment of their relationship with the Mursi more in accordance with my assessment of it as an 'objective observer', but have found no evidence of a Kwegu 'version' of the relationship which contradicts that of the Mursi.

19 Colin Turnbull, *Wayward Servants: The Two Worlds of the African Pygmies* (London: Eyre and Spottiswoode, 1966).

20 *Ibid.*, p. 50.

21 *Ibid.*, p. 13.

22 *Ibid.*, p. 3.

23 *Ibid.*, p. 37.

24 J. C. Woodburn, 'Egalitarian Societies', *Man* 17 (1982), pp. 431–51.

25 *Ibid.*, pp. 432, 445, 447.

26 This interpretation of 'Kwegu consent' conforms to a general hypothesis advanced by M. Godelier ('Infrastructures, Societies and History', *Current Anthropology* 19 (1978), pp. 763–72) to explain the origin of classes in classless societies:

> I should now like to formulate the following hypothesis: for relations of domination and exploitation to have arisen and reproduced themselves durably in formerly classless societies such relations must have presented themselves *as an exchange* and as an exchange

of *services* . . . We may even suggest that the formation of classes may have taken the form of an *unequal* exchange, one that looked more advantageous to the dominated than to the dominant, and it is perhaps this that we call an extreme case of alienation (pp. 767–8; italics in the original).

27 Paul Spencer, *Nomads in Alliance: Symbiosis and Growth Among the Rendille and Samburu of Kenya* (London: Oxford University Press, 1973); M. G. Kenny, 'Mirror in the Forest: The Dorobo Hunter-Gatherers as an Image of the Other', *Africa* 51 (1981), pp. 475–95; R. H. Blackburn, 'The Okiek and their History', *Azania* 9 (1974), pp. 139–57; 'Milk and Honey', pp. 283–305.

28 G. W. B. Huntingford, 'The Social Institutions of the Dorobo', *Anthropos* 46 (1951), pp. 1–48; 'The Political Organisation of the Dorobo', *Anthropos* 49 (1954), pp. 123–48.

29 Spencer, *Nomads*; J. L. Berntsen, 'The Maasai and their Neighbors: Variables of Interaction', *AEH* 2 (1976), pp. 1–11; R. van Zwanenburg, 'Dorobo Hunting and Gathering: A Way of Life or a Mode of Production', *AEH* 2 (1976), pp. 12–21; Cynthia Chang, 'Nomads without Cattle: East African Foragers in Historical Perspective' in Politics and History in Band Societies, ed. E. Leacock and R. Lee (Cambridge: Cambridge University Press, 1982).

30 Blackburn studied one of thirty-odd Okiek (i.e. Dorobo) groups living in the highland forest region of south-western Kenya. In his view, ethnographic and linguistic evidence supports the Okiek contention that, although now dispersed 'for at least several hundred years', they were once a single group, and that 'they were living in central Kenya prior to the arrival of any presently existing people' ('Milk and Honey', pp. 286–7). The fundamental reason for their survival is their adaptation to the forest, for which pastoralists have no direct use. But their relationship with the present Maasai, who invaded the area nearly one hundred years ago, has also been a formative influence on their culture. Steven Harvey, in 'Hunting and Gathering as a Strategic Adaptation: the Case of the Boni of Lamu District, Kenya' (Ph.D. thesis, Department of Anthropology, Boston University, 1978) describes a group of Boni hunters-cum-horticulturalists living in the Lamu district of Kenya, with Somali and 'Galla' neighbours. He sees the Boni as derived from a predominantly pastoral population which migrated into the area some two thousand years ago, and explains their present identity as, fundamentally, a product of adaptation to a forest environment. But he also suggests that an important factor may have been the external demand for ivory, which rapidly increased in the nineteenth century and in which Somali and 'Galla' acted as 'middlemen' between the Boni and Arab and European traders.

31 Kenny, 'Mirror in the Forest', p. 480.

32 D. A. Turton, 'Territorial Organisation'; 'A Journey Made Them: Territorial Segmentation and Ethnic Identity among the Mursi', in *Segmentary Lineage Systems Reconsidered*, ed. Ladislav Holy, Queen's University Papers in Social Anthropology, Vol. 4 (Belfast: Queen's University Press, 1979), pp. 119–43; 'War, Peace and Mursi Identity', in *Warfare Among East African Herders*, ed. Katsuyoshi Fukui and David Turton, Senri Ethnological Studies No. 3 (Osaka, Japan: National Museum of Ethnology, 1979), pp. 179–210.

33 This image is borrowed from J. Burton, 'Atuot Ethnicity: An Aspect of Nilotic Ethnography', *Africa* 51 (1981), pp. 496–507.

34 Leopard skins are an important trade good today, being exchanged usually for a rifle and/or ammunition. The external demand for leopard skin is, I presume, recent compared with that for ivory, and for this reason I think it can be safely ignored in the present argument.

35 R. W. Beachey, 'The East African Ivory Trade in the Nineteenth Century', *JAH* 8 (1967), pp. 269–90; Mordechai Abir, 'Caravan Trade and History in the Northern Parts of East Africa', *Paideuma* 14 (1968), p. 104.

36 Beachey, 'The East African Ivory Trade', pp. 269–70.

37 Abir, 'Caravan Trade', p. 104.

38 *Ibid.*, p. 111.
39 Vannutelli and Citerni, *Seconda Spedizione.*
40 *Ibid.*, p. 328 – 'alquanto abituata agli scambi'.
41 A. Donaldson Smith, 'An Expedition Between Lake Rudolf and the Nile', *GJ* 16 (1900), pp. 600–25.
42 Douglas H. Johnson, Chapter 9 of this volume.
43 Peter P. Garretson, Chapter 8 of this volume.
44 That they did not entirely escape these 'raids' is shown by the comments of the Kwegu quoted on p. 164.
45 Neil Sobania, 'A View of a Frontier from the Frontier: the Ethiopia–Kenya Frontier, *c.* 1875–1925' (Paper presented at the Society and History of Imperial Ethiopia Conference, Monterey, California, 1982).

7. Coffee in centre–periphery relations

1 The literature on this topic is extensive. General continent-wide analyses can be found in J. Forbes Munro, *Africa and the International Economy, 1800–1960* (Totowa, New Jersey: Rowman and Littlefield, 1976), and Immanuel Wallerstein, 'The Three Stages of African Involvement in the World-Economy', in *The Political Economy of Contemporary Africa*, ed. Peter C. W. Gutkind and Immanuel Wallerstein (Beverly Hills: Sage, 1976), pp. 30–57.
2 John Tosh, 'The Cash Crop Revolution in Tropical Africa: An Agricultural Reappraisal', *AA* 79 (1980), p. 79.
3 Unfortunately no thorough investigation of Gedeo social and political institutions has yet been accomplished. The material here is largely drawn from my own field work, which focused on other issues and was verified as much as possible by earlier Italian sources. See Charles W. McClellan, 'Reaction to Ethiopian Expansionism: The Case of Darasa, 1895–1935' (Ph.D. thesis, Department of History, Michigan State University, 1978), Chapter 1; Adolf E. Jensen, *Im Lande des Gada* (Stuttgart: Strecker und Schröder, 1936); Roberto Asinari di San Marzano, *Dal Giuba al Margherita* (Rome: L'Azione Coloniale, 1935). The Gedeo *gadaa* system was borrowed from the Guji and largely mirrors it, although in some aspects it is like that of the Sidama. For comparative material consult Bruno Lonfernini, *I Sidamo, un antico popolo cuscita* (Bologna: Nigrizia, 1971); John H. Hamer, 'Sidamo Generational Class Cycles: A Political Gerontocracy', *Africa* 40 (1970), pp. 50–72; John Hinnant, 'The Guji: Gada as a Ritual System', in *Age, Generation and Time*, ed. P. T. W. Baxter and Uri Almagor (New York: St. Martin's Press, 1978), pp. 207–43.
4 Richard A. Caulk, 'Adwa: How Much of a Challenge to Colonialism?' (Paper delivered to an Interdisciplinary Seminar of the Faculty of Arts and Education, Haile Selassie I University, Addis Abeba, 1970–1, mimeographed).
5 For a more developed discussion of this trend, see my 'Land, Labor and Coffee: The South's Role in Ethiopian Self-Reliance, 1889–1935', *AEH* 9 (1980), pp. 426–40.
6 Teferi's father, *ras* Mekonnen, had ruled Harergē from the time of its incorporation into Ethiopia in 1887 until his death in 1906. Balcha was given the post two years later on the death of Teferi's half-brother, Yilma. At the same time, Teferi was provided with a portion of Sidamo to rule over, undoubtedly because he was considered at that time too young and inexperienced to handle a province as important as Harergē.
7 Comparable data is hard to come by. Just prior to the railway's completion to Addis Abeba in 1916, A. Spaletta, in 'Il Caffè nell'Abissinia', *L'Agricoltura coloniale*, 11 (1917), p. 204, noted that a mule load of coffee from the capital to Dire Dawa cost MT$ 9 per 100 kilograms. A little later, the rail rate on 'Abyssinian' coffee (that from the interior provinces) was U.S. 9.¢ per ton-mile or a flat rate of U.S.$ 11.40 per ton (equivalent to MT$ 17.48 per ton if MT$ 1 = U.S. 65¢). At the flat rate, 100 kilos of coffee to Dire Dawa would cost around MT$ 1.75. See United States Department of Commerce, Bureau of Foreign and Domestic

Commerce, 'Abyssinia: Present Commercial Status of the Country', in *Special Consular Reports*, No. 81 (Washington, D. C.: Government Printing Office, 1918), p. 32.

8 Such an evolution was not untypical. Many of Ethiopia's major cities began as military centres; others were primarily commercial to begin with. Addis Abeba itself provides a prime example of the former. See Richard Pankhurst, 'The History of Shäwan Towns from the Rise of Menilek to the Founding of Addis Ababa', in *Modern Ethiopia From the Accession of Menilek II to the Present*, ed. Joseph Tubiana (Rotterdam: A. A. Balkema, 1980). See also Peter P. Garretson, 'A History of Addis Ababa From its Foundation in 1886 to 1910' (Ph.D. thesis, Department of History, School of Oriental and African Studies, University of London, 1974).

9 We do not as yet have a clear picture of the attempted coup in 1928. Hints and glimpses appear in the following: Haile Selassie I, *My Life and Ethiopia's Progress, 1892–1937*, trans. and ed. Edward Ullendorff (London: Oxford University Press, 1976); Tsehai Berhaneselassie, 'Menilek II: The Conquest and Consolidation of the Southern Provinces' (B. A. thesis, Department of History, Addis Abeba University, 1969), pp. 185–7; Bairu Tafla, 'Four Ethiopian Biographies', *JES* 7, 2 (1969), pp. 14–20; Pierre Mérab, *Impressions d'Ethiopie*, Vol. 3 (Paris: H. Libert, 1921), p. 180. See also the somewhat sensationalized account by Leonard Mosley, *Haile Selassie, the Conquering Lion* (London: Prentice Hall, 1964), p. 147.

10 I employ the terminology of 'patron–client' here, even though clients seldom had any real choice in who their patron would be. The relationship did involve mutual responsibilities: provisioning and labour services on one side, administrative, judicial and military obligations on the other. Patrons were theoretically obliged to keep the best interests of their clients in mind, and to care for them in times of need. Yet cultural, linguistic and religious differences between patron and client often made the patron less concerned about the plight of his *gebbar*, and the latter was reluctant to take his problems to a *neftennya* who really did not understand the nature of Gedeo society. While the southern *neftennya–gebbar* system was patterned upon the structures of northern society, it was more oppressive because of these basic differences. Clearly the same situation existed in northern society as well in its early years of evolution. Only over a period of centuries did assimilation of various ethnic groups there result in a new and singular community. The same process was undoubtedly under way in the south as well, but the extent of the peoples to be absorbed was so great and the process so long-term and tortuous that little comfort could be afforded to Gedeo caught up in the oppressive system at a particular point in time.

11 I present a statistical breakdown of *neftennya* origins in my article, 'The Ethiopian Occupation of Northern Sidamo – Recruitment and Motivation', *Proceedings of the Fifth International Conference on Ethiopian Studies*, ed. Robert L. Hess (Chicago: University of Illinois at Chicago Circle, 1979).

12 Gebre-Wold-Ingida Worq, 'Ethiopia's Traditional System of Land Tenure', *EO* 5 (1962), pp. 325–32; Mahteme Sellassie Wolde Maskal, 'The Land Tenure System of Ethiopia', *EO* 1 (1957), pp. 269–99.

13 J. G. Vanderheym, *Un expédition avec le Négous Ménélik* (Paris: Librairie Hachette, 1896) contains a heart-rending, first-hand account of the Welaita campaign. More general descriptions of the various campaigns can be found in Harold G. Marcus, *The Life and Times of Menelik II* (Oxford: Clarendon Press, 1975); R. H. Kofi Darkwah, *Shewa, Menilek and the Ethiopian Empire, 1813–1889* (London: Heinemann, 1975); and Tsehai Berhaneselassie, 'Menilek II'.

14 H. S. Mann *et al.*, *Field Study in Systems of Land Tenure and Landlord–Tenant Relationships (Tabor Woreda, Sidamo)* (Addis Abeba: Ministry of Land Reform, 1966), p. 1; see also Martino Mario Moreno, 'Il regime terriero nel Galla-Sidama', *Rassegna economica dell'Africa Italiana* 10 (1937), p. 1496; Berhanou Abbebe, *Evolution de la propriété fonçière au Choa (Ethiopie)* (Paris: Librairie Orientaliste Paul Geuthner, 1971), pp. 100–1; Mahteme

Sellassie, 'The Land Tenure System', p. 284.

15 *Kolla* land might sell as cheaply as MT$ 3–4 per *gasha*, while *woyna dega* (intermediate) land might go slightly higher at MT$ 5–10. West of Dilla, relatives of *dejazmach* Balcha were able to buy up to a thousand *gasha* of *kolla* land for only MT$ 320.

16 Gebre-Wold-Ingida Worq, 'Ethiopia's Traditional System', pp. 322–3; Mahteme Sellassie, 'The Land Tenure System', p. 287.

17 Some Gedeo were considered too poor to pay anything. They were assigned instead to the provincial *gibbī* (palace) for which they were to produce specified quantities of specialized commodities such as red pepper and ginger.

18 I found a few instances where a close acquaintance was assigned as a *gebbar* to a Gedeo collaborator. The *gebbar* found this relationship intolerable, unable to adjust to being subservient to one who had been a close companion. Transfer to other patrons was requested and granted.

19 A sizeable number of settlers in Sidamo were Shewan Gurage, who also consumed ensete as their traditional staple. Many Oromo settlers were also used to eating the commodity; Amhara-Tigrē were the most likely to be averse to it, but they also accepted quantities of it for themselves and particularly for their slaves and servants.

20 These iron bars, about half a metre long, bent at one end, and weighing about two kilograms, were widely exchanged throughout southern Ethiopia. The high-grade variety was used to fashion agricultural implements, while *wolanticha* was for other ornaments and jewellery. See the following: James J. Harrison, 'A Journey from Zeila to Lake Rudolf' *GJ* 18 (1901), p. 267; C. H. Stigand, *To Abyssinia Through an Unknown Land* (London: Seeley, 1910), pp. 296–7; M. S. Wellby, *Twixt Sirdar and Menelik* (New York: Harpers, 1901), pp. 141–2; Robert du Bourg de Bozas, *De la Mer Rouge à l'Atlantique à travers l'Afrique tropicale* (Paris: F. R. de Rudeval, 1906), pp. 260–1; Jules Borelli, *Ethiopie méridionale* (Paris: Ancienne Maison Quantin, 1890), p. 332; Getachew Kelemu, 'Internal History of the Aleta Sidanchos' (B. A. thesis, Department of History, Addis Abeba University, 1970), pp. 14–15; John Boyes, *My Abyssinian Journey* (Nairobi: W. Boyd, n.d.), p. 28.

21 In my survey of *gebbar* services, 87 per cent of the Guji and 79 per cent of the Gedeo reported herding livestock, while 67 per cent of the Guji and 75 per cent of the Gedeo cultivated crops for the *neftennya*. Since my Guji informants were at least partially dependent on settled cultivation, they were probably not completely typical of all Guji. I suspect that the disparities would have been even greater for the more pastoral Guji.

22 The value of this dispensation shifted with time, so that coffee-producing Gedeo after the 1920s might pay up to MT$ 50 to be free of all services. My survey showed that only 1 per cent of the Guji and 10 per cent of the Gedeo were able to purchase full exemption. Coffee seems to have made the big difference, and one suspects the Gedeo percentage may have been increased over time, in the earlier period being similiar to that of the Guji.

23 The government itself could conscript *gebbar* labour at any time for public works such as bridge-building or road-clearing. The *balabbat* and *korro* were responsible for seeing that sufficient labour turned up, penalizing *gebbar* who did not.

24 Of course, not all the labour within the extended family unit was fully and equally productive.

25 Only 50 per cent of Gedeo informants and 42 per cent of Guji reported such travel. Since such service might involve only one person within the *gibir*-paying unit, large numbers of Gedeo were unaffected by this task.

26 Ensete producers in Sidamo maintain 400 to 900 plants per family in various stages of development. See Eshetu Yimer, 'Land Use Study in Hanasho (Sidamo)' (B. A. thesis, Department of Geography, Addis Abeba University, 1968), pp. 60–1; Fantaye Berek, 'The Production and Consumption of Enset in Sidama' (B. A. thesis, Department of Geography, Addis Abeba University, 1968), pp. 26–7; Asres Kokebie, 'A Regional Study of Gerbicho' (B. A. thesis, Department of Geography, Addis Abeba University, 1967), pp. 43–4; Taye

Bezuneh and Asrat Felleke, 'The Production and Utilization of the Genus ensete in Ethiopia', *Economic Botany* 20 (1966), pp. 65–70. According to my informants, a man-load of *kocho* (a product of ensete) earlier in this century was worth one to two *mahalak* (12–16 per MT$). A man-load is equivalent to the product of three to four ensete plants. Using two *mahalak* as the base price and four plants per man-load, MT$ 5 would be equivalent to the product of 160 plants.

27 Birru reportedly amassed a fortune during his stint as governor of Wellegga. His Sidamo rewards were supposed to have considerably surpassed those of Wellegga. See San Marzano, *Dal Giuba*, pp. 219–20.

28 'Moyale District Handing Over Reports' (April, 1933), MLE/25. It was during Desta's administration that Sidamo and Borena provinces were consolidated into the present political entity. This unification was part of a longer-term endeavour to tighten control in Borena. The policy permitted greater exploitation of the area, and also sealed the international boundary more effectively to ensure that Ethiopian exports travelled to Addis Abeba rather than slipping illicitly across the border. See 'Memorandum on Mr. Thesiger's Journey to the Southern Frontier of Abyssinia and Nairobi', Enc. in No. 1, FO 371/1880/22457.

29 A prime historiographical debate over the intentions of Haile Selassie's modernization programmes seems to be emerging. We have little clear indication as yet as to what the emperor's perceptions of modernization were. Certainly his autobiography, *My Life and Ethiopia's Progress*, gives us few solid clues. In this developing debate, see Joanna Mantel-Niećko, *The Role of Land Tenure in the System of Ethiopian Imperial Government in Modern Times* (Warsaw: Wydawnictwa Uniwersytetu Warszawskiego, 1980) and Bereket Habte Selassie, 'The Dergue's Dilemma: The Legacy of a Feudal Empire', *Monthly Review* 17 (1980), pp. 1–23. The theme of a feudal Ethiopia trying to modernize itself can also be found in earlier works: Patrick Gilkes, *The Dying Lion: Feudalism and Modernization in Ethiopia* (New York: St. Martin's Press, 1975); John Markakis, *Ethiopia: Anatomy of a Traditional Polity* (Oxford: Clarendon Press, 1974); and Robert L. Hess, *Ethiopia: The Modernization of Autocracy* (Ithaca, N. Y.: Cornell University Press, 1970).

30 This assessment might be somewhat harsh, for landlords did play a rôle in getting coffee to market. Gedeo were unlikely to own any pack animals, and those few beasts that were present were most likely in settler hands. Imperial Ethiopian Government, *Report on a Survey of Sidamo Province* (Addis Abeba: Central Statistical Office, 1968), p. 35 reported that even in the 1960s pack animals were rare. In Gedeo *awrajja*, only seven in a hundred households possessed a mule, and only four in a hundred a donkey.

31 The former were referred to as the *barud bēt*, originally a highly disciplined and well-armed unit of Menilek's own soldiers sent by the emperor to assist *ras* Lu'ul Seged in the initial conquest of Sidamo, and to act as a watchdog and counterforce. Although under the provincial governor's command, the unit had its own revenues and reported directly to the emperor. The newcomers, often referred to as the *bēt lij*, were members of *dejazmach* Balcha's personal army and administration.

32 Louis A. Fuertes and Wilfred Hudson Osgood, *Artist and Naturalist in Ethiopia* (Garden City, N. Y.: Doubleday Doran, 1936), p. 85.

33 I am indebted to the late Volker Stitz and his 'Distribution and Foundation of Churches in Ethiopia', *JES* 13 (1975), pp. 11–36, for the ideas behind this methodology.

34 This data is based upon the official church records from the *awrajja* office in Dilla.

35 I.e. members of the *barud bēte*; see note 26.

36 Peter Schwab, *Decision-Making in Ethiopia* (London: Hurst, 1972), pp. 175–80, contains a cursory treatment of the 1968 disturbances.

37 About 20 per cent of my informants reported use of the *fird bēt* (court) at least once. In two-thirds of the cases, Gedeo were prosecutors, and 90 per cent of the cases involved land or its associated payments and services. *Ḳelad* involved more informants in legal action than any other single issue.

38 Connections are difficult to prove. Birru, in the meantime, lent valuable support to *ras* Mulugēta in the latter's campaign against *ras* Gugsa Welē in 1930, and thus in January of the following year, Haile Selassie appointed him War Minister. See Addison E. Southard to Secretary of State, Addis Abeba, January 26, 1931, No. 621, General Records of the Department of State Relating to the Internal Affairs of Ethiopia (Abyssinia, 1931–49), File 884.

39 Shibru Tekle Giorgis, trans., 'Compilation and Translation of Ethiopian Government Land Grant Orders' (Law Library, Addis Abeba University, 1969), pp. 1504–6; Mahteme Selassie, 'The Land Tenure System', pp. 295–6.

40 Tsehai Berhane Selassie, 'The Balabat and the Coffee disease: Politics and Ritual in Darasa', in *Working Papers on Society and History in Imperial Ethiopia*, ed. Donald L. Donham and Wendy James (Cambridge: African Studies Centre, 1980, mimeographed).

41 A survey of Limu, a coffee-producing region in western Ethiopia, reported that 60 per cent of the families hired external labour during the harvest, at the ratio of 3.5 labourers per household. See 'Limu Sample Survey, 1961–62', *Ethiopian Economic Review* 6 (1963), p. 108. Although I have no similar statistics for Gedeo, I never witnessed or was told about much migrant labour during the coffee season. In fact Gedeo had, to a degree, been a labour export area, with some Gedeo earning extra income by contracting to perform services for some Guji *gebbar* who could afford to pay them.

42 Gedeo *awraja* reported an absentee landlord rate of only 20 per cent as compared to the 25 per cent rate for the province as a whole. The neighbouring non-coffee-producing Jemjem *awraja*, by contrast, revealed a 56 per cent rate. Imperial Ethiopian Government, *Report*, pp. 20–1.

43 The Gedeo unit was called *hada* ('knife' in Oromo). A typical measured plot was two by three *hada* (of *c.* 50 metres each), thus about 15,000 square metres. It is interesting to compare this relatively small unit with the Amhara unit, *gasha*, at around 343,000 square metres (depending on the type of land being measured). Although I have been unable to confirm it, I suspect the Gedeo unit has been subordinated to that of the *gasha*. When more 'traditional' upland Gedeo areas were measured under *ras* Desta, no real surveying took place, but groups of five *gebbar* units were thrown together to create a *gasha* (see Moreno, 'Il regime', p. 1502).

44 The Italian war was instrumental in eliminating many of the earliest *neftennya*, and consequently reducing the importance of older garrison towns like Bule and Illalcha, which were not well-situated to develop commercial rôles. Overall, these events helped further to weaken the *neftennya–gebbar* structure, making abolition of the system after the war easier.

45 Gebre-Wold-Ingida Worq, 'Ethiopia's Traditional System', pp. 325–32; Mahteme Sellassie, 'The Land System', pp. 269–99.

46 This is not to suggest that northern peripheralization did not begin until that of the south was complete. James McCann, 'Ethiopia, Britain and Negotiations for the Lake Tana Dam, 1922–1935', *IJAHS* 14 (1981), pp. 41–60, complements this view. The north did have some items of potential export, e.g. hides and skins, but a restructuring of the collection and processing methods was needed to raise their quality and export value.

8. Vicious cycles

1 This song is taken from PRO FO 371/1043/9302, 27 July 1911.

2 Owen Lattimore, *The Inner Asian Frontiers of China* (New York: American Geographical Society, 1940).

3 See Harold Marcus, *The Life and Times of Menelik II, Ethiopia 1844–1913* (Oxford: Clarendon Press, 1975), pp. 7ff and 144ff. See also Mordechai Abir, *Ethiopia, the Era of the Princes. The Challenge of Islam and the Re-Unification of the Christian Empire, 1769–1855* (New York: Praeger, 1968).

4 Marcus, *Menelik II*, pp. 11, 64, 68–70, 156; Bairu Tefla, 'Three Portraits: Ato Aṣmä Giyorgis, Ras Gobäna Dachi and Ṣähafe Tezaz Gäbrä Selasse', *JES* 5, 2 (1967), pp. 133–50; Richard A. Caulk, 'Territorial Competition and the Battle of Embabo, 1882', *JES* 13, 1 (1975), pp. 65–88.

5 L. H. Gann and P. Duignan, eds., *The History and Politics of Colonialism 1870–1914*, Vol. 1 of *Colonialism in Africa, 1870–1960* (Cambridge: Cambridge University Press, 1970), p. 451. Richard Pankhurst, *An Economic History of Ethiopia, 1800–1935* (Addis Abeba: Haile Selassie I University Press, 1968), pp. 154–5.

6 A. K. Bulatovich, 'Dall'Abissinia al Lago Rodolfo per il Caffa', *BSGI* 37 (1900), pp. 121–42; I. Katsnelson and G. Terekhova, *Po Neīzvedannym Zemlyam Etiopii* [Through Unknown Lands of Ethiopia] (Moscow: Nauka, 1975); H. Darley, *Slaves and Ivory in Abyssinia: A Record of Adventure and Exploration Among the Ethiopian Slave-Raiders* (New York: Robert McBride, 1935), pp. 45 and 55.

7 Gorst to Grey, Cairo, 20 March 1909, Enclosure 2, and Capt. Kelly to Assistant Director of Intelligence, Khartoum, 10 February 1909, p. 8, PRO FO 371/597/9271.

8 C. P. Rosenfeld, *A Chronology of Menilek II of Ethiopia* (East Lansing: African Studies Center, Michigan State University, 1976), p. 139; R. Pankhurst, *Economic History*, pp. 154–5.

9 Song of the Soldiers, 27 July 1911, PRO FO 371/1043/9307.

10 R. S. O'Fahey and J. L. Spaulding, *Kingdoms of the Sudan* (London: Methuen, 1974), pp. 33–5, 59–60, 90–2; Mordechai Abir, *Era of the Princes*, pp. 97–108, 112–23; Sven Rubenson, *The Survival of Ethiopian Independence* (London: Heinemann, 1976), pp. 208ff.

11 See Peter P. Garretson, '*Shaykh* Hamdan Abu Shok and the Administration of Gubba, 1898 to 1937' in *Modern Ethiopia from the Accession of Menilek II to the Present*, ed. Joseph Tubiana (Rotterdam: A. A. Balkema, 1980).

12 S. Rubenson, *Ethiopian Independence*, pp. 208ff; *King of Kings Tewodros of Ethiopia* (Addis Abeba: Haile Selassie I University Press, 1966), pp. 15–46.

13 Thesiger to Gray, Annual Report of 1912, 10 January 1913, p. 2, PRO FO 371/1571/9283. See also the Diary of Azzaj Werḳineh (or Dr. Charles Martin), private ms. in the family's possession, 17 December 1899, for a long description of the traditional Ethiopian honours and prestige that accrued to the killer of an elephant. H. H. Kelly, 'Report on the Trade in Arms and Ivory on the Western Abyssinian Frontier', SIR 217, App. B. The Sudanese archives have been depended on so heavily because of the absence or inaccessibility of Ethiopian archives. The Sudan Intelligence Reports (SIR) and the Intelligence files (Intel) are extremely useful, in fact indispensable, and have always been confirmed from at least two sources.

14 H. Marcus, *Menelik II*, pp. 64, 185–7. Gebre Sillasē, *Tarike Zemen Za-Dagmawī Minilik, Nēguse Negest Za-Ityoppia* [A History of Menilek II, King of Kings of Ethiopia] (Addis Abeba, 1959, E.C.), pp. 276ff; C. C. Rossini, 'I Mekan o Suro nell'Etiopia del sudouest, e il loro linguaggio', *Rendiconti della Reale Accademia dei Lincei*, Classe Scienze, Morale Storiche, Series 5, 22 (1913), pp. 397–463 for an early introduction to the area; Bulatovich, 'Dall'Abissinia', p. 133 and *passim*; Katsnelson and Terekhov, *Etiopii*, pp. 105ff; C. W. Gwynn, 'A Journey to Southern Abyssinia', *GJ* 38 (1911), pp. 155ff. In the contemporary account published in the *BSGI* Bulatovich mentions a skirmish, but the unpublished papers in Katsnelson and Terekhov describe a 'bloody battle'. Tishana was the Amharic name for a supposed 'tribe', but actually the word *tishana* only means 'hello' in the languages of several contiguous peoples.

15 J. Barber, *Imperial Frontier, a Study of Relations between the British and Pastoral Tribes of North East Uganda* (Nairobi: East African Publishing House, 1968), pp. 93, 96–103; L. F. Athill, 'Extracts from a Paper Read at a Meeting of the Royal Geographical Society', Appendix, in H. Darley, *Slaves and Ivory: A Record of Adventure and Exploration Among the Ethiopian Slave-Raiders* (New York: Robert McBride, 1935), pp. 191–209. See also Enrico

Cerulli, *Peoples of South-West Ethiopia and its Borderland* (London: International African Institute, 1956), p. 91.

16 A. W. Hodson, *Where Lion Reign: An Account of Lion Hunting and Exploration in S. W. Abyssinia* (London: Skeffington, n.d., *c.* 1929), p. 109. Hodson's intelligence report from Maji, 21 July 1924 PRO FO 371/9994, pp. 70–6, contains a long and detailed description of the *gebbar* system in Maji.

17 C. Rossetti, *Storia diplomatica dell'Etiopia durante il regno di Menelik* (Torino: Società Tipografico-Editrice Nazionale, 1910), pp. 393–5.

18 Bulatovich, 'Dall'Abissinia', p. 126; Marcus, *Menelik II*, pp. 241–7; Hodson, *Where Lion Reign*, p. 109. See Barber, *Frontier*, p. 38 for Demtē as *dejazmach* in 1910. I. Guidi, *Vocabolario amarico–italiano* (Rome: Istituto per l'Oriente, 1953), p. 265; Peter P. Garretson, 'A History of Addis Abeba from its Foundation in 1886 to 1910' (Ph.D. thesis, Department of History, School of Oriental and African Studies, University of London, 1974); 'The *Naggadras*, Trade and Selected Towns in Nineteenth and Early Twentieth Century Ethiopia', *IJAHS* 12 (1979), pp. 416–39; H. H. Kelly, App. A, SIR 175 (February 1909).

19 For the above paragraph see Marcus, *Menelik* II, pp. 241 ff and Garretson, '*Shaykh* Hamdan Abu Shok'.

20 Marcus, *Menelik II*, p. 242; Darley, *Slaves*, pp. 25–6, 31, 35, 42–6, 55–7, 59, 61, 67, 83–5. See also the oral information cited by Richard A. Caulk, 'Armies as Predators: Soldiers and Peasants in Ethiopia, c. 1850–1935', *IJAHS* 9 (1978), p. 481ff; Martin Diary, 10 May 1910, SIR 209 (Dec. 1911); Hodson, *Where Lion Reign*, p. 160.

21 Darley, *Slaves*, pp. 67, 75–9; Athill, 'Extracts', p. 203; Cerulli, *Peoples*, p. 91; Alan R. Tippet, *Peoples of Southwest Ethiopia* (South Pasadena, California: William Carey Library, 1970), pp. 270–1; Record of Leading Personalities in Abyssinia, 18 March 1937, PRO FO 371/20940/6140, SIR 218 (September 1912), App. B. It is possible that Serie and Mwanga were the same person. It is difficult to be absolutely sure from the sources available, though my reading seems the most logical. It is interesting to note that Hodson lists the Serie as a sub-section of the Tishana 'tribe', *Where Lion Reign*, p. 40. Lomerio was leader of the Boma Murle and regent to a boy named Murungole, while Barikaring was leader of the Tirma-Lochipo.

22 Darley, *Slaves*, pp. 56, 66–7; SIR (February 1909), App. A, by H. H. Kelly; Barber, *Frontier*, pp. 112–24.

23 Consul Hodson Intelligence Report from Maji, 21 July 1924, PRO FO 371/9994.

24 Barber, *Frontier*, p. 112; Darley, *Slaves*, p. 85; John Lamphear, 'Aspects of Turkana Leadership During the Era of Primary Resistance', *JAH* 18 (1976), pp. 225–43; Martin Diary, 2 April 1910. Birru's mother was Tesemma's sister – personal communication from *dejazmach* Zewdie Gabre Sellassie, 2 July 1979. See also SIR 218 (September 1912), 209 (December 1911), App. B, 203 (June 1911); Marcus, *Menelik II*, p. 255. The *ḳurach* or relationship between lord and vassal in unclear.

25 Lawrence to Curzon, Addis Abeba, 30 May 1919, PRO FO 371/3496/9334.

26 Thesiger to Gray, Annual Report of 1912, 20 January 1913, PRO FO 371/1571/9283.

27 *Ibid.* SIR 209 (December 1911), App. B; 216 (July 1912); 218 (September 1912). This can be referred to as the first Tishana rebellion. SIR 333 (April 1922); Zaphiro to Rey, 6 June 1922, Rhodes House, MSS British Empire, S 384, C. F. Rey's Papers, Box 2.

28 SIR 263 (June 1916); Robert O. Collins, 'The Turkana Patrol', *UJ* 25 (1961), p. 31. 'Note on the Events on the Sudan–Uganda Frontier and the Latuka District Mongalla Province, 1913–1921', NRO Mongalla 1/7/43; SIR 317 (December 1920).

29 Marcus, *Menelik II*, pp. 280–1.

30 Thesiger to Wingate, Addis Abeba, 29 December 1916, and Thesiger to Balfour, Addis Abeba, 27 February 1917, PRO FO 371/2854/9334. See also Campbell to Balfour, Addis Abeba, 2 February 1918, p. 391, PRO FO 371/3126/9334.

31 'Note on Events', p. 10, 1 July 1943, NRO Mongalla 1/7/43. See also Collins, 'Turkana Patrol', p, 29.

32 See below, pp. 22–9.

33 SIR 292 (November 1918). Collins, 'The Turkana Patrol', pp. 28ff.

34 He was not replaced until after June 1922. See SIR 235 (June 1922); 339 (October 1922).

35 SIR 292 (November 1918).

36 SIR 297 (April 1919), 300 (July 1919), 317 (December 1920), 325 (August 1921), 330 (January 1922); Athill, 'Extracts', pp. 191–209. C. W. Hobley, 'Introduction' to Darley, *Slaves*, p. viii.

37 SIR 332 (March 1922), 333 (April 1922); M. S. Lush, 'Addis Abeba Monthly Intelligence Report', 30 April 1922, PRO FO 371/7152/9178.

38 Hodson to Russell, Maji, 2 August 1923, NRO Intel 1/5/22. While Hodson does not mention it in *Where Lion Reign*, p. 25, he indicates in this despatch that *neggadras* Desta was his source of information and that he had access to 'the official Abyssinian Register'.

39 Hodson to Russell, Maji, June 1923, NRO Intel 1/5/22. Hodson, *Where Lion Reign*, pp. 24, 31, 36, 82 and *passim*. Mekuriya's wife, *weyzero* Asselefech, was a good friend of the empress and had once been married to Teferi's brother Yilma. See also M. Perham, *The Government of Ethiopia* (London: Faber and Faber, 1947), pp. 332ff. SIR 344 (March 1923); 253 (December 1923).

40 Russell to MacDonald, Annual Report for 1923, 16 February 1924, p. 5, PRO FO 371/9993/9164; SIR 253 (December 1923), 364 (November 1924); Intelligence Report by Consul, Maji, 21 July 1924, p. 70, PRO FO 371/9994. See map by Hodson in Hodson to Russell, Maji, 26 June 1923, NRO Intel 1/5/22 indicating the extent of Tishana control. Hodson in *Where Lion Reign* gives two Tishana leaders as 'Cutler' and 'Kamale' of which the latter was the more important: see pp. 105–7, 114–16, 121–2, 135–6.

41 SMIR 374 (September 1925).

42 SMIR 367 (February 1925), 369 (April 1925), 370 (May 1925), (September 1925). See Hodson, *Where Lion Reign*, pp. 105–7, 114–6, 122, 135–6 for the previous year's offensive.

43 Personality Reports, 4 May 1937, PRO FO 371/20940/6140. Intelligence Report by Consul, Maji, 27 July 1924, p. 72, PRO FO 371/9994. In fact, his brother was collaborating with the Maji garrison in lowland raids among the Toposa.

44 SMIR 371 (June 1925).

45 R. E. Lyth, 'The Suri Tribe', *SNR* 28 (1947), p. 107.

46 Leading Personalities, 4 May 1937, PRO FO 371/20940/6140 (for *fītawrarī* Aggedew look under *ras* Desta Damatu); B. G. Steffanson and R. K. Starrett, *Documents on Ethiopian Politics*, Vol. 2: *The Consolidation of the Power of Haile Selassie, 1920–1929* (Salisbury, North Carolina: Documentary Publications, 1977), p. 72; SMR 19 (August 1930), 24 (February 1931).

47 Whalley dispatch of 8 September 1932 and 29 December 1932, British Embassy, Addis Abeba (I would like to record my gratitude to the late Richard Caulk for so kindly allowing me to consult his notes); Barton to Simon, 25 Jan. 1935, PRO FO 371/19189/9207; De Halpert papers S1459(1), p. 111, Rhodes House MSS. Afr. S1459.

48 SMIR 404 (March 1928), 407 (June 1928), 410 (September 1928), 411 (October 1928); Annual Report for 1929, Barton to Henderson, 28 July 1930, pp. 26ff, PRO FO 371/14598/9186.

49 See below, p. 26.

50 See Fig. 3.

51 See below, pp. 27–9.

52 Barton to Sion, 31 Jan. 1933, Encl. 1, 1st Annual Report on Slavery in Ethiopia, 1932, PRO FO 371/16996/9197. It is interesting to note that the previous Tishana revolts had had *balabbat* or potential *balabbat* leaders, but this revolt did not, and seems much more a movement among the *gebbar*. SMR 42 (July 1932), 41 (June 1932); Barton to Simon, Annual

Report of 1931, 20 January 1932, PRO FO 371/16101/9197; De Halpert Papers MS S1459 (11) p. 111, Rhodes House; Whalley despatch of 10 April 1932, British Embassy, Addis Abeba.

53 Perham, *Government*, p. 333; SMR 80 (September 1935), 89 (June 1936), 90 (July 1936); C. Sandford, *Ethiopia Under Haile Selassie* (London: J. M. Dent, 1946), pp. 50, 60–1; Whalley despatches of 26 September 1935, 27 February 1936, 27 March 1936, and 12 April 1936, British Embassy, Addis Abeba; Whalley to Civsec, 10 March 1937, Whalley to Governor, Juba, 21 January 1938, Walley to Civsec, Towoth Post, Boma, 24 and 25 November 1938, SRO EP 93/c/2/PH; De Halpert Papers S1459 (1), pp. 216–17, Rhodes House.

54 R. W. Beachey, 'The East African Ivory Trade in the Nineteenth Century', *JAH* 8 (1967), pp. 283–4, 287; see also SIR 175 (February 1909), App. A.

55 Abannik Ohure Hino, 'Latuka Resistance to Colonial Encroachment, 1821–1929' (B. A. thesis, Department of History, University of Khartoum, 1977), pp. 26ff; Darley, *Slaves*, p. 19.

56 See below.

57 Robert O. Collins, *Land Beyond the Rivers: the Southern Sudan 1898–1918* (New Haven: Yale University Press, 1971), p. 266.

58 Bulatovich, 'Dall'Abissinia', pp. 123ff. V. Bòttego, *Viaggi di Scoperta nel Cuore dell'Africa; Il Giuba Esplorato sotto gli auspici della Società Geografica Italiana* (Rome, 1895), pp. 374ff.

59 These are the terms usually used in the Sudanese, Ugandan, and British East African (later Kenyan) archives.

60 SIR 175 (February 1909), App. A, by H. H. Kelly.

61 Ethiopian hunters tended to have more success in the lowland areas in and around Illubabor province than to the north; also of course, in and around Wellegga.

62 M. Twaddle, 'The Founding of Mbale', *UJ* 31 (1966), pp. 31–2; Barber, *Frontier*, p. 99; AP:CR Vol. 69 (1913), No. 5163, p. 10 and Vol. 71 (1914–16), No. 5422, p. 7.

63 AP:CR Vol. 69 (1913), No. 5163, p. 10; British Foreign Office, *Abyssinia* (London: HMSO, 1920), pp. 80, 308; Barber, *Frontier*, p. 99; SIR 290 (December 1911), 217 (August 1912); Twaddle, 'Mbale', p. 37; but see especially W. D. Bell to Ormsby, D. O. Mbale, Muthingo, 28 February 1906, Rhodes House MSS Afr. S 1018.

64 SIR 175 (February 1909), App. A, by H. H. Kelly.

65 Garretson, 'Addis Abeba', pp. 267ff; see also Adrian Zervos, *L'Empire d'Ethiopie, le miroir de l'Ethiopie moderne 1906–1935* (Alexandria, Egypt: Imprimerie de l'école professionelle des frères, 1936), pp. 202–3, 500.

66 V. Harlow and E. M. Chilver, eds., *History of East Africa*, Vol. 2 (Oxford: Clarendon Press, 1965), p. 477.

67 Barton to Henderson, Annual Report for 1929, 28 July 1930, PRO FO 371/14598/9186; SIR 217 (August 1912), App. A. See also De Halpert Papers, Rhodes House MSS Afr. 51459 (1), p. 8.

68 SIR 217 (August 1912), App. A. The local traders were not all Shewans or Amhara, for Greek, Arabic, and Oromo names occasionally appear.

69 Darley, *Slaves*, pp. 45–7, 55, 66–7.

70 SIR 217 (August 1912), App. 8.

71 Whalley despatch of 13 March 1933, British Embassy, Addis Abeba.

72 'Note on Events', NRO Mongalla 1/7/43. See also Part III below.

73 SMIR 404 (March 1928); 407 (June 1928); 410 (September 1928); 411 (October 1928); 413 (December 1928).

74 See Figure 3. AP:CR vol. 71 (1914–16), No. 5422, p. 7; A. E. Southward, *Abyssinia*, Special Consular Reports No. 81 (Washington: United States Department of Commerce, 1918), pp. 29, 57–9; M. Boucoiran, 'La situation économique de l'Ethiopie, 1913–1917', *L'Afrique Française*, Supplement: Renseignements coloniaux 11, (1918), pp. 208–10.

75 Hodson, *Where Lion Reign*, pp. 109, 140.

76 AP:CR Vol. 92 (1900) No. 2531; Vol. 88 (1907) No. 3747, p. 24; Vol. 92 (1909) No. 4357; Vol. 90 (1911) No. 4759, p. 4 (figures from Jibuti, unlike the above, which were for Addis Abeba). The last figures may have suddenly jumped because then virtually all of Ethiopia's ivory exports went via Jibuti. The following sources are all for Jibuti: AP:CR Vol. 90 (1911) No. 4759, p. 4; Vol. 69 (1913) No. 5163, p. 10; Vol. 71 (1914–16) No. 5422, p. 7; A. I. Southard, *Abyssinia*, p. 57; Zervos, *L'Empire*, p. 164, for all figures between 1919 and 1934. Richard Pankhurst in *Economic History* cites some intervening years' statistics from Jibuti sources, but the figures on p. 401 do not agree with those on p. 432 and thus neither can be used. I have been unable to consult the official statistics.

77 Collins, 'Turkana Patrol', pp. 16–33; Barber, *Frontier*; J. Lamphear, 'Turkana Leadership', pp. 225–43.

78 Barber, *Frontier*, Chapters 3, 9, and 14 especially; Collins, 'Turkana Patrol'.

79 Lamphear, 'Turkana Leadership', *passim*.

80 *Ibid.*, p. 236 (for 1902 and before), pp. 239–40; Barber, *Frontier*, p. 117 for 1914, p. 171 for 1917; SIR 326 (September 1921); P. H. Gulliver, 'A Preliminary Survey of the Turkana: A Report Compiled for the Government of Kenya', *University of Capetown Communication from the School of African Studies* 7 (1951), p. 3. I do not intend to go into Ethiopian influence among the Turkana in any depth, but only to use the Turkana as an example to give perspective on Maji's influence on peoples in the Sudan. See also Hodson, *Where Lion Reign*, p. 131; L. F. Nalder, ed., *A Tribal Survey of Mongalla Province*, (New York: Negro Universities Press, 1970 [1937]), p. 74; SMR 19 (August 1930), 66 (July 1934), 69 (October 1934). But it must be remembered that in practice most Ethiopian influence was concentrated among the northern sections of the Turkana and was much less felt in southern sections, particularly as British administration moved north.

81 Hodson, *Where Lion Reign*, pp. 55, 131.

82 This comes out quite clearly, particularly in the 1930s when documentation is much more substantial. See R. Pankhurst, *Economic History*, pp. 74–5, 82, 99–112.

83 Nalder, *Tribal Survey*, pp. 62, 65, 67–8, 74; Barber, *Frontier*, p. 38; *PP* Command Paper No. 2553, March 1920; SIR 326 (September 1921); 348 (July 1923), SMIR 403 (February 1928).

84 SMIR 411 (October 1928); Equatoria Province, Oral Informant No. 1; SIR 313 (August 1920), 350 (September 1923). I would like to thank Gordon Lokipi, a Toposa, for pointing out the latter fact to me.

85 A. C. Beaton, 'Record of the Taposa Tribe', *SNR* 31 (1950), p. 132.

86 The Toposa had at various times control over major water holes on the route.

87 Nalder, *Tribal Survey*, p. 68.

88 Map of the Anglo-Egyptian Sudan, mounted by the Sudan Survey Department in January 1947: 'Sevatt Ambo' (seven springs) and 'Kilma Yahabesh'. Mt. Naita, sheet 78–U: 'Katima Waha' (water of Katima) and 'Cherosh Wonz' (end of river). Didinga sheet 78–0: 'Makonnen Cherosh' (end [death] of Mekonnen), 'Tulu Satan' (hill of Satan; this is the only Oromo place name) and 'Kilima Habash'. See also Hodson, *Where Lion Reign*, p. 168. A nagging suspicion still remains that many of the Ethiopian place names on these maps may have been the invention of Hodson's escort. For it was Hodson who was largely responsible for the Sudan Survey Department maps.

89 SIR 346 (May 1923); Nalder, *Tribal Survey*, p. 78; *PP* Command Paper No. 2553, July 1922.

90 Beaton, 'Record', p. 132; 'Note on Events on the Sudan–Uganda Frontier and in the Latuka District, Mongalla Province', App. 4 of S. H. Turpin, Intelligence Notes on Rudolf Province, 1 January 1917, NRO Mongalla 1/7/43.

91 J. W. Brooke, 'A Journey West and North of Lake Rudolf', *GJ* 25 (1905), p. 531; SIR 321 (April 1921); Hodson to Russell, Kullu, 14 August 1923, NRO Intel 1/5/22.

92 W. D. M. Bell, *The Wanderings of an Elephant Hunter* (London: Country Life, 1923), especially pp. 66ff; Darley, *Slaves*, pp. 17, 20–1.

93 Brooke, 'Lake Rudolf', p. 531; SIR 321 (April 1921); Hodson to Russell, 14 August 1923, NRO Intel 1/5/22.

94 SIR 322 (May 1921), 343 (February 1923); 364 (December 1924).

95 SMIR 402 (January 1928). See especially SMR 58 (October and November 1933) for overall implications of droughts.

96 Sudan Abyssinia Frontier Reports, January 1922 and April 1922, NRO Intel 1/16/78; SIR 218 (September 1912), App. B, 310 (May 1920), 324 (January 1923).

97 SIR 294 (January 1919), 309 (April 1920), 332 (March 1922); 'Note on Events', App. 4, NRO Mongalla 1/7/43; Darley, *Slaves*, pp. 83–5; Barber, *Frontier*. pp. 113–14; Sudan–Abyssinia Frontier Reports, January 1922–August 1923, NRO Intel 1/16/78. See also J. Driberg, 'A Preliminary Account of the Didinga', *SNR* 5 (1922), pp. 208–22; Nalder, *Tribal Survey*, p. 143.

98 The best recent historical study of the Latuka is by Abannik Ohure Hino, 'Latuka Resistance'. See also Collins, *Beyond the Rivers*, p. 226.

99 'Note on Events', NRO Mongalla 1/7/43. R. O. Collins, 'Sudan–Uganda Boundary Rectification and the Sudanese Occupation of Madial', *UJ* 26 (1962), pp. 140–53.

100 SIR 228 (July 1913), App. A, 249 (April 1915), 260 (February 1916), 276 (July 1917), 304 (November 1919), 333 (April 1922); SMIR 380 (March 1926); Abyssinia Monthly Report, April 1915, NRO intel 1/16/75.

101 SIR 249 (April 1918), 260 (February 1916), 276 (July 1917), 333 (April 1922), 305 (December 1919), 354 (January 1924).

102 Nalder, Tribal Survey, pp. 55, 80–1. G. Schweinfurth, F. Ratzel, R. Felkin, and G. Hartlamb, eds., *Emin Pasha in Central Africa* (London: George Philip, 1888), p. 242.

103 The best recent historical study of the Kakwa, one of the Bari-speaking peoples, is by Samuel Kenyi A. Bakite, 'A History of the Kakwa Tribe to 1910 – a Survey' (B. A. thesis, Department of History, University of Khartoum, 1978). See also Richard Gray, *A History of the Southern Sudan 1839–1889* (London: Oxford University Press, 1961), pp. 33–41, 54–8, 95–9, 107–10, and Robert O. Collins, *The Southern Sudan, 1883–1898: A Struggle for Control* (New Haven: Yale University Press, 1962), pp. 42–51, 55–92, 110ff and 156ff.

104 SIR 265 (August 1916), 318 (January 1921), 319 (February 1921); A. C. Beaton, Local Bari Histories, p. 110, SRO EP 66.A.3/2.

105 Oral interviews carried out among the elders of Beliniang, 1977. I would like to thank Sayyid Subek for all his assistance on finding informants and for acting as translator.

106 A most interesting recent work on the Sudan Acholi, including their contacts with the Päri, is by Kenneth Okenyi, 'A Reconstruction of Acholi History Through Oral and Documentary Material, 1861–1956' (B. A. thesis, Department of History, University of Khartoum, 1978). Also see Gray, *History of the Southern Sudan*, pp. 19, 35, 38.

107 Okenyi, 'Acholi History', *passim*; SMIR 385 (August 1926).

108 SIR 202 (April 1911), 354 (January 1924), 364 (November 1924).

109 Hodson, *Where Lion Reign*, p. 224.

110 B. A. Lewis, *The Murle, Red Chiefs and Black Commoners* (Oxford: Clarendon Press, 1972), map, pp. 25, 53–5.

111 *Ibid.*, p. 10; Darley, *Slaves*, p. 173.

112 Lewis, *The Murle*, pp. 9–10; 'Note on Events', NRO Mongalla 11/7/43.

113 SIR 215 (June 1912); M. H. Longan, 'The Beirs', *SNR* 1 (1918), p. 247; SIR 245 (December 1914), 293 (December 1918); SMR 85 (February 1936).

9. On the Nilotic frontier

1 Richard Gray, *A History of the Southern Sudan, 1839–1889* (London: Oxford University Press, 1961), p. 9; R. O. Collins, *Land Beyond the Rivers: The Southern Sudan, 1898–1918* (New Haven: Yale University Press, 1971), p. 48; E. E. Evans-Pritchard, *The Political*

System of the Anuak of the Anglo-Egyptian Sudan, LSE Monograph on Social Anthropology 4 (London: Lund and Humphries for London School of Economics, 1940), p. 13.

2 The total number of Anuak was estimated in 1947 to be 35,000, of which about 25,000 lived in Ethiopia (E. E. Evans-Pritchard, 'Further Observations on the Political System of the Anuak', *SNR* 28 (1947), pp. 64–5). The populations of other peoples living on or near the border in the Sudan were estimated in 1956 as: Jikany – 103,222; Lou – 103,638; Koma – 6,313; Murle – 44,849; Meban – 31,558; other 'Burun' (combined) – 50,901. See Republic of the Sudan, Ministry of Social Affairs, Population Census Office, *First Population Census of Sudan 1955/56. Notes on Omodia Map* (Khartoum: Ministry for Social Affairs, Population Census Office, 1958), pp. 22, 58–60.

3 Douglas H. Johnson, 'History and Prophecy among the Nuer of the Southern Sudan' (Ph.D. thesis, Department of History, University of California, Los Angeles, 1980), Chapters 2 and 3.

4 For an account of Shewan expansion I am particularly indebted to the following, especially the B. A. theses of Ethiopian historians in Addis Abeba: Terrefe Woldetsadik, 'The Unification of Ethiopia (1880–1885): Wälläga', *JES* 6, (1968), pp. 73–86; Atieb Ahmed Dafalla, 'Sheikh Khojele al-Hassan and Bela Shangul (1825–1938)' (B. A. thesis, Department of History, Addis Abeba University, 1973), pp. 27–8; Nagaso Gidada, 'The Impact of Christianity on Qelem Awraja, Western Wallaga, 1886–1941' (B. A. thesis, Department of History, Addis Abeba University, 1971), p. 5; Alessandro Triulzi, *Salt, Gold and Legitimacy: Prelude to the History of a No-Man's Land, Belá Shangul, Wällägga, Ethiopia (ca.1800–1898)* (Naples: Istituto Universitario Orientale, 1981), pp. 148–53, 'Trade, Islam, and the Mahdia in Northwestern Wälläggā, Ethiopia', *JAH* 16 (1975), pp. 67–9, 'The Background to Ras Gobäna's Expeditions to Western Wällägga in 1886–1888: A Review of the Evidence', in *Proceedings of the First United States Conference on Ethiopian Studies 1973*, ed. Harold G. Marcus (East Lansing: African Studies Center, Michigan State University, 1975), p. 143.

5 See Harold G. Marcus: 'Ethio-British Negotiations Concerning the Western Border with Sudan, 1896–1902', *JAH* 4 (1963), pp. 81–94; 'The Foreign Policy of the Emperor Menelik 1896–1898: A Rejoinder', *JAH* 7 (1966), pp. 117–22; *The Life and Times of Menelik II* (Oxford: Clarendon Press, 1975), Chapter 7. Also see George N. Sanderson: 'Contributions from African Sources to the History of European Competition in the Upper Valley of the Nile', *JAH* 3 (1962), pp. 69–90; 'The Foreign Policy of the Negus Menelik, 1896–1898', *JAH* 5 (1964), pp. 87–97; *England, Europe and the Upper Nile 1882–1899* (Edinburgh: Edinburgh University Press, 1965), Chapter 13.

6 Charles Michel, *Vers Fachoda à la rencontre de la mission Marchand à travers l'Ethiopie* (Paris: Plon, 1901), p. 447. F. I. Maxse, 'Topography and Recent Events in the Nuer Country', SIR 60 (May–December 1898), App. 58B, p. 99.

7 Wendy James, 'From Aboriginal to Frontier Society in Western Ethiopia', in *Working Papers on Society and History in Ethiopia: The Southern Periphery from the 1880s to 1974*, ed. D. L. Donham and Wendy James (Cambridge: African Studies Centre, 1980), mimeographed.

8 Consul Gorei to H. B. M. Minister Addis Ababa, 12 September 1933, NRO Dakhlia I 112/16/102; SIR 213 (April 1912), p. 3.

9 'Statement of Fitaurari Ammaia, brother of Dejaz. Joti and Lij Merdasa, son of Dejaz. Joti', SRO UNP SCR Gov.1 (note: all references to documents in the SRO are to their original file numbers); H. H. Kelly, 'Notes on the Anuak Country', SIR 217 (August 1912), App. A., p. 6; SIR 264 (July 1916), p. 6; Atieb Ahmad Dafalla, 'Sheikh Khojele al-Hassan', pp. 51–4, 61; Girma Mengistu, 'The Busase of Anfillo, Qellam, Wallaga (A Historical Study)' (B. A. thesis, Department of History, Addis Abeba University, 1973), p. 41. These events are also fully covered in Bahru Zewde, 'Relations between Ethiopia and the Sudan on the Western

Ethiopian Border Frontier (1898–1935)' (Ph.D. thesis, Department of History, School of Oriental and African Studies, University of London, 1976), pp. 261–9.

10 H. H. Wilson, 'Report on Itang Trading Station', SIR 116 (March 1904), App A, p. 6, 'Report on the Expedition to Gore, Saiu, Anfilo, Gidami, etc.', SIR 126 (January 1905), App. A, p. 10; H. E. D. O'Sullivan, 'Report on Gambeila Trading Post', SIR 136 (November 1905), App. B, p. 8.

11 Governor, Upper Nile Province to ADI, 1 July 1909, SRO UNP A.1.

12 H. E. D. O'Sullivan in 'Reports on the Finances, Administration and Condition of the Sudan, 1910', pp. 392–4. F. W. Woodward in 'Reports on the Finances, Administration and Condition of the Sudan', 1911, Vol. 2, p. 239. SIR 194 (September 1910), p. 4; 209 (December 1911), p. 4; 212 (March 1912), p. 3. Intelligence Department, 'Note on Military Action and Administration in the Nuer Country', NRO Dakhlia I 112/13/87.

13 Wingate to J. J. Asser, 1 February 1911, G. F. Clayton to Adjutant General, 12 December 1911, 'Extracts from Major Leveson's Report, 27 March 1912', A. E. M. Russell to Major Stack, 24 March 1917, all in NRO Intel 1/14/66; SIR 214 (May 1912), p. 3, 217 (August 1912), p. 3; C. E. Koebel, 'Report on the First Patrol into Garjak Country', 24 March 1913, J. A. Pollock to Officer Commanding Sobat Pibor District Akobo, 6 May 1913, G. S. Symes, Captain, Private Secretary, 5 November 1913, all in NRO UNP 1/12/101. Douglas H. Johnson, 'Tribal Boundaries and Border Wars: Nuer–Dinka Relations in the Sobat and Zaraf Valleys *c.*1860–1976', *JAH* 23 (1982), pp. 195–6.

14 SIR 234 (October 1914), p. 4, 250 (May 1915), p. 5, 257 (December 1915), p. 4. J. J. Bramble to Governor, Upper Nile Province, 6 January 1917, NRO UNP 1/12/101. C. R. K. Bacon, 'Patrol No. 71 – Political Report', 10 May 1920, NRO UNP 1/13/117. Intelligence Department, 'Note on Military Action and Administration in Nuer Country'.

15 Godfrey Lienhardt, 'Anuak Village Headmen: (II) Village Structure and "Rebellion"', *Africa* 28 (1958). Evans-Pritchard, *Political System*, pp. 43–7.

16 Evans-Pritchard, *Political System*, Chapters 3–5, Appendix 4, 'Further Observations', pp. 74–82.

17 Evans-Pritchard, 'Further Observations', p. 77.

18 *Ibid.*, pp. 66, 74–7, 91–2; Evans-Pritchard, *Political System*, p. 52.

19 Evans-Pritchard, *Political System*, pp. 11, 37, 89, 92–3, 'Further Observations', p. 81; Kelly, 'Notes on the Anuak Country', p. 5. See also Bahru Zewde, 'Relations between Ethiopia and the Sudan', p. 109; 'Twixt Sirdar and Emperor: the Anuwa in Ethio-Sudanese Relations 1902–35', unpublished paper, Addis Abeba University.

20 Evans-Pritchard, *Political System*, pp. 36–7; Kelly, 'Notes on the Anuak Country', p. 5; George Montandon, 'A Journey in South-western Abyssinia', *GJ* 90 (1912), pp. 383 and 385.

21 Evans-Pritchard, 'Further Observations', p. 8.

22 Evans-Pritchard, *Political System*, p. 13; Kelly 'Notes on the Anuak Country', p. 5.

23 Evans-Pritchard, *Political System*, p. 92; Kelly, 'Notes on the Anuak Country', p. 5.

24 Bahru Zewde, 'Relations between Ethiopia and the Sudan', pp. 128–31.

25 'Statement of Fitaurari Ammaia'; C. H. Walker to Civil Secretary, 18 June 1912, and Hamikam to Governor Kodok, 29 March 1913, both in SRO UNP SCR 9.3.1; C. H. F. Cox, 'Report', 8 August 1913, and C. P. Browne to ADI, n.d. (*c.* October 1912), both in SRO UNP File No. 7; Walker to Thesiger, 21 April 1913, SRO UNP A.1 'Gambela (continued)'; C. R. K. Bacon to ADI, 23 June 1916, SRO UNP SCR 5; H. H. Kelly, 'Report on the Trade in Arms and Ivory on the Western Abyssinian Frontier', SIR 217 (August 1912), App.B, p. 7; SIR 210 (January 1912), p. 7, 260 (March 1916), p. 8, 261 (April 1916), p. 3, 262 (May 1916), pp. 6–7, 268 (September 1916), p. 5; 'A brief account of Megid Abbud's second Expedition against a part of the Annuaks of the Yambo Province, Abyssinia, and the chief events which transpired after his removal from position up to his departure from Gambeila on 21st June, 1916', NRO Intel 2/23/183. Bahru Zewde gives a full account of these events,

including Magid Abud's own version, in 'Relations between Ethiopia and the Sudan', pp. 134–5 and 139–44, and in 'Twixt Sirdar and Emperor'.

26 C. R. K. Bacon, 'Kingship among the Anuak', *SNR* 4 (1921), pp. 162–3; SMIR 318 (January 1921), p. 4; Evans-Pritchard, *Political System*, pp. 95–9; 'Upper Nile Province Monthly Diary' [UNPMD] (March 1927), SRO BD 57.C.1; J. N. Grover, 'Succession of the Anuak Royal Emblems', n.d. (1943), SRO UNP 66.B.14/J.

27 J. N. Grover, 'Succession of the Anuak Royal Emblems'; UNPMD (August 1928), SRO BD 57.C.1 (I); UNPMD (May, November 1933 and January, March 1934), SRO BD 57.C.1 (II).

28 UNPMD (March 1936), SRO BD 57.C.1 (II); Grover, 'Succession of the Anuak Royal Emblems', J. N. Grover, A/DC Pibor, to Governor, Upper Nile Province, 26 November 1944, Governor, Upper Nile Province, to Civil Secretary, 4 December 1944, J. N. Grover, A/DC, Pibor, to Governor, Upper Nile Province, 8 May 1945, R. E. Lyth, A/DC, Pibor District, to Governor, Upper Nile Province, 2 March 1948, R. E. Lyth, A/DC, Pibor District, to Governor, Upper Nile Province, 13 January 1947, R. E. Lyth, A /DC, Pibor Post, to Governor, Upper Nile Province, 18 March 1950, all in SRO UNP 66.B.14/J.

29 Lienhardt, 'Anuak Village Headmen: (II)', p. 32.

30 UNPMD (February 1930), SRO BD 57.C.1 (I); UNPMD (March, April 1935), SRO BD 57.C.1 (II); R. E. Lyth, A/DC, Pibor District to Governor, Upper Nile Province, 12 December 1946, SRO UNP 66.B.14/J; Godfrey Lienhardt, 'Anuak Village Headmen: (I) Headmen and Village Culture', *Africa* 27 (1957), pp. 341–2.

31 Evans-Pritchard, *Political System*, p. 42; Lienhardt, 'Anuak Village Headmen: (I)', pp. 341–2, 250, 354, 'Anuak Village Headmen: (II)', p. 35.

32 Evans-Pritchard, 'The Nuer: Tribe and Clan', *SNR* 18 (1935), pp. 52–4; 'Abyssinian traders arrested in Mongalla Province', (1911), SRO UNP A.1. Governor Mongalla to Governor Kodok, 25 November 1911, SRO UNP SCR 5.5; Pollock to Governor, Upper Nile Province, 22 October 1913, and Governor, Upper Nile Province to Civil Secretary, 15 October 1913, both in NRO UNP 1/12/101.

33 SIR 223 (February 1913), p. 3.

34 'Note on the Country between Khor Jokau or Garre, and River Baro', SIR 202 (May 1911), App. A., p. 8.

35 C. H. Walker to Civil Secretary, 18 June 1912, and Kelly to Governor Kodok, 18 June 1912, both in SRO UNP SCR 9.3.1; SIR 215 (June 1912), p. 3, 216 (July 1912), p. 4, 219 (October 1912), p. 2, 220 (November 1912), p. 4, 225 (April 1913), p. 4, 233 (December 1913), p. 4; Koebel, 'Report on the First Patrol into Garjak Country', Koebel to Governor, Upper Nile Province, 23 November 1913, and Governor, Upper Nile Province to Civil Secretary, 15 October 1913, all in NRO UNP 1/12/101; C. E. Browne to ADI, n.d. (*c*. October 1912), SRO UNP File No. 7.

36 'Notes on the Nuer Country North of the Sobat and Baro Rivers', n.d. (*c*. 1917), NRO UNP 1/12/101; SIR 217 (August 1912), p. 2; Inspector Roseires to Governor Singa, 20 November 1915, SRO UNP CRR Gov. 2; 'Extracts from Monthly Report, Kurmuk, for February 1916', SRO UNP SCR 37; SIR 265 (August 1916), p. 7; Mamur Kurmuk, 15 November 1916, NRO UNP 1/12/101.

37 SIR 282 (January 1918), p. 2–3.

38 C. H. Stigand, 'Political Report of Patrol 42', 9 July 1917, NRO Dakhlia I 112/16/102; F. D. Corfield, 'The Koma', *SNR* 21 (1938), p. 136; 'Intelligence Summary July 24th (1920)', SRO END SCR 93.H.2/2, Vol. 1.

39 A G. Pawson, Governor, Upper Nile Province, 'Handing Over Notes' (1934), NRO Civsec 57/2/9.

40 Pawson, 'Handing Over Notes'; Bahru Zewde, 'Relations Between Ethiopia and the Sudan', p. 164.

41 C. H. Walker to H. B. M.'s Minister Addis Ababa, 12 September 1923, NRO Dakhlia I

112/16/102. A report of forty 'Fitawaris' appointed may really have only referred to the number of chiefs who were given Ethiopian clothes.

42 SMR 50 (February–March 1933), pp. 2–3. F. D. Corfield, 'Nasir District Notes: History, 1931–1935', NRO UNP 1/51/4; 'Return of Prominent Persons in Upper Nile Province, Eastern Nuer District (Nasir)', ENRC SCR 66.D.4/8.

43 Pawson, 'Handing Over Notes'; Corfield, 'Nasir District Notes'; SMR 59 (November–December 1933), pp. 2–3; Personality Reports, Upper Nile Province, NRO UNP 1/46/334; SMR 71 (November–December 1934), pp. 3–4.

44 Corfield, 'Nasir District Notes'; SMR 61 (January–February 1934), p. 7, 63 (February–March 1934), p. 5; M. W. Parr, Governor, Upper Nile Province, 'Handing Over Notes' (1936), NRO Civsec 57/2/9; UNPMD (October 1936), SRO BD 57.C.1 (II).

45 C. H. Stigand, 'Report on the Sobat Valley Nuers', NRO UNP 1/12/101.

46 Douglas H. Johnson, 'The Fighting Nuer: Primary Sources and the Origins of a Stereotype', *Africa* 51 (1981), pp. 514–15.

47 Johnson, 'History and Prophecy among the Nuer', Chapters 8 and 9.

48 Nagadaw, quoted in Triulzi, 'Ras Gobäna's Expeditions', p. 144.

49 R. H. Darkwah, *Shewa, Menilek and the Ethiopian Empire* (London: Heinemann, 1975), p. 134; Nagaso Gidada, 'The Impact of Christianity', p. 6; Girma Mengistu, 'The Busase', p. 39; Atieb Dafalla, 'Sheikh Khojele', pp. 43–4.

50 R. S. O'Fahey and J. Spaulding, *Kingdoms of the Sudan* (London: Methuen, 1974), p. 63; L. G. Massaia, 'Khartoum to the Gold Workings of Fazūghlī, 1851', in *The Opening of the Nile Basin*, ed. E. Toniolo and R. Hill (London: Hurst, 1974), p. 208; A. Brun-Rollet, 'Excursion de M. Brun Rollet dans la région supérieure du Nil', *Bulletin de la Société de géographie de Paris*, 4th series, 4 (1852), p. 412; Gordon to Khairy Pasha, 20 November 1875, in M. F. Shukry, *Equatoria under Egyptian Rule* (Cairo: University of Cairo Press, 1954), p. 317; J. M. Schuver, *Reisen im Oberen Nilgebiet*, Supplement No. 72 to *Petermanns Geographische Mitteilungen* (Gotha: Justus Perthes, 1883), pp. 20, 28–9, 39–40; H. H. Wilson, 'Report on the Dinkas of the White Nile', pp. 13, 17; F. W. Woodward, 'Report on Patrol in the Nuer Country', p. 6; Michel, *Vers Fachoda*, p. 372; C. Tappi, letter from Lull, 7 April 1901, *BSGI* 38 series 4 (Vol. 4), 1901, p. 585; 'Notes on the Country between Khor Jokau or Garre, and River Baro', p. 8. The Nuer (Abigar'?) found in Gidami explicitly involved in the ivory trade with Sudanese Nuer in 1905, may have been some of these original Dinka 'Abigar' (cf. Wilson, 'Expedition to Gore', p. 14).

51 SIR 106 (May 1903), p. 6; H. Gordon, 'Report on Nuers of the Sobat', SIR 107 (June 1903), App. D, p. 11; H. E. D. O'Sullivan, 'Report on the Burun People', SIR 134 (September 1905), App. B., p. 11, 'Lau Nuers', 14 March 1906, NRO Dakhlia I 112/13/87.

52 C. H. Walker to H. B. M.'s Minister Addis Ababa, 12 September 1923, NRO Dakhlia I 112/16/102; Gordon, 'Report on the Nuers of the Sobat', p. 11; Wilson, 'Expedition to Gore', p. 14; SIR 106 (May 1903), p. 3; O'Sullivan, 'Report on the Burun People', p. 11.

53 Wilson, 'Expedition to Gore', pp. 6, 10, 13; O'Sullivan, 'Report on Gambela', pp. 7–8; Bahru Zewde, 'Relations between Ethiopia and the Sudan', pp. 248, 251; H. H. S. Morant, 'Notes on the Situation of the Sobat and Baro, and on the Commercial Outlook at Itang', SIR 128 (May 1904), App. A, p. 6; H. H. Kelly, 'Report on a Journey from Malakal via R. Sobat to Gidami (Abyssinia) Kurmuk and Gelhak (W. Nile)', SIR 203 (June 1911), p. 9; G. S. Symes, ADI, 'Note on the Arms Traffic', 28 November 1911, SRO UNP SCR 5.5; 'Statement of Fitaurari Ammaia'; Girma Mengistu, 'The Busase', pp. 39, 41; Atieb Ahmed Dafalla, 'Sheikh Khojele', pp. 42, 51–3. See also Peter P. Garretson, Chapter 8 of this volume, and Neal Sobania, 'A View of a Frontier from the Frontier: The Ethiopia—Kenya Frontier *c.* 1875–1925' (Paper presented at the Society and History of Imperial Ethiopia Conference, Monterey, California, 1982), p. 19.

54 'Statement of Fitaurari Ammaia'; Governor, Upper Nile Province to ADI, 23 March 1909,

Governor, Upper Nile Province to ADI, 1 July 1909, 'Abyssinian Traders arrested in Mongalla Province', (1911), C. H. Walker to Civil Secretary, 27 February 1910, all in SRO UNP A.1; Kelly, 'Report on the trade in Arms and Ivory', pp. 8–9; SIR 202 (May 1911), p. 4, 188 (March 1910), p. 17; 'Notes on Conversation with Mr. Karsten', (*c*. July 1911), SRO UNP A.1 'Gambela (continued)'.

55 G. B. Wauhope, 'Gun Running', 4 May 1912, SRO UNP SCR 5.5; SIR 214 (May 1912), p. 3; Koebel, 'Report on the First Patrol into Garjak Country', Governor, Upper Nile Province to Civil Secretary, 15 October 1913, C. H. Stigand, 'Intelligence Notes. Nasser Merkaz', 20 April 1916, all in NRO UNP 1/12/101; SIR 280 (November 1917), pp. 2–3.

56 Wauhope, 'Gun Running'; C. E. Koebel to Governor Upper Nile Province, 19 April 1913, NRO UNP 1/12/101; P. Coriat, *The Gaweir Nuers* (Khartoum, *c*. 1923), pp. 11–2; J. W. G. Wyld, 'Arms Gun Running', 26 November 1925, NRO UNP 1/5/27; SMIR 352 (November 1923), p. 3.

57 E. Marno, *Reisen in Gebiet des Blauen und Weissen Nil* (Vienna: Gerold, 1874), pp. 394–5; SRO EHJP5, Ruot Diu (Gaawar), 22–3 May 1982; SRO EHJP6, Pok Tuot (Gaawar), 23 May 1982; SRO EHJP8, Kulang Majiok (Gaawar), 24 May 1982; D. H. Johnson, 'Ngundeng and the 'Turuk': Two Narratives Compared', *History in Africa* 9 (1982): 126, 128.

58 Figures are computed from the rates in Table 5 and from numbers of cattle and firearms reported in: SIR 106 (May 1903), p. 3; Governor, Upper Nile Province to ADI, 1 July 1909, SRO UNP A.1; Symes, 'Note on the Arms Traffic'; SIR 223 (February 1913), p. 3; Mostyn, 'Abyssinian Intelligence', January 1914, SRO UNP 'Abyssinian IRs'; Wyld, 'Arms Gun Running'.

59 'Reports on the Finances, Administration and Condition of the Sudan, 1908', pp. 25, 654; G. B. Wahab to Governor, Upper Nile Province, 25 March 1910, and C. H. Walker to Civil Secretary, 27 February 1910, both in SRO UNP A.1.

60 SRO EHJP2, Lueth Ayong Yor and Malok Lam (Duor Dinka), 21 May 1982; SRO EHJP5; SRO EHJP6; SRO EHJP8; SRO EHJP12, Twic elders, 25 May 1982. The remembered exchange rates for the period 1916–28 tally with the recorded figures.

61 P. P. Howell, 'A Note on Elephants and Elephant Hunting among the Nuer', *SNR* 26 (1945), pp. 100–1.

62 SRO EHJP5; SRO EHJP6; SRO EHJP8.

63 Evans-Pritchard, 'Further Observations', p. 73; Kelly, 'Report on the Trade in Arms and Ivory', pp. 8–9; Garretson, Chapter 8 of this volume; Cox, 'Report', 8 July 1913, SRO UNP SCR 5; 'Gambeila', 1 November 1917, SRO UNP 'Abyssinian IRs'.

64 Kelly, 'Report on the Trade in Arms and Ivory', p. 9, 'Notes on the Anuak Country' pp. 5–6; SIR 221 (December 1912), p. 4.

65 C. R. K. Bacon to ADI, 23 June 1916, SRO UNP SCR 5.

66 'The Ujang Tribe', *SNR* 5 (1922), p. 170; J. Stauder, 'Notes on the History of the Majangir and their Relations with other Ethnic Groups of Southwest Ethiopia', *Proceedings of the Third International Conference on Ethiopian Studies* (Addis Abeba: Addis Abeba University Press, 1970), p. 112.

67 SMIR 381 (April 1926), p. 9; Tierney, 'Handing Over Notes', 1931, SRO UNP 66.A.6.

68 Mostyn, 'Abyssinian Intelligence', January 1914.

69 Atieb Ahmed Dafalla, 'Sheikh Khojele', p. 57.

70 Inspector Roseires to Governor Singa, 20 November 1915, SRO UNP CRR Gov. 2; SIR 282 (January 1918), p. 3; Maxwell, 'Report on Eastern Frontier District, Upper Nile Province', 6 July 1927, SRO UNP G.

71 *Report on the Administration of the Sudan for the Year 1949*, Sudan No. 1 (1952) Cmd. 8434 (London: HMSO, 1952), p. 218.

72 SIR 106 (May 1903), p. 3; Gordon, 'Report on Nuers of the Sobat', p. 11. Wilson, 'Expedition to Gore', p. 14; SIR (May 1912), p. 3, 221 (December 1912), p. 5; 'Intelligence

Summary July 24th (1920)', SRO END SCR 93.H.2/2 Vol. 1; SRO EHJP5; Stauder, 'Majangir', p. 112; 'The Ujang Tribe', p. 170.

73 Gordon, 'Report on Nuers of the Sobat', p. 11; H. H. Wilson, 'Report on the Situation in the Sobat Valley', SIR 117 (April 1904), App. A, p. 10; C. H. Walker to Civil Secretary, 27 February 1910, SRO UNP A.1; Symes, 'Notes on the Arms Traffic'; Evans-Pritchard, *Political System*, p. 11; SIR 194 (September 1910), p. 11, 202 (May 1911), p. 4, 203 (June 1911), p. 3, 204 (July 1911), p. 3, 205 (August 1911), p. 4, 211 (February 1912), p. 4, 214 (May 1912), p. 3. F. W. Woodward, 'Anuak Raids, Illicit Ivory and Gun Running', SIR 207 (October 1911), p. 4. Kelly, 'Notes on the Anuak Country', p. 4–5.

74 C. P. Browne to ADI, n.d. (*c.* October 1912), SRO UNP File No. 7; Koebel, 'Report on the First Patrol into Garjak Country', SIR 235 (February 1914), p. 3, 236 (March 1914), pp. 4–5, 237 (April 1914), p. 5; C. E. Koebel to Governor, Upper Nile Province, 5 March 1914, NRO UNP 1/12/101.

75 SIR 261 (April 1916), p. 3.

76 SIR 283 (February 1918), p. 3; Governor, Upper Nile Province to D. C. Malakal, 3 June 1936, END 66.B.2/3; Evans-Pritchard, 'Further Observations', p. 72.

77 Upper Nile and Pibor District Monthly Diary, May 1922, NRO Civsec 57/3/12.

78 E. E. Evans-Pritchard, 'Ethnological Observations in Dar Fung', *SNR* 15 (1932), pp. 53–60; K. E. Ecsedy, 'An Unknown People of the Sudan: Four Months with the Maiaks', *The New Hungarian Quarterly* 14 (1973), pp. 143–50; Wendy James, '*Kwanim pa: The Making of the Uduk People* (Oxford: Clarendon Press, 1979); John M. Lee, 'Report on the Khoma Baruns', NRO Dakhlia I 112/16/102.

79 Gabrial Jal (SOAS), personal communication. C. W. L. Bulpett, *A Picnic Party in Wildest Africa* (London: Edward Arnold, 1907), p. 82; SIR 186 (January 1910), p. 4; Stigand, 'Political Report on Patrol 42'; ADC Upper Sobat to Governor, Upper Nile Province, 3 May 1923, SRO END SCR 93.H.2/2. Vol. 1.

80 'Notes on the Nuer Country north of the Sobat and Baro Rivers'; SIR 270 (January 1917), p. 4; Stigand, 'Political Report on Patrol 42'; Corfield, 'Nasir District Notes'.

81 Wendy James, 'From Aboriginal to Frontier Society', pp. 49–53.

82 J. Stauder, *The Majangir. Ecology and Society of a Southwest Ethiopian People* (Cambridge: Cambridge University Press, 1971), pp. 1–4, 143, 190; 'Majangir', pp. 109–11; J. N. Grover, A/DC Pibor to Governor, Upper Nile Province, 8 May 1945, SRO UNP 66.B.14/J.

83 SIR 311 (June 1920), p. 3. C. R. K. Bacon, 'Patrol No. 71 – Political Report' claims that the Gaajak habitually sold their Meban captives. This claim must be doubted, since all earlier contemporary accounts of Nuer raids on the Meban are explicit that the Nuer were after grain and livestock, not slaves. See SIR 192 (July 1910), App. A. p. 8, 262 (May 1916), p. 4, 293 (December 1918), p. 3. In fact, Meban captured in the 1918–19 raids were still to be found living among the Gaajak in 1936: UNPMD (March 1936), SRO BD 57.C.1 (II). Shaikh Bol Bodi, who was himself captured by Nuer during one of Mut Dung's raids and was raised among the Nuer, denied that the Nuer sold Meban captives to the Ethiopians. They did, however, sometimes exchange Meban girls for Dinka cattle: SRO Meban 1, Bol Bodi, 7 May 1983.

84 Woodward, 'Anuak Raids, Illicit Ivory and Gun Running', p. 5; SIR 236 (March 1914), p. 4; J. N. Grover, A/DC Pibor to Governor, Upper Nile Province, 8 May 1945, SRO UNP 66.B.14/J; Stauder, 'Majangir', p. 111.

85 Lienhardt, 'Anuak Village Headmen: (I)', p. 351.

86 UNPMD (August 1935), SRO BD 57.C.1 (II).

87 Asmarom Legesse, 'Ethiopian Colonists and Frontier Peoples: the Borana Case' (Paper presented at the Society and History of Imperial Ethiopia Conference, Monterey, California, 1982), p. 3; Almagor, Chapter 4 of this volume.

88 Legesse, 'Ethiopian Colonists', pp. 27–9; H. S. Lewis, 'Gada, Big Man, K'allu: Political Succession among the Eastern Mech'a' (Paper presented at the Society and History of

Imperial Ethiopia Conference, Monterey, California, 1982), p. 14; *cf.* Donald L. Donham in Chapter 3 of this volume; J. Bureau, 'Etude diachronique du deux titres gamo', *Cahiers d'études africaines* 18 (1978), pp. 279–91.

89 Sobania, 'The Ethiopia–Kenya Frontier', pp. 26–7.

90 Gatkek Bol Ngundeng, 31 March 1976 (interview transcribed by Simon Kun Puoc, translated by Simon Kun Puoc and myself). Field work among the Nuer was first undertaken in 1975–6 during research for a Ph.D. at the University of California, Los Angeles. Subsequent interviews among the Nuer, Dinka and Meban were recorded in 1982–3, during the collection of oral history for the Southern Records Office, research which was funded by a Fulbright-Hayes Senior Research Scholarship. Copies of these interviews are on deposit with the Southern Records Office in Juba, under the titles 'EHJP' (Ecology and History of Jonglei Province) and 'Meban'.

91 Michel, *Vers Fachoda*, pp. 444–55.

92 Gabrial Jal, personal communication.

93 The version cited here was told in response to a question about Haile Selassie's visit to Ngundeng.

94 L. P. and G. N. Sanderson, *Education, Religion and Politics in Southern Sudan 1899–1964* (London: Ithaca Press, 1981), p. 3.

95 *cf.* Johnson, 'Tribal Boundaries and Border Wars'.

96 Evans-Pritchard, *The Nuer*, p. 88, *Political System*, p. 11; Howell, 'A Note on Elephants and Elephant Hunting among the Nuer', p. 95. Both authors were aware of the 1903 SIR reports about the Zaraf trade, but neither seem to have been aware of other government sources outlining the scale and time-span of the ivory trade.

97 El Wathig Kameir, 'Nuer Migrants in the Building Industry in Khartoum: A Case of the Concentration and Circulation of Labour', in *Urbanization and Urban Life in the Sudan*, forthcoming; personal communication, Bernadette Trottier, Mefit consultant, Swamp Ecology Study, Jonglei Executive Organ.

98 E. E. Evans-Pritchard, *Nuer Religion* (Oxford: Clarendon Press, 1956), pp. 223–4.

99 Table 5 is compiled from figures contained in documents found in the following:
SIR: 85 (August 1901), p. 3; 107 (June 1903), p. 11; 207 (October 1911), p. 5; 221 (December 1912), pp. 4–5.
NRO: Files UNP 1/5/270 and 1/12/101; Civsec 1/2/6 and 112/3/10; Intel 1/16/75; Dakhlia I 112/16/102.
SRO: Files UNP A.1 and A.1, 'Gambela (continued)'; UNP 'Abyssinian IRs'; UNP File No. 7; UNP SCR 5.5; UNP 14.1; UNP SCR 15.10; UNP 66.A.6; BD 57.C.1.
Evans-Pritchard, *Political System*, p. 13.

Epilogue

1 E. E. Evans-Pritchard, *The Sanusi of Cyrenaica* (Oxford: Clarendon Press, 1949).

2 J. Vansina, 'A Comparison of African kingdoms', *Africa* 32 (1962), 325–35.

3 Starting with Vansina's advocacy of field work in African historical research, *De la tradition orale: Essai de méthode historique* (Brussels; Musée Royale de l'Afrique Centrale, 1961), some notable examples of field-based historical studies (many of which deal with African states) are: J. Vansina, *Kingdoms of the Savannah* (Madison: University of Wisconsin Press, 1966); D. W. Cohen, *The Historical Tradition of Busoga, Mukama and Kintu* (Oxford: Oxford University Press, 1972); J. Vansina, *The Tio Kingdom of the Middle Congo 1880–1892* (London: Oxford University Press for the IAI, 1973); S. Feierman [trained in both history and anthropology] *The Shambaa Kingdom, a History* (Madison: University of Wisconsin Press, 1974); J. C. Miller, *Kings and Kinsmen: Early Mbundu States in Angola* (Oxford: Oxford University Press, 1976); G. Prins, *The Hidden Hippopotamous: Reappraisal in African History: The Early Colonial Experience in Western Zambia* (Cambridge: Cambridge University Press, 1980).

Select bibliography

Abir, Mordechai, *Ethiopia: the Era of the Princes. The Challenge of Islam and the Re-Unification of the Christian Empire, 1769–1855*, London and New York: Longmans/Praeger, 1968

Addis Hiwet, *Ethiopia: From Autocracy to Revolution*, London: Review of African Political Economy, 1975

Almagor, Uri, *Pastoral Partners: Affinity and Bond Partnership among the Dassanetch of Southwest Ethiopia*, Manchester: Manchester University Press, 1978

Amborn, Hermann; Minker, Gunter; and Sasse, Hans-Jürgen, *Das Dullay: Materialen zu einer ostkuschitischen Sprachgruppe*, Berlin: Dietrich Riemer Verlag, 1980

Asmarom Legesse, *Gada: Three Approaches to the Study of African Society*, New York: Free Press, 1973

'Post-Feudal Society, Capitalism, and Revolution: The Case of Ethiopia', in *Symposium Leo Frobenius II*, Bonn: Deutsche UNESCO Kommission, 1980

Bahru Zewde, 'Relations between Ethiopia and the Sudan on the Western Ethiopian Frontier, 1898–1935'. Ph.D. thesis, University of London, 1976

Bairu Tafla, 'Four Ethiopian Biographies'. *Journal of Ethiopian Studies* 7, 2 (1969), 1–31

Bartels, Lambert, *Oromo Religion: Myths and Rites of the Western Oromo of Ethiopia – An Attempt to Understand*, Berlin: Dietrich Reimer Verlag, 1983

Bauer, Dan Franz, *Household and Society in Ethiopia*, East Lansing: African Studies Center, Michigan State University, 1977

Baxter, Paul, and Almagor, Uri, eds., *Age, Generation and Time: Some Features of East African Age Organisations*, London and New York: C. Hurst/St. Martin's Press, 1978

Bender, M. L., *The Non-Semitic Languages of Ethiopia*, East Lansing: African Studies Center, Michigan State University, 1976

and Bowen, J. D.; Cooper, F. L.; and Ferguson, C. A., eds., *Language in Ethiopia*, London: Oxford University Press, 1976

Berhanou Abbebe, *Evolution de la propriété fonçière au Choa (Ethiopie) du règne de Ménélik à la constitution de 1931*, Paris: Imprimerie Nationale, Librairie Orientaliste Paul Geuthner, 1971

Berry, LaVerle Bennette, 'The Solomonic Monarchy at Gonder, 1630–1755: An Institutional Analysis of Kingship in the Christian Kingdom of Ethiopia', Ph.D. thesis, Boston University, 1976

Braukämper, Ulrich, *Geschichte der Hadiya Süd-Äthiopiens von den Anfängen bis zur Revolution 1974*, Wiesbaden: Franz Steiner Verlag, 1980

Die Kambata: Geschichte und Gesellschaft eines Südäthiopischen Bauernvolkes, Wiesbaden: Franz Steiner Verlag, 1983

Bureau, Jacques, *Les Gamo d'Ethiopie: Etude du système politique*. Paris: Société d'Ethnographie, 1981

Caulk, Richard, 'The Origins and Development of the Foreign Policy of Menelik II, 1865–1896', Ph.D. thesis, University of London, 1966

'Armies as Predators: Soldiers and Peasants in Ethiopia, *c.* 1850–1935', *International Journal of African Historical Studies* 11 (1978), 457–93

Cerulli, Enrico, 'The Folk Literature of the Galla of Southern Abyssinia', *Harvard African Studies* 3 (1922), 11–228

Etiopia occidentale (dallo Scioa alla frontiera del Sudan): Note del viaggio 1927–28, Rome: Sindacato Italiano Arti Grafiche, 1933

Clapham, Christopher, *Haile Selassie's Government*, New York: Praeger, 1969

'Centralization and Local Response in Southern Ethiopia', *African Affairs* 74 (1975), 72–81

Cohen, John M., and Weintraub, Dov, *Land and Peasants in Imperial Ethiopia*, Assen: Van Gorcum, 1975

Conti Rossini, Carlo, *Principi diritto consuetudinario dell'Eritrea*, Rome: Tipografia dell'Unione Editrice, 1916

Crummey, Donald, *Priests and Politicians: Protestant and Catholic Missions in Orthodox Ethiopia, 1830–1868*, Oxford: Clarendon Press, 1972

'Abyssinian Feudalism', *Past and Present* 89 (1980), 115–38

Darkwah, R. H. Kofi, *Shewa, Menilek and the Ethiopian Empire, 1813–1889*, London: Heinemann, 1975

Department of History, eds., *Proceedings of the Second Annual Seminar of the Department of History*, Addis Abeba: Addis Abeba University, 1984

Donham, Donald L., *Work and Power in Maale, Ethiopia*, Ann Arbor, Michigan: UMI Research Press, 1985

and James, Wendy, eds., 'Working Papers on Society and History in Imperial Ethiopia: The Southern Periphery from the 1880s to 1974', photocopied; Cambridge: African Studies Centre, 1980. (Copies have been deposited in the collections of the following: African Studies Centre, Cambridge; Institute of Social Anthropology, Oxford; School of Oriental and African Studies, London; Stanford University; African Studies Center, Michigan State University; Institute of Ethiopian Studies, Addis Abeba University; National Records Office, Khartoum.)

Ege, Svein, 'Chiefs and Peasants: The Socio-Political Structure of the Kingdom of Shäwa in about 1840', Hovedoppgave i historie, University of Bergen, 1978

Evans-Pritchard, E. E., *The Political System of the Anuak*, Monographs on Social Anthropology No. 4, 1940, reprint; London: Percy Lund, Humphries & Co. Ltd., 1977

Ellis, Gene, 'The Feudal Paradigm as a Hindrance to Understanding Ethiopia', *Journal of Modern African Studies* 14 (1976), 275–95

Fecadu Gedamu, 'Ethnic Associations in Ethiopia and the Maintenance of Urban/Rural Relationships, with Special Reference to the Alemgana-Walamo Road Construction Association', Ph.D. thesis, University of London, 1972

Fukui, Katsuyoshi, and Turton, David A., eds., *Warfare Among East African Herders*, Senri Ethnological Studies, No. 3, Osaka: National Museum of Ethnology, 1979

Gamst, Frederick C., *The Qemant: A Pagan–Hebraic Peasantry of Ethiopia*, New York: Holt, Rinehart and Winston, 1969

Garretson, Peter, P., 'A History of Addis Abeba from its Foundation in 1886 to 1910', Ph.D. thesis, University of London, 1974

Gebre-Wold-Ingida Worq, 'Ethiopia's Traditional System of Land Tenure and Taxation', *Ethiopian Observer* 5 (1962); 302–39

Gebru Tareke, 'Peasant Resistance in Ethiopia: The Case of *Weyane*', *Journal of African History* 25 (1984), 77–92

Gilkes, Patrick, *The Dying Lion: Feudalism and Modernization in Ethiopia*, London and New York: Julian Friedmann/St. Martin's Press, 1975

Grottanelli, Vinigi L., *Ricerche geografiche ed economiche sulle popolazioni*, Vol. 2 of *Missione di studio Lago Tana*, Rome: Reale Accademia d'Italia, 1939

'I Pre-Niloti. Un'arcaica provincia culturale in Africa', *Annali Lateranensi* 12 (1948), 281–326

Haberland, Eike, *Galla Süd-Äthiopiens*, Stuttgart: W. Kohlhammer Verlag, 1963

Untersuchungen zum Äthiopien Königtum, Wiesbaden: Franz Steiner Verlag, 1965

Haile Sellassie I (Emperor), *My Life and Ethiopia's Progress, 1892–1937*, translated and edited by Edward Ullendorff, London: Oxford University Press, 1976

Hallpike, Christopher R., *The Konso of Ethiopia: A Study of the Values of a Cushitic People*, Oxford: Clarendon Press, 1972

Hess, Robert L., *Ethiopia: The Modernization of Autocracy*, Ithaca, N.Y.: Cornell University Press, 1970

ed., *Proceedings of the Fifth International Conference of Ethiopian Studies. Session B, 1978*, Chicago: University of Illinois at Chicago Circle, 1982

Hickey, Dennis, 'Ethiopia and Great Britain: Political Conflict in the Southern Borderlands, 1916–1935', Ph.D. thesis, Northwestern University, 1984

Hoben, Allan, *Land Tenure among the Amhara of Ethiopia: The Dynamics of Cognatic Descent*, Chicago: University of Chicago Press, 1973

Hultin, Jan, 'Political Structure and the Development of Inequality Among the Macha Oromo', *in Pastoral Production and Society*, Equipe écologie et anthropologie des sociétés pastorales, Cambridge: Maison des Sciences de L'Homme and Cambridge University Press, 1979

James, Wendy, '*Kwanim Pa: the Making of the Uduk People. An Ethnographic Study of Survival in the Sudan-Ethiopian Borderlands*, Oxford: Clarendon Press, 1979

Jensen, A. E., ed., *Altvölker Süd-Äthiopiens*, Stuttgart: W. Kohlhammer Verlag, 1959

Johnson, D. H., 'History and Prophecy among the Nuer of the Southern Sudan', Ph.D. thesis, University of California at Los Angeles, 1980

Klausberger, Friedrich, *Woga-Recht und Gesellschaft in Süd-Äthiopien*, Frankfurt am Main: Peter D. Lang, 1981

Knutsson, Karl Eric, *Authority and Change: A Study of the Kallu Institution Among the Macha Galla of Ethiopia*, Goteborg: Etnografiska Museet, 1967

Lange, Werne J., 'Gimira (Remnants of a Vanishing Culture)', Ph.D. thesis, Johann Wolfgang Goethe-Universität, Frankfurt am Main, 1976

History of the Southern Gonga (Southwestern Ethiopia), Wiesbaden: Franz Steiner Verlag, 1982

Levine, Donald N., *Wax and Gold: Tradition and Innovation in Ethiopian Culture*, Chicago: University of Chicago Press, 1965

Greater Ethiopia: The Evolution of a Multiethnic Society, Chicago: University of Chicago Press, 1974

Lewis, Herbert S., *A Galla Monarchy: Jimma Abba Jifar, 1830–1932*, Madison: University of Wisconsin Press, 1965

Lewis, I. M., *A Pastoral Democracy: A Study of Pastoralism and Politics Among the Northern Somali of the Horn of Africa*, London: Oxford University Press, 1961

Lienhardt, R. G. 'Anuak Village Headmen: (I) Headmen and Village Culture', *Africa* 27 (1957), 341–55, '(II) Village Structure and "Rebellion" ', *Africa* 28 (1958), 23–36

Lydall, Jean, and Strecker, Ivo, *The Hamar of Southern Ethiopia*, 3 vols, Hohenschaftlarn: Renner Verlag, 1979

Mahteme Sellassie Wolde Maskel *Zikre Neger*, Addis Abeba: Netsanet Press, 1942 E.C.

Mantel-Niećko, Joanna, *The Role of Land Tenure in the System of Ethiopian Imperial Government in Modern Times*, Warsaw: Wydawnictwa Uniwersytetu Warszawskiego, 1980

Marcus, Harold G., ed., *The Modern History of Ethiopia and the Horn of Africa: A Select and Annotated Bibliography*, Stanford: Hoover Institution Press, 1972

ed., *Proceedings of the First United States Conference of Ethiopian Studies*, East Lansing, Michigan: African Studies Center, Michigan State University, 1975

Ethiopia, Great Britain, and the United States, 1941–1974, Berkeley: University of California Press, 1983

The Life and Times of Menelik II: Ethiopia 1844–1913, Oxford: Clarendon Press, 1975

Markakis, John, *Ethiopia: Anatomy of a Traditional Polity*, Oxford: Clarendon Press, 1974

and Nega Ayele, *Class and Revolution in Ethiopia*, London: Review of African Political Economy, 1978

McCann, James C., 'Householders, Peasants, and Rural History in Lasta, Northern Ethiopia, 1900–1935', Ph.D. thesis, Michigan State University, 1984

McClellan, Charles W., 'Reaction to Ethiopian Expansionism: The Case of Darasa, 1895–1935,' Ph.D. thesis, Department of History, Michigan State University, 1978

Merid W. Aregay, 'Southern Ethiopia and the Christian Kingdom, 1508–1708, with Special Reference to the Galla Migrations and their Consequences', Ph.D. thesis, University of London, 1971

Messing, Simon David, 'The Highland-Plateau Amhara of Ethiopia', Ph.D. thesis, University of Pennsylvania, 1957

Mockler, Anthony, *Haile Selassie's War*, Oxford: Oxford University Press, 1984

Pankhurst, Richard, *Economic History of Ethiopia, 1800–1935*, Addis Abeba: Haile Sellassie I University Press, 1968

Perham, Margery, *The Government of Ethiopia*, London: Faber & Faber, 1947

Quirin, James A., 'The Beta Israel (Felasha) in Ethiopian History: Caste Formation and Culture Change, 1270–1868', Ph.D. thesis, University of Minnesota, 1977

Reminick, Ronald A., 'The Manze Amhara of Ethiopia: A Study of Authority, Masculinity, and Sociality', Ph.D. thesis, University of Chicago, 1973

Rubenson, Sven, *The Survival of Ethiopian Independence*, London: Heinemann, 1976

ed., *Proceedings of the Seventh International Conference of Ethiopian Studies*, East Lansing: African Studies Center, Michigan State University, 1984

Samatar, Said S., *Oral Poetry and Somali Nationalism: The Case of Sayyid Mahammad 'Abdille Hasan*, Cambridge: Cambridge University Press, 1982

Shack, William A., *The Gurage: A People of the Ensete Culture*, London: Oxford University Press, 1966

'Urban Ethnicity and the Cultural Process of Urbanization in Ethiopia', in Aidan Southall, ed., *Urban Anthropology*, New York: Oxford University Press, 1973

Sobania, Neil, 'The Historical Tradition of the Peoples of the Eastern Lake Turkana Basin, *c.* 1840–1925', Ph.D. thesis, University of London, 1980

Ståhl, Michael, *Ethiopia: Political Contradictions in Agricultural Development*, Stockholm: Rabén & Shörgren, 1974

Stauder, Jack, *The Majangir: Ecology and Society of a Southwest Ethiopian People*, Cambridge Studies in Social Anthropology 5, Cambridge: Cambridge University Press, 1971

Stitz, Volker, *Studien zur Kulturgeographie Zentraläthiopiens*, Bonn: F. Dummlers Verlag, 1974

Straube, Helmut, ed., *Westkuschitische Völker Süd-Äthiopiens*, Stuttgart: W. Kohlhammer Verlag, 1963

Taddesse Tamrat, *Church and State in Ethiopia, 1270–1527*, Oxford: Clarendon Press, 1972

Terrefe Woldetsadik, 'The Unification of Ethiopia (1880–1935): Wallaga', *Journal of Ethiopian Studies* 6 (1968), 73–86

Trimingham, J. Spencer, *Islam in Ethiopia*, London: Oxford University Press, 1952

Triulzi, Alessandro, *Salt, Gold and Legitimacy: Prelude to the History of a No-Man's Land, Belā Shangul, Wälläggā, Ethiopia (ca. 1800–1898)*, Naples: Istituto Universitario Orientale, 1981

Tsehai Berhane Selassie, 'The Political and Military Traditions of the Ethiopian Peasantry (1800–1941)', D.Phil. thesis, Oxford University, 1981

Tubiana, Joseph, ed., *Modern Ethiopia from the Accession of Menilek II to the Present. Proceedings of the Fifth International Conference of Ethiopian Studies. Nice, 1977*, Rotterdam: A. A. Balkema, 1980

Turton, David A., 'A Journey Made Them: Territorial Segmentation and Ethnic Identity among the Mursi', in *Segmentary Lineage Systems Reconsidered*, edited by Ladislav Holy, Belfast: Queen's University Press, 1979

Weissleder, Wolfgang, 'The Political Ecology of Amhara Domination', Ph.D. thesis, University of Chicago, 1965

Zawde Gabra-Sellase, *Yohannes IV of Ethiopia: A Political Biography*, Oxford: Clarendon Press, 1975

Index

Aba Bulcho (Gumuz village), 131–9, 140, 141
Aba Timbaho, Chief, 127, 128
Abbay lands, 23; Dinka trade, 231; gold, 38; Gumuz in, 44, 119–23 *passim*, 126, 127, 129–47 *passim*
Abigar, *see* Nuer people
Abir, Mordechai, *quoted*, 168–9
Abu Ramleh, 122
Abu Shok, *see* Aghib, Shaykh
Abyssinia (pre-Menilek II era), 3, 4–24, 247; Abyssinianization, 10–11, 47–8; military ethos, 7, 33–4; old border with Sudan, 12, 196, 225; ṭowns, 15, 20; *see also under* agriculture; class systems; economy
Acholiland, 197, 211, 216
Adafa, 20
Adal, 21
Addis Abeba, 20, 31, 85, 199, 259; growth, 32–3, 34; railway, 27, 30, 77
Addis Alem, 62
Addis Hiwet, 24, 26
Adwa, battle of (1896), 23, 24, 77, 177
Afodu 63
Agaw people, 13, 14, 34, 119, 126, 147
Agere Mariam (garrison town), 183
Agere Selam (provincial capital), 178
Aggedew, *fītawrarī*, 206
Aghib, Shaykh (Abu Shok), 121, 124–5, 126, 139
Agole, 65
agriculture, 28, 33, 166, 189; Abyssinia, 4, 8, 14, 15, 255; cultivation, 4, 8, 47, 75, 99, 112–13, 149, 150, 154, 155, 161, 255, 259, 269; modern, 32, 269; *see also* cash crops; cattle; coffee; ensete; maize; pastoralism; sugar; tobacco
Ahmad ibn Ibrahim al-Ghazi, 47
Akobo region, 226, 238
Aksumite empire, 20
Akwei-wa-Cam, 225, 226, 231, 237, 238, 240
Alabdu people (Guji Oromo), 176, 177, 184
Aliab, 235
Allidina Visram, 210
Alvarez, Francesco, 15
American aid, 28, 78
Amhara (ethnic category), 12, 13, 34, 35, 96–7, 101, 107–15, 228–9, 268
Amharic (language), 11, 12, 19, 21, 23, 96, 144, 259
Anderson, Perry, 13–14
Anfillo, 56, 220, 226, 231, 232, 237
Anglo-Egyptian government in Sudan, 197, 209, 211, 219–33 *passim*, 238–45 *passim*; border treaties, 98, 201, 220, 221; inflexibility, 46, 220–1, 231, 240, 241–2, 244, 245; Nuer people, 43, 228, 229, 230, 231; and slave raids, 213, 217, 232; trading posts, 30, 222, 223; tribute, *see under* tribute; *see also* British; Sudan
Anokhosia, Chief, 104–5, 110
anthropology and history, link between, 4, 69, 93–4, 147, 247, 248
Anuak people, 37, 219, 220, 221, 222; defeat Majid, 226, 230; leadership, 224–8, 241, 242; Nuer relationships, 223–4, 225, 238–40; population (1947), 288; *see also under* class systems; trade
Arjo, 52, 56, 57, 67
arms, 75–6, 140, 184; Dassanetch, 98, 101, 103–4, 112, 114, 268; Kwegu, 149, 152–3, 167, 170; Maji, 170–1, 197, 200, 204, 206, 208, 210, 211, 213–17 *passim*; Sudan–Ethiopian border, 43, 213, 226, 228, 229, 233–7 *passim*, 244
army, professional, 25, 27, 194, 256; provincial, *see ketema*; *neftennya*; *see also* Abyssinia, military ethos; Dergue
Arregude, King, 81–3, 89, 94
Arsi, 44, 46, 259
Asbe Hailu, 39–40
Asefe, *dejazmach*, 206
Asmarom Legesse, 34; *quoted*, 42
Asmera, 32

Asosa, 65, 229, 231, 237, 240
Asselefech, *weyzero*, 205
Athill, Major, 205
Atol, Chief, 106
Ausa, 37–8
Awash valley, 42, 47
awraja (sub-provinces), 27, 38, 78, 188
Azande people, 246

Baderg, Chief, 140, 143
Baeteman, J., 12, 251, 259
Bahr al-Jabal, 245
Bahr al-Zaraf, 232, 235
Bahru Zewde, 24–5, 28
Bailo, Chief, 92, 93
Bakare Godana, 51–2, 60
Bakare ruling family, 52, 57, 130, 216, 260; *see also* Bakare Godana; Gebre Igzīabihēr; Moroda Bakare
Bako (garrison town), 81
Bako province, 213; and Maale, 78, 81, 82, 83, 84, 85, 87, 92, 94, 170·
Balabbat, 38, 39, 40, 42, 44, 266; Dassanetch chiefs, 45, 101–7 *passim*, 109, 110, 111, 113, 115; Gedeo, 180, 181, 183, 186, 190, 193; Maale, 44, 69, 70, 76, 84, 85, 88, 90, 93; Maji, *see kure*; *see also under* taxation
Balcha, *dejazmach*, 177–8, 186, 280
Bandits and outlaws: aristocratic, 20, 200, 225, 227; Maji, 204, 206, 209–10, 211, 213, 214, 215; *see also* cattle raids
Banja, *dejazmach* (Shaykh Hamdan Abu Shok), 121, 122, 127, 128, 139–40
banks, 29, 77, 210
Bantu villagers of Ituri forest, 160–2
Bar, 229
Barber, J., 212, 282, 286
Bari people, 204, 213, 215, 216
Baro river, 222, 226, 230, 231, 233, 238, 240
Barros, João de, *quoted*, 14–15
Basarote, Chief, 122, 124
Baumann, Gerhard, 271
Beachey, R. W., *quoted*, 168
Begemdir, 21, 23, 202, 253
Beggi, 229, 233
Beke, Charles T., 121
Bela Shangul, 37–8, 47, 129, 220; rule of, 51, 58, 59, 63, 64, 65, 67, 68; trade, 231, 237
Beliniang, 216
Belodiya people, 201, 202
Bender, M. Lionel, 11, 272
Beri Hill, 122, 123, 126, 127, 128, 139, 143
Bertha people, 63, 122, 140
Bicad (Gumuz leader), 139, 140
Billo, 62
Bio chiefdom, 83, 84, 85, 88
Birru Haile Mariam, *dejazmach*, 202, 203, 204, 210, 215, 230, 239
Birru Welde Gebriēl, *ras*, 186–7
Blue Nile, *see* Abbay lands
Bobo, Chief, 140, 143
Bodi people, 163
Bola chiefs, 70, 74, 75, 84; conflict with royalty, 82, 89, 91, 92; *see also kati*
Boma plateau, 207, 210, 217; imperial rule, 201, 202, 204, 206, 212, 213
Bonga, 206
Bor, 197, 207; Bor Dinka people, 235
borders, *see* frontiers
Borelli, Jules, 265
Borena people (Oromo), 42, 108, 109, 184
Bosuma (headman of Aba Bulcho), 137, 140, 142, 143
Bòttego, Vittorio, 169
Bourdieu, Pierre, 272
Boya people, 204, 211
Braudel, Fernand, 21
British administration, 42, 98, 197, 200, 209, 211; in Ethiopia, 27, 28, 205, 206, 207; *see also* Anglo-Egyptian; Kangalla
British East Africa, 98, 197, 211; *see also* Kenya
Bruce, James, 119, 121, 146, 247
Bulatovich, A. K., 201
Bule (garrison town), 188
Bulls, *see* Dassanetch; provincial domination
Bunka, 83, 84, 85, 89, 92, 93
Bure, 222, 226, 232, 237
Bureau, Jacques, 44
Burji (Maji leader), 206
Bwangani (trader), 207, 208

'Cai' people, *see* Koma; Meban
Cam-war-Akwei (Anuak noble), 226–7
capitalism, 25, 27–8, 186, 194, 210
cash crops, 125, 127, 149, 175, 176, 181; *see also* coffee; tobacco
cattle, 231; disease (1888–92), 60; raids, 42, 202, 209–10, 216; trade, 119, 167, 170, 181, 213, 214, 216, 223, 228, 229, 231–7 *passim*; *see also* pastoralism
Caulk, Richard, 15
Cerulli, Enrico, 9
Chaliya, 62
Cheesman, R. E., 126, 127–8
Chelenko, battle of, 23, 24, 256
Chercher province, 207
Chichu (garrison town), 183
chikashum, 69, 70, 76
Chimburu Shunde, *balabbat*, 190
chisennya, *see* tenancy
Christianity, 13, 17; and *gebbar* system, 12, 78, 254; monasteries, 12, 21; Orthodox, 6, 11–12, 26, 40, 42, 47, 78, 81, 188, 193, 201; Protestantism, 45, 46, 145–6, 260, 269

Ciec Lam, Stephen, 242–3
civet, 23, 27, 199
Clapham, Christopher, 35, 37
class systems, 28, 95; Anuak, 224–5; Dassanetch, 99, 100, 106, 113; Gedeo, 176, 180, 182, 183; Gumuz and highlanders, 120–1, 124, 145, 147; Kwegu and Mursi, 148, 150, 151, 154–62 *passim*, 164, 165, 168; Maale, *see kati*; traditional Abyssinian, 4, 5, 7, 8, 9, 10, 11, 25, 33, 34, 35, 252, 253
coffee, 105, 181, 231; exports, 23, 27, 31, 175, 184; Gedeo, 41, 175, 176, 177, 178, 181, 184, 186–94 *passim*
Collins, R. O., 212
colonists, *see neftennya*
commerce, *see* trade
communications, 77, 176, 177, 194; problems of, 17, 20, 21, 101; *see also* railways; roads, steamer traffic
Conti Rossini, Carlo, 11
cotton, 119, 144, 181
crops, *see* agriculture; cash crops; coffee; ensete; maize; sugar; tobacco
Crosby, Oscar T., 126–7
Crummey, Donald, 8–9, 15, 252–3, 254
cults, religious, 45–6
customs gates (*kella*), 34, 61, 62, 63–5; *see also* imports; taxation

Dabus river, 56, 65, 66, 129
Daga valley, 230, 239
Dahlak Islands trade route, 21, 24
Dapo, 56
Darasa people, *see* Gedeo
Daraso, *ras*, 52
Darley, Henry, 203, 210
Dasifi (nineteenth-century village), 124, 125–6, 127, 139, 142; *see also* Datsipa
Dassanetch people, 37, 96–115 *passim*, 267; Bulls, 45, 100, 103, 106–7, 109, 110, 111, 113, 114, 115; relations with settlers, 47, 96, 97, 107–9, 111, 112, 114, 115; *see also under* arms; *balabbat*; class systems; domination, imperial; ethnicity; kinship; Menilek II; Mussolini; pastoralism; provincial domination; taxation
Datsipa (Gumuz section), 142
Debbebe, *dejazmach*, 206
Debo, *fītawrarī* (also *balabbat* and *kure*), 202
Dekereya sections (of the Gumuz people), 141
Demissew, *ras*, 61, 63, 64
Demtē, *fītawrarī* (later *dejazmach*), 199, 201
Deng Lakka (Nuer leader), 231, 235
Derēssa, *blatta*, 54–5, 56
Dergue (military government from 1974), 34, 145
Desē, 29, 32
Desta Birru, *dejazmach*, 203, 204, 205
Desta Damtew, *ras*, 187
Dewaro, 21
Diddessa river, 52, 56, 130
Didinga people, 203, 204, 211, 213, 215, 217
Dilla, 193
Dinka people, 220, 238, 291; trade, 228, 231, 232, 233, 235, 236
Dire Dawa, 30, 32
Dishigishi (Gumuz section), 143
Dizi-speaking peoples, 197
domination, imperial, 37, 38, 42–3, 47, 120; Dassanetch, 101, 102; Gedeo, 179, 182, 183, 184, 185, 186, 188, 191, 192, 194, 195; Gubba chiefs, 122, 123–4, 128; Maale, 76, 85; Mursi, 149, 167, 168, 170–1; Nekemte, 51, 55, 59, 67, 68; *see also* provincial domination
Donaldson Smith, A., *quoted*, 169–70
Dorobo people, 164
Dorze, 81
Dual Diu (Nuer leader), 231, 236
Dukunza sections (of the Gumuz people), 141
Dukunzilla (Gumuz section), 135–40, 141, 142, 143; *see also under* migration
Dura valley, 127

economy, 37, 204; Abyssinian political, 15–17, 33–4, 251, 255; cash crop revolution, 175; Dassanetch social, 99; and exchange marriage, 146–7; Gedeo, 176, 179, 182, 183, 184, 187, 191; Gubba political, 121; Gumuz social, 131, 145; Kwegu, exploitation of, 148; Maale, political, 71, 74, 93, 94; Maji political, 197; Mursi, 149, 152, 154, 157, 158, 167, 170; Nuer political, 244–5; subsistence, 144, 146, 175, 176, 182, 183; Woodburn's 'systems', 161; world, 175, 177; *see also* capitalism; taxation
education, 35, 76, 87, 93, 145
Egyptian rule, 23–4, 200, 232; *see also* Anglo-Egyptian; Turco-Egyptian
Egzaw, Chief, 127
Eisenstadt, S. N., 96–7, 99
Elele (Dassanetch section), 99
elephants, depletion of, 27, 177, 209, 233, 235; *see also* hunting; ivory
Embabo, battle of (1882), 23, 52, 54, 199, 256, 261
empire, *see* domination, imperial; imperial rule
ensete, 176, 181, 183, 184, 185
Ergetē, *dejazmach*, 206
Eritrea, 24, 31, 257

ethnicity, 12–13, 17, 34–5, 37, 40, 176; Dassanetch and settlers, 45, 47, 107–9; Gumuz exchange marriage, 120, 130, 147; highlanders, 20; hunters and herders, 164–5; Kunama and Tigrai raids, 258; Kwegu and Mursi, 150–1, 166–7, 171; Nilotes, 240, 244; *see also* Amhara; Galla; marriage; Shankilla
Evans-Pritchard, Sir Edward E., 43, 219, 245, 246, 247
exports, 23, 27, 31, 175, 184, 186, 209, 210, 211, 217; *see also* trade

Fagage, 98
Famaka, 122, 127
famine, 60–1, 83, 111, 129, 144, 185, 244, 271; crop failure, 74; drought, 184, 185, 274; ecological degradation, 15, 63, 170, 189; Great Famine (1890s), 38, 60, 262; impoverishment and depopulation, 122, 126–8, 182; overpopulation, 124, 189
farming, *see* agriculture; cash crops; cattle; coffee; ensete; maize; pastoralism; sugar; tobacco
Fashoda, 243
Fazoghli, 122, 232
Feseha Gennet, 194
Fetegar, 21
feudal societies, 8–9, 13–14, 15, 42, 253, 255, 259
fiefs, *see gult*
firearms, *see* arms
fishing, 148, 149, 152, 153, 154, 245
frontiers, 3, 251; border treaties, 98, 201, 220, 221–2, 226–7; migration across, 42, 230, 231, 239; Sudan–Ethiopian, *see* arms; *gebbar*; hunters; Mussolini; *neftennya*; as a vantage point, 4, 120, 196
Funj (historical dynasty), 121, 125, 139, 145, 200; *see also* Sennar

Gaajak (Nuer people), 225, 226, 228, 229, 243; trade, *see under* trade; *see also* Mut Dung (Gaajak leader)
Gaawar (Nuer people), 224, 231, 235, 236, 237
gadaa (Oromo ritual system), 52, 176, 193
Gai Jang (Nuer leader), 228, 231
Galata Sheshemo, *grazmach*, 145
Galla (ethnic category), 12, 13, 55, 56, 68, 199, 254; *see also* Oromo
Gallajira (Tishana leader), 205
Gambela, 29, 30–1, 216, 223
Gamo-Gofa province, 78, 148
Gamo highlands, 44
Garretson, Peter P., 121, 122, 124, 128
garrison towns, *see ketema*
gebbar system, 35, 37, 38–42, 67, 113, 259; abolition, 87, 207; and Christianity, 12, 78, 254; Gedeo, 37, 178–95 *passim*, 278; Gumuz, 120, 124; Maale, 83, 84, 85, 88; Maji, 197, 199, 201, 202, 203, 204, 206, 207, 210, 217, 218; Nekemte, 61; Oromo, 258; Sidamo (pre-1920), 179–84; Sudan–Ethiopian border, 221, 226, 240; *see also gult*; *ketema*; *neftennya*; *rist*; slavery; tribute
Gebre Igziabihēr, *dejazmach* (Kumsa Moroda), 51, 57, 67, 68, 130, 199; *quoted*, 55, 56, 59, 60, 61, 62, 63, 64, 65, 66
Gebre-Wold-Ingida Worq, 58
Gedeo people (Darasa), 41, 175–95 *passim*; *see also under balabbat*; class systems; coffee; domination, imperial; economy; *gebbar*; *kelad*; kinship; migrations; *neftennya*; provincial domination; *rist*; taxation; tenancy; tribute
Gero chiefdom, 84, 93
Getachchew Abbate, *ras*, 206
Ghol Dinka people, 233
Gibe region, 52, 56
Gidami, 52, 221–2, 228, 232, 233, 237; governor of, 226, 229
Gilo region, 238
Gimira, 199, 204, 205
Ginte chiefdom, 83, 84, 88
Girpe, King, 89, 90, 91
Gluckman, Max, 15, 16, 17
Gobena Dachi, *ras*, 52, 54, 55, 56, 65, 66, 199
Goddo, 81, 84, 85
Gofa, 44, 79, 80, 81, 85
Goha, 63
Gojjam, 122, 129; Gumuz in, 119, 121, 130, 139, 142, 143, 147; *rist* 16; Shewan dispute, *see under* Shewans
gold, 38, 55, 119, 129, 199; export, 23, 27; and Nilotes, 231, 232, 233, 237; tax, 60, 62–3; tribute, 58–9, 64
Golda, 202
Gollo chiefdom, 84
Gonder, 20, 119
gonderē, *see neftennya*
Gonja people, 17
Goody, Jack, 4–5, 8, 15–16, 251, 255; Gonja people, 17
Gore, 31, 216, 226, 232, 240
government, *see* Anglo-Egyptian; Dergue; Egyptian; imperial rule; Turco-Egyptian
Grottanelli, Vinigi L., 120, 146, 147, 269
Grühl, Max, 15, 254–5
Gubba, 121, 122–3, 139, 143; chiefs, *see under* provincial domination
Guek Ngundeng (Nuer leader), 231, 236
guerrilla fighters, 27, 98
Guidi, Ignazio, 12

Guji people (Oromo), 46, 176, 177, 182, 184
Gulbak (Gumuz leader), 139, 140; place name, 273
gult (fiefs), 5, 8, 9, 10, 11, 13, 15, 16, 40; abolition, 41; for churches, 12; enforcement, 39; insecurity of, 14, 17; Maale, 39, 83, 88; Sibu, 66; unsettled lands, 259; *see also gebbar*; tribute
Gum Gum, 127
Gumuz people, 37, 43–4, 119–47, 271; Dukunzilla section, *see* Dukunzilla; *see also under* class systems; domination, imperial; marriage, exchange; economy; ethnicity; *gebbar*; Gojjam; migration; *neftennya*; provincial domination; slavery; Sudan; Wellegga
guns, *see* arms
Gurafarda, 216
Gurage people, 34, 35, 46, 47, 199
Gute Dili, battle of, 55, 129
Gwynn, C. W., 98, 139

Haberland, Eike, 130
Habesha people, 23, 34, 35; 'Habash' as Gumuz category, 141; *see also* Amhara; Tigrinnya
Habte Mika'ēl, *dejazmach*, 206
Hadiya, 21
Haile Selassie I (1930–74 formerly *ras* Teferi Mekonnen), 24–5, 111, 204, 229, 253–4; abdication, 34, 69; imperial bodyguard, 27, 256; Nekemte rule, 51, 59, 61, 66; policies, 28, 33, 77, 78, 177, 178, 186, 187, 194, 206–7; reforms (1941), 26, 27, 38, 41, 85, 87
Hamar-Bako *awraja*, 148
Hamdan Abu Shok, Shaykh, *see* Banja, *dejazmach*
Hana, 148
Harer, 23, 24, 31, 32, 46, 256
Harergē, 178, 253
Hawkins, Major, 205, 207
herders, *see* pastoralism
highlands and lowlands: centre–periphery relations, 37, 42–4; *kelad*, 87; lowland migration, 40, 120; social boundaries, 12, 19, 21, 23, 35, 200, 201, 222, 240
Hilla, *grazmach*, 88, 89, 90–1, 92, 265–6
history and anthropology, *see* anthropology
Hoben, Allan, 5–6; *quoted*, 16
honey, 59, 75, 149, 153, 155, 181
hunters, 20, 37, 97, 129, 184; and herders, 164–5, 276; Kwegu, 43, 148, 149, 150, 152–3, 154, 155, 167, 168, 171; Maale, 75, 87; Maji, 207, 210, 282; Sudan–Ethiopian border, 225, 232, 236, 237; Woodburn's views on, 161; *see also* elephants; ivory

Idi Wad Sheru, 210
Ilemi Appendix, 98
Illalcha, 183, 188
Illubabor, 199, 204, 220, 221, 222, 230
immigrants, *see* migration; *neftennya*
imperial rule, 9–10; centralization, 25–6, 27, 28, 33, 34, 77, 78, 85, 95, 178, 186, 191, 192, 194, 206–7; devolution of power, 77–8, 93, 202, 204, 217; finance policies, 25, 26–7, 28, 29, 30–1, 33, 34, 78, 87, 88, 175, 177, 184, 186, 194, 207, 210; *see also under* Boma plateau; Murle; Sibu; Sudan; *see also* domination, imperial; economy; Haile Selassie; Menilek II; taxation; tribute
imports, 211; *see also* customs gates
industry, 23, 28, 32–3, 55, 129
Inkabelo (Dassanetch section), 99, 100
Inkoria (Dassanetch section), 99
Irbo, 84
Irgudo, Chief, 104, 110
Islam, 21, 26, 34, 45, 47, 260
Italy, in Eritrea, 24, 31; Menilek II's defeat of, 3, 24, 77; occupation (1936–41), *see* Mussolini; supplies arms, 112
Itang, 223, 238
ivory trade, 30, 38, 120, 187, 199; exports, 23, 27, 211; Maale chiefs, 75–6, 81, 84–5; Maji, 197, 200–17 *passim*; Mursi and Kwegu, 43, 149, 152–3, 167–70; Nilotes, 43, 207, 213, 223, 225, 226, 227, 228, 231–7 *passim*, 243, 244; slump, 27, 177, 186, 204, 210, 211; *see also* elephants; hunters
Iyasu, *lij*, 26, 77, 80, 203, 204, 229, 256; and Nekemte rule, 51, 59, 66, 68

Jabal Abur, 139
Jabal Kathangor, 206
Jabal Lafon, 213, 215, 216
Jagasien, Chief, 124
Jammoa (Gumuz section), 141, 142, 143
Jara Biftu, *fītawrarī*, 140
Jato chiefdom, 84
Jensen, A. E., 265–6
Jibuti, 27, 30
Jifar, *dejazmach*, *quoted*, 55
Jikany (Nuer people), 224, 228, 230, 232, 235, 237, 238; population (1956), 288
Jimma, 47, 84, 85, 199, 206
Jinka, 93, 101, 103, 105, 106
Jote Tullu, *dejazmach*, 55, 199, 220; deposed, 226, 228; *see also under* trade

Kadalo people, 123
Kaiemothia, 98
Kalam, 98, 104, 105, 109, 110, 114
kallu (spirit medium), 45

Kamba, 81
Kambata, 46, 47
Kangalla, battle of (1918), 204, 205
Karamojong, 197, 203, 211, 212
Kara people, 169, 170
kati (Maale kingship), 77, 80, 81–5, 90–2, 94; abolition, 93; as landlords, 45, 70, 88–9, 93; limited power of, 44, 70, 71–6; *see also* Bola chiefs; Makana chiefs
Kebbede Mengesha, *ras*, 206
Kefa, 201, 202, 203, 204, 206, 220; ivory trade, 210, Shewan conquest, 199, 205, 207
ḳelad (measured land), 41, 66, 67, 264; in Gedeo, 179–80, 188, 189, 190–1, 192, 280, 281; in Maale, 87, 91–2
Ḳelem, 52, 56, 220
kella, *see* customs gates
Kenya, 42, 98, 212; *see also* British East Africa
ketema (garrison towns), 39, 63, 180, 183, 184, 263; Agere Mariam, 183; Bako, 81; Bule, 188; Chichu, 183; Maale, 81; Maji, 201; *see also neftennya*
Khartoum, 29, 30, 207
Khojali al-Hassan, 65, 66, 239, 240; and Jote's land, 222, 229, 233; and trade, 237
Khor Adar, 232
Kibish, 98
Kichepo people, 206
kingship, Anuak, *see* Anuak, leadership; Maale, *see kati*; *moti*, 51
kinship, bilateral descent system, 4, 7–8, 11, 16; Dassanetch, 100, 102, 106, 113; Gedeo, 176, 191, 193; Gumuz, *see* marriage, exchange; Kwegu and Mursi, 155, 156, 160, 163–4; Nilotes, 225, 236
Kokuru, 98
Koma people, 221, 229, 232, 239, 240, 244; population (1956), 288
Koro (Dassanetch section), 100
korro (subordinate of *balabbat*), 180, 183
Koryom Tut, *fītawrarī*, 239
Kumsa Moroda, *see* Gebre Igziabiher
kure (Maji chief), 106, 199, 201, 202, 217
Kwara, 197, 200
Kwegu people, 37, 43, 148–68 *passim*; *see also under* arms; class systems; economy; ethnicity; hunters; ivory; kinship; marriage; Omo river; provincial domination; tribute

Lak (Nuer people), 235
Lamphear, John, 203, 212
land tenure, *see gebbar*; *gult*; *ḳelad*; *madbet*; *maderia*; marriage; *rist*; taxation; tenancy
language regions of Abyssinia, 21–2, 256; *see also* Amharic; Oromo; Tigrinnya
Lasta, 23, 256
Lattimore, Owen, 196
Latuka people, 204, 207, 211, 213, 215, 216
League of Nations, Ethiopia enters the, 205
Leinhardt, Godfrey, 241
Leḳa people (Oromo): Neḳemte, 51–2, 54, 56, 62, 68; Ḳelem, 52, 56, 220; *see also* Bakare ruling family; Jote Tullu
Lemo chiefdom, 83, 84, 88
le Roux, Hugues, *quoted*, 129–30
Lévi-Strauss, C., 43, 120, 146–7
Levine, Donald, 7, 252; *quoted*, 8
Liwan, 98
Lokomarinyang, 98
Lopit (Lafit) mountains, 215–16
Lorienatom Range, 98
Losanga, Chief, 206
Lou (Nuer people), 216, 223, 228, 231, 238, 242–3; population (1956), 288; trade, 233–4, 237
lowlands, *see* highlands
Lozi people, 17
Lumuromoi, Chief, 106
Lu'ul Seged, *dejazmach*, 188, 203, 280

Maale people and kingdom, 69–95; early history, 265; incorporated into Ethiopia, 264; kings, *see kati*; *see also under* Bako; *balabbat*; domination, imperial; economy; *gebbar*; *gult*; hunters; ivory; *ḳelad*; Menilek II; Mussolini; *neftennya*; provincial domination; revolution; *rist*; taxation; tenancy; tribute
McCann, James, 251, 255, 256
madbēt (land supplying the palace), 54, 55, 56, 60, 206
maderia (form of rights over land and labour), 179, 188, 189, 194
Mago river, 148
Mahdiyya, 24, 216, 220; Gubba, 121, 122; Gute Dili, 55, 129; ivory trade, 207
Mahteme Sellassie Wolde Maskal, 58, 67, 80
maize, 149, 181, 184
Majangir people, 237, 239
Maji, 37, 196–218; *kure*, *see kure*; *see also under* bandits; domination, imperial; economy; *gebbar*; hunters; ivory; Mussolini; *neftennya*; provincial domination; Shewans; slavery; Sudan; trade; tribute; Welde Gīyorgis
Majid Abud, 226, 230, 238, 289
Makana chiefs, 74, 75, 84; conflict with Royals, 82, 89, 91, 92; *see also* Bola; Makana
Makaro, 158–9, 160
Makwei region, 238
Mantel-Niećko, J., 67

Mao people, 239, 269
Marchand expedition, 220, 243
Marille people, 213
Markakis, John, 76; *quoted*, 33, 42
marriage: between ethnic groups, 12, 13, 17, 34–5, 150–1, 165, 214, 238, 244; exchange marriage (general), 119–20, 146–7; exchange marriage and the Gumuz, 43, 120, 130–8, 140–4, 145, 147; exchange marriage and the Mbuti, 161; Gubba Shaykhs, 124–6; and land rights, 4, 5, 11, 16, 176; Lévi-Strauss' views on, 146–7; and Mursi domination over Kwegu, 155–6, 160
Marsabit, 42
Mbale, 207, 209, 210
Mbuti pygmies, 160–2
Meban people, 229, 232, 238, 239, 240, 293; population (1956), 288
Mecha people (Oromo), 35, 51–2
Meillassoux, Claude, 156
Mekonnen, *ras*, 58, 129, 220
Mekuriya, *dejazmach*, 205
mekwannint (noble status), 5, 6, 24
Mendi customs gate, 62, 63–5
Mengesha Yilma, *dejazmach*, 206
Menilek II (King of Shewa, 1865; Emperor, 1889–1913), 51, 80, 231, 232, 233, 247; Dassanetch conquest, 97–8, 101, 114; illness, 25, 39, 68, 77, 202, 258; Maale, 81, 82, 88; Mursiland occupation, 148, 163, 169, 170; Nekemte, 54–66 *passim*, 262; policies, 29, 77, 177; Shewan expansion, 3, 23–4, 129, 197, 199, 208, 220, 239
Menz, 197
Merid Habte Mariam, *dejazmach*, 78, 79, 80, 83, 84
Merid Wolde Aregay, 14, 258
Meshesha, *fitawrari*, 204, 205, 206
migrations, 20, 265; across international borders, 42, 196, 215, 230, 239, 241; Addis Abeba, 34, 259; Dukunzilla Gumuz, 139–40, 142, 143; Gedeo people, 184–5, 186, 191, 192; to lowlands, 40, 120; Nilotic, 42, 220, 230, 241, 245; to south, 40, 78; *see also neftennya*; Wellegga Gumuz, 44, 120, 121–2, 123–4, 126–30, 138–43 *passim*
military, *see* Abyssinia, military ethos; army; Dergue; *ketema*; *neftennya*
Mirba (Tishana leader), 205
missionaries, 45, 46, 145–6, 260, 269
Mohamedally Company, 210
monasteries, 12, 21
Moroda Bakare, *dejazmach*, 51, 60, 65, 68, 129, 130; and Shewans, 52, 54, 55, 56, 57, 261
Muhammad Ablikaylik, Sultan (of Sennar), 196
Muhammed ibn 'Abd Allah Hasan, 46
Mulegeta, *dejazmach*, 63, 204
Murle people, 202, 207, 211, 215, 216, 240, 288; and Dassanetch, 108; imperial influence, 201, 204, 206, 212, 213
Mursi people, 37, 43, 148–71 *passim*; *see also under* class systems; domination, imperial; economy, ethnicity; ivory; kinship; marriage; Menilek II; Mussolini; pastoralism; provincial domination; trade; tribute
Muslims, *see* Islam
Mussolini, Benito (fascist dictator of Italy 1924–43), 26, 38, 44, 177, 194, 281; Dassanetchland, 98, 268; local rulers' collaboration, 28; Maale, 148, 163; religious change, 46; Sudan–Ethiopian border, 23
Mut Dung (Gaajak leader), 229–30, 231, 239
Mwanga (Boma leader), 202, 283

Nagaw Ashana, *fitawrari*, 229
Namuraputh, 98
Naritch (Dassanetch section), 99
Nasir, 232
neftennya 39, 40, 67, 78; abolished, 87, 207; Dassanetchland, 96, 97–8, 101, 105, 107–8, 109, 110, 111, 113, 114; Gedeo, 176, 178–95 *passim*; Gumuz, 120, 123, 124, 126, 127, 129–30; Maale, 70, 76, 77, 81, 85, 91, 92, 94; Maji, 197, 199, 202, 204, 205, 206, 207; Nekemte, 55, 58, 59, 60, 61, 66, 263; Sudan–Ethiopian border, 221, 240; *see also under* Shewans; *see also gebbar*; *gult*; *ketema*
neggadras (imperial trade official), 61, 62, 201
Nejjo, 55, 59, 67, 129
Nekemte: rule, 37–8, 51–68 *passim*; *see also under* domination, imperial; *gebbar*; Haile Selassie; Iyasu; Leka; Menilek; *neftennya*; taxation; Tesemma; tribute
Ngaba ('Funj' or Sudanese) Shaykhs, 139, 140
Ngundeng (Nuer prophet and leader), 231, 235, 236, 242–3, 244
Nilotes, *see* Anuak; Dinka; Nuer; Shilluk; *see also under* ethnicity; gold; ivory; Jote Tullu; kinship; migration
Nole Kabba, 52, 56, 57
northern soldier–settlers, *see neftennya*
Nuba Mountains, 237
Nuer people, 37, 219, 220, 221, 222, 224, 288; and Anuak, 225, 238–40; leadership, 43, 228–31, 241; *see also under* Anglo-Egyptian; economy; slavery; trade; *see*

Nuer people (*cont.*)
also Gaajak: Jikany: Lak: Lou
Nyamumery settlement, 110
Nyangatom people, 213
Nyigoc lineage (Anuak), 225, 227
Nyiudola lineage (Anuak), 227

Okiek people, 164
Omo river, 96, 99, 158; Delta, 213; ferry, 111; Kwegu peoples by, 149–50, 151, 152, 153–4, 155, 157, 158–9, 162–3; Lower Omo, 97–8, 101, 112, 113, 148, 163, 167
Oro (Dassanetch section), 100
Oromo people, 23, 26, 34, 35, 63, 239, 256; *gebbar* (own system), 258; language, 21–2, 247; religion, 44, 45, 46; Wellegga highlanders near Abbay, 120–1, 122, 123, 124, 126, 128, 129, 130, 141–2, 144, 145, 147; *see also* Borena; Galla; Guji; Leḳa; Tulema
outlaws, *see* bandits

Pankhurst, Richard, 58; *quoted*, 253
Päri people, 215, 216
pastoralism, 20, 42, 84, 87, 164–5, 166, 167, 170, 185, 259, 276; Bodi, 163; Dassanetch, 96, 98, 99, 102, 113; Guji, 182, 184; Mursi, 149, 150, 151, 154, 164, 166, 170; Nilotes, 219, 220, 230; *see also* cattle
peasants, 3, 9, 12, 27, 28, 76; and aristocracy, 5, 6, 8, 10; and military ethos, 7, 33–4, 258; northern, 24; and technology, 14, 15; *see also gebbar*; *nefṭennya*; tenants
Pibor river, 220, 238
Plowden, Walter C., *quoted*, 7, 253
poachers, *see* bandits; cattle raids
provincial domination, Dassanetch Bulls, 45, 98, 106–7, 110–11, 113, 114, 115; Gedeo, 186, 187–8, 189–90; Gubba chiefs (Gumuz), 38, 43, 121–2, 124, 125, 126, 127, 128, 139–40; Maale, 77, 81–2, 91; Maji, 197–218 *passim*; Mursi over Kwegu, 43, 148, 149, 152, 154, 157, 158, 160, 161, 162, 164, 167, 171

railways, 27, 29–30, 77, 177, 186
Randal (Dassanetch section), 99–100
reforms (1941), 26, 27, 38, 41, 85, 87
refugees, *see* migrations
religion, changes in, 44, 45–6; *see also* Christianity; cults; Islam; missionaries; monasteries; Oromo
revolts: Didinga, 215; Kefa, 199, 205, 207; Menilek II's illness, 39, 258; Tigrai, 28; Tishana, 201, 202–3, 204, 205, 206, 211–12, 282, 284
revolution (1974), 27, 34, 78, 95, 195; in Maale, 69, 93
Riele (Dassanetch section), 99–100
Rift valley, 21, 32, 175, 184, 258
rist, 5, 11, 14, 16, 41, 259; Gedeo, 179, 194; governors in possession of, 10, 253–4; Maale, 88; Sibu, 66; *see also gult*
roads, 28, 177, 187, 193, 194

Sago, King, 75
Sahle Sillasē (1821–47), 197, 199
Salt, Henry, 121, 147
Sandford, Daniel, 206
Sayo, 37–8, 220, 230, 239, 240, 243; trade, 222, 232, 237
schools, 35, 76, 87, 93, 145
Schuver, Juan Maria, 122, 125, 126, 232; *quoted*, 123–4; manuscript source, 271
Segale, battle of (1916), 204
Sennar, 121, 123, 196, 232
Serie (Belodiya leader), 202–3, 283
Ses, 122
Shabo chiefdom, 84
Shack, William, 35, 47
Shangama, 82
Shanḳalla, *see* Gumuz
Shanḳilla (ethnic category), 17, 19, 35, 119; as slaves, 12–13, 23, 254, 256
Shasha (military post), 205
Shewans, 32–3, 45, 77, 253, 259; Bela Shangul, 63, 220; crucial battles, 23, 24, 256; Gojjam dispute, 23, 51, 52, 54, 55; Maji, 197, 199, 201; *nefṭennya*, 38, 179, 199; reassertion (1916), 26, 258; strategic position of kingdom, 21, 23; *see also* imperial rule; Menilek II
shifta, *see* bandits
Shilluk people, 220, 233, 246
Shils, E., 11
Shinasha people, 122–3
Shubatari (northern hunters), 97
Siba Jorgo, 56
Sibu: *ḳelad*, 66; *kella*, 62, 63–5; local versus imperial rule, 51, 52, 55, 56, 57, 59, 62, 65, 67, 88
Sidama people, 184, 188
Sidamo province, 175–95; *gebbar* (pre-1920), 179–84; governor, change of 177; military occupation, end of, 178; Oromo in 46; *see also* Gedeo
Slavery, boom, 126, 204, 205, 210, 213; decline, 27, 186; epidemic, 204; export, 27; *gebbar* link, 38, 81–2, 120, 122, 128, 139, 170, 197, 200, 210, 217, 218, 233, 237, 262; *gebbar* slaves, 40, 83, 202; Gumuz slaves, 38, 43, 119, 122, 126, 128, 139, 144, 147, 270; and Maji, 197, 200, 202, 204–5, 206, 210, 211–12, 213, 214, 217, 218; and Nuer, 213, 217, 232; pressure

against, 11, 177, 205; for tax payment, 42, 120; trading complex, 205, 206, 211–12, 217, 218; other references, 3, 5, 12, 20, 23, 34, 126, 184, 187, 231, 232, 238; *see also under* Anglo-Egyptian; Shankilla
Sobania, Neil, 97
Sobat river, 220, 223, 232, 238
Somali, 43, 46
steamer traffic, 29, 30
Stigand, C. H., 98, 231
Stitz, Volker, 17
Sudan, 38, 145, 196; Gumuz flight to, 126, 129; imperial influence, 43, 170, 219–49 *passim*; Maji influence, 170, 196, 197, 200, 201, 202, 203, 204, 206, 207, 209–18 *passim*; Turco-Egyptian, 121, 122, 124; *see also* Anglo-Egyptian; arms; frontiers; Kangalla; Khartoum; Upper Nile Province
sugar, 28, 42, 47
Suk people, 203
Susenyos, Emperor, 196
Swahili people, 203, 205, 212; bandits, 209–10, 215; traders, 206, 207, 208, 211, 214

Taddesse Tamrat, 9, 11, 120, 273; *quoted*, 10
Talodi, 235
taxation, 120, 122, 230; *balabbat*'s duties, 42, 44, 101, 102; centralization of, 27, 34, 41, 88; Dassanetch, 101, 102, 103, 111, 114, 267, 288; Gedeo, 179, 181, 182, 183, 184, 186; gold, 60, 62–3; land, 25, 33, 69, 87, 179, 180; Maale, 69, 85, 87, 88, 92; Nekemte, 58, 60, 61, 62, 63, 64, 68; slavery, 42, 120; trade, 30, 60, 61, 62, 63, 64, 85, 184, 186, 217, 223
Taytu, Empress, 26, 62, 66, 202
Tchoki hill, 129
Teferi Mekonnen, *see* Haile Selassie
tenancy, 3, 5, 10, 42, 259; Gedeo, 41, 187, 188, 189, 190, 191–2, 193, 194; Maale, 87, 88, 89
Terrefe Woldetsadik, 54
Tesemma, *ras* (also *dejazmach*), 203, 220, 222, 223, 232, 233, 243; death, 204; Nekemte, 61, 68
Tēwodros II (1855–68), 3, 24, 200
Tid people, 201, 202, 206
Tigrai, 23, 28, 253; and Kunama raids, 258
Tigrinnya-speaking peoples, 19, 21, 23, 256
Tirma people, 201, 206
Tishana people, *see under* revolts
tobacco, 28, 125, 127, 149, 232
Toki, 62
Toposa people, 204, 212, 213–14, 215; trade, 206, 207, 211, 217
Tosh, John, 175, 176
towns, 14; Abyssinian, 15, 20; Ethiopian, 31–2, 35; *see also ketema*
trade, 63, 219, 220, 221; Anuak, 207, 213, 225, 226, 227, 232–8 *passim*; Bela Shangul, 231, 237; Dinka people, 228, 231, 232, 233, 235, 236; Gaajak (Nuer people), 224, 232, 233, 236; Jote Tullu, 222, 223, 229, 231, 232–3, 237; *ketema* markets, 184, 201; Khojali al-Hassan, 237; Lou (Nuer people), 233–4, 237; Maji, 101, 105, 197, 200–17 *passim*; Mursi, 153, 171; Nuer people, 43, 223, 224, 228, 229, 232–8 *passim*, 242, 243, 244, 245; routes, 20, 30, 46, 168–9, 216, 217; Sayo, 222, 232, 237; Sudanese trading posts, 30, 222, 223; Swahili, 206, 207, 208, 211, 214; Toposa people, 206, 207, 211, 217; Turkana people, 211, 214, 217; Wellegga, 23, 144–5, 237; *see also* arms; cash crops; cattle; civet; coffee; cotton; exports; gold; ivory; slavery; taxation; tobacco; tribute
transport, *see* communications; railways; roads; steamer traffic
tribute, 15, 24, 39, 120, 122, 128, 226, 231; British Sudan, 220, 221, 222, 223, 224, 228, 239, 242; Gedeo, 181, 182; gold, 58–9, 64; Kwegu and Mursi, 152, 157, 167, 170; Maale, 71, 75, 76, 81; Maji, 40, 170, 197, 201, 202, 206, 213, 214–17; Nekemte, 55, 56, 58, 59, 60, 62, 63, 64; trade link, 38, 58, 59, 62, 64, 181, 183, 219, 222, 223, 224, 237, 244; *see also gebbar*; *gult*
Trimingham, J. Spencer, 260
Tsemai, 84, 85
Tulema people (Oromo), 199, 254
Turco-Egyptian government, 121, 122, 124
Turkana people, 98, 104, 197, 203, 204, 212, 213; and Dassanetch, 108; trade, 211, 214, 217
Turnbull, Colin, 160–1
Twij Dinka people, 233, 235

Uba, 81
Udiel-wa-Ngenya, 225, 226, 237, 238
Uganda, 200, 210, 211, 212
Uliimi-war-Agaanya, 225, 226
United States aid, *see* American aid
Upper Nile Province, 220, 224, 236, 242

Wag, 23
Wambera, 123, 126, 127
Warragarra region, 221–2, 232
watersheds, 20–1, 30, 39
Weber, Max, 9–10, 253
Wedajo, *dejazmach*, 55
Welaita, 45, 80–1, 199, 260
Welde Giyorgis, *ras*, 80–1, 122, 258; Maji,

Welde Gīyorgis (*contd.*)
199, 201, 202, 204, 207, 210
Wellegga, 51, 58, 62, 67, 230; gold, 23, 55, 129; Gumuz in, 44, 119–23 *passim*, 126, 129–47 *passim*; highlanders, *see* Oromo; incorporated into Ethiopia, 120–1, 199, 220; missionary, 45; trade, 23, 144–5, 237
Wello, 26
Wesenē, *fītawrarī*, 205–6
White Nile, 238
women: as *balabbat* 44; and exchange marriage 136–8; as slaves, 120
Woodburn, James, 161
Wunakoi, 228

Yaringhe hill, 125, 126, 129, 139
Yebirka, King, 88, 89, 90, 91, 92–3, 94
Yerar, Chief, 104
Yggezu, *neggadras*, 61, 62
Yirga Cheffe, 194
Yohannis IV (1871–89), 3, 23, 24

Zagwe dynasty, 20
Zanni, L., 121
Zaraf valley, 223, 232, 236
Zeggheldu, Shaykh, 121
Zerefu, *ato*, 229
Zervos, A., 58
Zewdē Ayyelle, *fītawrarī*, 206
Zewditu, Empress, 26, 44, 66, 77, 178, 188–9
Zhogwadze (Gumuz leader), 139, 140